Microsoft®*Press*

Microsoft®
Exchange
Server 5.5
Administrator's
Companion

PUBLISHED BY
Microsoft Press
A Division of Microsoft Corporation
One Microsoft Way
Redmond, Washington 98052-6399

Library of Congress Cataloging-in-Publication Data
Greenwald, Rick.
    Microsoft Exchange Server 5.5 Administrator's Companion / Rick
Greenwald, Walter J. Glenn.
      p. cm.
    ISBN 0-7356-0646-3
    1. Microsoft Exchange server. 2. Client/server computing.
 I. Glenn, Walter J. II. Title.
 QA76.9.C55G76 1999
 005.7'13769--dc21   99-22855
                                    CIP

Printed and bound in the United States of America.

1 2 3 4 5 6 7 8 9   WCWC   4 3 2 1 0 9

Distributed in Canada by Penguin Books Canada Limited.

A CIP catalogue record for this book is available from the British Library.

Microsoft Press books are available through booksellers and distributors worldwide. For further information about international editions, contact your local Microsoft Corporation office or contact Microsoft Press International directly at fax (425) 936-7329. Visit our Web site at mspress.microsoft.com.

Acquisitions Editor: David Clark
Project Editor: Barbara Moreland
Technical Editors: David Smith, Bret Alexander, Sean Wallbridge

For LuAnn Greenwald, the wind under my wings; and Elinor Vera YuXiu Greenwald, the light of my life, who can make even corny song's lyrics ring true.—Rick

For my dogs, Belle and Jasmine, for knowing absolutely nothing about Exchange Server 5.5.—Walter

Contents at a Glance

Table of Contents

Part II
Planning

Part III
Deployment of Exchange Server

7   Installing Exchange Server 5.5   102

Part IV
Deployment of Exchange Clients

Part V
Maintenance

Rick Greenwald has worked in the data processing field for more than 15 years, in positions with Data General, Cognos, and Gupta. He is currently a principal with Strategic Computing Services. Mr. Greenwald has spoken on computing concepts and implementation at conferences throughout the United States, as well as in Asia, Australia, South America, and Africa. He is a certified Microsoft Visual Basic instructor, and he has written three books and dozens of articles on computing technology.

Walter J. Glenn is also a veteran of more than 15 years in the computer industry. He is a Microsoft Certified Systems Engineer (MCSE) and Microsoft Certified Trainer (MCT), who currently splits his time between consulting for small to medium-sized companies and writing on computer-related topics. His publications include *Exchange Server 5.5 MSCE Study Guide*, *Teach Yourself MCSE Windows NT Server 4.0 in 14 Days*, and *Teach Yourself MCSE TCP/IP in 14 Days*.

Melissa Craft and **Stace Cunningham** also contributed to chapters throughout the book. Melissa, a consulting engineer for MicroAge, concentrates on designing infrastructure and messaging systems for complex or global network projects. Stace is a systems engineer with SDC Consulting in Biloxi, Mississippi, where he works with all aspects of networks—design, engineering, and installation. Both have extensive technical credentials, and we are grateful for their important additions to the book.

Acknowledgments

The creation of a book such as the one you are holding is a collaborative task. Although the authors labor long and hard to create the basic substance of the book, they are aided and abetted by many hands along the way.

The folks at Microsoft Press were essential guides in the formative stages of this project. Anne Hamilton, David Clark, Barbara Moreland, and Bill Teel all helped to make sure that this book was aimed in the right direction. The responsibility for any subsequent failures in hitting the mark is assumed by the co-authors. The crew at Syngress Media were our most important companions on this particular journey. Amy Pedersen and Matt Pedersen were there at all the right times, and Anne Marie Walker served as not only a crackerjack editor, but as a valued advisor in the ways of all things publishing. We were blessed with not one, not two, but three excellent technical editors — David Smith, Bret Alexander, and Sean Wallbridge — who significantly increased the depth and robustness of this book and, occasionally, our blood pressure. Many thanks to all of them.

We also feel we should publicly thank some of the folks who gave us technical help along the way. Ken Reitz and Thomas Rizzo were always ready to respond to our questions. Randy Zellner in tech support provided some crucial answers at just the right time. The entire Exchange community benefits from the discussions in the public news groups on Exchange and Outlook hosted by Microsoft. And we would be remiss if we did not point out that there are several Web sites, most notably *http://www.slipstick.com* and *http://www.cdolive.com*, that are a terrific source of information on many aspects of Exchange and Outlook.

Perhaps most importantly, the authors would like to thank Studio B, their literary agency. The wonderful folks at Studio B were there every step of the way, helping us to navigate the sometimes turbulent waters of the project. Most importantly, Studio B guided the two happy co-authors into their first, but hopefully not last, collaboration, and for that, both Rick and Walter are truly grateful.

The manuscript for this book was prepared and galleyed using Microsoft Word 97. Pages were composed by Syngress Media using QuarkXPress 3.32 for Macintosh, with text in Sabon and display type in ITC Franklin Gothic. Composed pages were delivered to the printer as electronic prepress files.

Principal Compositor: Reuben Kantor
Principal Proofreader: Mildred Rosenzweig
Indexer: Robert A. Saigh

Part I
Introduction

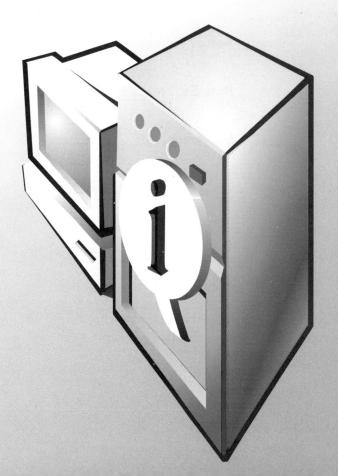

Chapter 1
Introducing Exchange

Microsoft Exchange Server is one of Microsoft's most successful BackOffice products, and the new Exchange 5.5 version builds on the superior performance and features Exchange users have come to expect.

In this chapter, we start looking at the architecture of an Exchange Server system. We look at the components of the architecture, examine how those components are organized, and learn how they interact to provide a comprehensive messaging system. Exchange Server is a complex program, but with a little dissection, it becomes clear how its complexity benefits an enterprise that implements it.

What Is Exchange?

As an IT professional, you know that Exchange is one of the most popular components of Microsoft's BackOffice package, which runs on Microsoft's NT Server operating system. But functionally, how would you define Exchange? Is it an e-mail system, a groupware product, something in between, or something altogether different? Exchange does sport some characteristics of each of these possibilities:

- **An e-mail system?** You are no doubt familiar with electronic mail, or e-mail, systems, which have become one of the dominant communication methods over the past couple of decades. You can use e-mail to communicate within your company or with people across the planet. Exchange is one of the most popular e-mail systems in the world, but it is much more than a simple e-mail system.

- **A type of groupware?** In the 1980s, the term *groupware* became popular. The term was interpreted in various ways, but it generally meant a product that could be used to create collaborative applications, in which people shared access to a collection of centralized documents. Groupware has evolved to not only include shared information, but also workflow tracking, process automation, and workgroup-based knowledge management. Exchange lets you store virtually any type of document within the

Exchange system, which in turn allows the document to be shared among a wide variety of people. Exchange can also automatically send copies of documents to different physical information stores, making the use of shared documents across an organization much more efficient. Sharing documents in a common storage area is only one aspect of groupware. Exchange includes a full collection of application samples and development tools with which to create collaborative, automated applications.

- **A common repository of information?**   One thing that Exchange must do is store information. Even if you are using Exchange only for e-mail, Exchange still must store the messages sent in a logical structure. Through the use of shared information stores, you can extend the capabilities of Exchange to act as a general repository for a wide variety of information, including documents, presentations, and multimedia. You can leverage Exchange's capabilities to provide a logical storage system for all your complex data. You can then use other Exchange features to provide distributed storage for your data, replication of data between different Exchange Servers, and varying levels of secure access to the data.

- **A platform for creating interactive applications?**   You can use Exchange as the basis for creating applications and systems to address the specific needs of your organization. For example, you can create forms that extend the capabilities of a simple message and attach application logic to these forms. Then you might configure Exchange to route these forms to specific users or destinations, where they can undergo further modification. Additional tools allow you to access and manipulate the information stored in Exchange or to take advantage of Exchange's Directory and Delivery Services.

- **A scalable and extensible platform?**   Many people use Exchange's messaging and groupware as is. Others purchase other applications that plug into Exchange and take advantage of its technology to provide best-in-class applications.

As you can see, Exchange is a multifaceted and complex product. By the time you complete this book, you will have a full understanding of how to use Exchange to implement all these types of functionality. You will be able to exploit the capabilities of Exchange to their fullest extent.

Basic Terms

Before moving to the specifics of Exchange, you need to understand some basic concepts that form its foundation.

Client/Server Systems

You might be using Exchange to replace an earlier e-mail system that is already installed at your company, such as Microsoft Mail. The key difference between Exchange and some of these earlier systems is that Exchange is a client/server system rather than a shared file system.

A shared file e-mail system, as shown in Figure 1-1, works fairly simply. Someone sending an e-mail places the message in a shared location. Someone attempting to receive an e-mail checks the shared location for any new messages. These types of systems are inherently passive, in that it is up to the messaging software running on the client machine to carry out the operations of the e-mail transaction. In contrast, the Exchange system, shown in Figure 1-2, is a *client/server* system. Each individual client interacts with the messaging database on the Exchange Server.

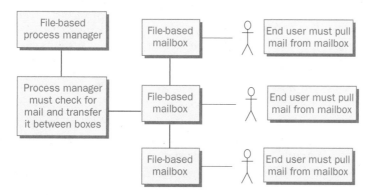

Figure 1-1. *A shared file e-mail system.*

The client/server process is active; it dynamically receives the message and delivers it to a location that individual users can access to retrieve their messages. The client does not have to do all the work. The server does most of the work in the system.

For example, each Exchange Server:

- Manages the messaging database
- Manages the connections to other Exchange Servers and messaging systems
- Indexes the messaging database for better performance
- Receives new messages and transfers them to their destinations

To provide these services and more, Exchange Servers are typically based on more powerful server machines than shared file e-mail systems, which means that a client/server system such as Exchange is inherently more scalable than a

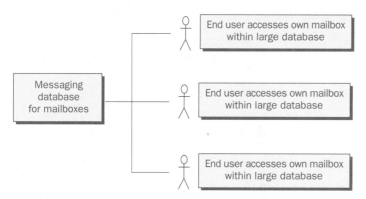

Figure 1-2. *The Exchange client/server system.*

shared file system. In fact, as you see later in the chapter, the server-based agents that implement Exchange can also provide a higher level of security, reliability, and scalability than a simple shared file e-mail system can. All these features allow Exchange to support many more users than simple file-based systems can.

As the name implies, a client/server system has two logically and physically distinct components: a client and a server. The client and the server use a specific interface to cooperate. The fact that Exchange Server distributes functions between the client and the server means that more processing power is available systemwide for messaging in general. In comparison, a shared file system depends on the client to constantly check and pull mail, a process that can result in poorer performance as well as heightened network traffic on a workstation client. You will see in Chapter 16 that many types of clients can be used to access the power of Exchange Server.

Note This book is primarily about Exchange Server, so most of the information applies specifically to the use of the server component of the Exchange system. Because the server does not exist in a vacuum, however, you also learn about the clients that participate in an Exchange system.

Many clients can access a server at the same time. As a result, a server must be implemented with an architecture that can simultaneously handle many types of requests from many sources.

The requirement to service many clients is one of the primary factors that led to the architecture used to implement Exchange, which implements several separate processes in the server that cooperate to handle client requests. These server processes and the way that they interact are detailed later in this chapter. Each Exchange process is responsible for implementing one type of task. This means that Exchange can execute different functions simultaneously rather than linearly, as would be found in a monolithic, single-process messaging architecture. The overall result is that Exchange Server can be a robust system and an improvement over legacy messaging architectures.

Messaging Systems

An e-mail is certainly a type of message, but an electronic messaging system can provide more functionality than just delivering e-mail. When you talk about a messaging system, you are describing a more generalized process that can be used to deliver many different types of information to many different locations. A messaging system has several specific characteristics. First, it involves the participation of at least two parties: the sender and one or more recipients. When a sender dispatches a message, the sender can count on the guaranteed delivery of the message. If a message cannot be delivered to the recipient immediately, the messaging system continues to try to deliver the message. If, for some reason, the messaging system cannot deliver the message, the least it will do is to inform the sender of this failure so that the message can be re-sent at a future date.

Although a standard messaging system can guarantee the reliable delivery of messages, it cannot guarantee exactly how long a message will take to be delivered. The sender and recipient(s) of a message can be located near each other or very far away from each other. A letter sent from New York to Chicago usually arrives faster than a letter sent from New York to Tokyo because of the distances involved. But under certain circumstances, the letter sent to Tokyo may arrive before the letter sent to Chicago. Even if a letter arrives in Chicago faster than it arrives in Tokyo, it might not be read and acted on by the recipient sooner than the Japan-bound message. The uncertainty implicit in this process is due to the asynchronous nature of a messaging system. In an asynchronous system, two related events are not dependent on each other; the sending of a message and the receipt of the message are not tied together in any fixed span of time.

When you send a message in Exchange, it is received by the Exchange Server immediately, and you can go on to another task. You don't have to wait for the message to be delivered, wherever it is going. Guaranteed delivery gives you confidence that a message will be delivered, but the asynchronous nature of messaging systems makes it impossible for you to know exactly when it will be received. This fact makes messaging systems ideal for some types of interactions and less than perfect for other types.

Messaging systems, in general, are implemented with a two-stage architecture, which includes a distribution hub and a number of clients. This structure is shown in Figure 1-3. The clients in the system act as the senders and recipients of messages. Each client connects to a single distribution messaging server, which receives the messages sent by the client and collects the messages sent to the client. If the system has more than one messaging server, the servers coordinate the exchange of messages between them with no additional interaction from the sender or the recipient. To make this distribution possible, some type of common directory must associate each client with a particular messaging server. In Exchange, each Exchange Server acts as a distribution messaging server, and the directory information used to distribute information is shared across multiple servers.

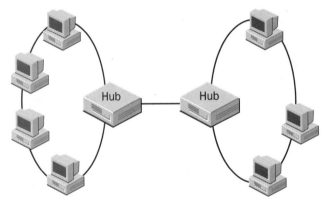

Figure 1-3. *A messaging system.*

Note Keep in mind that in a messaging system, the distribution hubs described in this section are logical entities. All clients must access a distribution hub to interact with the system, but the particular hub could be associated with a different physical location at different times.

The last characteristic of a messaging system is its information store. Because the messages in a messaging system are delivered asynchronously, and because the delivery is guaranteed, a messaging system must have a place to store messages. These message stores might hold messages only until a recipient retrieves them, or they might hold messages in archives for individual recipients. In some advanced messaging systems, such as Exchange, message stores can be used to hold information that can be shared by many recipients. The ability to share information among users improves efficiency in a network environment. Being able to share that information in a common storage area extends the capabilities of the messaging system into groupware functionality, which may include collaborative applications.

Now that we have reviewed the characteristics of messaging systems, you can see how this description can be applied to an Exchange system. Exchange can be used as a generic messaging system because you can access its services and information stores in a wide variety of ways—even from outside the Exchange environment.

This book won't revisit either of these topics, although you need a thorough understanding of the basic concepts that underlie messaging systems to provide a context for the operation of Exchange. From now on, the book refers to Exchange as an e-mail system or as a messaging system. But remember that Exchange is built with two basic architectural blueprints — client/server systems and messaging systems — and that much of the power of Exchange flows from the strengths and virtues of these two concepts.

The Organization of an Exchange Environment

An Exchange environment is built on multiple structural levels, as shown in Figure 1-4. Each level has specific features and supports different types of interactions with the other levels in the environment.

Figure 1-4. *The Exchange environment, as seen in the Exchange Administrator.*

Exchange offers a hierarchical architecture upon which to develop your directory of mailboxes and messaging servers. The top three levels of the Exchange environment — the organization, the sites, and the servers — make up the *topology*, or overall structure, of the environment. The organization, sites, and servers describe the arrangement of the components that make up an Exchange hierarchy. The other elements of Exchange identify mailboxes, folders, storage areas, connectors, and other messaging resources available to Exchange users established in the directory.

Organization

The top level in an Exchange environment is referred to as the *organization*. An organization contains all the elements in an Exchange environment. It is the starting point for the hierarchical directory structure that specifies your

Exchange environment. The boundaries of the organization define the boundaries of your Exchange environment. You cannot see anyone outside your organization in this directory structure without specifically creating a link to that person. This does not prevent an Exchange user from sending messages to external systems if Exchange has taken advantage of connectors such as the Internet Mail Service, an X.400 or FAX connector.

Exchange Server is a messaging system that sits on top of Microsoft Windows NT Server. The NT Server environment offers single logon authentication through its domain architecture and subsequent trust relationships. NT domains are groups of NT Servers, and a common directory of users is allowed to access any specific NT domain. When one domain trusts a second domain, the second domain's users can access the first domain's servers.

Exchange Server's hierarchy is outside yet integrated with the NT domain structure. An Exchange organization (the object at the top of the Exchange system's hierarchy) can span multiple NT domains. An Exchange site (the next-level object in the Exchange system hierarchy) must have some special security relationships set up that allow it to span multiple NT domains, a process that is discussed in Chapter 3 of this book.

Sites

The *site* is the basic administrative unit of the Exchange environment. Most of the administrative functions within Exchange can be performed at the site level, which means that you can set parameters and defaults for all the lower levels in the Exchange environment on a site-by-site basis. Although rules and policies are implemented on the basis of the organization of your company, site implementation is typically based on the physical infrastructure. An Exchange site is usually separated from other sites by WAN links so that intra-site bandwidth consumption is kept to a minimum across low-bandwidth links.

A site cannot span multiple Windows NT domains unless the domains have established a trust relationship, so the topology of your Windows NT network will, to some extent, determine the topology of your Exchange environment. For more information on the interaction between Windows NT and Exchange, refer to Chapter 3.

Exchange Servers generate more network traffic within a site than between sites. Servers within sites frequently interact in order to synchronize and replicate information. For this reason, your site will operate most efficiently if it is contained within a single *local area network* (LAN) or a high-speed *wide area network* (WAN). Balancing the physical requirements of sites with the organizational requirements of distributed companies is one of the high arts of designing and implementing large Exchange systems. For more information on the issues involved in creating the topology for an Exchange organization, refer to Chapter 6.

Servers

Server is the term used in the Microsoft Exchange topology to refer to an individual machine that has the Microsoft Exchange Server messaging application installed and running on it. A server is contained within one — and only one — site. The name of the server typically is the same as the name of the Windows NT computer that hosts the Exchange application.

There are no hard and fast rules as to how many servers you should have within a particular site. The size of the machine acting as the server will have some bearing on how many users and how large a store can be supported on the machine. In addition, when individual users on the same server communicate through Exchange, there is no need to use extra network bandwidth to enable the communication, because there is no need to move the message between separate physical machines. Some thought should be put into which servers to place users on. If users are grouped according to how they interact with each other, the Exchange Server's performance, and even the performance of the entire messaging system, can be improved. In terms of using Exchange, however, there is one critical component of the Exchange organization: the recipient.

Recipients

As the name implies, a *recipient* is an entity that can receive an Exchange message. Most recipients are associated with a single, discrete mailbox, although this mailbox can be represented by several addresses, depending on the addressing types implemented within Exchange. Each recipient's mailbox is associated with a single server. Public folders and distribution lists are also recipients in Exchange.

The *Global Address List*, which is the master list of recipients, custom recipients, distribution lists, and public folder addresses, is maintained for an entire Exchange organization. For example, a recipient on a server in Tokyo (in the Japan Exchange site) is located in the Global Address List along with a recipient on a server in London (in the United Kingdom site). When a mailbox is moved from one server to another, the Global Address List appears unaffected. When a mailbox is created for a user in Exchange, the mailbox becomes an Exchange recipient. If a mailbox does not exist in the Exchange organization but is available through connectors to another messaging system, the administrator can configure a *custom recipient* so Exchange users can send mail to it. A custom recipient has an e-mail address that shows up in the Global Address List but has no Exchange mailbox. Custom recipients can receive e-mail from Exchange users, just like standard Exchange recipients, after their addresses are defined in the Exchange system's Global Address List. Through the use of custom recipients, you can integrate external recipients into the address list of your Exchange system.

Address Lists

An *address list* is simply a list of Exchange recipients. The Global Address List is the list of all Exchange recipients in the entire Exchange organization. The recipient is the lowest level of the Exchange hierarchy. An Exchange system can have hundreds of thousands of recipients, making it hard to manage when a user is merely trying to locate an individual recipient's name. Exchange uses address lists to hold and organize the names of the recipients associated with the system.

The primary purpose of an address list, from a user's point of view, is to provide access to an e-mail address for a recipient. E-mail addresses can be somewhat cryptic. Various legacy messaging systems have restrictions for the length of the user's mailbox name; some administrators assign puzzling mailbox names, too. All in all, it is difficult to guess a user's e-mail address. When the Exchange Administrator creates a custom recipient, the name of the person — not a cryptic e-mail address — shows up in the Global Address List. This makes it easier for Exchange users to send mail to custom recipients.

Exchange maintains a Global Address List that contains all the recipients in the entire system. Individual users can create their own personal address books. Personal address books can contain a portion of the Global Address List, as well as other custom addresses added by the user, to make it easier to access the most frequently used addresses.

Connectors

You should understand one more piece of the Exchange topology before moving on. A *connector* is a piece of software that acts as a gateway to another Exchange site or to a non-Exchange mail system. By using a connector, you enable the Exchange system to interact directly with a foreign e-mail system, as though its users were part of your Exchange system. Connectors can integrate foreign address lists into the Global Address List, enable message exchange, provide access to shared messaging folders, and make available other functions. Some connectors simply enable a consistent mail-forwarding and receipt operation. Not only can a connector provide linkage between Exchange and other messaging systems, but a connector can be extremely useful if you are in the process of migrating to Exchange or connecting to non-messaging systems such as fax or voice mail.

Storage

Exchange uses several types of *stores* to hold the messages that make up the information environment of Exchange. Within the messaging stores, Exchange organizes the messages themselves in folders. A folder has the same relationship to its messages that a directory in a file system has to its files. Because Exchange manages the storage of its own data, there is not a strict one-to-one relationship between a folder in an Exchange store and a directory in the operating system. Exchange systems can use three types of stores: Public Information Store, Private Information Store, and Personal Information Store.

The Public Information Store is a database that can exist on an Exchange Server. This database stores public folders, indexes their contents, and assists in the replication of the folders with other Exchange Servers.

The Private Information Store is a database that usually exists on an Exchange Server. The Private Information Store contains all the mailboxes of every Exchange user associated with that Exchange Server. The Private Information Store manages the data within the mailboxes, tracking deleted messages and mailbox sizes and assisting in message transfers. The Private Information Store is sometimes considered the holder of private folders, which is another name for the individual folders within mailboxes.

Public Folders

As the name implies, a *public folder* is accessible to more than one user. You can define the specific security restrictions on a public folder to limit the types of users who have access to it. Public folders are the basis of a great deal of Exchange's functionality.

Like the Global Address List, public folders appear to be a single entity to an Exchange user. When exploring public folders, the user does not need to determine which Exchange Server houses which public folder. Instead, the user simply explores a single hierarchy of public folders.

Public folders are ideal places to keep information that is accessed by large numbers of people. If, for example, your organization has marketing materials or human resources policies that you want to make available to everyone as soon as they are created, you can put them in a public folder. Public folders are maintained in a separate *Public Information Store*. When you install an Exchange Server, you have to specify locations for the Public Information Store and the Private Information Store. Each store acts as a database for all the objects that it contains: mailboxes for the private store and public folders for the public store.

The reason for this separation between the public store and the private store lies in the way that Exchange automatically treats the information in the public store. Because public folders can be accessed by everyone on what could be a widely dispersed site, Exchange allows you to set up automatic replication of the contents of public folders. Exchange handles the replication of documents in a public folder with no intervention on the part of an administrator after the replication is defined. Users who request a document in a public folder retrieve it from the closest copy of the public folder, rather than all users having to reach out for a single copy of the requested document. In this way, public folders help expand the scalability of Exchange by reducing the bandwidth requirements for the access of common documents.

Private Folders

A *private folder* holds information that is available only to a single Exchange user and to others to whom that user has granted access permissions. A private folder is a secured folder component within a mailbox for an Exchange recipient.

Exchange maintains private folders and their container mailboxes within the Private Information Store of the associated Exchange Server. The word "secured" refers to the fact that an Exchange user must have an account and password to access each mailbox. That security does not exclude mailboxes from being managed in Exchange. Like Public Information Stores, Private Information Stores are included in standard Exchange backup and recovery operations.

Exchange users are not limited to Outlook or Exchange clients. Private stores can also be accessed through POP3 and IMAP4, which are Internet mail protocols, if the Exchange environment is configured to allow those types of access. When Exchange is configured for these protocols, a POP3 or IMAP4 client can be used in place of a standard Exchange client.

Personal Folders

A *personal folder* is a folder that has been taken out of the Exchange Server system and placed in a location that is controlled by an individual user. Typically, a personal folder is kept on the user's personal machine. This arrangement can be very handy because it allows users to access information from an Exchange client when they are not connected to the Exchange Server.

Personal folders are created when a user maintains Exchange data in a separately managed database. Personal folders are typically used as a separate place to retain mailbox contents. In addition, a user can replicate the contents of public folders to their personal folders.

After materials are placed in a personal folder, they are the exclusive responsibility of the user. Other users cannot access the materials in a personal folder, so if users create or modify any of the documents in the personal folder, they have to explicitly place these documents in a private or public folder in order to put them back under the care of an Exchange Server. Exchange Servers typically include backup and recovery services. When mail is placed outside an Exchange Server into a personal folder, users must handle any backup and potential recovery operations on their own.

This chapter introduced the most basic elements of storage. Chapter 4 examines the Exchange storage architecture in depth.

Server Processes

From the outside, Exchange looks like a single, monolithic software system. Internally, Exchange uses four key services to implement functionality: directory service, information store service, message-transfer agent service, and system attendant service. A *service* is a piece of software that runs in the background, performing its tasks without requiring any specific administrative intervention. For Exchange, agents are Windows NT Server processes known as services, as shown in Figure 1-5.

When you install Exchange, you must specify an NT account that the Exchange Server processes will utilize to access the NT Server system. NT accounts can be granted varying levels of NT Server access. When an Exchange Server service accesses the NT Server, it must be able to act as part of the NT system. The NT account that you specify as the Exchange service account will be granted extended access to the NT Server in order to perform this function on the behalf of Exchange.

All Exchange services normally utilize the same service account. The service account and its agents act as an intermediary between Exchange users and operating system files, so the service account requires a much higher level of access to the operating system and the server files than a standard user does. The following sections describe the four basic Exchange services, which are illustrated in Figure 1-5.

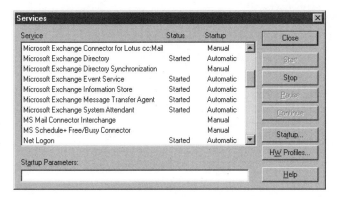

Figure 1-5. *Exchange Server processes in the Windows NT Services window.*

Directory Service

Earlier in this chapter, you learned that the Exchange Directory contains a listing of all the main objects known to an Exchange organization, including recipients, custom recipients, and distribution lists. Each Exchange Server contains a Directory object that lists the server's contents. The object is typically called Server Recipients. The Directory Service was developed to link all the different Exchange Server Directory objects into a cohesive Global Address List, to replicate the information throughout the Exchange system, and to resolve names to mailboxes. The Directory Service of Exchange acts as the intermediary to the physical store of the Directory objects on each Exchange Server. When a request for an address comes in, the Directory Service resolves the request to the correct Exchange Server and Directory object and then returns the address that can be used to access the recipient's location. For this reason, the Directory Service is involved in most Exchange interactions.

By providing a single interface to all Exchange objects, the Directory Service also makes it easier to manage all Exchange entities from a single interface, such as the Exchange Administrator. The Directory Service agent is called Microsoft Exchange Directory in the Windows NT Services window.

Information Store Service

The information stores, just like the Exchange Directory, are kept as database files that are managed by an Exchange Server. The Information Store Service is responsible for storing and retrieving information from any of those stores. The Information Service is involved in sending messages, and it is also involved in automatic functions of Exchange, such as replication. The Directory Service agent is called Microsoft Exchange Information Store in the Windows NT Services window.

Message-Transfer Agent Service

The most active part of an Exchange Server is the Message-Transfer Agent (MTA) Service. When the MTA shuts down, the Exchange Server no longer moves mail through the system. The MTA is responsible for coordinating the transfer of messages between Exchange Servers. It acts as a traffic cop and a crossing guard combined, directing messages to their next destinations as well as ensuring that the messages arrive safely. If a message is sent from one user on an Exchange Server to another user on the same server, the MTA is not involved in the transaction. The Directory Service agent is called Microsoft Exchange Message-Transfer Agent in the Windows NT Services window.

System Attendant Service

The System Attendant (SA) is the background manager for the Exchange system. The SA maintains the routing tables that are used by the MTA for message delivery, makes sure that the directories on separate servers are consistent, monitors the connections between servers, and collects feedback that is used by other monitoring tools. These unseen tasks are vital to the continuing successful operation of your Exchange environment. The SA is called Microsoft Exchange System Attendant in the Windows NT Services window.

Additional Exchange services can be running on your system because some optional features of Exchange create their own services, such as a key management server service, which provides an additional level of security for your Exchange system. To show you how these agents work together, the last section of this chapter walks you through a typical user interaction with Exchange and explicitly describes the services that are used throughout the process.

How Exchange Works

To understand how the different server processes work together, let's take a high-level view of the process of sending a message and the ways in which these services participate in this process (Figure 1-6).

1. A user creates a message and sends it.
2. The Exchange Server receives the message, and the Information Store Service stores it on the receiving Exchange Server. By storing the message immediately, Exchange in effect guarantees the partial completion of the message-delivery process. Regardless of what problems occur after this point, the

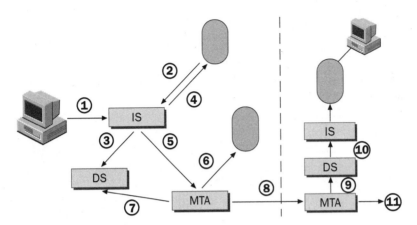

Figure 1-6. *Process flow and Exchange services.*

message has been safely received and stored on an Exchange Server, so corrective actions can be implemented with no additional user interaction.

3. The Information Store Service queries the Directory Service to determine where the message should be sent.

4. If the message is addressed to a recipient whose mailbox is on the same Exchange Server, the Exchange Information Store Service moves the message directly into the recipient's mailbox, and the delivery process ends.

5. If the message is addressed to a recipient whose mailbox is on a different Exchange Server, the Information Store Service transfers the message to the MTA Service.

6. The MTA stores the message in a message-transfer database. Just as the information store initially stores a message when it is received to act as a fail-safe, the MTA stores a message so that it can handle any delivery issues without further interaction with other services. When the message is successfully sent, the message is deleted from the message-transfer database.

7. Upon receiving the message, the MTA queries the Directory Service to determine whether the recipient is local or remote.

8. If the recipient is remote, the MTA determines how to best route the message: via a remote procedure call (RPC) or a connector. The MTA then delivers the message to the remote MTA.

Note An RPC is a session layer Application Programming Interface (API) that is used to make remote applications appear as though they are working locally. Much of the interaction of Exchange—whether between client and server, or between server and server—uses RPCs.

9. The remote MTA queries the Directory Service to determine whether the recipient is local or remote.

10. If the recipient is local, the MTA hands the message off to the information store, which then queries the Directory Service, places the message in the recipient's mailbox, and notifies the recipient's client.

11. If the recipient is not local, the MTA Service determines the best connection to use to deliver the message to the recipient's server and delivers the message to the information store of the target server, which continues the process of identifying the eventual local server for the recipient.

You can see from this discussion that the agents used by Exchange have the overall effect of dividing the operations of Exchange into circumscribed arenas. The Information Store Service handles all storage operations, from storing an incoming message temporarily to transferring a message to the MTA to delivering a message to a recipient's mailbox. When a message is handed off to the MTA, the Information Store Service that gave the message to the MTA is relieved of further proactive tracking of the message. The MTA explicitly notifies the Information Store Service if any subsequent problems occur with the delivery of the message.

The use of services in Exchange makes it easier for developers to modify existing functionality and to add new functionality to Exchange. By focusing on the specific tasks for each service, Exchange can optimize the server to deliver performance and functionality without interfering with the rest of the Exchange product. By isolating Exchange users from directly interacting with the storage files used by Exchange, the agents allow an administrator to implement a more robust security scheme for information contained in Exchange stores than is available for normal Windows NT files. The Exchange information stores act as a database so that Exchange itself uses a single operating system file for the storage of information but provides access to only a part of it for each user, as appropriate. For most users, the separation of actions among services is transparent, but as an Exchange Administrator, you need to understand exactly how Exchange and its services respond to user requests. Exchange services raise Exchange to the level of an enterprise product by providing the isolation necessary for enterprise scalability.

Summary

Exchange Server is a client/server system that provides messaging and groupware functionality. Although the name of the software package is Exchange Server, it can be and is typically implemented as more than a single stand-alone messaging server.

Exchange organizes multiple Exchange Servers into a hierarchical structure that has, at its top, the Exchange organization. All components held within this organization make up a single Exchange Server messaging environment. Because Exchange Server is installed on Windows NT Servers, the Exchange system must be able to integrate with multiple NT domain structures. NT domains are groups of Windows NT Servers that share a common security access, or group of users. An organization can span multiple NT domains.

The Exchange organization is a container that has within it other containers, called sites. Sites are groups of one or more servers. Within a site, the contained Exchange Servers transfer a significant amount of traffic with each other. Sites can also span NT domains, but only if those domains have trust relationships with each other so that the Exchange Servers within the sites can exchange information.

Within each site Exchange Servers represent actual Windows NT Servers that have been installed with the Exchange Server software. Servers hold the actual information stores used to organize messages and data. They also contain directory objects or address lists of their recipients. Connectors are used to connect various sites with each other and to connect to external messaging systems.

There are two basic types of recipients in Exchange. One type of recipient is an Exchange object—whether mailbox, directory list, or public folder—that can receive messages. The other type of recipient is a custom recipient. This type of recipient is not representing any type of Exchange object; it represents an external messaging system address. The custom recipient object makes a sometimes cryptic e-mail address much more easily accessible by Exchange users, because it appears in the Global Address List and uses a real name, not an e-mail address. The correct connector(s) must be configured in order to send mail to a custom recipient.

Exchange information is stored in two types of information store on an Exchange Server:

- Public Information Store
- Private Information Store

The Public Information Store is seen by Exchange users as a group of public folders. On the server, it is a database that manages these folders and their contained information. Each Exchange Server's Public Information Store is indexed into a common directory of public folders that users can access without concern over the location of the originating server.

Private Information Store contains mailboxes. Each mailbox is separate and integrated with NT Server through a specific NT user account and password. The Private Information Store is separate from the Public Information Store because it requires extended security. Mailboxes themselves contain a list of private folders, including an Inbox, Deleted Items, Sent Items, Notes, and more.

Personal folders are stored outside an Exchange Server. They are accessible from an Exchange client and are contained in their own database file. A personal folder file must be maintained by an end user because the file is not part of an Exchange Server database file.

Server processes are services that Exchange Server creates on an NT Server to manage the Exchange Server processes. There are four key services:

- Directory Service
- Information Store Service
- Message-Transfer Agent Service
- System Attendant Service

The Directory Service manages the directory objects of an Exchange Server. It ensures that recipients are replicated into the Global Address List throughout the Exchange organization.

The Information Store Service manages the messages and information within both the Public Information Store and the Private Information Store on the Exchange Server.

The Message-Transfer Agent Service handles the movement of messages throughout the Exchange Server system. It handles traffic and transmissions.

The System Attendant Service monitors and manages the Exchange Server background operations. One of the System Attendant Service's task is to handle the routing tables for the MTA.

The overall hierarchical structure of Exchange, along with the interaction of the Exchange Servers and their internal services, enables it to provide a scalable, reliable architecture for messaging and groupware.

Most of the topics covered in this introductory chapter are explained at much greater length in the remainder of this book. For now, you have enough of a foundation to move on to further exploration of Exchange 5.5.

Chapter 2
What's New in Exchange Server 5.5?

Microsoft Exchange has been a leading collaborative product since its introduction in April 1996. With each new release, Microsoft has added new functionality to enhance Exchange's capabilities.

In this chapter, we look at the new features and functions available in Exchange Server 5.5. We look at how Exchange Server integrates Internet functionality, examine the types of Internet protocols that can be used with it, and learn how other new components help Exchange to integrate with applications and systems. Exchange Server has many facets, and with some configuration, it can become an enterprise's greatest asset in accessing the outside world.

The improvements in Exchange Server 5.5 fall into four basic categories, each of which is discussed in this chapter.

- **Internet functionality** The Internet has become the new standard computing environment. Many of the new features in Exchange 5.5 revolve around making Exchange fit into the Internet environment.

- **Extended Exchange functionality** Not all the advances move into new areas of functionality; some of the enhancements are simply extensions of existing features. Don't downplay these enhancements simply because they build on the existing foundation. These features may be some of the most welcome additions to Exchange.

- **Integration with other products and standards** Although Exchange provides a complete messaging solution, other products and standards are part of the overall computing world. As Exchange becomes more popular, organizations need increased integration to the outside world to take advantage of Exchange in all types of environments.

- **Changes under the hood** Quite a few of the advances in Exchange 5.5 are not as readily apparent as those described in the previous paragraphs, but they probably are the most important improvements in Exchange.

Embracing the Internet

The Internet has revolutionized the world, providing an unprecedented level of interconnection among computer users. The primary purpose of Exchange is to enhance the communications capabilities of the people and organizations that use it. It is only natural that as Internet standards have evolved, Exchange has grown to embrace them.

The largest single area of increased capability in Exchange 5.5 is the capability to use Internet standards—from communications protocols to client access. The following sections discuss the main enhancements from version 5.0 and 5.5 that improve the capability of Exchange to work in an Internet environment.

HTML Support

Although the Outlook Web Access client was available for use with Exchange 5.0, it is a new feature to early Exchange adopters. Microsoft has extended the reach of Exchange with the Outlook Web Access client, which allows access to many Outlook features via HTML in a Web browser. Users can now access Outlook's contact and calendar information from any Web browser.

The Active Server Platform

The Active Server platform is a movement that Microsoft is continuing to develop within Exchange. In one sense, the Active Server platform that is part of Exchange 5.5 is primarily a way to extend the capabilities of Exchange, as discussed later in this chapter.

The Active Server platform not only works within Exchange for automating applications, but it can utilize Hypertext Transfer Protocol (HTTP). HTTP is the protocol that is used for Web browsers on the Internet. The result is that Exchange's Active Server platform is extensible to the Internet.

HTML Forms Converter

This new feature, which is included in Exchange Service Pack 1 (SP1), provides a wizard, which, with a few simple prompts, walks the user through converting Outlook forms to HTML and Active Server Page (ASP) components. This feature allows users to view the forms in a browser with no additional development work.

The implication of the HTML Forms Converter is that it integrates Microsoft Exchange Server with the Internet for application development. Exchange forms are the main means of development for groupware/collaborative applications. Unlike many groupware systems, the Exchange forms development process is easy to learn and use. Now that those forms can be converted to HTML, the HTML development for a Web site can be greatly shortened. Additionally, the groupware functionality is extended to non-Exchange users, enabling a unique Internet or intranet presence.

POP3 Protocol Support

Support for Post Office Protocol 3 (POP3) was available in Exchange 5.0, but it is an important feature of Exchange, so it bears mentioning here. Although Simple Mail Transport Protocol (SMTP) is the most common Internet messaging protocol, POP3 is used for retrieving mail transmitted over the Internet. By supporting POP3, Exchange 5.5 allows any standard POP3-capable Internet mail client to use Exchange as its mail server.

NNTP Protocol Support

The Network News Transport Protocol (NNTP) is the standard protocol for Internet newsgroups. *Newsgroups,* which are referred to as *Usenet newsgroups,* are servers on the Internet that provide a discussion service in which people read about a variety of topics and add their own comments on those topics. Exchange 5.0 and later versions supports the NNTP protocol so that newsgroups in Exchange can be extended to the Internet.

Exchange 5.5 lets you access discussion groups on your Exchange Server using a standard Internet newsgroup reader application. It also allows you to import discussion groups into your Exchange environment. After importing the contents of a newsgroup into an Exchange public folder, you can utilize the standard Exchange replication methods to propagate the newsgroup throughout your distributed Exchange environment. The newsgroup support in Exchange 5.5 allows you to pull information in from a newsgroup and push messages added to an internal Exchange public folder back to the original Internet newsgroup. In fact, your Exchange Server actually has the capability to act as a full-blown hub for a Usenet user group.

Newsfeed Configuration Wizard

Exchange 5.5 does more than simply give you the capability to use Internet newsgroups. Another new feature in this release is a wizard that helps you set up the way that your Exchange Server receives information from Internet newsgroups.

Many administrators fret over how to manage Internet traffic so that Internet links are not clogged with duplicated transmissions. Because workgroups tend to access the same types of information, an administrator can take advantage of both public folders and Exchange Server's single-instance storage by creating a public folder *newsfeed*.

In this scenario, the administrator discovers which newsgroups are required by multiple users. Then the administrator verifies that the newsgroups are accessible and that the newsgroup addresses are correct. After that, the administrator uses the Newsfeed Configuration Wizard on the public folders that will contain the newsgroup information. Then, the administrator performs a quality-assurance test to ensure that the newsgroup is accessible and timely and that the process of posting messages works properly. Finally, the administrator simply needs to notify the Exchange users that the newsgroup information is available and how to access it.

SSL Support

Although not as new as other features, the SSL feature extends the Internet functionality of Exchange. *SSL* stands for *Secure Sockets Layer*, which is one method of securing communications over the Internet. By providing SSL support, Exchange ensures secure communications with Outlook Web Access, a POP3 mail client, an Internet news reader, or an LDAP client.

> **Note** SSL is one of the Internet standards that people use without even realizing it. When transmitting financial information over the Internet, most people are using SSL. They needed a way to transmit personal and credit information without putting their customers at risk. SSL came to the rescue.
>
> You can easily determine when SSL is being used when you access a Web site. On the Microsoft Internet Explorer browser, an icon that looks like a yellow padlock appears on the status bar at the bottom of the browser window whenever SSL is being used. Additionally, the Web site's URL will begin with *https://* rather than *http://*.

LDAP Support

LDAP stands for *Lightweight Directory Access Protocol*, which is a standard protocol used for accessing directory information from a variety of sources. Exchange now supports LDAP queries on the Exchange Directory, which makes it easier for standard applications and custom programs to extract information about the Exchange environment.

A directory is a listing of network users and/or network resources that is used by operating systems and applications to organize and secure access to them. The Exchange Server Directory is used to manage messages, recipients, servers, connectors, protocol support, directory lists and sites, and so on. An Exchange user perceives the directory as the Global Address List of recipients, while an administrator perceives the directory through the Exchange Administrator as the entire hierarchical architecture.

LDAP was intended as an open standard. It is meant to access multiple directories simultaneously. The older X.500 standard for Directory Service was an exceptional standard and provided a hierarchical structure that Exchange emulates. However, when developed, X.500 clients tended to be on the heavy side, meaning they used a lot of network bandwidth. Hence, LDAP was developed and named "lightweight" to indicate its network bandwidth utilization improvement.

LDAP clients are able to access any directory that is LDAP-compatible. If, for example, a user wanted to access an LDAP-compatible UNIX Directory and also access the Microsoft Exchange Directory, the user could access both at the same time with an LDAP client.

The LDAP client sees each LDAP-compliant directory as a separate heading in a global directory. LDAP can access Domain Name System (DNS) directories of Internet information, too. Instead of DNS simply mapping the addresses to IP addresses in the background, the DNS domain directory can be browsed from an LDAP client. Microsoft's new Active Directory Service will also be LDAP-compliant, further enabling LDAP client usage on the network.

Internet Locator Server

Exchange users can take advantage of Microsoft's Internet Locator Server (ILS) for looking up addresses through the standard Exchange Directory Services. ILS is a feature of Microsoft NetMeeting that tracks users who are available to participate in a collaborative session with NetMeeting. Exchange 5.5 automatically links names in an Exchange address book to the names in NetMeeting's ILS, so there is no need to maintain two separate address books for NetMeeting and Exchange.

Junk Mail Prevention

When commercial businesses began to use the Internet, many new marketing schemes developed. One of these marketing schemes is sending mass e-mailings to thousands of people's mailboxes. Some Web sites collect data on people so that they can sell the e-mail addresses to companies that will use them for mass e-mailings. Those mass mailings of unsolicited commercial e-mail are collectively called *spam*; in other words, spam is the junk mail of the Internet. It can fill mailboxes with unwanted and unread messages. Not only is spam unwanted, but when a large amount of it is mass-mailed to Exchange users, it can eat up a lot of server space. SP1 for Exchange 5.5 allows Exchange Administrators to implement rules that help to block spam from users' mailboxes.

Chat Server

The Exchange Chat Server enables an Exchange Server to host real-time chat sessions that use Internet Relay Chat (IRC) services with the client (IRCX) extensions. The Exchange Chat Server also provides a set of advanced features, such as automatic transcription of conversations to disk, support for multiple languages, profanity filters, and a very high level of scalability.

Extending Existing Exchange Functionality

Exchange 5.5 extends some of the functionality of previous versions of the product, as detailed in the following descriptions. From enhanced e-mail capabilities to automated applications and Internet integration, Exchange 5.5 extensions provide even greater benefits to veteran Exchange users.

Active Server Components

Not only are Active Server components an Internet enhancement in Exchange 5.5, but the Active Server platform, as shown in Figure 2-1, is also a robust programming platform. The Active Server components in Exchange allow a developer to use Exchange features in Active Server Pages on the Web. The new Active Server components, such as Collaboration Data Objects, make it easier to integrate Exchange into outside applications or to write applications that extend the reach of Exchange into the enterprise and outside, to the Internet. Chapter 27 deals specifically with creating applications on the Active Server platform.

The Active Server platform is an exciting enhancement. It means that any Exchange groupware application that can be converted with Active Server components will be able to run on any computer that has a Web browser and TCP/IP. It literally provides universal accessibility.

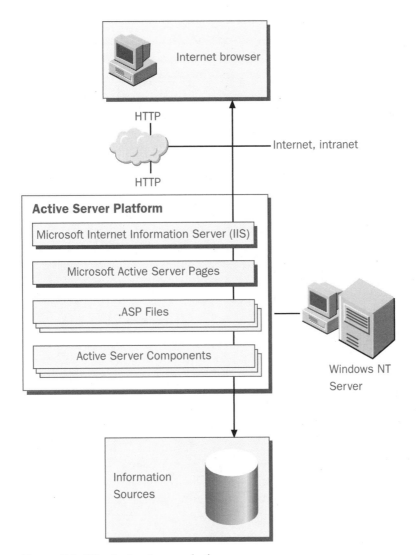

Figure 2-1. *The Active Server platform.*

Scripting Agent

Exchange 5.5 introduces a Server Scripting Agent, which intercepts certain server-side events and allows you to attach scripts that fire when the events occur. Scripts can use Microsoft VBScript or JavaScript. Not only can Exchange Server events cause a script to execute, but the Scripting Agent integrates with SQL Server and enables SQL events to cause a script to fire. Event-driven scripts execute when some action is taken on an Exchange folder, such as when a message is posted. The Scripting Agent also executes time-driven scripts. A time-driven script executes periodically — for example, every Friday.

In SP1, Microsoft introduced a set of routing objects that are built on the event architecture. You can use these objects to implement basic routing functionality into an Exchange form, which you will learn how to do in Chapter 23.

Person-to-Person Key Exchange

Key Management Server (KMS) is the encryption service offered within Exchange Server. KMS encrypts messages using a key encryption. A *key exchange* attaches to a message a key that encodes the contents of the message. A *person-to-person key exchange* allows key exchanges with people inside and outside the Exchange organization. Once an administrator assigns a key to a user, the user can send encrypted messages.

Address Book Views

In earlier versions of Exchange, administrators had to give users access to the entire Global Exchange Directory. Typically, users created their own individual address books. The display of all the users and resources in an Exchange system, however, could be disconcerting — for administrators, who wanted to be able to segregate access to the directory, and for users, who could be overwhelmed by the large amounts of information in the Global Directory. Exchange 5.5 allows administrators to create address book views, which show a subset of the Global Directory, and to use these views in place of the Global Directory for individual users. By using address book views, administrators can create a virtual organization whose members can see only the resources within their own virtual organization.

Outlook for Windows 3.x and Macintosh Clients

Exchange 5.5 includes a version of the Outlook client for 16-bit Windows machines and Macintosh computers. Outlook replaced the Exchange client as the preferred method of access for an Exchange Server. Outlook was originally released as part of the Microsoft Office suite of applications for 32-bit Windows. The Outlook application, its features, and its ease of use have made it exceptionally popular.

In mixed environments, where legacy 16-bit Windows is still used and where Macintosh clients exist, the addition of Outlook clients makes Exchange Server easier for users to work with and for administrators to support.

Integrating with the Outside World

Exchange 5.5 includes enhancements that improve integration with the messaging world outside an Exchange organization. Messaging is an integral part of business for many enterprises. Messaging is not only used to conduct business within the enterprise but to conduct business with partners, vendors, and customers as well. Exchange provides various links to external systems to facilitate this type of messaging connectivity.

Connectors

Many enterprises use the proprietary and legacy messaging systems utilized by mainframes and networks. Some applications have been developed to access and utilize the connectivity that their messaging infrastructures provide. Exchange Server provides connectors to access these types of systems.

Connectors enable Exchange to co-exist and interconnect with Lotus's cc:Mail systems, from version 2 through version 8, and provide support for IBM's PROFS and SNADS systems. Exchange also has connectors for popular Lotus Notes groupware and IBM's OfficeVision messaging systems.

Migration Tools

Migration is the ability to move a set of mailboxes from one messaging system to another. Depending on the type of connectivity and the support of the connector, varying types of migration can occur. Either the migration will simply carry over a set of users and mailboxes, or it will move those and include collaborative applications and shared data. Exchange 5.5 provides a set of migration tools for moving users and mail from existing Novell GroupWise (originally introduced in 5.0), Netscape Collabra (also introduced in 5.0), and UNIX SendMail systems. The SP1 release of Exchange 5.5 introduces enhanced support for migrating mailboxes and calendars from Lotus Notes and Lotus Domino servers. New enhancements include an IMAP/LDAP Migration option as well.

Changes Under the Hood

There are two categories of under-the-hood enhancement in Exchange 5.5. One category incorporates performance and capacity enhancements. The other category addresses administrative tasks.

Performance and Capacity

The following improvements either contribute to the enhanced performance of Exchange 5.5 or increase the capacity of Exchange systems using 5.5:

- **Unlimited message stores** As many current users of Exchange know, the information stores of Exchange can grow far beyond your calculations. Exchange 5.5 Enterprise Edition places almost no limit on the size of the Public and Private Information Stores (16TB).

- **Improved backup performance** The larger data stores get, the longer it takes to back them up. Backup performance in Exchange 5.5 has been improved up to 25GB an hour.

- **Support of Clustering Service** Clustering Service is a feature of Windows NT Enterprise Edition that allows two Windows NT machines to appear to be a single machine. If one of the two machines fails, the other machine automatically kicks in. The Clustering Service provides a new level of reliability in a Windows NT-based system such as Exchange.

Administration

Other under-the-hood improvements in Exchange 5.5 deliver an increased ability to administer and manage an Exchange system:

- **Public folder subsites** A public folder can be replicated to many servers in an Exchange site. Defining a subsite, which contains a corresponding subset of public folders, can help direct users to copies of public folders that they can access more rapidly. This improvement was initially introduced with Exchange 5.0.

- **Attribute filtering for intersite replication** By default, all attributes of Exchange objects are automatically replicated among sites in an organization. This new feature in Exchange 5.5 allows administrators to replicate specified directory attributes, which can improve the overall performance of directory replication.

- **Internet Mail Wizard**   Exchange 5.5 includes a wizard for setting up the Internet Mail Service, which allows Exchange Servers to send and receive mail over the Internet. This service was originally introduced in Exchange 5.0.

- **Information store free space**   The SP1 release for Exchange 5.5 includes an enhancement that calculates the amount of free space in Public and Private Information Stores on a daily basis. By checking this calculation, administrators can decide when they should defragment the data stores.

- **Deleted Item Recovery**   Version 5.5 allows administrators to keep items on the Exchange Server, even after they have been deleted by a user.

Real World   Deleted Item Recovery

The Deleted Item Recovery feature may seem like overkill. In an Outlook 98 client, for instance, deleting an item just moves it to the Deleted Items folder, where it can remain for a period of time the user sets. Why add what seems to be an identical function to the server?

For a few very simple reasons: Users make mistakes. Users do not have the long view of an administrator. This fail-safe function makes it easy for an administrator to keep an item around, even after users think they are completely finished with it. Most servers have a large amount of disk space, so maintaining these messages a little longer is not very costly. And when users find that they are able to salvage that crucial message that they thought was gone for good—well, let's just say that you will look like a real hero!

- **Move Server Wizard**   SP1 for Exchange Server 5.5 includes a wizard that makes it easy to move an Exchange Server between existing sites or organizations, to create a new site or organization, to create a new site in an existing organization, or to merge existing Exchange Servers. The wizard makes all of these processes less prone to error.

- **Interorganization replication**   Prior to Exchange 5.5, two different Exchange organizations could not share some information with each other. They had two separate trees that did not "know" that the other existed, nor could the organizations see each other's trees. They had two separate address lists that they could not automatically update. With this version, Exchange organizations can share directory and collaborative information.

Updating Exchange to the Next Version

Exchange 5.5 is not a major release, but it provides a significant number of new features and advances. Keep in mind that Microsoft continually adds new features with each incremental service pack for Exchange, so you should periodically check the main Exchange Web site, *http://www.microsoft.com/exchange*, for announcements of new service packs and their features, such as SP2, released in January 1999.

The next release of Exchange, 6.0, looks as though it will be an even greater advance. But that's in the future. For now, let's focus on giving you all the information that you need to use and administer Exchange 5.5 in the most effective way possible.

Summary

Exchange 5.5 delivers a raft of improvements in four basic areas:

- Integrates with the Internet and its protocols and standards
- Extends existing Exchange functionality
- Integrates with external mail systems
- Enhances Exchange under the hood

The Internet explosion has affected many applications, especially those in the area of messaging. Internet e-mail is one of the basic functions required for Internet connectivity. Exchange Server enables use of standard Internet e-mail applications by its integration of POP3, HTTP, and IMAP4 protocol support. It also expands its Internet integration through the use of Active Server components and scripting tools.

Exchange Server 5.5, although not a major release, extends capabilities from earlier versions. The capabilities that were introduced in Exchange 5.0 have been enhanced to provide a wider range of resources of which end users can take advantage.

Connectors are the means that Exchange uses to integrate with other messaging systems. Exchange can support connections to PROFS, SNADS, and OfficeVision, all from IBM. Exchange also provides connectors to Lotus cc:Mail and Lotus Notes. Connectors can provide simple messaging or extend to sharing calendaring information and collaborative applications.

Under the hood, Exchange 5.5 has enhanced administrative capabilities. From the ability to recover deleted items to the management of free space in the information store, Exchange 5.5 is easier than ever for an administrator to manage.

Exchange Server 5.5 is an ever-evolving product. It can provide messaging and collaborative applications and any messaging requirements for enterprises today, even those on the leading edge of the Internet. The next version of Exchange, a major release, will further expand the horizons of Exchange Server in terms of messaging, connectivity, groupware, and Internet capabilities.

Chapter 3
Integration with the Operating System

Microsoft's Exchange Server 5.5 and the Microsoft Windows NT Server network operating system platform are closely linked. Both products' heritage gives them a similar look, feel, and design philosophy, making it easy to apply knowledge about one of these products to using the other.

In this chapter, we look at Microsoft Windows NT Server and its linkage to Exchange Server 5.5. We look at how Exchange Server incorporates Windows NT's interface, examine Exchange's security integration through NT accounts, and learn how Exchange utilizes various Windows NT features. If we take advantage of the robust performance of Windows NT, Exchange becomes more effective and scalable.

Microsoft Windows NT is the only network operating system platform that Exchange Server runs on. The interaction between Exchange and Windows NT, however, goes a bit beyond that simple statement. Exchange is intertwined with Windows NT in three ways:

- Exchange runs in a Windows NT environment.
- Exchange uses the features and functionality of Windows NT.
- Exchange is integrated with Windows NT security.

This chapter examines the connections between Exchange and Windows NT, and explores how the two products will become even more closely united through advancing technologies.

Running on Windows NT

The Exchange Server provides a single-server application that can be installed only on the Microsoft Windows NT Server network operating system. Exchange Server provides client applications that are compatible with Windows,

Macintosh, and Windows NT. There is also a Web browser client that can be accessed from any Web browser, regardless of the operating system. Exchange is implemented as a series of Windows NT services. If you open the Windows NT Control Panel and double-click on the Services icon, you see the Services window, shown in Figure 3-1.

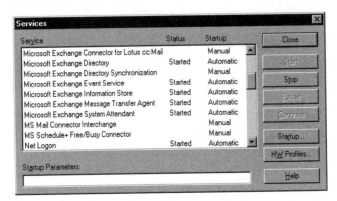

Figure 3-1. *The Windows NT Services window.*

Figure 3-1 displays the main Exchange services — Directory, Information Store, Message-Transfer Agent, and System Attendant — showing that they are implemented as separate Windows NT services. Other, more specialized functions of Exchange, such as Directory Synchronization and the Exchange Event Service, are also implemented as individual Windows NT services. Each Exchange Server is configured according to the enterprise's individual requirements, so the number and types of Exchange services running differ from server to server.

Exchange Server integrates with Windows NT Server's security account management system, which is organized in the form of domains. A *domain* is a group of computers that share a common security scheme and database. The operation of domains is controlled by a computer designated as the primary domain controller (PDC). The PDC contains the security account database. Because Exchange depends on the security services offered by a domain, an Exchange Server cannot be installed in a network that does not include a PDC. An NT domain can contain one or more NT Servers that have been installed as backup domain controllers (BDC) for redundancy; however, BDCs are not necessary for Exchange Server to function. The remaining NT Servers in a domain, if they are not PDCs or BDCs, are called member servers.

Exchange Server 5.5 participates in the Windows NT domain model security through corresponding Exchange mailboxes with NT user accounts. For users to access an Exchange mailbox, they must log on to the Windows NT domain under a valid Windows NT user account. This user account can exist in the same domain as the Exchange Server computer or in any trusted domain. Even a user with an Outlook Web Access client, POP3, IMAP, or LDAP client will be authenticated to an NT domain prior to accessing the services. The user may not even realize it, but that is where the account must reside for Exchange.

When a trust relationship exists between two domains, one domain can directly access the resources of the other domain. A trust relationship must be explicitly defined between two domains, and each trust relationship operates in only one direction. If Domain A is configured to trust Domain B, the users in Domain B can be granted permissions on resources in Domain A. If users in Domain A need to be granted permissions on resources in Domain B, the administrator has to explicitly define a separate trust relationship in which Domain B trusts Domain A.

Real World   Site Service Account and Multiple Domains

If you have the appropriate trust relationships set up among multiple domains in an Exchange site, it is best to give the Exchange Site Service account exactly the same name and password in both domains. Because each domain maintains its own isolated directory of users and passwords, there is not necessarily any coordination between the Site Service accounts in two different Windows NT domains. If you choose not to create identical Site Service accounts in each domain, you must specify certain rights and permissions in each domain for the other domain's Site Service account.

It is good practice to create an NT user account in each domain that participates in an Exchange organization for a specific Site Service account. This will prevent any problems with determining and granting rights and permissions to accounts later on.

Using Windows NT

Because your Exchange Server participates in a Windows NT environment, all the information associated with Exchange is stored in the Windows NT file system. This fact may seem so simplistic that it is not worth mentioning, but because Exchange uses the Windows NT file system, it also can use a modified form of the Windows NT backup program to safely store all the data in Exchange as part of a Windows backup. Check out Chapter 21 for advice on backing up and restoring Exchange Server data.

The Exchange application itself does not authenticate users; it leaves that job to the Windows NT security system. Exchange concentrates on enforcing a security scheme based on an already authenticated and identified Windows NT user. What this means is that the mailbox is separate from the user account, because the mailbox is provided by Exchange and the user account is provided by a Windows NT Server domain.

Exchange integrates with other Windows NT utilities, such as Performance Monitor and Event Viewer. For example, if you launch Performance Monitor and click Add Counter, you see Exchange objects that can be added to the Performance Monitor window, as shown in Figure 3-2.

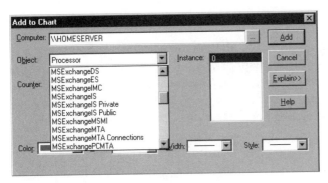

Figure 3-2. *Categories of Exchange counters in Windows NT Performance Monitor.*

Each of these objects has several counters, so you have a great deal of flexibility in the types of monitoring that you can enable. In fact, Exchange comes with its own set of predefined Performance Monitor views, which are described in more detail in Chapter 20. These views are implemented as instances of the Windows NT Performance Monitor, with several appropriate counters enabled, as shown in Figure 3-3.

You can also set up Windows NT alerts that are sent when a problem occurs with any Exchange service. Exchange Server extends to the Windows NT Event Log, which can track changes made in the messaging system that you specified previously.

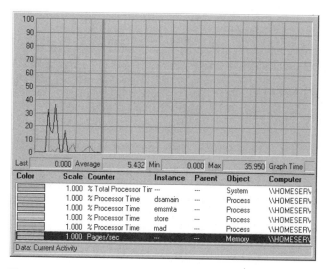

Figure 3-3. *An Exchange Performance Monitor.*

Integrating with Windows NT

The Exchange Server lives in the Windows NT environment and uses the services of Windows NT. But after you install Exchange on your Windows NT Server, you will find that Exchange and Windows NT start to act as an integrated system.

One way in which the administrative functions of Exchange and Windows NT are integrated involves the definition of a new user for either system. Exchange Server integrates mailbox creation with NT user account creation tools. The NT Server User Manager for Domains can be used to create an Exchange mailbox and NT user account simultaneously, as well as link the mailbox and NT account. When you define a new mailbox recipient in Exchange Server 5.5 or a new user account in Windows NT, you are asked whether you also want to define the other entity.

Linking a Windows NT Account with an Exchange Mailbox

As an example of the integration between a Windows NT account and an Exchange mailbox, consider creating a new mailbox in Exchange Administrator. When you create a new user by choosing New Mailbox from the File menu in Exchange Administrator, you see the Mailbox property sheets shown in Figure 3-4.

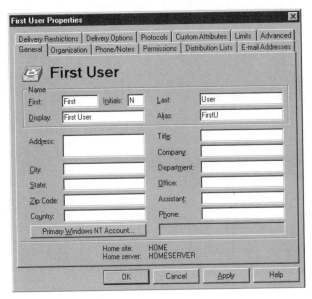

Figure 3-4. *The General property sheet for defining a new user.*

At the bottom of the General property sheet is a button labeled Primary Windows NT Account. When you click this button, you are given the option to select an existing Windows NT account as the primary account or to create a new account. If you choose to use an existing account, a dialog box allows you to select a Windows NT user or group as the primary account. If you choose to create a new account, you are asked for the username and domain for the new Windows NT account.

The Permissions tab of the Mailbox property sheets allows you to give more than one Windows NT account permission to access a particular Exchange mailbox. Normally, however, the Permissions tab does not appear as part of the property sheet for a mailbox. You add this tab to the property sheet by choosing Options from the Tools menu in Exchange Administrator and then selecting the Permissions tab. When you check the box labeled Show Permissions Page for All Objects, the Permissions tab shows up in the property sheet for a mailbox, as shown in Figure 3-5.

You assign additional users in the Windows NT Accounts with Permissions area at the center of the Permissions tab. After you give users permission to look at a mailbox other than their own, they can simply choose Open Other User's folder from the Open or File menu in the Outlook client to bring up another window that displays the Inbox of the second user.

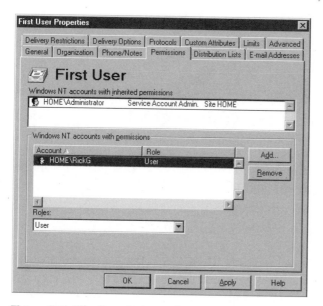

Figure 3-5. *The Permissions tab.*

The Permissions property sheet in the Options screen of Exchange Administrator contains two other options related to the association between an Exchange user and a Windows NT user. The last check box on the page tells Exchange Administrator to automatically search for a Window NT user account when you create a mailbox in Exchange. This option means that Exchange Administrator will search the Windows NT accounts in the domain for a username that matches, or almost matches, the name that you assigned in the top part of the General tab of the User Definition window. By the time you finish entering the information, Exchange Administrator will have already found and suggested a user account to the mailbox. If you do not want to use the suggested account, you have the option of selecting or creating another account. This feature is enabled by default.

The other option related to Windows NT accounts is represented by the check box labeled Delete Primary Windows NT Account When Deleting Mailbox. This check box is somewhat more dangerous because it removes the underlying Windows NT account when you delete a mailbox from Exchange. Because Windows NT has a broader range of functionality than simply hosting Exchange, this option is deselected by default, and you should carefully consider the implications before you change the default setting.

Linking a Mailbox with a Windows NT Account

Just as you can associate a Windows NT account with a new Exchange mailbox, after you install Exchange in a domain, you can automatically create an Exchange mailbox when you create a new Windows NT account.

You create new Windows NT accounts by using User Manager for Domains, which is one of the administrative tools that comes with Windows NT. When you open the User Manager for Domains, you see an Exchange menu on the main menu bar. This menu contains two commands. The PROPERTIES command displays the Exchange property sheet for the user that you selected in the main window of the User Manager for Domains.

The other command in this menu, OPTIONS, displays the dialog box shown in Figure 3-6. This dialog box contains check boxes that allow you to always create an Exchange mailbox when you create a new Windows NT user and to automatically delete an associated mailbox when you delete a user. By default, both of these check boxes are checked. You probably will want to add Exchange mailboxes on an ongoing basis as you add new accounts to your Windows NT domain. When that option is selected, the standard property sheet for an Exchange mailbox appears as soon as you create a new user in the User Manager.

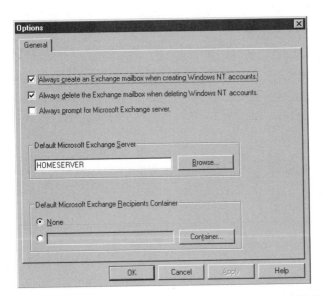

Figure 3-6. *The Exchange options in the Windows NT User Manager for Domains.*

If you decide that you do not want to create an Exchange mailbox for the newly defined Windows NT user, click the Cancel button. Because the Windows NT user is directly associated with an Exchange mailbox, it makes sense to delete the mailbox as soon as you delete the user from the domain.

The process of creating recipients for Exchange is covered in more detail in Chapter 9. Chapter 9 also discusses the Exchange Import utility and the Windows NT User Extraction tool, which allow you to create an Exchange mailbox for all or some of the Windows NT user accounts on your server.

Real World   Why Not Both?
In the real world, you typically have a Windows NT user account and an Exchange mailbox for all users on both systems. Exchange facilitates communication, and the more inclusive that communication, the more powerful it is.

However, in cases like the following, you might want to have a Windows NT account or an Exchange recipient, each without the other:

- **Windows NT user and no Exchange recipient**   Exchange provides messaging and collaboration services for Windows NT users, so you probably want to give all your Windows NT users access to Exchange. But you might have some Windows NT accounts that are not really part of your organization (such as guest accounts that can be used by many people), and you might want to exclude those accounts from your Exchange organization. If you are implementing Exchange for the first time, you might want to add users to the Exchange environment gradually, so you would not want to create mailboxes for all the Windows NT users on your server. You could still use the Windows NT Account utility to create a complete export of your Windows NT users and then edit the file manually.

- **Exchange recipient and no Windows NT user**   You can define an Exchange mailbox without assigning it to a Windows NT account. But why would you do this? You might want to create a dummy user, which you could then use as a template to define other users. This template would not necessarily need to have a Windows NT user account associated with it.

After your Exchange installation becomes a mature implementation, you generally will want to create a new Exchange user for every new Windows NT account, and vice versa.

Exploring the Future of Exchange and Windows 2000 Server

As you may have already heard, the future of Windows NT is Windows 2000. The release that was once anticipated as Windows NT 5.0 Server has been renamed Windows 2000 Server. Although the name will be different, the Windows 2000 release remains part of the same Windows NT family.

Windows 2000 aims to deliver a seamless computing environment to the enterprise. This goal implies convergence and expansion. In this context, convergence means that many of the applications that run on Exchange will be integrated much more tightly with Windows 2000. Exchange Administrator, for example, will be part of the Microsoft Management Console, rather than a stand-alone program.

One of the most important new features in Windows 2000 is the Active Directory Service, which will give developers and users a uniform view of *all* the resources available in Windows 2000—from directories and drives to mailboxes and users. As you can imagine, these capabilities will allow Exchange to appear much more like an integrated piece of the Windows 2000 operating system. In effect, the new release of Windows 2000 and the next release of Exchange will make Exchange seem like a simple extension of Windows 2000. This tight integration will, in turn, help simplify all of your administrative and management tasks. With Windows 2000, the distinctions among Exchange running on a platform, using the services of the platform, and being integrated with a platform will blur.

The expansion of Windows 2000 will provide even more scalability, expanding the resources that are available to Windows 2000 and making it easier to manage large numbers of these resources. Windows 2000 will make it easier for applications such as Exchange to integrate with the management capabilities of Windows 2000. Therefore, as management features are added to the Windows 2000 environment, the benefits of these features will be available to Exchange automatically.

The next release of Exchange is scheduled for 90 days after the production release of Windows 2000, so you will not have to wait long to see the benefits of the increased integration of Windows 2000 and Exchange.

Summary

In many ways, Exchange Server is integrated with Windows NT. Exchange Server was developed as a Windows NT application. It integrates with the NT network operating system and utilizes many of the services and features of Windows NT.

Exchange Server is tightly integrated with Windows NT security account data. An Exchange Server is intended to participate in the security of an NT domain, and as such, it requires a primary domain controller (PDC) in its NT environment. The domain structure of Windows NT affects the way you implement your Exchange organization. Trust relationships should be planned between domains in order to enable Exchange Servers to interconnect.

As an administrator, you can configure Exchange and Windows NT so that you will be able to create both an Exchange mailbox and a Windows NT user account at the same time — from either the User Manager or the Exchange Administrator.

Exchange Server utilizes a distinctive user account, known as the Site Service account, to access the NT system. The Site Service account is an NT user account that, to avoid issues, should be identically named and granted identical passwords in each NT domain of the Exchange Server environment.

The Exchange Server application integrates with other parts of NT Server. Both Performance Monitor and Event Log, which are NT Server tools, are extended to manage Exchange Server processes and events.

The next release of Windows NT, called Windows 2000, will feature an even closer integration between Exchange and its host operating system. This will appear in a new integrated management application. Active Directory 2000's new security management database will affect the way that Exchange mailboxes and user accounts are linked, as well as how the Exchange Server system is designed.

Chapter 4
Organizing Information in Exchange

Exchange is composed of two basic areas of operation:

- The active services, which Exchange uses to implement functionality such as message delivery
- The storage of information in various physical locations

In this chapter, we explore the organization of information in an Exchange Server system. We look at the storage components of the architecture and how those storage components work together. We learn how they are organized both logically and physically to provide a comprehensive groupware system. Exchange Server can manage a great deal of information, and with Exchange's strong organizational system, it becomes clear how distributing Exchange data—without users being required to know where it is physically located—facilitates enterprise-wide accessibility.

This chapter examines the capabilities of one of the most important features of Exchange: the public folder. The public folder is the organizational container for shared data. The public folder is also the logical area that houses collaborative applications. An Exchange user experiences public folders as a single storage area, even when public folders are distributed across many physical public information stores on Exchange Servers. The distribution, replication, and security of public folders must all be designed correctly for the intended users to be able to access them.

Understanding Physical Storage in Exchange

Exchange separates the physical storage of information from the logical organization of the same information. This separation enables Exchange users to access information based on the logical organization, while allowing administrators to deal with the physical organization in their maintenance tasks.

The primary unit of physical organization in Exchange is the *information store*. Because the physical storage of information in Exchange is closely associated with the Exchange Server, most Exchange administrative functions operate on the underlying physical storage areas of Exchange. Based on this association, the information stored in an Exchange organization follows the topology of the underlying Exchange Servers and sites.

Exchange uses two information stores: one public, one private. You have the choice of placing the Public Information Store and the Private Information Store on the same server machine and disk, or on different disks, or even on different machines.

A typical Exchange Server is implemented with both a Private Information Store and a Public Information Store. However, Exchange Servers can be configured as dedicated mailbox servers with only a Private Information Store, or they can be installed as dedicated public folder servers with only a Public Information Store. Some Exchange Servers have both the Private and Public Information Stores, but they are configured to hold each store on different physical storage devices (either a separate physical hard drive or a separate RAID array).

An administrator might implement Exchange Server in any configuration for a variety of reasons. For one, selecting separate physical devices for the Private Information Store and the Public Information Store can enhance the server's performance. This enhancement is mainly caused by the way Exchange manages each of these stores. Even further performance enhancements can be realized by using separate servers dedicated to either a mailbox or a public folder task. Another reason to dedicate servers to a particular task is to divide administrative responsibilities and to maintain security; granting administrative access to a dedicated public folder or dedicated mailbox server is more secure than granting it to a combined server.

Each information store is a database. An Exchange Server handles the storage and differentiation of information from multiple users in a single physical file. Any requests to the information store are implemented by the Exchange Information Store Service.

An Exchange Server is allowed one Private Information Store and one Public Information Store. When the server is installed, it can be dedicated to supporting one type of store, in which case the other store would simply not be installed. The Private Information Store contains the mailboxes for each Exchange user configured on that server. Each recipient in an Exchange organization is associated with one server and, subsequently, that server's Private Information Store, which possesses the user's mailbox.

The Public Information Store holds public folders. A replica of each public folder can exist on more than one server in an Exchange organization (a topic that is covered in greater depth later in this chapter). Each individual Exchange Server, however, is responsible for delivering a complete representation of the hierarchy of public folders throughout the entire Exchange site, whether or not the content of the particular public folder exists within its own Public Information Store.

Note A *folder* is an object that contains other objects—primarily Exchange items and other folders. A *public folder* is specifically held in the Public Information Store on an Exchange Server, then enabled across the Exchange organization through replication and granting of rights. A *private folder* is held within the Private Information Store and is seen as a folder within a user's mailbox. A *personal folder* is held outside the Exchange Server and managed by an Exchange user.

Public folders in Exchange consist of two elements: the hierarchy and the content. Because the hierarchy is replicated across the organization automatically, each public folder appears to exist on every server in the organization. What the administrator or Exchange designer must decide is whether the content of a public folder is replicated to multiple servers.

Note Even though information is stored on servers across WAN links, the user accesses that information in the same way that the user accesses local information. The process is transparent to the user. However, the WAN link could cause some performance issues—usually in the form of slow access.

To understand how information stores relate to an Exchange organization, you need to understand the way that the contents of these information stores are displayed in the Exchange Administrator.

The view of the Exchange environment in the Exchange Administrator application consists of a series of containers that are displayed in the container pane of the Administrator window. *Containers* are the objects that arrange an Exchange system into a hierarchy. The Organization object is a container. Also, each Site object is a container. Within each container, there are other objects — either container objects or resource objects. Resource objects represent connectors, mailboxes, distribution lists, and so on.

The Exchange Administrator application is divided into two panes. The left-hand side of the application is the container pane. The right-hand side of the application displays the contents of any container selected in the container pane. These contents include resources, properties, and other containers.

To understand the role that information stores play on an individual server within an Exchange site, open the container for that server in the container pane on the left side of the Exchange Administrator window, as shown in Figure 4-1.

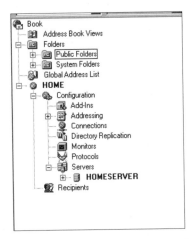

Figure 4-1. *Containers displayed in the Exchange Administrator container pane.*

You see that the Private Information Store includes a Mailbox Resources entry. The entries below this heading list all the mailboxes in this server's Private Information Store and the resources used by each of the mailboxes. There is a mailbox for each of the recipients listed in the Server Recipients container, as well as a mailbox for the System Attendant, which is a system entity used as part of Exchange's internal administration services. Each Exchange Server includes a container called Server Recipients. This container holds the mailboxes for all users that are associated with that particular Exchange Server.

You should also look at the entries inside the Public Folder Resources container in the Public Information Store. These entries list all copies, or replicas, of public folders that have been replicated to the Public Information Store for this particular Exchange Server. The other headings have to do with the replication of public folders. For detailed information on public folder replication, see Chapter 13.

Both the Public and Private Information Stores have a Logons container. A *logon* refers to the users who are accessing the two different information stores on the server. You can't really tell from Exchange Administrator what a user is doing in either the Public or Private Information Store; all you really know is that this user is accessing the appropriate store on this server. As the information store accepts a request for information in the store, it reports this information back to Exchange Administrator.

> **Note**   While looking at the Logons list, did you try to access a mailbox or pub-
> lic folder and still didn't see any changes in the Exchange Administrator display?
> To see any new entries for a group in Exchange Administrator, you have to press
> F5, which refreshes the display.

Exchange Administrator also provides a global view of the information about public folders and users throughout an entire Exchange organization. You can view all the public folders for a site or in an entire Exchange organization through Exchange Administrator. If you go to the top of the Hierarchy container pane in Exchange Administrator, you can see containers for Public Folders (inside the Folders container) and for the Global Address List, whose location in the hierarchy is shown in Figure 4-2.

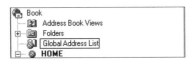

Figure 4-2. *Global views in Exchange.*

Although the physical storage for individual users and replicas of public folders are kept on individual Exchange Servers, Exchange delivers a complete view of the directory for the entire organization, including all recipients. The Exchange Directory Service creates a global view of recipients by incorporating the information from each individual server. When you create a new user on an individual Exchange Server, the mailbox for that user is stored on the server and represented in the Server Recipients container, the site-level Recipients container, and the Global Address Book. In the same way, when you add a public folder to the Public Information Store on an individual server, the folder is represented in the Public Folders and Global Address List (GAL) containers for the Exchange organization. Note that by default, public folders are hidden from the Global Address List. If the administrator "unhides" a public folder and it is seen in the GAL, users will find that it is just as easy to send a message to the public folder as it is to send a message to another user.

Real World   Unhiding a Public Folder from the GAL
If you want to enable a public folder so that it is seen in the Global Address List (GAL), you can change it in the Exchange Administrator. Go to the public folder that you want unhidden and select its properties. Select the Advanced property sheet. Then uncheck the box for Hide from Address book.

Both of these organizational collections are a bit more than simple aggregates of the items from individual Exchange Servers. It is possible to hide recipients so that they do not appear in the GAL. More important, the Public Folders container imparts a complete view of the public folders across an organization, regardless of how those public folders are replicated across multiple servers. Even if a replica of a public folder is kept on many servers in your Exchange organization, you still see only one copy of the folder below the Public Folders container.

Keep in mind that many Exchange administrative functions—including backup, recovery, and replication—are performed on information stores. These operations are covered in later chapters of this book. For now, understanding that these functions relate to the physical storage of information is a key to comprehending how they are used.

Although some administrative functions are handled from the Exchange Administrator application for public folders, most of them are performed from within an Exchange client. Outlook, the Exchange client, is the application that users utilize to create, manage, and access public folders.

Real World **Defining a Public Folder**

Why do you need to define a public folder in an Exchange client? After all, doesn't the Exchange Server handle the information in public folders? The creation of public folders is the exclusive domain of Exchange clients. As logical representations, folders make sense to users. The information that exists in folders, however, is physically maintained as part of an information store on an Exchange Server. The management of the logical entity—the folder—takes place in the client, whereas the physical representation of that entity takes place on the server.

Up to this point, this chapter has discussed the information kept on the Exchange Server. In fact, three additional types of storage involved in an Exchange system are not kept on a server: personal folders, personal address books, and offline storage folders.

Outlook, the primary client for Exchange, can keep files on a client machine or on a network shared disk as personal information. This information is known as personal folders. Outlook can also maintain folders that can be accessed when the client is not connected to Exchange. This type of storage is known as *offline storage folders*. Offline storage folders (which are created with the extension .OST) have an advantage over personal folders (which are created with the extension .PST). Offline storage folder data is actually stored on the Exchange

Server and replicated to the OST file, which means that the data is backed up by administrators.

Understanding Logical Organization in Exchange

The logical organization of information in the Exchange environment loosely parallels the physical organization of information in Exchange. Just as the primary unit of physical storage is the information store, the primary unit of logical organization of information in Exchange is the folder.

As a logical unit of organization, the representation of public folders exists on the clients in an Exchange system, as shown in the folder list in Outlook 98 in Figure 4-3. An administrator can view the logical representation of the Exchange information stores in the Exchange Administrator application.

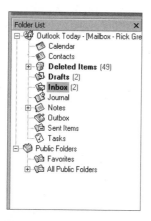

Figure 4-3. *Folder organization in Outlook.*

Mailboxes

Mailboxes in an Exchange client such as Outlook are logical entities that are kept for a user in the Private Information Store on the home Exchange Server. Private folders organize the data in each Exchange user's mailbox.

In Figure 4-4, the Outlook 98 mailbox is shown below the heading Outlook Today, which is a top-level view of the mailbox that contains all the private folders for a user. Each of the folders listed in the mailbox performs a specific function for the Outlook client. The Inbox receives incoming mail for the user, the Outbox holds outgoing mail until it is actually sent to the Exchange Server, the Deleted Items folder holds all the items that have been deleted from the other private folders, and so on. You learn more about the specific functions of private folders in Chapter 18.

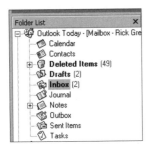

Figure 4-4. *Private folder organization in Outlook.*

Real World   The Deleted Items Folder

The Deleted Items folder holds the items that have been deleted from the Outlook client. You can set up a rule to specify how long items will remain in the Deleted Items folder. Outlook can also periodically clean up any old deleted items.

In addition to this client-based control, an administrator can control how long an item is maintained in the Exchange Server's Private Information Store *after* a client has deleted it. An administrator can also use tools to purge old deleted items. It is good practice to exercise this option only after checking with the Exchange users who might be affected.

Each folder within the mailbox serves double duty. It is an actual private folder as well as a template for creating the same type of folder. For example, the Notes folder contains items that utilize a particular Exchange form (a "note"). The note form provides for the particular set of functions appropriate for a note. A user can create a new folder inside any of the private information folders, and that "child" folder inherits the capabilities and structure of its parent, unless specified as a different folder type. You can delete from your mailbox any folder that you have created, but you cannot delete any of the default folders that appear in your mailbox as part of the Outlook environment.

Public Folders

The other basic type of folder is the public folder. Figure 4-5 shows the public folders in an Outlook 98 folder view.

The two entries below the Public Folders heading are Favorites and All Public Folders. The Favorites entry is useful because an Exchange organization might contain thousands of public folders. (Public folders are the primary means of sharing information among users, so it makes sense to have a public folder for

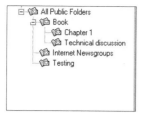

Figure 4-5. *Public folders in Outlook 98.*

each topic that requires shared information.) Individual users, however, might be interested in only a few public folders, and the Favorites entry allows them to highlight the folders that they access most frequently. In addition, users need to add a public folder to their Favorites list if they want to work with the information in the folder offline.

The All Public Folders entry lists all the public folders that are available to the user and contains a default folder called Internet Newsgroups. By default, users can create a public folder directly below the top level of the hierarchy of All Public Folders. Administrators typically change the default setting to restrict Exchange users from creating public folders at the top level; this is an attempt to manage the placement and design of public folders by forcing users to request this access. To truly control the public folder scheme, the administrator should make this change prior to enabling Exchange for users. A public folder acts as both a true folder and as a template for any child folders.

Real World   Granting Privileges for Creating Public Folders

Administrators should carefully evaluate whether to allow users the default privilege of being able to create a public folder at any level. Because public folders immediately become part of the global Exchange environment, unrestricted creation of these folders can rapidly lead to an unmanageably large number of public folders. In addition, users create public folders with little knowledge of the physical location of the data. If a user in one site intends to create a public folder for use in another Exchange site, the default behavior of Exchange requires additional administrative steps to be taken. The user's action will be somewhat unsuccessful for the other site, and a lot of time and effort will be wasted in trying to resolve the issue before, finally, an administrator is asked to solve the problem. The user will have created the public folder, but the rest of the administrative actions will not be completed, because the user will not have created—nor should the user have the ability to create—the trusts, the site affinity, the site connectors, or the replication required.

Both mailboxes and public folders are organized into a single hierarchical view for an Exchange user. The hierarchy is a logical organization of the folders that the Exchange user can access. A parent folder (for example, a folder that contains other folders) initially acts as a template for all child folders created below it. But keep in mind that this hierarchy is a logical one imposed by the logical unit of a folder. Physically, all the private and public folders are organized as part of the larger information store, whether that is the Private Information Store or the Public Information Store.

Working Offline

The mailbox and public folders in Outlook map to the private and Public Information Stores on an Exchange Server. Outlook supports two additional types of information storage: offline folders and personal folders.

Offline Folders

The first type of additional storage is referred to as offline folders. As the name implies, these folders allow Outlook users to work when they do not have a direct connection with an Exchange Server, such as when they are traveling with a laptop. The ability to work offline in the same Outlook environment that is used while connected can greatly improve the productivity of Exchange users.

An *offline folder* is a folder normally available in an Exchange message store that has been copied to your local disk drive so that you can use it when you are not connected to an Exchange Server. By default, all the basic private folders—such as your Inbox, Outbox, and Deleted Items folders—are copied to your machine when you decide to download folders for offline use. You can specify whether you want to include in the download any of the private folders that you created or any existing public folders. Offline folders are stored on a local disk drive in a file with the .OST extension.

When you use a folder offline, you can work with the folder and its functionality even though you are not connected to an Exchange Server. Upon reconnecting to an Exchange Server, you must go through the process of synchronization. *Synchronization* transfers the changes that you made in your offline folders to the source folders on the Exchange Server. For more information about setting up and using offline folders, see Chapter 18.

Personal Folders

One more type of storage can be used for information in an Outlook client, either connected to an Exchange Server or offline. A personal folder, which belongs to an individual user, is kept on a disk drive accessible to the user—either through a local drive or a shared network drive. Personal folders are unique in that they can be created and used without the Outlook user ever having connected to an Exchange Server.

A *personal folder* is merely an external information store that has been added to the Outlook environment. The folder is a file that is identified by the extension .PST. You can add an existing personal folder to your Outlook environment by choosing File, selecting Open, and clicking on a personal folders file (which has the extension .PST). Alternatively, you can use the New menu choice in place of the Open choice to create a new .PST file to contain personal folders.

When you open a personal folder, it appears as a normal set of mailbox folders in the Outlook Directory pane, as shown in Figure 4-6. You can move the folders inside a personal folder to one of the standard Exchange information stores by dragging them in the Outlook Directory pane to the mailbox or to the Public Information Store's hierarchy.

Figure 4-6. *A personal folder in the Outlook Directory pane.*

Personal folders are outside the realm of the Exchange environment. The Exchange Server has no awareness of the existence of any personal folders. Personal folders are not backed up or restored through an Exchange administrative process. Because personal folders act just like private and public folders, you might find them ideal for creating and testing folders before introducing them into the Exchange environment. Keeping valuable information in a personal folder on a permanent basis, however, is considered bad practice. Information in personal folders is inherently less secure than the information stored on an Exchange Server, which is typically subject to more regular backup and monitoring than the information on a client.

Managing Public Folders

Public folders are among the primary mechanisms for dispersing information within Exchange. A public folder, as the name implies, typically is open to the

Exchange user public. However, security features within Exchange can be used to limit which users might access certain folders. In addition, the administrator must configure replication to ensure that the public folder is available to users on different servers and in different Exchange sites while maintaining acceptable performance levels.

Replication enables public folder access for users on different servers so that a user accesses a local copy of the public folder rather than using a copy that is physically distant or on a busy server. The result of using a physically distant public folder or one that is on a busy server is usually poor or slow performance. A public folder can exist in more than one physical location. A single logical representation of a public folder can exist physically in several locations, as shown in Figure 4-7.

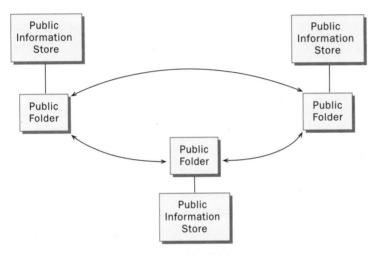

Figure 4-7. *The topology of a public folder.*

When you create a public folder on a specific Exchange Server, you specify when and where it is going to be replicated. When anyone changes the information in a public folder in any location, the changes are replicated automatically to all the other physical locations of the public folder.

> **Note** You don't necessarily have to replicate public folders to make them available to everyone in your Exchange organization. One good thing about public folders is that you can replicate them at will, to address configuration and performance needs, without changing anything for users.

This key capability makes public folders one of the ideal ways to share information over a widely dispersed organization. An intranet is another method that is used to distribute information in dispersed organizations. Because Exchange integrates with the Internet, it can extend collaborative applications into an intranet. You might want to put company announcements in a public folder that is replicated across the country, for example. Each individual user could go to the nearest location of the public folder, which would be much more efficient than having everyone go to a single location.

Like private folders, public folders support a hierarchy. A public folder can be the parent of another public folder. When you create a child public folder, it inherits most of the properties, rules, and forms that are associated with its parent folder.

As mentioned earlier in this chapter, each Public Information Store acts as a public folder hierarchy server. Each Public Information Store Service is aware of the closest location of all available public folders. If a request comes in for an item in a particular public folder, the Public Information Store Service first checks to see whether the folder is available on the server. If not, the service routes the request to the server that can be accessed most efficiently.

All changes in the public folder hierarchy are replicated throughout an Exchange organization automatically. Whenever a client logs on to Exchange, it requests a copy of the public folder hierarchy from the nearest Public Information Store. You can configure the replication of the actual content in public folders, which can have a significant effect on both the use of bandwidth and the timeliness of the material across multiple servers, but every server always acts as a hierarchy server for its clients.

You can send a mail message to a public folder or post a message to a public folder. The basic difference between mailing and posting is that you can specify multiple recipients for a mail message, whereas a posting goes only to a specific folder.

> **Note** By default, a public folder is not shown as part of the Global Address List. To make a public folder visible in the Address Book, you have to go to the Advanced tab of the Properties dialog box for the folder in Exchange Administrator and uncheck the Hide From Address Book check box.

Public folders are the foundation of much of the extended functionality of Exchange, so they are discussed in detail throughout the rest of this book.

Administering Folder Properties

You use Exchange Administrator to set many properties of folders, as discussed in Part III of this book. You can also set some properties of folders through an Exchange client such as Outlook. Because this type of administration is not covered elsewhere, this section briefly describes the configuration options that are available from an Outlook client.

To set properties on a folder through Outlook, right-click a folder and then choose Properties from the shortcut menu. This action displays the Properties dialog box, which contains several tabs. The available tabs depend on the capabilities of the underlying folder and on the Exchange Server that holds the folders. If a folder can be used offline, for example, the Synchronization tab allows you to set the synchronization options. If your Exchange Server is running the Events Service, an Agents tab appears.

The four tabs that are common to most folders are General, Administration, Forms, and Permissions. The General tab, shown in Figure 4-8, lets you name the folder, provide a meaningful description and other information about the folder, and specify whether Exchange should generate the normal set of standard views for the folder. You can also indicate that you want to use a particular form to post messages to the folder. This form will act as the customized interface to the folder. The Folder Size button displays information about the amount of data that is currently in the folder.

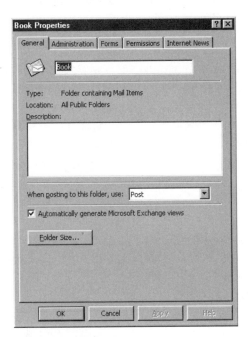

Figure 4-8. *The General tab.*

The Administration tab, shown in Figure 4-9, gives you the ability to specify some basic administrative options, such as the initial view of a folder and the effect of dragging an item to the folder.

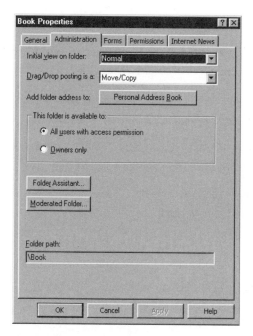

Figure 4-9. *The Administration tab.*

Two command buttons allow you to specify rules for the folder. The Folder Assistant button lets you specify rules that operate on items when they are delivered to a folder. The Moderated Folder button lets you set up a folder with a specific set of rules that allow a moderator to receive messages before those messages are moved to a public folder. These two buttons are available only for public folders and private folders that you create. You can create rules for some of the default private folders by using the Rules Wizard.

The Forms tab, shown in Figure 4-10, simply lets you indicate the forms that are associated with a particular folder. You learn more about forms in Part VI of this book.

Clicking the Manage button brings up the Forms Manager, which is shown in Figure 4-11. You can use the Forms Manager to adjust the properties of individual forms, as well as to copy, update, and delete the forms.

The last of the four common tabs probably is the most frequently used of the four. The Permissions tab, shown in Figure 4-12, allows you to give other users access to the items in a folder.

In the top part of the tab, you can select the user or role to which you want to assign access permissions. Two roles are predefined and apply only to public folders:

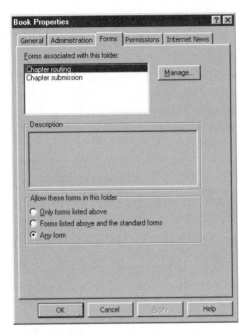

Figure 4-10. *The Forms tab.*

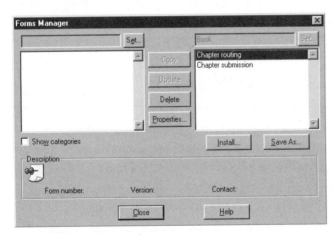

Figure 4-11. *The Forms Manager.*

- Default, which assigns permissions to all users who are not specifically named in the user listing
- Anonymous, which applies to users who might log on to Exchange without specifying a username

Figure 4-12. *The Permissions tab.*

To add a user, click the Add button to the right of the user list box; to remove a user, select the user and then click the Remove button to the right of the list box. After you select a user, you can assign individual permissions in the lower part of the form. The tab lists several predefined user roles, such as Owner, Author, and Editor. Each role is a collection of privileges. If you select a role for a user and modify the privileges associated with that role, the name of the role changes to the role whose privileges match the selected privileges. If no role matches the selected privileges, the role changes to Custom.

The security that you assign through the Permissions tab in Outlook, you can also assign through Exchange Administrator (by clicking the Client Permissions button in the General tab of the Properties dialog box). Wherever you assign security, it is always enforced through the Exchange Server.

Summary

Exchange Server uses database storage to store messaging and collaborative application data. Exchange Server stores public folders into a database called the Public Information Store. It stores mailboxes into a database called the Private Information Store.

An Exchange user sees a single logical hierarchy of public folders, even though the physical location of the public folders can be on different servers. Exchange users see only their own private folders in their mailboxes. Users create public folders from within the Exchange client, Outlook. The Outlook application is also used to manage the properties of the public folders. An administrator uses the Exchange Administrator application to manage the replication of public folders to other servers.

Mailboxes are the set of private folders created for each Exchange user. The private folders contain different types of information, which is displayed in specific forms. For example, calendar information is shown in various calendar and scheduling views in the Calendar folder; note information is displayed in a free-form "Post-it" note format.

One specialized mailbox folder is called Deleted Items. Whenever a message or other private folder item is deleted, it is moved to the Deleted Items folder. A user can configure the Deleted Items folder to automatically empty the deleted items upon exit from the client, or the user can manually empty the folder.

Users can create personal folders to store information outside of an Exchange Server. A user never needs to connect to an Exchange Server in order to install and use personal folders. Another type of folder that a user can create outside of the Exchange Server is the offline storage file. An offline storage file enables a user to work on Exchange when not connected to an Exchange Server, such as when traveling with a laptop.

Part II
Planning

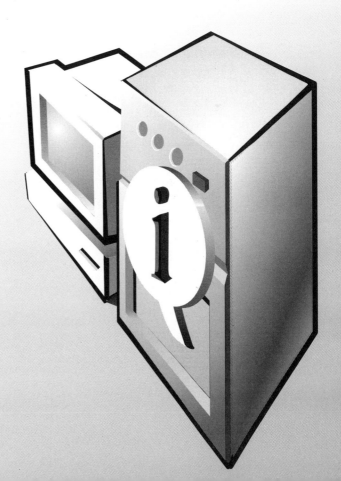

Chapter 5
Assessing Needs

Proper planning is valuable in any project. In a Microsoft Exchange Server 5.5 deployment, planning is critical. Many Exchange Server 5.5 components are difficult or impossible to change after installation. Poor planning can cause problems that range from inadequate performance to outright failure of components.

In this chapter, we review the strategy for implementing an Exchange Server. We look at the business requirements of the enterprise, examine how to assess the needs of future Exchange users, and learn how to evaluate the resources of the current environment for the new messaging system. Exchange Server is a complex program, but with suitable preparation, implementation of the new Exchange organization becomes an easy task.

This book breaks the discussion of planning into two chapters. This chapter discusses how to assess your users' needs as well as the needs of the resources on your current network. Chapter 6 discusses how to plan certain elements of your Exchange organization based on those assessments.

If you are reading this book straight through, you might want to skim these two planning chapters and then go on to read the rest of the book. After you have a firm understanding of the way that the various components in an Exchange organization work, come back and read these two chapters more carefully. In the real world, planning should always come before implementation, but it helps to understand the implementation before working on your plan.

Defining User Needs

Your first step in designing any system should be determining what that system needs to accomplish. Goals include gathering business requirements and understanding the corporate culture and the technical environment—inclusive of network topology and desktop systems—where you will place Exchange. In designing an Exchange organization, this step also means establishing the services and functionality required by your users. After you discover the answers to the questions presented in the following sections, you can effectively group users according to their needs. Then you can use those groups to plan Exchange resources to accommodate user needs. Chapter 6 covers that level of planning. This chapter is concerned with gathering information.

Messaging

Exchange Server is typically implemented as a messaging system. Odds are that future Exchange users will want the ability to send e-mail to each other. You might ask several questions to help describe the specific needs of your users:

- **To whom will most users be sending messages?** Messaging on most networks behaves according to a fairly typical pattern. Users tend to send messages primarily to other users in their own workgroup. Occasionally, users also need to send messages to other workgroups or to outside recipients, such as people on the Internet. Developing a picture of these traffic patterns can help you effectively plan user and server placement.

- **How much e-mail do users expect to generate and receive?** Some users rarely use e-mail; others send and receive dozens of messages per day. Knowing the average volume of messages for your users allows you to effectively plan the capacity of your servers, the limits on your information stores, and the bandwidth requirements of your network.

- **Will user messages primarily be stored on an Exchange server or in local personal folders?** If server-based storage is to be the primary repository of user messages, how much space do you intend to allot for your Private Information Stores? Your organization might have business policies that require mail to be stored for long periods of time. For example, some government units must store e-mail forever. Such information can help you plan hardware capacity for both servers and clients.

Public Folders

Public folders are the foundation for collaboration within Exchange Server 5.5. They enable public access to, and collaboration on, centralized messaging information. Public folders require considerable planning. In addition to planning storage capacity for the Exchange Servers that will hold public folder replicas, you must plan public folder replication and user access to public folder servers. The following questions will assist you in assessing public folder usage in the new Exchange environment:

- **Which users will need access to which public folders?** Some workgroups will collaborate on certain documents and messages more than others. This information helps you decide where replicas of certain folders need to be placed and how often replication needs to occur.

- **Which users should be allowed to create public folders?** By default, top-level public folders are created on the home server of the user who creates them. Subfolders are created on the same server as the top-level folder in which they are created. By restricting which users can create top-level folders, you can govern the placement of public folders on servers.

- **How much information do users expect to post within those public folders?** Both the type of information—documents, forms, executables, or simple messages—and their typical size help you determine the storage capacity required for Public Information Stores.

- **How long will the average message need to remain in a public folder?** This information helps you determine the storage space that your Public Information Stores will consume and the load that will be placed on your servers by users accessing the public folders.

- **How often will users access the public folders?** This information helps you further determine the load that your public folder servers will have to meet and to schedule public folder replication.

Connections to Other Systems

Will any of your users need to access the Internet or an existing messaging system? Having this information can help you plan the placement of users and foreign messaging connectors. If one group of users tends to use a connector heavily, you might want to place those users on the server on which the connector is installed, to reduce the number of hops that messages have to take from your users to the foreign system. Any Exchange Server on a site can host a foreign messaging connector, and that messaging connector can be made available to all sites in the organization. You might want to configure more than one connector to a foreign system to help balance the messaging load to that system.

You must decide between connector types when multiple connectors can support the same system. Planning connectors can be impacted by the types of foreign systems and the types of connectors that they support, as well as the performance that those connectors will be expected to provide. For example, an X.400 connector is highly reliable, but to be reliable, it has a 20-percent higher overhead that impacts performance. The X.400 connector also has the capability to send and receive mail at scheduled times, thus reducing the impact e-mail has on other network applications.

Connectors also have variable capabilities when it comes to additional services. A connector that enables use of shared storage may be preferable to one that enables only e-mail between users.

If a connector is used only for migrations, it will be a temporary addition to the Exchange system. In this case, the connector that is chosen should enable the easiest transition for the users. In many cases, you can migrate the users transparently, with little interruption to their daily business, just by selecting the right connector.

Remote Access

Often, you want to allow users to access private and public folders from a remote location. In planning an Exchange organization, you need to take the needs of these users into account. This information can help you plan the placement of users, as well as plan a remote access service (RAS) or virtual private network (VPN) server for your network. Various manufacturers offer solutions that can enable access to Exchange. This information is also valuable in security planning. Ask these questions to assess the remote access needs of the organization:

- Which users need to be able to access the Exchange organization remotely?
- Will users dial in to a RAS server or access it over the Internet?
- Where will you locate your RAS server?
- Where will you locate your Internet Mail Service?

Custom Applications

Do your users have special needs that can be met only by custom-tailored applications? If so, can these applications be designed by the users themselves, or will you need to hire special personnel? The time to think about custom applications is during the planning stage. The use of custom applications could change many of the answers that you have already come up with to the questions we've examined so far. For more information on the types of applications that can be designed for Exchange Server 5.5, see Part VI of this book.

Training and Support Services

Your users will likely need special training in using the new system. Don't make the mistake of assuming that e-mail is simple to use. Outlook and Exchange Client are sophisticated programs. Users may need to be taught how to use public folders or how to sign and encrypt messages. Do you plan to have users install the mail clients themselves? If so, they will need training, and you may need to set up a convenient method for them to do so.

Remember that users are often called upon to learn all kinds of new things, including new versions of operating systems and software. Take the time to make sure that your users understand the system you are putting in place, as well as who they should go to with questions or problems. Public folders actually make a great place to store training materials so that they are available to all users. You could also use a public folder to list the contact information for support personnel. A public folder can utilize the same forms and views that are found in a user's mailbox folders. In this case, a public folder that stores contact information and uses the Exchange Contact form is ideal for a list of support personnel contacts.

Defining a Geographic Profile

The next step in planning your organization is assessing your current resources. To make this assessment, you must put together three diagrams: a diagram of your company's geographic profile, a diagram of your network topology, and a diagram of your Microsoft Windows NT domain model.

The easiest place to start is with the geographic profile of your company. Get out a pen and paper, and start drawing maps. If your network is global, start with all the countries in which your company is based. Work your way down through states, cities, buildings, and even in-building locations. After you have a firm idea of how your company is laid out geographically, gather information on how users and resources are located within those geographical regions. All this information helps you determine where the users are, where the computers are, whether the computers are ready for Exchange, and how many licenses you are going to need. The following are a few things to think about along the way:

- Where are existing servers located?
- What are the servers' names and functions?
- What versions of which software are installed on the servers?
- How many workstations are in each location?
- What operating systems and software are used on those workstations?
- How many users are in each location?
- What are users' needs?

Real World   Systems Management Server

Ideally, you already have a detailed inventory of your existing network assets. A comprehensive inventory includes a list of all the hardware and software on all the computers on your network. The inventory should also take into account how your network is constructed and maybe even some of the network's use statistics.

If you don't already have a network inventory, you could actually go to all the computers on your network with notebook in hand. A better method is an automatic inventory system such as Microsoft System Management Server (SMS). You can use SMS to automatically gather hardware and software information from computers on your network. You can also use SMS to push installations of software (such as Exchange clients) to workstations throughout the network from a central location, control and support client software remotely, and even keep track of licensing information on your network. SMS is really must-have software for any up-and-coming Exchange administrator.

Note SMS is not a simple install-and-run application. Instead, it is a comprehensive, enterprise-capable network management software package. SMS requires SQL Server to provide the underlying database to capture and manage the network's data. To implement SMS and SQL Server, you should have defined and executed a project plan and systems design.

Defining a Network Topology

After you create diagrams of your company's geographic profile, you need to diagram your company's network. Unlike the geographic profile, network topology tells you exactly how your network is physically put together. When reviewing the geographic topology of the network, make sure to mark out the wide area network (WAN) links between the various locations and their bandwidths. This will help in assessing the site boundaries, connectors required between sites, and replication schedules.

A clear definition of your network's topology allows you to effectively plan site boundaries, site connections, server placement, and replication issues. Whether your network is a single local area network (LAN) within one office building or a WAN connecting thousands of users around the world, you should design the Exchange system to optimize its messaging functions over the network topology. Areas that can be optimized include:

- Site definition
- Server placement
- Message routing
- Public folder replication

The first step in defining a network topology is determining the size of your network. The size of your network determines how you make many planning decisions, and even whether you need to make them at all. On a large WAN, for example, especially one that is geographically dispersed, you might want to consider setting up multiple sites. Using multiple sites means that you have to consider such things as messaging connectors, directory replication, and public folder replication among sites. If you are setting up a relatively small LAN, you may decide to configure only one site in your organization, in which case, many of these decisions will be much easier.

In a small company, all your computers could be connected on one high-speed LAN. In larger companies, networks usually consist of many small LANs connected in various ways to form larger, interconnected LANs or WANs. In the diagram of your network topology, you need to include all the segments that comprise your network. For each segment, ask yourself the following questions:

- How big is the segment? How many computers are there? How large a geographic area does the segment cover?
- How is the segment wired? Does it use thin or thick Ethernet, shared or switched Ethernet, 10Mbps or 100Mbps, Fiber Distributed Data Interface (FDDI), Token Ring, or something else?
- What is the bandwidth of the segment? Determine what the optimal bandwidth is according to the type of network being used.

Real World   Determining Bandwidth

Although it can be somewhat tricky to figure it out, you need to determine the available bandwidth of each segment. *Available bandwidth* is the amount of data that can be transmitted after taking into account the consumption of bandwidth by network activity. For example, if the throughput of a WAN link is 1.544Mbps, and the consumption of that link can peak at 1.544Mbps but averages around 512Kbps (equivalent to 0.5Mbps), then the available bandwidth will be 1.544Mbps – 0.5Mbps, or 1.044Mbps. The peak value is not subtracted, but the average is, because all network links experience peaks that do not represent the common network bandwidth consumption.

- How is the segment connected to other segments? Is the network segment connected to the rest of the network directly, through a router, switch, or bridge, or is it connected through a WAN link? Is the connection permanent or switched? What is the bandwidth of the connection?

- What are the traffic patterns on the network segment? At what times of day is network traffic highest? What application and operating system functions account for this traffic?

- What are the traffic patterns between this segment and other segments? At what times of day is network traffic highest? What application and operating system functions account for this traffic?

- What protocols are used on the network segment? Microsoft Windows NT Server supports TCP/IP, NWLink, and NetBEUI. Protocols might determine what applications can and cannot be used.

Defining a Windows NT Domain Model

Exchange Server 5.5 and Windows NT Server are tightly integrated. Windows NT Server gives Exchange Server 5.5 security features and access to user account information. Furthermore, many Exchange Server 5.5 components run as Windows NT services. The configuration of your Exchange organization depends heavily on the configuration of your Windows NT network. The final step in assessing your current situation is diagramming the Windows NT domains on your network.

Windows NT Domains

Although a full discussion of Windows NT domain models is beyond the scope of this book, this section reviews basic domain models before discussing how

Exchange Server 5.5 fits in. A *domain* is a logical grouping of users, computers, and resources that have a common security database. This security database consists of computer and user accounts in the domain. Permissions to use resources within a domain can be granted to any user account defined in that domain. Domains can be linked by means of trust relationships. A *trust relationship* gives a user in one domain permissions on a resource in another domain. Trust relationships work in one direction. However, for example, assume that a trust relationship is defined so that Domain A trusts Domain B. Users in Domain B can then be assigned permissions on resources in Domain A. For users in Domain A to be assigned permissions to resources in Domain B, a second trust relationship has to be established between the two domains in the opposite direction.

Microsoft defines four basic domain models, which represent the ways that domains can be configured on a network:

- Single domain model
- Single master domain model
- Multiple master domain model
- Complete trust domain model

Single Domain Model

The single domain model, shown in Figure 5-1, is the simplest of the domain models. Only one domain is defined for the entire network. All user accounts and resources exist within this domain.

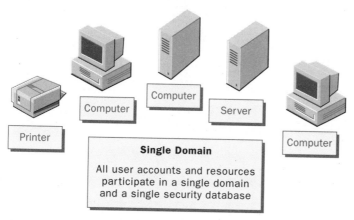

Figure 5-1. *All resources and user accounts exist in one domain.*

Single Master Domain Model

In the single master domain model, shown in Figure 5-2, multiple domains are defined on a network and are linked by trust relationships. All user accounts on the network are configured in one domain: the master domain. Resources on the network are configured in any number of resource domains, each of which is configured to trust the master domain.

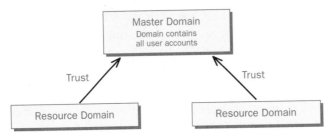

Figure 5-2. *All user accounts exist in one master domain, but resources exist in other domains.*

Multiple Master Domain Model

In the multiple master domain model, shown in Figure 5-3, multiple domains that contain user accounts for the network are configured. Each of these domains is considered a master domain. There are also multiple resource domains on the network. In the purest example of this model, each master domain trusts every other master domain, and each resource domain trusts every master domain.

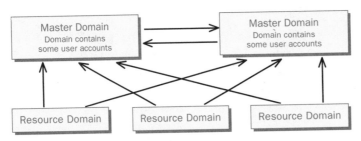

Figure 5-3. *User accounts exist in multiple master domains, and resources exist in other domains.*

Complete Trust Domain Model

In the complete trust domain model, shown in Figure 5-4, multiple domains exist on a network. Each domain contains both user accounts and resources. Every domain on the network is configured to trust every other domain.

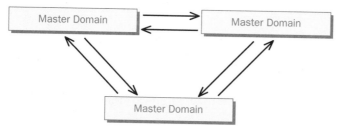

Figure 5-4. *Every domain trusts every other domain.*

More Info   For more information on Windows NT domains and domain models, consult *Running Microsoft Windows NT Server 4.0* (1997) by Charlie Russel and Sharon Crawford, available from Microsoft Press.

Exchange Sites and Windows NT Domains

Although Exchange sites and Windows NT domains are different entities, resources on sites rely on domains to perform essential security operations. For example, a user must log on to a domain with a valid user account to access an Exchange Server 5.5 mailbox. Because Exchange Server 5.5 services are Windows NT services, they, too, need to be authenticated by a domain before they can perform their functions. Each site in an Exchange organization is configured with a special user account called the Site Services account, which is used to validate Exchange services.

When you plan your Exchange organization, you must take into account the domain model used on your network. Again, constructing a diagram is helpful. Whereas the topology diagram illustrates the layout of your network at a physical level, the domain model diagram illustrates the layout of your network at a logical level. It helps to use the same kind of diagramming techniques that you see in the illustrations of the various domain models in the preceding section. Use an oval to represent the domain and a single arrow to represent a trust relationship.

If your network follows the single domain model, your task is easy. If your network consists of multiple domains, for each domain on your network, ask the following questions:

- What is the name of the domain?
- Is the domain a master or resource domain?
- What domains does this domain trust?

- What domains trust this domain?
- How many user accounts are configured in this domain?
- What resources are configured in this domain?
- Who are the administrators of this domain?
- In what domain are the user accounts of the administrators configured?

After you diagram the domains on your network, it is helpful to see how the domain model diagram, the geographic diagram, and the network topology diagram fit together. No real rule defines how Exchange sites should correspond to Windows NT domains. It is tempting, and sometimes appropriate, to simply create a site for each domain. However, this approach does not always work. A single domain might span several geographic regions that a site might not be able to span, due to the topology of your network. You may end up with one site spanning several domains. You may end up with one domain spanning several sites. These decisions are more an art than a science—an art that is the topic of the following chapter.

Summary

Good planning can make or break your deployment of Exchange Server 5.5. This chapter covered the first stage of planning an Exchange organization: assessing your current situation. The first step in this assessment is determining your users' needs. After you establish what Exchange services your users need and the expected levels of use, you can effectively group users according to those needs to help plan server capacity and placement.

Your next step in planning the organization is assessing your current resources. This step involves first defining the geographic profile of your company. You should list all the physical locations, from countries down to building locations, in which your company exists. You should then inventory all the users and resources in each location. Next, you should define your network topology. This step involves diagramming the physical layout of your network. Determine the size of your network, how network segments are designed, how segments are connected, and what traffic patterns exist within and between network segments.

Finally, you need to diagram the Windows NT domain organization of your network. This diagram represents the logical layout of the network. Find out how many domains exist on the network, and for each domain, list information such as whether the domain is a master or resource domain, how many users are defined in the domain, what resources exist in the domain, and what trust relationships are configured for the domain.

Now that you have collected the information you need about your users and the existing resources of your network, it's time to put that information to work. In Chapter 6, you will learn how to plan the actual Exchange organization based on the information you have learned to collect in this chapter.

Chapter 6
Planning for Deployment

In Chapter 5, you learned how to assess the needs of your users and how to take stock of your current network situation. In this chapter, you learn how to put that information to use.

We will break Exchange organization planning into three distinct tasks: constructing the overall Exchange organization, planning the location of Exchange sites, and placing individual Exchange Servers in those sites to optimize the messaging system. The Exchange Server hierarchy entails an intricate architecture of sites and servers, but with appropriate preparation, the hierarchy develops into a logical placement of sites and servers created with users' needs in mind.

At the organizational level, you establish organization-wide naming conventions, determine the number of sites you need and the boundaries of those sites, and plan how to link those sites. At the site level, you plan the services that the site must provide. You also plan public folders and gateways. At the server level, you determine the functions each server will perform and plan the server hardware to accommodate those functions.

Planning the Organization

The best place to start planning an Exchange organization is at the top — with the organization itself. Planning at the organization level primarily involves determining the number of sites that you need in the organization and where the boundaries of those sites go. You also need to plan the messaging and directory replication links between those sites. However, before you get started on these plans, you need to establish a convention for naming the various elements of the organization.

Establishing Naming Conventions

When you create objects in the directory of an Exchange organization, those objects can have several types of names. All objects created in Exchange Server 5.5 have at least two names: a display name and a directory name.

The *display name* of an object is the name that appears in Microsoft Exchange Administrator and in address books. Display names can be changed easily at any time.

The *directory name* of an object is the actual name for the object that is stored in the Exchange Directory Information Tree (DIT). Directory names are used to uniquely identify objects in the directory and to generate e-mail addresses for those objects. Pay attention to the word "unique" in this context. Objects in the hierarchy must have unique names. No two sites and no two servers can have the same name. No two objects (mailboxes, connectors, directory lists, and so on) can have the same name within any container.

The requirement for uniqueness of names is common in any system with a directory of users, resources, and servers. Because Exchange Server provides various migration tools, there can be duplication when two different systems are migrated to the same Exchange system. An administrator should review the systems for possible duplication and take appropriate precautions—such as changing a name or deleting old accounts—prior to migrating multiple systems to Exchange.

Another common requirement for network and messaging systems is to avoid *illegal characters*, characters that some systems do not understand. Other systems misinterpret them as special codes (sometimes called *escape sequences*) and then try to interpret the remainder of the name as a command of some sort. The result, of course, is failure to communicate electronically and, perhaps, errors on the network or messaging systems. Although the list of illegals can vary, most systems consider some or all of the following, along with the "space" (using the spacebar on the keyboard), illegal characters:

\ / [ ] : | < > + = ~ ! @ ; , " ( ) ' # $ % ^ & * - _

Avoid using them in any names, even if Exchange will allow you to do so.

Exchange systems can grow to include hundreds of thousands of users worldwide and many sites and servers. Directory names cannot be changed after an object is created. In general, you should make the display name and directory name of any given object the same. Certain objects, such as user mailboxes, have other types of names as well. Before you install your first Exchange Server, you need to establish a convention for naming the four primary types of objects in your Exchange organization: the organization, sites, servers, and mailboxes.

Establishing a naming convention for distribution lists, as well as for mailboxes and custom recipients that appear in the Global Address List, is a great help to Exchange users. Furthermore, if administration is distributed among multiple administrators at different sites, it can also help to apply a naming standard to connectors and other Exchange objects.

Organization

The organization is the largest organizational element of Exchange, and its name should reflect the largest organizational element of your company. Typically, an organization is named after the enterprise itself. Organization names can be up to 64 characters long, but to facilitate administration, it is good practice to limit the length of the organization's name. Keep in mind that users of external messaging systems might need to enter the organization name manually, as part of the Exchange users' e-mail addresses, so limiting the name assists those users.

> **Note**   When you install the first production Exchange Server, be careful that the organization name is the absolutely correct one. If this means that you wait for management's approval, so be it. Changing the organization name later requires a huge amount of work, so you want to be absolutely certain that you use the correct name. Also, be aware that the organization and site names are used by default with the Internet Mail Service's SMTP address space to construct e-mail addresses for the Internet. The SMTP address space can be changed, but changing it can be both a hassle and a cause of confusion for other Exchange administrators later.

Sites

The convention for naming sites varies, depending on how the site boundaries are established. In a typical Exchange system design, sites are named by geographic region or department because site boundaries are determined based on WAN links and workgroup data flow. Like the organization name, site names can be 64 characters long, but the advisory regarding name length also applies to site names. Again, some external messaging systems may require the external users to enter the name of the site, as well as the organization, to identify the intended Exchange recipient.

Servers

The server name for an Exchange Server is the same as the NetBIOS name of the Microsoft Windows NT Server on which Exchange Server 5.5 is installed. Therefore, you should establish naming conventions for servers before installing Windows NT Server. You can determine the name of a Windows NT Server in the Identification property sheet of the Network utility in Control Panel. NetBIOS server names cannot be more than 15 characters long.

If the Exchange Server is being installed on the first NT Server in an enterprise network, one recommendation for naming the server is to use its location or the type of function that server will provide. This name can be used along with one or two digits to allow multiple NT Servers in the same location providing the same network function. For example, an Exchange Server in a company's London office could be named LON-MAIL01. In addition, if the Exchange Server is the first NT Server, the domain in which that server participates requires a name. Domain names are typically reflective of geographic or organizational boundaries. Because a user must type the domain name when he or she logs on and will see it whenever he or she logs on, the domain's name should be short, concise, and easy to remember.

Mailboxes

Mailbox names work a bit differently from the names of the three objects discussed in the preceding sections. Mailboxes actually have five key names, as shown on the property sheets of the Mailbox object in Figure 6-1.

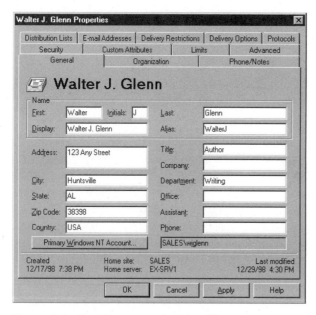

Figure 6-1. *Creating names for a mailbox.*

- **First Name**   This name is the full first name of the user.
- **Initials**   This is the middle initial or initials of the user.
- **Last Name**   This name is the full last name of the user.

- **Display Name**   The display name is automatically constructed from the user's first name, last name, and middle initial or initials, using rules that you will learn in Chapter 8. The display name appears in address books and in Exchange Administrator, so it is the primary way in which users in Exchange search for other users. Display names can be up to 256 characters long.
- **Alias Name**   Alias names are automatically derived from the user's other names. Alias names are used to construct the addresses that users of foreign messaging systems use to send e-mail to your users. Aliases can be up to 64 characters long.

A naming convention should take into account the outside systems to which Exchange may be connecting. Many legacy messaging and scheduling systems restrict the length allowed for recipients within their address lists. If Exchange Server allows longer mailbox names, the names can be truncated or rejected by the legacy system, resulting in duplicates or missing recipients. In turn, messages could show up in the wrong mailboxes or might not be transmitted at all. A common length restriction in legacy systems is eight characters. Many problems can be avoided if you keep mailbox names to eight characters or fewer.

Keep in mind that a mailbox's name and the key names of the associated user that appear in the Global Address List are not necessarily the same. The mailbox name is assigned to the Exchange mailbox object; the names appearing in the Global Address List are the key names. The mailbox name is usually the same as the NT user account and can simply assume whatever naming conventions were established in Windows NT for user accounts. An administrator does not have to use the same mailbox and NT user account name, but if different names are used, administration becomes difficult.

Real World   Naming Conventions and Addressing

The names that you establish for objects in your Exchange organization govern the way that users of external messaging systems will address messages sent to them.

Foreign systems do not always use the same addressing conventions that Exchange Server 5.5 does. Therefore, Exchange Server 5.5 must have a way of determining where an inbound message from a foreign system goes. For each type of messaging system to which it is connected, Exchange Server 5.5 maintains an address space, which is information on how foreign addressing information should be used to deliver messages within the Exchange organization.

Suppose that you have set up the Internet Mail Service in Exchange Server 5.5 so that your users can exchange e-mail with users on the Internet. A user on the Internet addresses messages to your users using the typical SMTP format — something like *user@site.organization.com* or maybe simply *user@organization.com*. (You will learn how address spaces work in Chapter 14. For now, just understand that the way you name the objects in your organization has fairly far-reaching effects.)

Defining Sites

In general, you want to keep the number of sites in your organization as low as possible. If you can get away with having just one site, you should do so. Many of the communications between servers on a site, such as directory replication and message transfer, are configured and used automatically, greatly reducing administration on your part. However, there are many good reasons to consider using multiple sites. The following sections cover some of these considerations.

Geographic Profile

If your company is spread over two or more geographic regions, you might want to consider implementing a site for each region. There are two excellent reasons for dividing an organization into multiple sites:

- Managing network bandwidth consumption
- Distributing administrative responsibilities

A single site is easy to connect because much of the communication between an Exchange site's servers happens automatically. Unfortunately, this automatic communication consumes a considerable amount of bandwidth, which grows with the size of the site. If there are wide area network links, which typically have a smaller amount of bandwidth available, the best decision an Exchange administrator can make is to divide the organization so that an Exchange site does not span a WAN link.

An enterprise may want to distribute administrative responsibilities because it has multiple administrators placed at different locations or because it requires enhanced security for specific security reasons. For example, human resources information is considered highly confidential, and often a specific administrator is assigned to manage confidential or sensitive information. Each distinct Exchange site can be administered separately, without concern that another administrator will have access to the site and its information.

Network Topology

Several physical factors determine the possible boundaries of a site. All Exchange Servers within a site must be able to communicate with one another over a network that meets certain requirements:

- **RPC connectivity**   Exchange Servers within a site use remote procedure calls (RPCs) to exchange directory information. Therefore, a site cannot span connections that do not support RPCs. RPCs are session-layer APIs that can run over several different protocols, including NetBIOS, Banyan Vines, Novell's IPX/SPX protocol stack, and the TCP/IP stack that is used on the Internet.

- **Permanent connectivity**   Because of the constant and automatic communication between Exchange Servers within a site, these servers must be able to communicate over permanent connections—connections that are always on line and available. If you have network segments that are connected by a switched virtual connection (SVC) or dial-up connection, you must implement separate sites for those segments.

- **Relatively high bandwidth**   Servers on a site require enough bandwidth on the connections between them to support whatever traffic they generate. Microsoft recommends that the minimum connection between servers support 128Kbps. Keep in mind that a network link that provides 128Kbps but is highly utilized will not be sufficient for Exchange Server traffic. The network link should have a fair amount of bandwidth available for new traffic generated by Exchange, if an Exchange site will span that link.

Windows NT Security

As you learned in Chapter 5, computers on a Windows NT network are grouped in domains, according to one of four domain models: single domain, single master domain, multiple master domain, and complete trust domains. Exchange Server 5.5 uses Windows NT security to validate both users and services. All servers in a site must be able to authenticate Exchange users and services. In addition, all Exchange services within a site must use the same Site Service account. Therefore, Windows NT user accounts must be in the same domain as the servers or in domains trusted by the servers' domains.

A single Exchange site can span multiple domains if all the other requirements for creating a site are met. A single domain can also span multiple sites. If an NT domain structure has been designed so that domains do not span WAN links and are separated for administrative purposes, the simplest way to set up an Exchange organization across multiple domains is to create one site per domain. Using the one-site-per-domain model is also the most common method.

More Info Planning an Exchange organization involves more detail than two chapters of this book can cover. For organizations that have a large number of sites, site design involves many additional factors, such as whether to use mesh or hub-and-spoke architecture. For more information on advanced planning of Exchange organizations, see *Deploying Exchange Server 5.5* (1998) in the *Notes From the Field* series by Microsoft Press.

Planning Site Links

After you determine how many sites will be in your organization and what the boundaries of those sites will be, you need to plan how those sites will be linked. Sites are linked by two different types of connectors. The first type of connector used to link sites is a *messaging connector*, which allows the transfer of messages between users and services on different sites. The second type of connector used to link sites is the *directory replication connector*, which allows the sharing of directory information between sites.

Messaging Connectors

Exchange Server 5.5 provides four types of messaging connectors that you can use to link two Exchange sites: the site connector, the X.400 connector, the dynamic RAS connector, and the Internet Mail Service. These connectors are covered in detail in Chapters 11 and 14. This section provides a brief introduction.

Site Connector The site connector is used only to connect Exchange sites to other Exchange sites. The site connector is by far the easiest of the messaging connectors to set up, but it also has some of the strictest use requirements. The site connector requires a relatively stable, RPC-capable connection that supplies relatively high bandwidth. All other things being equal, the site connector is the fastest of the messaging connectors. The site connector can be configured to communicate with a remote site in either of two ways:

- **Target servers** The site connector maintains a list of servers on the other site, to which messages can be sent directly. Any server in the local site can send messages to any target server using the site connector. If the first server on the list isn't available, others are tried, in order, until the message is successfully sent.

- **Bridgehead servers** One server on the local site — the bridgehead server — is designated to send all messages to the remote site. Other servers on the local site send messages to the bridgehead server, which then sends the messages to target servers on the remote site. By implementing only one target server on the remote site and by designating that target server as the remote site's bridgehead server, you can effectively channel all messages between the two sites using only those two servers.

X.400 Connector   The X.400 connector can be used to connect two Exchange sites or to connect an Exchange site to a foreign X.400 messaging system. In connecting two Exchange sites, the X.400 connector is generally slower than a site connector because of additional communication overhead. However, the added flexibility in configuring the X.400 connector often makes it more efficient and effective than a site connector. You can schedule the times at which the X.400 connector is available and control the size of messages that can be transferred — two things that you cannot do with a site connector. Any X.400 connector link must use designated bridgehead servers. Because of X.400's scheduling capabilities and reliability, it is often used for links with low available bandwidth.

Dynamic RAS Connector   The dynamic RAS connector can be used only to connect two Exchange sites. It is used primarily when no permanent network connection exists between the two sites, and as its name implies, it relies on the Windows NT remote access service (RAS) to provide dial-up functionality. Both sites require that RAS be installed. Like the X.400 connector, the dynamic RAS connector can be configured only to use bridgehead servers. As you can with the X.400 connector, you can control the scheduling and messaging parameters for a dynamic RAS connector.

Internet Mail Service   The Internet Mail Service (IMS) can be used to connect two Exchange sites or to connect an Exchange site to a foreign system. Although it is installed as part of the Exchange Server application, the IMS is actually a Windows NT service that allows Exchange Server 5.5 to act as an SMTP host. Use of the IMS requires that TCP/IP be configured on your network. The IMS can be used to connect two Exchange sites over the Internet.

Multiple Messaging Connectors

Between any two Exchange sites, you can configure multiple messaging connectors. Generally speaking, the simplest solution is to configure only one messaging connector between any two Exchange sites. Multiple connectors can be used to provide fault tolerance in case one connector fails or to balance the messaging load over different network connections.

Each messaging connector that you create on a site is assigned a cost value. Cost values range from 1 to 100. A messaging connector with a lower cost is always preferred over a connector with a higher cost. This approach allows you to designate primary and backup connectors between sites. When the Message-Transfer Agent determines which connector it should send a message over, it takes into account the cumulative cost of the entire messaging path. In Figure 6-2, for example, a message could move from Site 1 to Site 4 by either transmitting through Site 2 or transmitting through Site 3. The path through Site 2 has a cumulative cost of 4, while the path through Site 3 has a cumulative cost of 2. Thus, the Site 3 path is preferred over the path through Site 2.

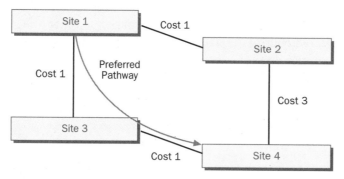

Figure 6-2. *Costs are used to determine message routing.*

Multiple connectors should be used whenever the physical networking between sites is unreliable. For a small or medium-size network with high-bandwidth links between sites, using a single connector between sites provides a consistent messaging pathway. This consistency is valuable in developing an accurate picture of network traffic and in troubleshooting message delivery problems. In midsize to large networks that have inconsistent traffic patterns or restricted bandwidth availability as well as multiple, redundant links between sites, using two connectors between sites for backup or load balancing can enhance the messaging system's reliability.

Directory Replication Connectors

After you link sites using a messaging connector, users and services can exchange messages between the two sites. No mechanism is yet in place for sharing Exchange directory information between those sites. Within the boundaries of a single site, servers replicate directory information automatically. Between sites, you have to set up special directory replication connectors for this purpose.

Directory replication connectors take advantage of existing messaging connectors to transfer directory information between sites. When you create a directory replication connector, you create that connector on two servers—one in each site that you are connecting. These servers, referred to as the *directory replication bridgehead servers,* are responsible for the transfer of all directory replication messages between the two sites.

Directory replication between the two bridgehead servers happens according to a predefined schedule. At specified times, a directory replication bridgehead in one site pulls directory information from its partner bridgehead server in the other site. You can have multiple bridgehead servers in a single site, as long as each server maintains a connection to a server in a different site. A single bridgehead server can even have multiple directory replication connectors configured on it, as long as each connector points to a different site. The point is that any single pair of sites can have no more than one directory replication connector configured between them.

When you have only two sites in an organization, directory replication is fairly straightforward. The process gets a little more complicated when you have three or more sites in your organization. Unfortunately, setting up directory replication between multiple sites is not as simple as just connecting all the sites. The primary reason is that directory replication connectors are transitive. Suppose that you have three sites, A, B, and C, as shown in Figure 6-3. If you set up one directory replication connector between Sites A and B and another between Sites B and C, a transitive connection is automatically provided between Sites A and C.

> **Note** Remember that you should always send a test e-mail, using a manual address, before you establish directory replication. This will ensure that your messaging connector is working.

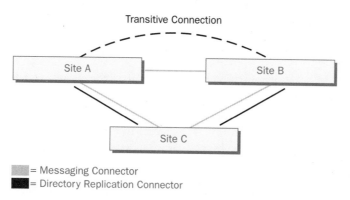

Figure 6-3. *Directory replication connectors are transitive.*

When you set up a multisite organization, it is important that no two sites have more than one directory replication pathway between them. The optimal way to set up directory replication in an organization is to use a single-line pathway, as shown in Figure 6-4. Notice that the directory replication connectors throughout the site form a single pathway throughout all the sites in the organization.

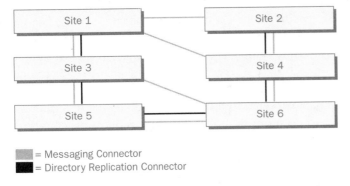

= Messaging Connector
= Directory Replication Connector

Figure 6-4. *Creating a directory replication pathway.*

Planning Sites

After you establish the number of sites that your organization will contain and determine how those sites will be linked, you are ready to design the sites themselves. Several elements go into a good site design. You need to establish a public folder strategy. You also need to plan the services, such as foreign gateways, that your users will need. Many of these determinations are made based on the assessment of user needs that you learned how to collect in Chapter 5.

Designing Your Sites

A good portion of the design for your Exchange sites involves planning the servers that will be members of that site. Planning Exchange Servers themselves is discussed a bit later in this chapter. The following are a few guidelines for deciding how to distribute the services among the servers in a site:

- If your goal is to isolate messaging traffic from other network traffic, put users and their home servers on the same network segment in a workgroup configuration. It is important to have high-bandwidth connections between mail clients and servers for the best performance.

- If your goal is to use a hierarchical physical network structure, in order to utilize its inherent security by grouping servers together, put servers on intermediate network segments that route traffic to the network backbone, and route traffic to the geographically located workgroup segments.

- Put the mailboxes for all users in a workgroup on the same server. Users tend to send the most mail to other users in their own workgroup. Keeping all the mailboxes on the same server means less network traffic and less server disk space consumed.

- When possible, create duplicate services on multiple servers to provide fault tolerance. Always place Exchange Servers on servers that have fault-tolerant hardware.

Planning Public Folders

Public folders in Exchange Server 5.5 can be put to several uses, including use as discussion forums, public collections of documents, and even the basis for custom applications. When a public folder is created, it is created on one Exchange Server. When a top-level folder is created, it is created on the home server of the user who created the folder. When a lower-level folder is created, it is created on the same server as the folder in which it is created. The content of a public folder can be stored on a single server, or it can be replicated to other servers in the site and organization. Public folder creation, storage, and replication are discussed in detail in Chapters 4 and 14. A few aspects of public folders are pertinent to site planning:

- Decide whether to distribute public folders on multiple servers throughout your site or whether to maintain them all on a single server.

- Decide whether to dedicate specified servers to public folders by having only Public Information Stores or to have servers with both Public and Private Information Stores that contain mailboxes.

- Determine which users will be using public folders for collaborative applications and whether those applications will require other services or special security.

- If users in remote sites need to access public folders in a local site, you need to decide whether to configure affinity between the sites so that remote users can access the content from a local server or alternatively, to replicate the content to a server in the remote site.

- If you replicate public folder content to multiple servers in the same site, consider grouping servers in the site into server locations, to make client access to public folder content more efficient.

- Consider which users should be allowed to create top-level folders. Limiting the permissions to create top-level folders allows you to control both the servers on which public folders are created and the basic organization of the public folder hierarchy.

Planning Gateways

Any server in a site can be configured with a connector to a foreign system. All other servers in the site will be able to route messages over that gateway. When possible, you want to create foreign messaging connectors on the servers that maintain the actual physical connection to the foreign systems. Also, if one group of users makes primary use of a foreign connection, consider placing those users on the server on which the connector is installed.

Planning Servers

After you plan the general structure of your organization and sites, you can plan the servers in those sites. The number of servers needed depends on the number of users in the site and the services that you plan to provide to those users. As you've learned throughout this chapter, you accomplish part of server planning while planning your organization and sites. By the time you have planned your sites, you should have a fairly good idea of the services that each site needs to offer and the number of servers that you need to offer those services.

Depending on your needs and resources, you are likely to have decided whether to use just a few powerful servers and concentrate your site's services on those few or instead distribute those services among a larger number of less powerful servers. There really is no guideline for the number of servers that you need or the power of those servers. What is important is that you make a plan. After you make that plan, you can begin to estimate the hardware requirements for your servers.

When estimating the performance of an Exchange Server, you need to consider four distinct categories of hardware: disk, processor, memory, and network.

Disk

Your server needs to have adequate disk space for Windows NT Server, Exchange Server 5.5, directory information, transaction logs, and Public and Private Information Stores. The amount of disk space that you need is only one consideration. The speed at which Exchange Server 5.5 can access your disks is another important consideration.

SCSI drives generally are faster than IDE drives. Consider using a caching disk controller with a high-speed bus, such as PCI. Adding more drives allows Exchange Server 5.5 to distribute the workload, reading and writing to multiple drives at the same time. Also consider placing your transaction logs on a separate physical disk. Using a separate disk allows transaction logs to be written sequentially, increasing performance.

If you use multiple drives, you might also want to consider Windows NT software-based *Redundant Array of Inexpensive Disks* (RAID), including disk striping with parity (RAID 5) or disk mirroring (RAID 1) to offer some level of fault tolerance. Windows NT software-based RAID is configured in the Disk Administrator utility. The Disk Administrator allows the administrator to create a *volume set*, which is a group of hard disks that are treated as though they are a single hard drive by the NT operating system. Yet another option is implementing a form of hardware-based RAID, which can be costly but offers the best performance and fault tolerance available.

Although it may seem tempting to throw as much storage space at the Exchange Server as you can, don't do it. Instead, think about the storage needs over time and the capability of the backup system. If the storage space might exceed the capacity of the backup system, consider that you may need additional servers instead. Many gigabytes of data can accrue on an Exchange Server. This data does not appear immediately after the server is installed but grows over time. The server can be configured to limit the size of users' mailboxes in order to avoid inordinate growth of the information store. The main concern about a large information store is that it can grow to be too large for the backup system. When defining the storage for a server, ensure that the backup system is adequate to fully back up the information stores, transaction logs, and operating system files. A large information store can take several tapes, and a very long time, to back up on a daily basis. A restore of the information store can take several hours! Multiple servers with smaller information stores provide an inherent tolerance to failure; the failure would affect fewer users for a shorter period of time because the restore process is shorter.

As the amount of data grows on an Exchange Server, performance can diminish. Exchange manages a number of background tasks for the information stores. These tasks take longer to execute when there are more messages in the information store to manage; hence, performance degrades across the server as a whole.

Processor

Using multiple processors also significantly increases a server's performance. The increase in performance on a server is not an automatic doubling when there are two processors. Instead, the performance is increased by only a percentage because the processors share a motherboard, adapters, storage, and other components. Data will face a bottleneck in these components, even though two or more processors do increase the server's performance.

Memory

Memory (RAM) is used to run active processes on a computer. When physical memory is not sufficient, it is supplemented through the use of a paging file on the computer's hard disk. Ideally, you should have enough physical memory on a server to avoid excessive accessing of the paging file. Right now, memory is the cheapest way to increase the performance of any computer. We recommend using at least 128MB RAM on any Exchange Server as the bare minimum; use 256MB RAM from the start if at all possible.

Network

Network interface cards on your servers should be fast enough to handle traffic coming from and going to clients and other servers. High-speed network adapters, such as those that use a PCI bus, are best. Fast servers can take advantage of multiple network interface cards, providing the ability to host connections to several other clients or servers at the same time. Furthermore, many server platforms allow you to merge network interface cards into a pool; should one of the cards in the pool fail, another card takes over.

Fault Tolerance

Some standard precautions can be taken to ensure that Exchange Servers stay online, even when there are failures. An *uninterruptible power source* (UPS) is a common way to ensure that the server does not go offline if the power in the building fails. A UPS can also prevent power surges from damaging the server components.

As we have stated already, a server can have multiple hard drives, multiple processors, and multiple network interface cards. These redundant components provide increased performance, load balancing, and failover options, depending on how they are configured. A server can have dual power supplies, controller cards, and error-correcting RAM as well. Whenever a server has redundant internal components, the server is able to better tolerate faults in those components. Server-class machines typically come with software that is able to monitor the servers' hardware components from a central management machine.

Redundancy can be established not only for server components but for the server itself. Exchange Servers can be configured to take advantage of a shared storage system using Microsoft Cluster Server. This is a system in which multiple servers are configured in a cluster so that if one server has a problem, the system fails over to the redundant server.

Real World   **Load Simulator**

The *Microsoft BackOffice Resource Kit* comes with a wonderful utility called Load Simulator (LOADSIM.EXE), which allows you to simulate the load caused on an Exchange Server by a specified number of users sending and receiving messages over a given period. Load Simulator cannot tell you exactly what hardware a server needs to provide a set of services. It can, however, answer one important question for you: What kind of average load will a certain number of users put on your server hardware?

Load Simulator can be set to perform five separate tasks:

- The Inbox task (a user reading new mail)
- The Browse task (a user reading old mail)
- The Send Mail task
- The Schedule+ task
- The Public Folder task

Each individual simulated user performs the selected tasks a specified number of times per simulated day. You can specify the number of simulated days that you want Load Simulator to run. Load Simulator can run many simulated days in a fraction of a real day. You can get Load Simulator and detailed information on using it from the *Microsoft BackOffice Resource Kit*.

For a copy of the latest version of LoadSim, check Microsoft's Web site at *http://www.microsoft.com/exchange*.

Summary

In this chapter, you learned how to take information about the needs of your users and the current assessment of your network and put that information to use designing an Exchange organization. The design of an organization happens at three distinct levels: the organization level, the site level, and the server level.

At the organization level, you determine the number of sites needed in your organization and where the boundaries of those sites should be placed. You also determine how those sites should be linked to one another. Once you have planned your organization, you plan each of the sites in that organization. Planning a site includes setting a public folder strategy and planning for other services, such as gateways to foreign systems, that the site will provide.

Once you have planned your organization and sites, you need to plan the servers that go in your sites. You need to decide whether to use fewer, more powerful servers or many, less powerful servers. This decision depends upon the services your site needs to provide. Once you have decided how many servers will be in a site and what services each of those servers will provide, you must plan the hardware for each server.

Part I of this book introduced you to some of the vital concepts of using Exchange Server 5.5. The past two chapters have shown you how to collect and use information about your situation in planning your Exchange organization. Chapter 7 begins a series of chapters that look at the deployment of Exchange Server 5.5. In Chapter 7, you will learn how to install Exchange Server 5.5.

Part III
Deployment of Exchange Server

Chapter 7
Installing Exchange Server 5.5

So far, you've learned a good bit about how Microsoft Exchange Server 5.5 works and how to plan your Exchange organization. In this chapter, you actually get your hands dirty and install Exchange Server 5.5. The setup of Exchange Server 5.5 happens in four basic stages:

- First, make sure that your server is prepared for the installation.
- Second, run the Exchange Server 5.5 Setup program, click a few buttons, and supply some information about your environment.
- Third, optimize the installation and verify that the new Exchange services are up and running.
- Fourth, apply other software that may need to be integrated with Exchange, such as Exchange service packs, the NT option pack, backup software, and Exchange server virus-detection software.

In this chapter, we examine the three stages of Exchange Server installation. We review server preparation and how that preparation is required for installation, and you learn how to install the Exchange Server application as the first or subsequent server within the Exchange messaging system. Exchange Server is not difficult to install when you select the right options, but if you choose the wrong options, often the only way to repair the results is to reinstall the server. For anyone involved in installing Exchange Server, this is a critical chapter.

Preparing for the Installation

Although it's tempting (and easy enough) just to plug in the Exchange Server CD-ROM and run the Setup program, a few chores are best taken care of first. You should verify that your server is correctly configured, gather some information, and set up special accounts. If you created a good deployment plan, you probably have all the information you need.

Real World   Taking Exchange Server 5.5 for a Test Drive

If you are considering upgrading your Exchange organization to Exchange Server 5.5 from a previous version, we recommend trying version 5.5 on a non-production server first to get a feel for its new features. You may also want to test drive the software even if you are not upgrading. Testing Exchange Server 5.5 before deployment can help you plan the best ways to implement some of the features offered by the new version as those decisions come up during the "real" installation.

If you do decide to take Exchange Server 5.5 for a test drive, we recommend setting up a test network that is physically separate from your actual network. If you do not have the resources for a separate network, you can test Exchange Server 5.5 on a server on your existing network. However, if you have an existing Exchange organization, you will need to install Exchange Server 5.5 using a different organization name. This will prevent unwanted interactions between existing servers and your test server. It will also prevent you from changing the existing Exchange Server.

The following is a checklist of critical questions that you should answer before starting an Exchange Server installation. The answers to some of these questions may seem a bit obvious, but take the time to answer them before you begin, to prevent problems during or after installation:

- Does the computer running Windows NT Server 4.0 meet the hardware requirements for running Exchange Server 5.5?

- Have you installed Windows NT Server 4.0 with Service Pack 3 or a later version?

- Does your server have access to a primary or backup domain controller?

- If your new Exchange site will cross Windows NT domain boundaries, have appropriate trust relationships been established?

- If you plan to support Internet protocols, is TCP/IP correctly configured on your Windows NT Server, and do you have access to WINS and DNS servers?

- Is Internet Explorer 4.0 or later installed on the server?

- What are the names of the organization and site that you will create or join?

- If you are creating a new site, what is the name and password for the Site Services account of the site you are creating?

- If you are joining an existing site, what is the name of one other Exchange Server in the site you are joining, and what is the name and password for that site's Site Services account?

- For what connectors will you need to install support during your Exchange Server Setup?

- What is the disk configuration of the computer on which you are doing the installation?

- Do you have the 10-digit key number from the back of the Exchange Server CD-ROM jewel case?

- If you plan to install Outlook Web Access, have you installed the rollup hotfix for Service Pack 3 or installed Service Pack 4 or 5? (A *hotfix*, a fix for a specific software problem, is made available to the public. When a new service pack is issued, recent hotfixes are included with it.)

- If you plan to install Outlook Web Access, is Internet Information Server (IIS) 3.0 or later, with Active Server Pages, running on the computer?

- If you plan to install Key Management Server, is Microsoft Certificate Server running on your computer? Note that if you choose to install the Key Management Server component of Exchange Server 5.5, the Key Management Server installation will actually happen after the Exchange Server 5.5 installation has completed. We cover the installation and use of Key Management Server in Chapter 15.

- If you plan to use the connector for MS Mail for AppleTalk networks, is Windows NT Services for Macintosh correctly configured?

Note Exchange Server 5.5 comes in two editions: the Standard Edition and the Enterprise Edition. The two products are nearly identical in function, but the Enterprise Edition does include a few features that the Standard Edition does not. The Enterprise Edition adds the following:

- Unlimited database storage. Databases in the Standard Edition are limited to 16GB, but databases in the Enterprise Edition are not limited at all.

- X.400 connector. The Enterprise Edition provides an X.400-compliant messaging connector.

- IBM OfficeVision/VM/SNADS connectors.

- Support for Windows NT clustering technology.

Verifying Hardware Requirements

To run Exchange Server 5.5, you must first make sure that your machine meets the minimum hardware requirements. Table 7-1 details what Microsoft has published as both the minimum and recommended configurations for a computer running Exchange Server 5.5. Keep in mind that these requirements represent only servers on which Exchange Server will run, not what it will run on *well*. In real implementations, many Exchange Servers require more processors and more memory to execute the desired services.

Table 7-1.   Minimum and Recommended Hardware Configurations for Exchange Server 5.5

Hardware	Minimum	Recommended
Processor	Pentium 60 or Digital Alpha AXPTM	Pentium 300 or Digital Alpha AXPTM
Memory	24MB (32MB for RISC-based system)	128MB
Disk space	250MB after Windows NT installation; space for paging file (50MB + RAM)	Space for e-mail and public folders; space for paging file (100MB + RAM); multiple physical drives configured as a stripe set or stripe set with parity

Note   In order to absolutely verify that your hardware is compatible with Microsoft Windows NT Server, Microsoft publishes a hardware compatibility list (HCL). Because the HCL is published for various Microsoft operating systems and applications and is updated often, Microsoft publishes it online as a search utility at *http://www.microsoft.com/HWTest/HCL/default.htm*.

From this Web page, you can explore additional compatibility list links. Of particular interest are the BackOffice hardware and software compatibility lists. These two lists describe hardware and software products that have passed the BackOffice logo tests. Because Exchange Server is a component of the BackOffice package, the products on these two lists have successfully passed a run of difficult tests to verify that they take advantage of BackOffice technology.

If you plan to add future enhancements, such as a fax service, to the Exchange Server environment, check the BackOffice software compatibility page to help select a compatible application.

Using Service Packs

Microsoft provides its service packs online for free and on CD-ROM for a small charge. A *service pack* is an update to an operating system or application that encompasses the solutions for multiple problems. In contrast, hotfixes, or *patches*, are solutions to single, immediate problems with an operating system or application. Even when the latest service pack has been applied, a glitch in the millions of lines of code that make up an operating system can still adversely affect system performance. Some systems experience problems that others do not because the hardware, software, configuration, and utilization methods vary from system to system, network to network, and enterprise to enterprise. Service packs and hotfixes assure you quick access to the latest improvements for your operating system or applications.

To get the latest service pack or set of hotfixes from Microsoft, downloading is the way to go. However, be aware that although hotfixes are usually small and quick to download, a service pack is typically several megabytes in size and can take a very long time to download, even with a fast Internet connection.

Most — but not all — service packs include the contents of past service packs within them. Check to make sure that the service pack you are downloading does include past service packs, if you do not already have those past service packs installed on your system. This information will be in the README file.

Once you have downloaded a service pack, it is important that you test it on another system before implementing it in your production environment. It should be tested on the exact same type of hardware that you have running in your environment.

Defining Your Server's Role

Unfortunately, even Microsoft's recommended Pentium 133 with 32MB RAM is not sufficient for anything but a small organization — and even then, performance depends on what you're doing with the server. Optimally, you should run your Exchange Server on a computer that is *not* also functioning as a primary domain controller (PDC) or a backup domain controller (BDC) for your network. All domain controllers, whether they are PDCs or BDCs, experience some capacity loss to the overhead required to manage the security account management (SAM) database for the domain. The amount of this overhead is determined by the size and activity of the domain.

An Exchange Server operates at a higher performance level if it is running on a machine that is dedicated to Exchange messaging and does not handle domain management. But in small networks, running both on one machine is not an uncommon configuration, because it saves the expense of an extra machine.

However, saving on a machine in this way may result in meager performance for both Windows NT and Exchange.

If you're running a small network or a test lab, you may not have the option of dedicating a server to Exchange. If your computer does play the roles of both Exchange Server and domain controller, you need hardware more powerful than that detailed in Table 7-1. Also, Exchange running on the domain controller requires that administrators of that machine will be administrators on all domain controllers. Furthermore, there is a security risk in that anyone who uses the Web connector will need the right to log on locally at the server, which is generally not a privilege allowed for users on a domain controller.

The Exchange Server architecture was developed to participate in a Windows NT domain system. The NT domain system can have one or more domains in it. Each Exchange Server must be a member server, or a domain controller of the domain, and must be able to access a primary domain controller or backup domain controller in order to function. Before installing Exchange, it is recommended that you execute a NET VIEW \\PDC or NET VIEW \\BDC command from a command prompt window on the future Exchange Server to verify the domain controller's accessibility. Another way to verify accessibility is to open the Network Neighborhood and look for the PDC or BDC listing in the Exchange Server's domain.

The role that a server plays in a network is more than its configuration as a domain controller or member server. It also includes specifying the services that the server will provide to the network. One of these services is the Internet Information Server (IIS). Hardware capacity is even more critical if your server is also running IIS or other network applications. IIS, which is required to run on the network if you want to allow Outlook Web Access to your Exchange Server, utilizes all the memory and processing power it can get, depending on its configuration. For example, if IIS is configured to provide FTP service as well as Outlook Web Access, it utilizes many more CPU cycles and much more hard drive space than if it did not provide those services. IIS can be installed on the Exchange Server or on another server, so you have options as to where to provide these services. You should list the services that the server will host and the various applications' hardware requirements when you determine how much hardware you're going to need. Start with the largest hardware requirements of any of the applications, and then increment the RAM, processor speed, and storage capacity for each additional service by a portion of its own recommendation. You will then have a fair idea of your server's hardware needs.

For more information on planning your server hardware, see Chapter 5.

Optimizing Hardware through Configuration

Increasing the speed of your processor and the amount of storage and memory on your computer are effective ways of making your Exchange Server more powerful. You can also optimize your existing hardware to help boost the performance of an Exchange Server if you configure the operating system in the following ways:

- If possible, use one physical disk for your operating system and another for your page file. You can also increase the size of your page file to 50MB or 100MB beyond the size of your physical memory.

- Exchange Server logs all transactions to disk. You can use a utility called Performance Optimizer to designate separate physical disks to house your Information Store and transaction log files after installing Exchange Server. This step allows your log files to be written more quickly to disk. Keep in mind that logs are written to disk sequentially, while the Exchange database is written randomly. When the logs and the database are on the same physical disk, the hard drive performance is affected by the extra time taken to continually reposition the head. Furthermore, keeping the logs on a separate disk can assist you if the database disk crashes, because the logs are used in recovery of the database. Because the log files are relatively small (5MB of storage space), you can increase speed even further by formatting the disks with the file allocation table (FAT) file system. On partitions smaller than 500 MB, the FAT file system is usually quicker than the Windows NT File System (NTFS). Note that NTFS has other advantages that may outweigh the need for speed, plus it performs well on partitions larger than 500MB. Choose this optimization only when it is relevant to your situation.

- You can also use a stripe set consisting of multiple physical disks to house the Exchange Information Stores and other main components, allowing the various components to be accessed most efficiently. Using a stripe set with parity adds the additional advantage of providing fault tolerance. Because messaging data is considered critical to most businesses, striping without parity should be avoided, because the chances of losing all data at once increases. Hardware RAID using striping with parity provides higher performance than software RAID, because the operating system is not taxed with managing the disk activity.

Verifying System Requirements

In addition to making sure that your computer's hardware can handle Exchange Server 5.5, you need to check certain other settings before proceeding with your Setup.

Windows NT Server

Exchange Server 5.5 can be installed only on Windows NT Server 4.0 or later, and you must also install NT Service Pack 3 or later. If you are running Service Pack 3 and you plan to install Exchange Server 5.5 with the additional Outlook Web Access component, you also need to install a rollup hotfix. The hotfix is available at *ftp://ftp.microsoft.com/bussys/winnt/winnt-public/fixes/usa/nt40/hotfixes-postSP3/asp-memfix/*. If you are running Service Pack 4 or later, you do not need this hotfix.

You also need to make sure that the NetBIOS name given to your Windows NT Server is the name that you want your Exchange Server to have. It is simple enough to change the name of an NT member server before installing Exchange Server, but it's nearly impossible afterward. You can change the name by using the Identification tab of the Network Control Panel applet, shown in Figure 7-1. For more information on Exchange Server's dependence on Windows NT Server, see Chapter 3.

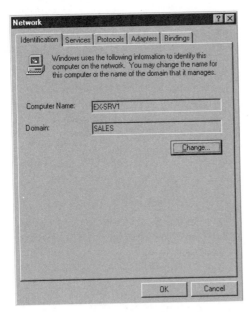

Figure 7-1. *Changing the name of your Windows NT Server.*

Windows NT Domains

When you install Exchange Server for the first time, you also create a new Exchange site and organization. If you are installing on a single-domain network or if your new Exchange site will not cross any domain boundaries, you should have no problems. However, if your new site will cross domain boundaries, you need to make sure that appropriate trust relationships have been established before Setup. For more information on how sites and domains interact, see Chapter 5.

TCP/IP

Exchange Server 5.5 includes support for many Internet protocols, including Simple Mail Transfer Protocol (SMTP), Network News Transfer Protocol (NNTP), and Hypertext Transfer Protocol (HTTP). All these protocols rely on the TCP/IP suite to operate. To install support for the optional Internet protocols, you need to ensure that TCP/IP is correctly configured on your Windows NT Server. To do so, use the TCP/IP tabs of the Network Control Panel applet, or use the Ipconfig utility, shown in Figure 7-2. Note that each server's IPCONFIG output reflects the actual IP configuration of that server—and varies widely from machine to machine.

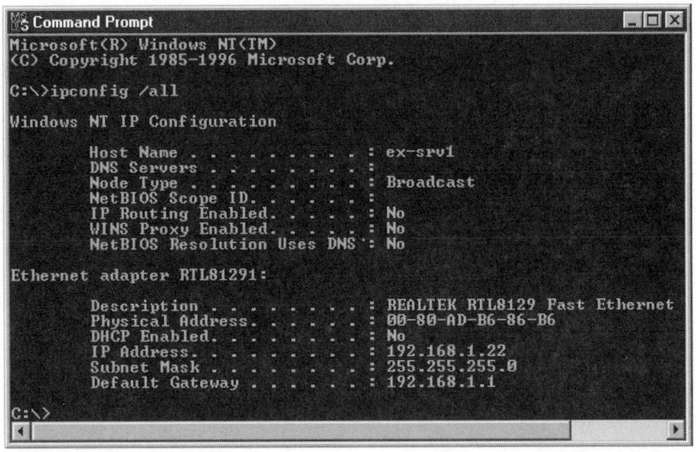

Figure 7-2. *Using the Ipconfig /ALL command to verify TCP/IP configuration.*

Internet Information Server

When you install Exchange Server 5.5, you have the option of installing a component called Outlook Web Access (OWA). OWA provides a way for clients to use a simple Web browser to access certain Exchange Server resources, including server-based inboxes, public folders, and the Global Address List. OWA accomplishes all these tasks using a technology called

Active Server Pages, which is a component of IIS 3.0 and later. For this reason, you must first make sure that IIS 3.0 or later is installed on the same network as your Exchange Server.

Microsoft Key Management Server

In addition to taking advantage of the built-in security of Windows NT Server, Exchange Server 5.5 provides advanced security in the form of an optional component called Key Management (KM) Server. KM Server works in conjunction with the Directory Service to manage the encryption keys used to encrypt e-mail messages. KM Server integrates with Microsoft Certificate Server in order to provide services.

KM Server is typically installed after Exchange Server has been installed. It can be installed on a server that is running Microsoft Certificate Server, or it can be installed with the Certificate Server client that is configured to access the Microsoft Certificate Server on the internetwork.

For more information on configuring and supporting KM Server, see Chapter 15.

Microsoft Cluster Server

The Enterprise Edition of Windows NT Server 4.0 provides support for clustering technology, in which two Windows NT Servers, called *nodes*, can be grouped to act as a single network unit. Clustering is designed to provide reliability through hardware redundancy. If one server in a cluster fails, another server in that cluster can take over, providing near-continuous access to network resources. To install Exchange Server, you must ensure that a cluster has a single network name and IP address as well as a shared disk that is part of an external disk array.

> **Note** A hotfix for Service Pack 3 that must be installed before installing Exchange Server 5.5 on clustered servers is now available. This hotfix is available at *ftp.microsoft.com/bussys/winnt/winnt-public/fixes/usa/nt40/hotfixes-postsp3/roll-up/*. If you are using Service Pack 4, you do not need to install this hotfix. If you are running an Intel server, you need the hotfix named ROLLUPI.EXE. If you are running an Alpha server, you need the hotfix named ROLLUPA.EXE.

Certain components of Exchange Server 5.5—including the four main components (Directory Service, Information Store, Message Transfer Agent, and System Attendant), the Internet Mail Service, and the Event Service—are designed to take advantage of clustering technology. Exchange Server must be installed on both the primary and secondary nodes of the cluster server. Installation on the first node of the cluster goes much like the typical installation outlined in this chapter.

When you run Setup on the second node of the cluster, you are presented with an Update Node option. You must choose this option, which copies the already installed Exchange Server files to the appropriate directories on the second node.

Real World   The Clustered Environment
The four main Exchange components (Directory Service, Information Store, Message Transfer Agent, and System Attendant), along with the Internet Mail Service and Event Service, are supported in a clustered environment. Many additional Exchange components, however, cannot be used on clustered servers because they were not designed that way. These components include the following:

- Dynamic RAS connector
- Internet Mail Service using dialup connection
- Internet News Service using dialup connection
- Outlook Web Access
- StarNine Mail for AppleTalk Networks
- Exchange Connector for Lotus Notes
- Exchange Connector for SNADS
- X.400 connector using X.25
- X.400 connector using TP4
- Exchange Connector for IBM OfficeVision OV/VM (PROFS)
- Third-party connectors and gateways

Note   Whenever you add components to or remove components from the clustered Exchange Server installation, you run the Setup program on the first node as usual. You must then run Setup again on the second node and choose the Upgrade Node option.

Windows NT Services for Macintosh

Exchange Server 5.5 provides support for a connector that allows Exchange Server and Microsoft Mail for AppleTalk Networks to transfer messages and share Directory information. To install this optional component, you must ensure that Windows NT Services for Macintosh is installed and configured correctly on the soon-to-be Exchange Server computer.

Creating Special Accounts

Your last task before starting Exchange Server Setup is creating some special user accounts. The first account, the Site Services account, is required. The second, a special Exchange Administrator's account, is helpful for distribution of Exchange administration responsibilities.

Before creating the accounts, you should run two tasks to ensure that the system is recoverable to the same state in which it started. One of these tasks is to create a rescue disk. Windows NT has a utility, called RDISK, for creating these disks. Simply open a command prompt window, execute RDISK, and follow the prompts. If the standard prompts are acceptable, you can also use RDISK –S.

The second task is to back up the server. Most administrators select a tape backup system for backing up their servers on an ongoing basis. However, many of these tape backups only back up recently changed files. The best thing to do at this point is to execute a full system backup.

Creating a Site Services Account

Each of the main components of Exchange Server acts as a Windows NT Service. For these components to communicate with one another, communicate with services on other Exchange Servers, and access parts of the Exchange Directory Information Tree (DIT), all the services within a site must have a common security context. This common context takes the form of a Windows NT user account called the Site Services account.

When you install the first Exchange Server in a site, thus creating the new site, you are asked to specify this Site Services account. Although you can specify any existing user account, it is highly recommended that you create a special account for this purpose instead of using a normal user account.

You can create this new account via User Manager for Domains, assuming that you have administrative privileges in the domain in which you'll be installing Exchange Server. In the User Manager for Domains window, click on the User menu and choose New User. In the New User dialog box (Figure 7-3), enter an

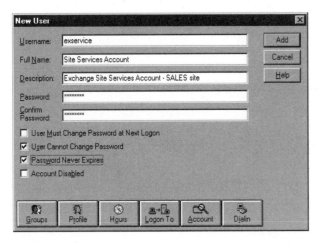

Figure 7-3. *Setting up the Site Services account.*

appropriate username, a full name, and a password. Because the Site Service account has considerable access to the network, select a complex password that cannot be guessed easily. This step further secures your network. (Be sure to write down the username and password, because you need to know them during the installation.) You also need to disable the User Must Change Password At Next Logon option and select both the User Cannot Change Password and Password Never Expires options so that this account does not encounter authentication problems. When you're done, click Add to create the new account. Other rights required by the new Site Services account will be assigned during Setup.

Note Once you create a Site Services account, you can change the password for it. Unfortunately, the procedure for changing the password is not as simple as simply changing it in User Manager for Domains. You first must change the password on the SERVICE ACCOUNT PASSWORD property sheet of the *Configuration* object in Exchange Administrator. Following this step, you must change the password in User Manager for Domains. The full procedure for changing the Site Services account password is covered in Chapter 10.

Creating the Exchange Administrator's Account

Exchange administration and Windows NT administration are handled separately. Just because an account has administrative permissions in Windows NT does not mean that same account will have administrative permissions in Exchange. When you install Exchange Server, one user account is given permission to administer Exchange: the account that you are logged on with when you started the installation. If you want to enable other Exchange administrators, you must do so manually, using the Exchange Administrator utility.

For this reason, make sure that when you start Exchange Server Setup, you are logged on from the account that you want to use for Exchange administration. This account can be the preconfigured Administrator account, your own account, or a special one that you create just for the task. Later, you can assign administrative rights to other accounts or groups.

Installing Exchange Server

Finally! After all this explanation and planning, you actually get to run Exchange Server Setup. You can run Setup from either the Exchange Server CD-ROM or a shared network installation point. If you are using the CD-ROM, you only have to insert the disk and watch Setup start automatically. If you're installing over the network, you have to find and run the Setup program yourself. There could be multiple versions of the installation files for different processors (Intel and Alpha), for different encryption levels, and for different languages. Be sure that you find the right files for your situation.

If you insert the Exchange Server 5.5 CD-ROM and the Autorun feature is enabled on your system, you see a splash screen like the one shown in Figure 7-4. From this window, you can run the main Exchange Server Setup program, or you can install support for chat services and other optional features and connectors. If Autorun is disabled, you will need to manually run SETUP.EXE from the CD-ROM. In this case, the splash screen is bypassed and the main Setup program is launched directly. This section details the main Exchange Server 5.5 Setup option.

Note The first thing that you'll see when you run Setup is a warning to shut down any other applications that are running. The single most common reason Exchange Server installation fails is that other MAPI-based applications are running in the background while Setup is running. These applications can include e-mail programs, Web browsers, and even components of Microsoft Office. Use the Processes tab of Windows NT's Task Manager to find and close any such applications. You also need to shut down all instances of Performance Monitor monitoring the server, whether Performance Monitor is running locally or on a remote machine. Finally, you also need to make sure that Event Viewer is not running on the server.

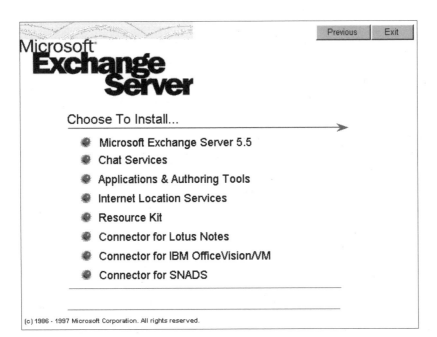

Figure 7-4. *Choosing which setup to run.*

Choosing an Installation Type

After you make sure that no other programs are running, read Microsoft's End-User License Agreement (EULA) and enter your 10-digit CD-Key. Setup then searches for any components of Exchange Server that may already be installed on the computer. If another installation is found, you are prompted to perform an upgrade. If no previous installation is found, you see the dialog box shown in Figure 7-5.

You can do two things in this dialog box. The first option is to specify the installation directory, which by default is C:\EXCHSRVR. Unless you have a good reason for changing this directory, you should leave it alone. The second thing that you can do in this dialog box is choose one of the three available installation types:

- **Typical**   Only the four core Exchange components — IS, DS, MTA, and SA — and the Exchange Administrator utility are installed, along with the online documentation. None of the additional connectors (such as the X.400 or dynamic RAS connector) or components (such as the Internet News Service) is installed. This type of installation is often useful for installing additional servers on an existing site.

Figure 7-5. *Choosing an installation type.*

- **Complete/Custom**   You can select any or all of the components available
  to Exchange. These components include the core components and the
  Exchange Administrator utility as well as additional connectors, Outlook
  Web Access, and extended online documentation. Table 7-2 provides a
  detailed list of components that can be installed. The Complete/Custom
  installation is useful for installing the first server on a site and for installing
  only the Exchange Administrator utility.

- **Minimum**   Only the four core components are installed. The Exchange
  Administrator utility and optional components are not installed.

Note   Unlike the rest of the Exchange Server components, the Exchange
Administrator utility can be installed by itself on Windows NT Server or
Windows NT Workstation using the complete/custom installation type. This
option is required to manage your Exchange organization remotely.

For the first Exchange Server on a site, it usually is best to run a Complete/Custom
installation and install all available components. Even though optional components are installed with this choice, they generally won't be active until you specifically configure them by using Exchange Administrator. However, should you
need the component at some point, you won't have to return to your CD-ROM
to reinstall it.

Table 7-2.   Components Included in Available Installation Types

Component	Minimal	Typical	Complete/Custom
Core components	X	X	X
Exchange Administrator		X	X
Online documentation		X	X
Outlook Web Access			X
MS Mail connector			X
cc:Mail connector			X
X.400 connector			X
Event Service			X
Key Management Server			X

Setting Up Outlook Web Access

If you chose to install Outlook Web Access, Setup informs you that it needs to stop all of the running Internet Information Server services. Then the Setup program installs OWA and restarts the IIS services.

Creating a New Site

In the next phase of installation, you get to create the new site and organization that you've been planning. As Figure 7-6 illustrates, this is the point at which you get to join an existing site or create a new one. To create a new site, you simply select that option and enter Organization and Site names. Remember, though, not to take these names lightly. After you click OK, Setup creates the new items, and you will not be able to change them without reinstalling Exchange Server.

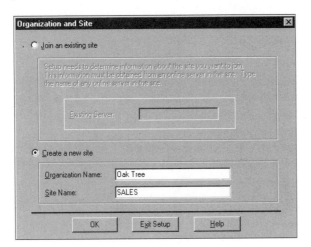

Figure 7-6. *Creating a new organization and site.*

Note If you are creating a new site in an existing organization, enter the name of the current organization and the name of the new site. Setup will not verify or attempt to join the organization, but it will create the new site. You will manually connect the two sites later.

Choosing a Site Services Account

Remember the Site Services account that you created earlier? The Site Services Account dialog box, shown in Figure 7-7, is where you get to use it. Be careful, though. By default, the account selected for use is the user account under which you are currently logged. In this dialog box, you want to select the Site Services account that you created instead. Do this by clicking Browse and selecting the new account. Enter the password (which you remembered to write down, right?), and click OK.

Note If you get to the point where you need to choose a Site Services account and realize that you forgot to create one, don't panic. Just press Ctrl-Esc (or the Windows key, if you have one) and run User Manager for Domains. It's not too late to create the account.

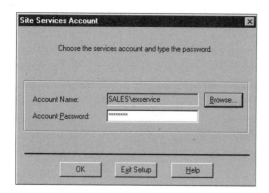

Figure 7-7. *Choosing a Site Services account.*

After you assign the Site Services account, Setup grants it three new rights:

- Logon as a service
- Restore files and directories
- Act as part of the operating system

This point is the final step in installing Exchange Server. Setup begins copying files. When Setup completes that task, the new Exchange services start and Setup finishes.

You are now given a chance to run Performance Optimizer, a utility that optimizes Exchange Server 5.5 for use on your hardware. Performance Optimizer is discussed in "Optimizing and Verifying Your Installation" later in this chapter. First, though, this section covers two other installation methods that are a little different from those outlined earlier. The first method is installing Exchange Server on an existing Exchange site. The second method is upgrading from a previous version of Exchange Server.

Real World   Automating Exchange Server 5.5 Setup

If you plan to deploy a large number of Exchange Servers in your enterprise or if you need to deploy servers remotely, you will be glad to know that there is a way to automate the Setup process. All the information that controls the file-copying process during Setup is contained in a file called SETUP.INI. The file is customized for a particular installation when you make choices in the various Setup windows outlined in this chapter.

You can create your own SETUP.INI files based on samples found on your Exchange CD-ROM. Go to Server, select Support, and then select Batsetup. The samples will be found in the Setup folder. You can then create a batch script that runs the Setup program, using the information in your customized file. If you are deploying Exchange Server to existing Windows NT Servers in your enterprise, you can also use Microsoft System Management Server or a similar application to further automate the process.

If you want to learn more about automating Exchange Server Setup, including all the parameters for customizing the SETUP.INI files, consult the online product documentation or *Deploying Microsoft Exchange Server 5.5* (1998) from the *Notes from the Field* series published by Microsoft Press.

Installing in an Existing Site

Installing Exchange Server 5.5 in an existing Exchange site is a nearly identical process to installing it as the first server on a site. However, a couple of peculiarities exist. You start Setup the same way: from either the CD-ROM or a network installation point. The first difference that you encounter is in the dialog box shown in Figure 7-8.

This time you select the Join An Existing Site option and enter the name of an Exchange Server on the site that you are attempting to join. Notice that this

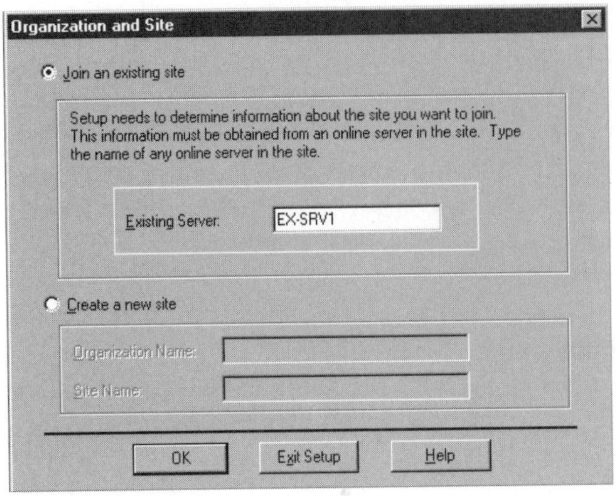

Figure 7-8. *Joining an existing site.*

dialog box has no convenient Browse button. You must know the name of an existing server in order to join the site. After you enter that name and click OK, you see a confirmation dialog box like the one in Figure 7-9.

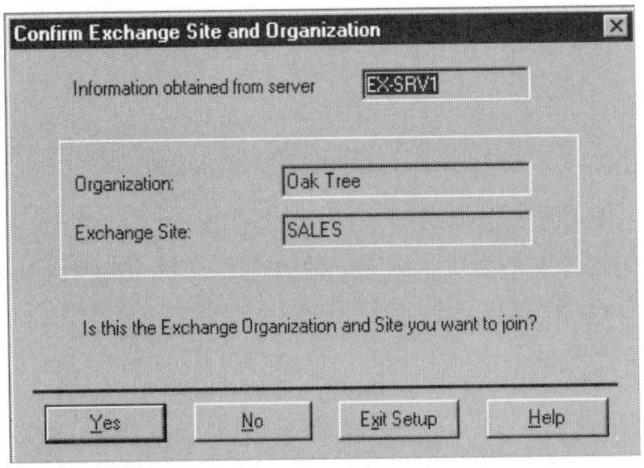

Figure 7-9. *Confirming existing site information.*

When you proceed, you are prompted for the password of the existing site's Site Services account, as shown in Figure 7-10. Notice that you are not given the option to select a different account this time.

After this point, installation proceeds the same way as when you are installing the first server on a site. Setup copies files, starts services, and prompts you to run Performance Optimizer.

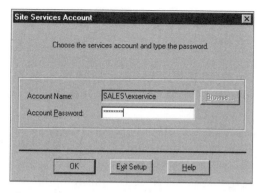

Figure 7-10. *Entering the Site Services account password.*

Upgrading an Existing Server

Exchange Server 5.5 supports the direct upgrade of existing Exchange Servers running versions 4.0 and 5.0. Before you begin an upgrade from either version, you should take certain precautions. The first precaution is to back up your current Exchange Server, which will allow you to revert to the old version should something go wrong. The second thing you need to do is turn off any server monitors that are running on your current servers. (For more information on using server monitors, see Chapter 22.) Third, you will need to update (or create) the Emergency Repair Disk (ERD) for your server. To create an ERD, simply enter RDISK.EXE at the command prompt and follow the instructions on the screen. Finally, you should test and repair the existing Exchange information stores using the Information Store Integrity tool (ISINTEG.EXE) and the Offline Defragmentation tool (ESEUTIL.EXE), both of which are discussed in Chapter 22.

> **Note**   When you are upgrading a server from a previous version of Exchange Server Enterprise Edition, you want to make sure you upgrade to Exchange Server 5.5 Enterprise Edition. If you want, you can also upgrade a server running a previous version of Exchange Server Standard Edition to the Exchange Server 5.5 Enterprise Edition. However, upgrading a server from a previous version of Exchange Server Enterprise Edition to Exchange Server 5.5 Standard Edition is not supported.

To start an upgrade, run Exchange Server 5.5 Setup as usual. Setup detects the previous version and walks you through the installation. If you are upgrading from Exchange Server 5.0, you are given the choice of two types of upgrades:

- **Standard**   This method upgrades your existing Information Stores in their current locations, one large piece at a time. If Setup fails for any reason, the existing information stores are rendered unusable and must be restored from backup.

- **Fault-tolerant**   This method upgrades one Information Store (IS) file at a time, making a backup copy before the upgrade. If Setup fails, it can begin again where it left off (after you reboot and run Setup again). When Setup finishes, the backup copies of the IS files are deleted. The fault-tolerant method requires twice as much disk space as the standard method and can take place only on a local drive.

The fault-tolerant method is available only when you are upgrading from Exchange Server 5.0 to 5.5. If you want to use the fault-tolerant method when you upgrade from Exchange Server 4.0, you must first upgrade to 5.0 and then to 5.5.

> **Note**   You can determine what version of Exchange Server and the current Service Pack revision you are running by using the Exchange Administrator utility. Simply view the properties of the *Server* object for the server in question. You'll learn more about using Exchange Administrator in Chapter 8.

Upgrading a server can take some time; how much time depends primarily on the size of the Information Store databases that are being converted. For servers that have particularly large Information Stores, an upgrade can easily take more than a day. During the upgrade, the server is unavailable to the organization. It is best to plan the upgrade of your servers carefully so that users experience the least amount of downtime. A good practice is to notify users of the expected outage, and then execute the upgrade during an evening or over the weekend. For more information on deployment planning, see Chapter 6.

Real World   **Upgrading Multiple Servers from Exchange Server 4.0**

If you are upgrading multiple servers in an organization from Exchange Server 4.0, you must take some special steps. The procedure Microsoft recommends is to make sure that all Exchange Servers in your organization are upgraded to Exchange Server 4.0 with Exchange Service Pack 2. Then you can upgrade the servers to Exchange Server 5.5 in any order you please.

That said, you can use an alternative procedure if you can't install Service Pack 2 on all your servers. Start by upgrading any Directory Replication Bridgehead Servers (which you'll learn about in Chapter 12) on each site to Exchange Server 5.5. Then restart all servers that are still running Exchange Server 4.0 and wait for directory replication to occur throughout your organization. When this replication happens, you can upgrade your remaining servers to Exchange Server 5.5 in any order you please.

Optimizing and Verifying Your Installation

Exchange Server has been installed, but don't pat yourself on the back just yet. You still need to perform some post-installation tasks. The first task is running a handy utility called Performance Optimizer. The second task is checking on the newly installed Exchange services to make sure that they're all running as they should be.

Running Performance Optimizer

No matter how you installed Exchange Server 5.5—by creating a new site, joining a site, or upgrading a server—you are prompted at the end to run Performance Optimizer (Figure 7-11). Although this procedure is optional, it is highly recommended. Performance Optimizer is a clever little tool that scans your system, collects some information from you about your needs, and optimizes Exchange Server based on that data.

Figure 7-11. *Running Performance Optimizer.*

When you click Next, Optimizer stops all the Exchange services that Setup just started and presents the dialog box shown in Figure 7-12. This dialog box asks for some basic information about how your Exchange Server will be used. This information includes how many users are on the server and in the organization and which services the new server will provide to those users.

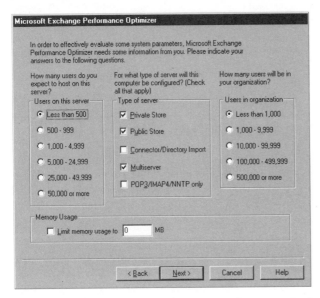

Figure 7-12. *Entering information in Performance Optimizer.*

After you enter all this information, Performance Optimizer scans your system and displays a page like the one shown in Figure 7-13. This page shows the locations that Performance Optimizer has determined are best to hold the various components of your Exchange Server. You can change any or all of these locations. If, for example, you have a small FAT-formatted drive or partition, you might want to move your Information Store logs and Directory Service logs there for faster access. When you are satisfied with the locations, click Next. Performance Optimizer makes the changes and restarts all your Exchange services. For more information on using Performance Optimizer to fine-tune Exchange Server performance, see Chapter 22.

Note Performance Optimizer should always be run on a newly installed Exchange Server. You should also run it whenever you add or remove components or change hardware on an existing server. Furthermore, you can use this utility to experiment with moving components to different locations to see how the changes affect performance.

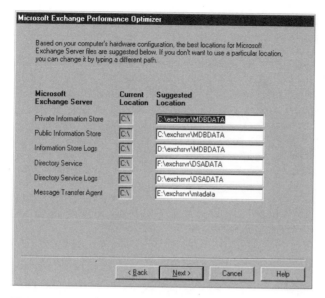

Figure 7-13. *Changing component locations in Performance Optimizer.*

Checking the Exchange Services

Now that you have finished the installation of your new Exchange Server, you should make sure that everything is running well. The very first thing you should do is restart your server. Once the server has restarted, you can check the Windows NT Event Log for any problems. Each of the Exchange components that make up your new server run as standard Windows NT Services. You can verify that these services are running using the Services applet from Windows NT Control Panel. The Services dialog box is shown in Figure 7-14.

You should see the following services listed:

- Microsoft Exchange System Attendant
- Microsoft Exchange Directory
- Microsoft Exchange Information Store
- Microsoft Exchange Message Transfer Agent

Depending on the optional components that you installed with Exchange Server, you may also see several other Microsoft Exchange services running. Microsoft releases service packs for Exchange Server, just as it does with Windows NT. In order to avoid possible problems later on, it is now time to install the latest Exchange Server service pack.

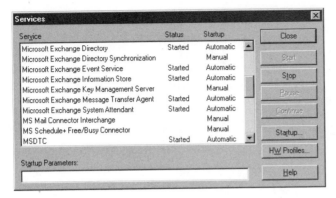

Figure 7-14. *The Services dialog box.*

After the service pack installation is complete, you should restart the system. When the server is back online, again check the Services applet in the Windows NT Control Panel to ensure that the Exchange Server services are up and running. Your new Exchange Server is ready to be configured. *Now* you can pat yourself on the back.

Note To verify that services are running on a remote Exchange Server, you can use the Windows NT Server Manager utility. You can also configure Server Monitors to keep watch over services for you by using Exchange Administrator. You learn how to set up these monitors in Chapter 20.

Summary

In this chapter, you learned to install Exchange Server 5.5. Before you install Exchange Server 5.5, you must make sure that your Windows NT Server is ready for the installation. This includes ensuring that the proper version of Windows NT Server and any service packs are installed, Windows NT domains and trust relationships are properly established, and required support for any optional Exchange Server 5.5 components is established. You will also need to verify that the hardware on your Windows NT Server meets requirements for installing Exchange Server 5.5 in the desired configuration. Finally, you need to create a Site Services account for use by the Exchange services in the site.

There are three basic contexts for installing Exchange Server 5.5: as the first server in a site, as a server joining an existing site, and as an upgrade to an existing server. When you install the first server in a site, you actually create the new site (and possibly a new organization) in the process. When you join an existing site, you need to provide the name of the existing site, the name of a server in that site, and the password for that site's Site Services account.

You can upgrade to Exchange Server 5.5 from versions 4.0 and 5.0. When you upgrade from version 5.0, you can choose between a standard and a fault-tolerant upgrade. When you upgrade from version 4.0, no fault-tolerant upgrade is available.

Once you have performed the installation, you are automatically given the chance to run Performance Optimizer, a program that collects information about how you intend to use the new server (as well as hardware information about your server) and optimizes Exchange Server 5.5 based on that data.

Chapter 8
Using Exchange Administrator

The primary tool that you will use to administer Microsoft Exchange Server is Microsoft Exchange Administrator, which provides a graphical environment for configuring the various services and components of an Exchange organization.

In this chapter, we start studying the Exchange Administrator program. We will look at how to start the Exchange Administrator and connect to an Exchange Server, how the Exchange Administrator window and its menus are organized, and how to use its many functions to manage an Exchange organization. The Exchange Administrator offers an almost overwhelming view into the entire Exchange system. With an understanding of its features, you'll see that Exchange can be a complete messaging support system.

Starting Exchange Administrator

Exchange Administrator is a sophisticated program that allows you to manage all the components of an entire Exchange organization from a single location. The program is installed when you perform a typical or custom installation of Exchange Server 5.5. You can also install it separately on any computer running Microsoft Windows NT Workstation 4.0 or Server 4.0 or later.

By default, Exchange Administrator is installed in the Exchange Server program group. You can get to it by clicking on the Start menu, choosing Programs, choosing Microsoft Exchange, and then choosing Microsoft Exchange Administrator.

Whenever you run Exchange Administrator, the program must connect to a specific Exchange Server in your organization. When you start Exchange Administrator, it prompts you to connect to a server. If you want to connect to another server, you can go to the File menu, choose the Connect To Server option, and then provide the name of the desired Exchange Server.

Exchange Administrator interoperates with the Exchange Server 5.5 program using local procedure calls (LPCs) or remote procedure calls (RPCs). A *procedure call* is an application program interface (API) that connects to another program and runs using various data interface points. LPCs run on the same machine, so when you run Exchange Administrator on the Exchange Server to which you are connected, you have invoked LPCs. RPCs run as a session-layer API between two different networked computers. RPCs are an open standard and can run over multiple protocols such as NetBEUI, SPX, Banyan Vines, and TCP/IP. When you run the Exchange Administrator on a computer that is different from the Exchange Server to which you are connected, you have invoked RPCs. This means that to connect to a server, Exchange Administrator must be installed on the Exchange Server computer itself or must be connected to an Exchange Server via a network connection that supports RPCs.

In order to administer an Exchange system with the Administrator, you must be logged on to Windows NT under a domain user account with administrative permissions in the Exchange site where the server is located. Until you specifically grant other user accounts permissions to administer Exchange Server, the only account with permission to do so is the account under which you were logged when you installed Exchange Server 5.5 and the Site Services account.

You can grant a user account different types of administrative permissions. If you grant permissions to a site, that user account can add mailboxes and administer recipients. If you grant permissions to a configuration container, that user account can configure the servers, connectors, and site properties. If you want to grant full permissions to an account at the site level, you grant permissions to both the site and the configuration container.

Permissions are generally granted through the use of roles. A *role* is a group of individual permissions within Exchange that can be applied to any user. The roles that can be assigned are Admin, Permissions Admin, Service Account Admin, View Only Admin, User, Send As, and Search. Roles are a timesaving device, but you should understand what each role means when it is applied to an account. The Service Account Admin role grants the most wide-ranging permissions. The View Only Admin role grants the lowest level of permission. To make a user account able to administer the organization, use the Admin role. For more information on how to assign permissions within Exchange Server, see Chapter 15.

The first time you run Exchange Administrator on a newly installed server, you encounter the Connect to Server dialog box, shown in Figure 8-1. You can enter the name of the server to which you want to connect, or you can browse the network to find the server. You can also specify that the selected server be the default connection. If you choose this option, you do not see this dialog box when you run Exchange Administrator in the future; instead, you connect to the default server automatically. Then you can connect to different servers from within Administrator.

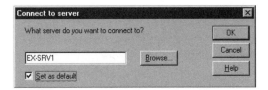

Figure 8-1. *Choosing an Exchange Server.*

Note   You can connect to only one Exchange Server at a time within a single instance of Exchange Administrator. However, you can run multiple instances of Administrator on the same computer and connect to a different server with each instance. To do so, run Exchange Administrator a second time or choose Connect To Server from the File menu of Administrator.

Real World   Starting Administrator from the Command Line
Like most Windows NT programs, Exchange Administrator can be run from the command line. Simply enter the command ADMIN at the command prompt to start Administrator from the command line. This technique can be useful for executing Administrator functions from batch files and for running Administrator in certain ways that are difficult to run from a graphical interface. The command-line switches for Exchange Administrator are as follows:

- **/r**   Starts Administrator in Raw mode, which provides access to all the directory attributes in the Exchange schema. Raw mode is an advanced mode of Exchange Administrator in which you can make privileged changes directly to the Directory Information Tree. A wrong move in this mode can completely devastate an Exchange organization, even forcing a reinstallation of all the servers into a new tree. For this reason, we suggest that you do not use Exchange Administrator in its Raw mode unless you are required to execute specific commands or you are testing Raw mode on a lab system. You can think of Raw mode changes in the same light as registry changes. The user interface will not protect from errors.

- **/h**   Starts Administrator and displays a help file containing information on available command-line switches.

- **/s <server name>**   Starts Administrator and connects to the specified server.

- **/m [Site]] *monitor name| server name***   Starts Administrator and starts the Exchange Monitor specified by *monitor name*. The optional *Site* parameter specifies the directory name of the site that contains the monitor to be run. The required *server name* parameter specifies the name of the server on which the monitor is configured.

- **/t**   Temporarily suspends an Exchange Monitor on a server that is to be taken down for repair. This command can be used with the optional additional switches **n**, which suspends notifications of problems found during maintenance, but initiates repairs; **r**, which suspends repairs but sends notifications; and **nr**, which suspends both notifications and repairs. You will learn more about monitors in Chapter 22.

- **/i**   Runs the command-line Directory Import utility.

- **/e**   Runs the command-line Directory Export utility.

Exploring the Main Administrator Window

Exchange Administrator provides a graphical view of all the resources and components of an Exchange organization. No matter how many sites and servers you have set up, you can manage them all from a single Administrator window, as shown in Figure 8-2. Use this window to navigate the Exchange organizational hierarchy and perform the various tasks associated with Exchange administration.

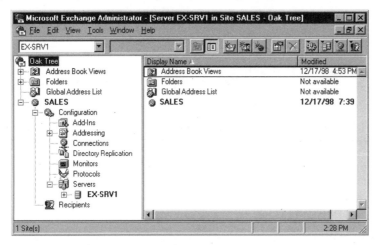

Figure 8-2. *Finding your way around the main Administrator window.*

The first thing to notice is that the window is divided into two panes. The pane on the left is called the *container pane*. The pane on the right is called the *contents pane*. These panes work much like the familiar dual-paned Windows Explorer. When you select a container in the container pane, its contents are displayed in the contents pane.

Exchange Server is a great example of an object-based, hierarchical directory environment. All the little bits and pieces that make up Exchange are objects that interact with one another to some degree. All the objects that you see in the container and contents panes can be divided into two types:

- **Leaf objects**   A leaf object represents a messaging resource or account. Some common leaf objects with which an administrator works daily include mailboxes, distribution lists, and connectors. These objects do not contain other objects. Leaf objects appear only in the contents pane of Administrator.

- **Container objects**   Container objects can contain both leaf objects and other container objects. The container pane of Administrator displays only container objects. Container objects can also appear in the contents pane. Container objects are used to logically group all the objects that make up an Exchange organization. An administrator uses the container objects to organize the tree and then to navigate through it. Two container objects are *Organization* and *Site*. In fact, if you take a close look at the container pane shown in Figure 8-3, you'll see that each level of the Exchange hierarchy is displayed.

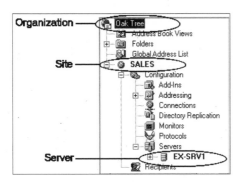

Figure 8-3. *Viewing the Exchange hierarchy in the container pane.*

The actual objects that you encounter in Exchange can be confusing if you do not know what their functions are. The top of the hierarchy in the container pane is the Exchange organization. It has a small globe icon with a letter in front of it. All other Exchange objects are contained within the organization.

The second container that you run into is the Address Book Views container. This holds the various configurations that you designate for the Global Address List.

The next container in the hierarchy is usually Folders. The Folders container holds the public folders hierarchy and properties, but not their contents. It also contains the system folders, a list of folders that Exchange users do not see. The system folders hold the Offline Address Book and other system configuration objects.

After that, you see the Global Address List (GAL). The GAL is the container of the recipient list for all servers within the Exchange organization. The GAL is a separate list from the server recipients because it incorporates all recipients and replicates between servers in order to be updated consistently.

Finally, you see all the site containers, listed by their names. Each site contains further containers for:

- **Servers** The actual Exchange Servers
- **Protocols** The protocols that the site is configured for
- **Monitors** The tools that an administrator can create and configure to watch Exchange messaging activity
- **Directory replication** The configuration of directory updates
- **Connections** The connectors that are configured for the site
- **Add-ins** The additional components plugged into Exchange
- **Addressing** The address templates and generators for consistent names

You will use both container and leaf objects to administer an Exchange organization. Most objects in the Exchange Administrator window—both container and leaf—have a set of property sheets that allow you to configure various parameters for that object and make it act in the way that will best serve the organization's needs. You can open an object's property sheets by selecting the object in the main window and choosing Properties from the File menu. Figure 8-4 shows the property sheets for the server EX-SRV1. Notice that each of the tabs contains options for different configuration details. Property sheets are used to both configure and administer Exchange.

There are property sheets for both container and leaf objects. The sheer number of property sheets that you will encounter when administering Exchange Server 5.5 can seem daunting, but don't let it intimidate you. Take the time to play with the program. You probably won't be able to remember exactly where to go to accomplish every administrative task in Exchange Server. It helps to think about what the task will involve. If you need to manage communication between two

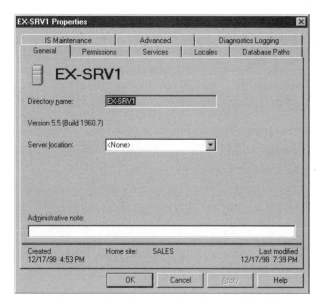

Figure 8-4. *Examining a server's property sheets.*

sites, use the Connections container. If you need to manage communication between two servers, use the Servers container and check out the Message Transfer Agent (MTA). If you need to configure the Global Address List, look at the Global Address List container, the Server Recipients container, or Directory Replication. As you can see, there are many different places to configure messaging. Each component handles a different aspect of the configuration, so multiple components might be involved with a single configuration or administration task. As you use the program and get used to the Exchange environment, it will become easier to navigate the program and find exactly the object or objects that you need to administer.

Learning the contents and layout of the various property sheets in Administrator is a key part of learning how Exchange works. After you learn how to organize tasks that match the way that Exchange is structured, you will find that your administrative tasks flow more easily.

Using the Toolbar

The toolbar of Exchange Administrator, shown in Figure 8-5, provides quick access to some of the most commonly used administrative features. The toolbar is visible by default when you start Administrator; you can hide it by choosing the Toolbar command from the View menu.

Figure 8-5. *Using the Exchange Administrator toolbar.*

The items available by default on the toolbar include the following:

- **Server box**   The Server box contains a list of the 20 servers most recently accessed from Exchange Administrator. You can use the drop-down menu to connect to any of these servers.
- **View Filters box**   The View Filters box lets you specify what types of recipients you want to view: mailboxes, distribution lists, public folders, custom recipients, or all recipients.
- **Up One Level**   This button bumps the current contents-pane view up one level.
- **Container Pane**   This button toggles the view of the container pane on and off.
- **New Mailbox/Distribution List/Custom Recipient**   These three buttons let you create new recipients quickly.
- **Properties**   This button displays the property sheets for the currently selected object.
- **Delete**   This button deletes the currently selected object (if it can be deleted).
- **Switch to Configuration/Servers/Connections/Recipients**   These buttons allow you to switch to the respective containers quickly.

You can also customize the toolbar by specifying what items appear on it. Open the Customize Toolbar dialog box (shown in Figure 8-6) by choosing Customize Toolbar from the Tools menu or by double-clicking the toolbar background. The left window shows available commands for which buttons may be added to the toolbar; the right window shows commands that are already represented by buttons on the toolbar. Use the Add and Remove buttons to move commands between these two windows.

Note   Sometimes multiple users log on to the same computer to manage Exchange Server 5.5. Most of the customization features of Exchange Administrator are saved in the profile of the user account that is logged on when the program is customized. Storing these changes in the user profile enables customized window layouts of Administrator that are maintained separately for each user. The customization options include toolbars, default views, default server connections, and customized columns in the contents pane.

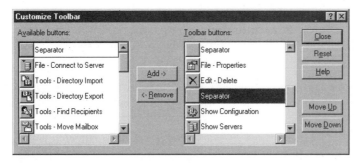

Figure 8-6. *Customizing the toolbar.*

Exploring the Administrator Menus

Many commands are available in the menus of Exchange Administrator. Most of these commands perform tasks that are covered in other chapters of this book. However, some commands are of a more general nature, so they are covered in this section.

File Menu: Connect to Server

This command opens the Connect to Server dialog box. (Refer to Figure 8-1 earlier in this chapter.) Use this command to change the server to which Exchange Administrator is currently connected. To administer a site in an Exchange organization, you must be connected to a server in that site. When you connect to a server in a different site, you view the Exchange Directory structure from that site's perspective.

> **Note**   You can view, but not administer, directory information from another site without being connected to a server on that site if directory replication is configured between the two sites.

File Menu: Save Window Contents

This command allows you to save the contents of the contents pane of Administrator to a comma-separated value (.CSV) file. For example, Save Window Contents is useful if you want to see a list of all the recipients in a particular recipient container. The .CSV file can be printed or opened in a spreadsheet application such as Microsoft Excel.

View Menu

The primary function of the View menu is to allow you to filter the way that you view recipients in the Administrator window. You can choose to view only recipients of a certain type or to view all recipients. You can also specify whether to view hidden recipients. For more information on recipients, see Chapter 9.

View Menu: Columns

The COLUMNS command displays the Columns dialog box, shown in Figure 8-7. This command is available only when the contents pane displays a container that has columns, such as the Recipients container. Using the Columns dialog box, you can specify the columns that appear, the order in which they appear, and their on-screen width.

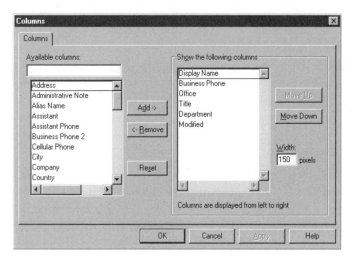

Figure 8-7. *Changing the way that columns are viewed.*

Tools Menu: Save Connections

The Tools menu actually contains two SAVE CONNECTIONS commands: SAVE CONNECTIONS NOW and SAVE CONNECTIONS ON EXIT. These commands save all connections that are currently open to other Exchange Server computers in the organization; the only difference is the time at which they save these connections. The connections are reestablished the next time Exchange Administrator runs. If you want to keep open multiple connections to different Exchange Servers, this feature saves you from having to manually reconnect to all of them each time you start Administrator.

Tools Menu: Options

This command opens the Options dialog box, which has three tabs: Auto Naming, Permissions, and File Format. Each of these tabs is discussed in this section.

Auto Naming Tab The Auto Naming tab, shown in Figure 8-8, lets you specify how display names and alias names are generated whenever you create a new recipient. A recipient's *display name* is the name shown for the *Recipient* object in the Exchange Administrator window. The *alias name* is typically a shortened version of the recipient name that can be used to address messages to that recipient. Many of the services in Exchange use the alias name instead of the full recipient name, since the alias is unique.

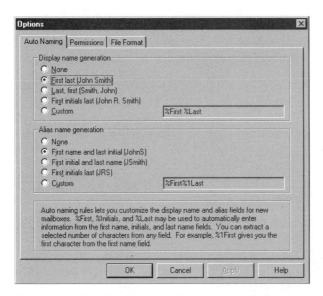

Figure 8-8. *Configuring Auto Naming in Administrator.*

You can specify how each type of name is generated individually. By default, the display name is generated from the recipient's full first and last names (for example, John Smith). The alias name is generated based on the recipient's full first name and last initial (JohnS). You can configure Auto Naming several ways, including specifying a custom generation scheme.

These custom schemes are based on three simple variables:

- **%First**   Recipient's first name
- **%Last**   Recipient's last name
- **%Initial**   Recipient's middle initial

You can further customize the %First and %Last variables by specifying how many characters of that name are to be used. For example, to use the first two letters of the first name, specify the variable %2First. These variables can be combined in just about any way you like. To create a custom display name that uses a recipient's first initial, middle initial, and first six letters of the last name, you specify the following string:

```
%1First%Initial%6Last
```

You should use your naming convention when creating the custom generation scheme. It will guide you in how to establish your string.

Permissions Tab   The Permissions tab, shown in Figure 8-9, lets you configure where and how administrative permissions can be assigned to objects in Administrator. The top section of this tab, labeled Windows NT Domain Defaults, lets you designate default options for choosing user accounts to which to assign permissions. The Default Windows NT Domain box indicates the domain from which the list of users is displayed whenever you assign permissions to an object. You can also specify whether to display user accounts from that default domain or from the domain to which Administrator is connected at the time.

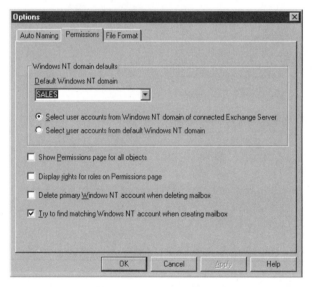

Figure 8-9. *Enabling permissions for Administrator objects.*

You can assign permissions individually to every object in Exchange using the PERMISSIONS property sheet for each object. Figure 8-10 shows an object's property sheet.

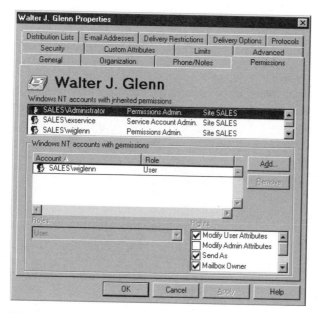

Figure 8-10. *Viewing permissions for an object.*

By default, however, the PERMISSIONS property sheet is not displayed for most objects. To specify that it be displayed for all objects, select the Show Permissions Page For All Objects check box in the Permissions tab of the Options dialog box. (Refer to Figure 8-9 earlier in this chapter.)

After you assign permissions to a user, you can customize that user's rights by assigning certain roles. You can use any of several predefined roles or customize these roles with certain rights. Like the PERMISSIONS property sheet itself, the rights for the roles are not displayed by default. To specify that they be displayed on every Permissions page, select the Display Rights For Roles On Permissions Page check box in the Permissions tab of the Options dialog box. (Refer to Figure 8-9 earlier in this chapter.) For more information on rights and permissions, see Chapter 15.

When you create a mailbox in Exchange Administrator, you usually associate a Windows NT user account with that mailbox. The last two options on the Permissions tab deal with how that feature is implemented. You can specify whether Exchange Administrator should automatically try to find a matching Windows NT user account whenever you create a new mailbox. Administrator performs this action by default. You can also specify that Administrator automatically delete an associated user account whenever a mailbox is deleted.

Administrator does not make this deletion by default. For more information on creating recipients, see Chapter 9.

File Format Tab   The File Format tab (Figure 8-11) is used to define the default settings used for importing and exporting Exchange Directories and for saving the window contents of Exchange Administrator. You can specify whether to use the ANSI or Unicode character set and which character should be used as the value separator.

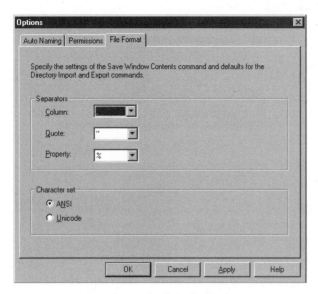

Figure 8-11. *Specifying the default file format.*

Summary

This chapter provided a basic introduction to the Exchange Administrator program, which is your primary interface to all administrative tasks within Exchange Server 5.5. The rest of the chapters in Part III describe using Exchange Administrator to accomplish particular tasks.

In this chapter you learned that when launched, Exchange Administrator must connect to a single Exchange Server. In addition, you must be logged on to

Windows NT under a user account with administrative permissions in the site where that server is located. Each instance of Exchange Administrator can connect to only one server, but multiple instances of Exchange Administrator can be run simultaneously.

There are two panes in the Exchange Administrator main window: the container pane, in which all container objects are displayed, and the contents pane, in which the contents of any container selected in the container pane are displayed. Containers may hold other containers. You manage an Exchange organization primarily using the property sheets of objects within Exchange Administrator.

Chapter 9
Creating and Managing Recipients

Sending and receiving information is the foundation of messaging, groupware, and, of course, Exchange Server. In this chapter, we start looking at the message transfer process within an Exchange system. We examine the mailbox repositories, how those mailboxes and other network resources are Exchange recipients, and how to manage those recipients. Exchange Server is based on a multitude of messaging components, but with some analysis, it becomes apparent how those components interact to create an enterprise-wide messaging system.

Recipients are objects in Exchange that reference resources that can receive messages. Such a resource might be an inbox in the Private Information Store where one of your users gets mail, a public folder where information is shared among many users, or even a newsgroup on the Internet.

However, no matter where a resource resides, a recipient object for that resource is always created on an Exchange Server in your organization. One of your main tasks as an administrator is to create and maintain these recipient objects. This chapter explains how to create and manage various types of messaging recipients; it also discusses tools that allow you to search for and organize recipients.

Understanding Recipient Types

It is tempting to think of a recipient as a mailbox or simply an object that can receive a message, and as you administer your organization, it may be convenient to take that view. But it is important to understand how the underlying architecture affects how you work with recipients in Exchange.

In Exchange, a recipient object does not receive messages. Instead, a recipient object is a reference to a resource that can receive messages. This is a subtle but important distinction. Recipient objects are contained in and maintained by the Directory Service. The resources that those objects reference could be anywhere. One resource might be a mailbox for a user in your organization. A mailbox resource would be contained in the Private Information Store of the associated

Exchange Server and maintained by its Information Store Service. Another resource might be a user on the Internet. In this case, the recipient object would contain a reference to that resource, along with rules governing the transfer of messages.

Four types of recipient objects are available in Exchange.

- **Mailbox** A *mailbox* is a private storage area in which an individual user can send and receive messages. Each mailbox is typically associated with a Microsoft Windows NT user account and a single user within your organization. A mailbox recipient object references that mailbox and is used to configure its properties.

- **Custom recipient** A *custom recipient* is a pointer to a mailbox in an external messaging system linked to a person outside the organization. This type of recipient points to an address to be used to deliver messages sent to that person and the properties that govern how those messages are delivered. Custom recipients are most often used for connecting your organization to foreign messaging systems, such as Microsoft Mail (also known as MSMail), Lotus cc:Mail, or the Internet. An administrator creates custom recipients so that often-used e-mail addresses are available in the Global Address List (GAL) as real names. This makes it easier to send mail because users do not need to guess at cryptic e-mail addresses.

- **Public folder** A *public folder* is a public storage area, typically open to all users in an organization. Users can post new messages or reply to existing messages in a public folder, creating an ongoing forum for discussion of topics. Public folders can also be used to store and provide access to just about any type of document. The concept of a public folder as a recipient is difficult to grasp because the repository for information is shared. One way that a public folder is used as a recipient is when it is configured for Network News Transfer Protocol (NNTP) newsfeed. In this scenario, the information from the newsgroup is sent to the public folder recipient and then viewed by Exchange users in the organization.

- **Distribution list** A *distribution list* (DL) is a list of other recipients. Messages sent to a distribution list are redirected and sent to each member of that list. Distribution lists can contain any combination of the other types of recipients, including other DLs. These lists allow users to send messages to multiple recipients without having to address each recipient individually. A typical distribution list is one for Everyone. All Exchange recipients are made members of the Everyone DL. When a public announcement is made, the sender of the announcement simply selects the Everyone DL and is not forced to select every user's mailbox from the GAL.

Although a public folder is a type of recipient, it is composed of many more functions than just the transfer or receipt of messages. This chapter focuses on message sending and receiving by the three recipient types other than public folders: mailboxes, custom recipients, and distribution lists. A full review of the features, functions, and administration requirements for public folders is included in Chapter 13.

Understanding Recipient Containers

Recipients can be located anywhere — in an Exchange Information Store on a particular Exchange Server or on a foreign messaging system. Recipient objects reference those recipients and appear in specific places within Exchange Administrator. These specific places are called *Recipient containers*. Exchange Server uses Recipient containers to construct address books, and Exchange Administrator uses Recipient containers to organize recipient objects for easier administration.

> **Note**   The word *container* makes it sound as though recipient objects are actually stored inside recipient containers. This is not really the case. A recipient container is merely a group of references to recipient objects. Recipient objects all have their specific places within the Exchange Directory Information Tree (DIT). However, a single recipient object might be viewed in multiple recipient containers within Exchange Administrator. You can think of different recipient containers as different ways to view the recipients in an organization. A single mailbox object, for example, can be viewed in the server recipient container on its home server, the site recipient container of its site, and the GAL.

There are four types of Recipient containers in Exchange Administrator, as depicted in Figure 9-1:

- **Global Address List**   The GAL is a master Recipient container for an entire Exchange organization. It contains a list of every recipient configured in the organization — on all sites and on all servers. Note that some recipients are hidden; they cannot be seen by users but they are still there. This is the default behavior for public folders, and this default can be configured for other types of recipients.

- **Site Recipient Containers**   Site Recipient containers allow you to group recipients that belong to a specific site. When you create a new Exchange organization with the first server installation, you see only one site Recipient container, named Recipients. Although the Recipients container cannot be deleted, it can be renamed and will remain the default container for new users. All new recipients created in the site are visible in this container. You can, however, create new recipient containers and subcontainers at the site level. You will learn about this process later in the chapter.

- **Server Recipient containers**   Each Exchange Server that has a Private Information Store has one recipient container, called Server Recipients. All mailboxes that reside on that server have corresponding recipient objects that can be viewed in this container. Other types of recipients are not represented in server recipient containers.

- **Public folder containers**   Public folder containers are specialized Recipient containers used only to view the public folders in your organization.

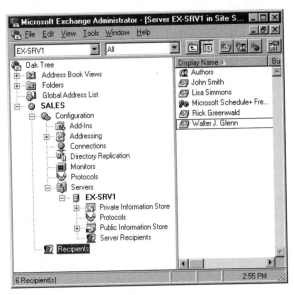

Figure 9-1. *Viewing recipients in the Recipients container.*

Note   You probably won't see any public folders in the Recipients container when you first open it because, by default, public folders are hidden from the address book when they are created. You can choose Hidden Objects from the View menu of Administrator to make hidden recipients visible.

The only type of Recipient container that you can actually create or modify is the site Recipient container. You can create a new Recipient container for the site or create a subcontainer for an existing site container.

To create a new Recipient container for a site, choose New Other, and then select Recipients Container from the File menu of Exchange Administrator. You will be prompted for the location where you want to create the new Recipient container. This command opens property sheets for the new container, as shown in Figure 9-2. Supply the Display Name and the Directory Name, and then click OK. You can modify a container's properties later by opening its property sheets. Remember that after you create the new Recipient container, the only thing you'll be able to change is the display name.

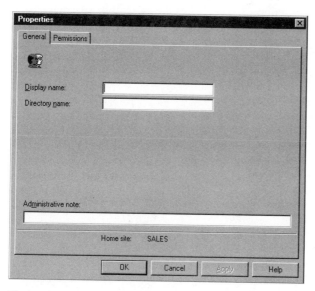

Figure 9-2. *Creating a new Recipients container.*

Note   Keep in mind that after you create a Recipient in a Recipient container, you cannot move it to another container without exporting the mailbox and then importing it into the new container. For this reason, it is important that you carefully plan your containers before creating your recipients. Having multiple containers can be quite useful. For example, you might choose to create all custom recipients for Internet users in a container separate from the main Recipients container. Two tools that are used to move mailboxes around the Exchange organization are the Mailbox Migration tool and the Move Mailbox option. The Mailbox Migration tool is used to move a mailbox between sites. The Move Mailbox option is used for moving a mailbox between servers within the same site. To use the Move Mailbox option, simply go to the Advanced tab for the mailbox and select a different server in the site.

Using Mailboxes

Mailboxes — the mainstays of any messaging system — are private, server-based storage areas in which user e-mail is kept. Every user in your organization must have access to a mailbox to send and receive messages. Most enterprises require the ability for all associates to be able to participate in sending and receiving e-mail, because it is one of their primary communication methods. One of your principal tasks as an administrator is to create and configure mailboxes for users.

Many administrators manage the network server tasks as well as the messaging system tasks. In an Exchange system, the administrator might be placed in charge of creating the Windows NT new user accounts and the mailboxes for Exchange Server. Exchange Server's tools integrate these two tasks into a single automated function.

Creating Mailboxes

There are several ways to create mailboxes for Exchange users. You can create a mailbox by using Windows NT's User Manager for Domains. Alternatively, you can create a mailbox with Exchange Administrator. You can also create mailboxes by importing user account information from a Windows NT Server or Novell NetWare server using the migration tools provided with Exchange, such as the Exchange Migration Wizard.

Creating Mailboxes with User Manager For Domains

When Exchange Server 5.5 is installed, several extensions for the User Manager For Domains program are installed as well. The most important extension added (in the form of a file named MAILUMX.DLL) is one that allows you to create a new mailbox at the same time that you create a new user account. To see this new extension in action, choose New User from the User menu of User Manager For Domains. This command displays the New User dialog box, shown in Figure 9-3.

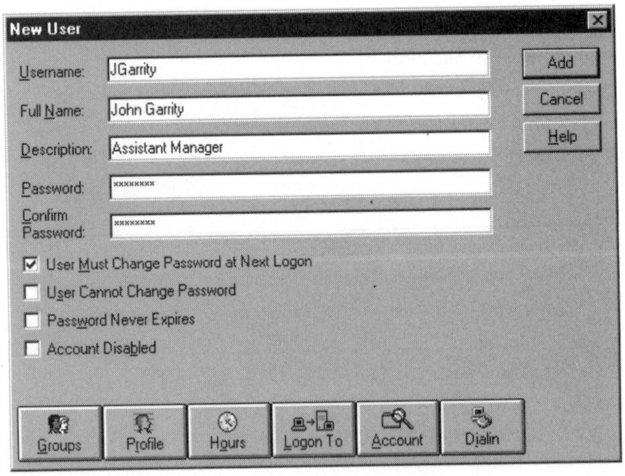

Figure 9-3. *Creating a new user account with User Manager For Domains.*

If you have worked with Windows NT, you are probably familiar with this dialog box. Here's what's new, though. After you fill in the new user account information and click Add, User Manager For Domains automatically displays the property sheets for the new mailbox, as shown in Figure 9-4. These property sheets enable you to immediately associate a new mailbox with the user account. After you complete the information for the new mailbox, click the OK button. The mailbox is created, and you are given the chance to create more new user accounts in User Manager For Domains.

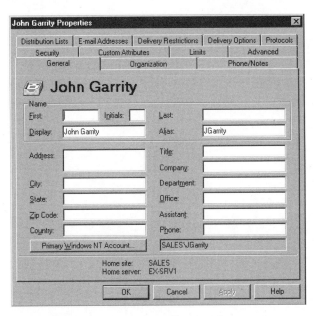

Figure 9-4. *Associating a mailbox with a new user account.*

> **Note** Remember that a user account with domain or account administrator privileges in NT is not necessarily granted administrator privileges in Exchange Server. It is also true that a user account can have administrator privileges in Exchange but not in Windows NT Server. Any Windows NT domain or account administrator can create a new user account by using User Manager For Domains. To use the new User Manager For Domains extension provided by Exchange to create a new mailbox, that administrator must also have the rights of the Permissions Admin role in the Exchange Server organization or custom rights at the Site level or even the Recipients container level that allow mailbox creation. For more information on assigning permissions in Exchange, see Chapter 15.

Creating Mailboxes with Exchange Administrator

Not only can mailboxes be created through User Manager For Domains, but mailboxes can be created by using Exchange Administrator. The process is similar to creating mailboxes with User Manager For Domains, but in reverse. To create a mailbox within Administrator, choose New Mailbox from the File menu. This command opens a blank set of mailbox property sheets like the one shown in Figure 9-5.

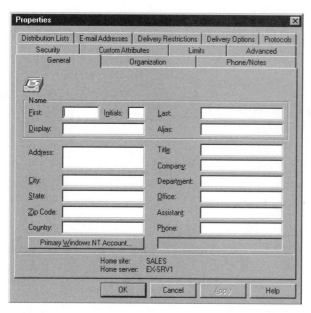

Figure 9-5. *Creating a mailbox in Exchange Administrator.*

After you fill in the new mailbox information, click Primary Windows NT Account. The dialog box shown in Figure 9-6 appears. In this dialog box, you have the choice of associating this new mailbox with an existing Windows NT user account or creating a new user account.

Figure 9-6. *Associating a user account with a new mailbox.*

If you choose the option to use an existing Windows NT user account, you are shown the list of domain users with a suggested user account. Exchange looks for a user account with the same or similar name and suggests the closest approximation to the mailbox you created. The domain selected will be the one in which your Exchange Server participates.

If you choose to create a new Windows NT account with which to associate the new mailbox, the Create Windows NT Account dialog box opens (Figure 9-7). In this dialog box, you can select the domain and account name for the new account. The domain suggested in this dialog box is the one to which Exchange Administrator is currently connected or the default domain set within Administrator. The suggested user account name is the alias name of the new mailbox.

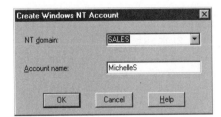

Figure 9-7. *Creating a new Windows NT user account.*

Caution Although you can create a new user account when you create a mailbox in Exchange Administrator, doing so as a general practice is not recommended. The new user account is created with a name only—not with a password. Although the administrator is warned of this situation and the user is required to supply a password at first logon, creating a new user account from Exchange Administrator is not a secure way of managing accounts. You still have to go to User Manager For Domains to configure information about the new account.

Creating Mailboxes with Directory Import

Being able to create individual accounts with User Manager For Domains or Exchange Administrator is great. Many enterprises that implement Exchange already have an existing network operating system with user accounts completely configured. If you already have all your user accounts set up on your network, can't you create new mailboxes for all of them at the same time? In a word, yes.

You can quickly create groups of mailboxes based on Windows NT or LAN Manager user account lists, NetWare account lists, or other Exchange Server account lists. The process is simple:

1. Extract the user information from its source.

2. Import that extracted information into Exchange Server, creating the new mailboxes.

Extracting User Information No matter how you choose to extract user account information or where you extract it from, this information should always be extracted to a comma-separated values (.CSV) file, which can then be imported into Exchange Server. However, you must use different tools to extract the information from different sources. To extract Windows NT, LAN Manager, NetWare, and Exchange Server account lists, you can use tools in Exchange Administrator.

Extracting Windows NT Account Lists To extract account lists from Windows NT or LAN Manager, choose Extract Windows NT Account List from the Tools menu of Exchange Administrator. This command opens the Windows NT User Extraction dialog box, shown in Figure 9-8. You must provide the domain from which to extract the account list and the name of a primary or backup domain controller (PDC or BDC) in that domain. You must also specify the name of the .CSV file to which the information should be extracted. This extraction works the same way whether you name a Windows NT Server or a LAN Manager server.

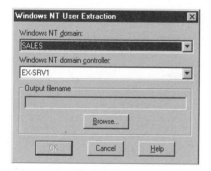

Figure 9-8. *Extracting Windows NT user accounts from a domain controller.*

When you click OK, extraction begins. Even in domains that have many users, this process should go fairly quickly. In fact, extractions for several thousand users can take mere minutes.

Extracting NetWare Account Lists Extracting account information from a NetWare server is just as easy as extracting it from a Windows NT Server. You can extract user accounts from NetWare 2.x, 3.x, 4.x, or 5.x. If you are using NetWare 4.x or NetWare 5.x, the NetWare server must be running bindery emulation.

To begin the extraction, choose Extract NetWare Account List from the Tools menu of Exchange Administrator. This command opens the NetWare User Extraction dialog box, shown in Figure 9-9.

Figure 9-9. *Extracting user accounts from a NetWare server.*

You must provide the name of a NetWare server as well as the name and password of a user account with Supervisor privileges on that server. Notice that the dialog box has no convenient drop-down menu or Browse button; you must type this information. As you do in a Windows NT extraction, you also need to designate a .CSV file to receive the extracted information.

Note   Whether you extract user lists from Windows NT or NetWare, the format of the resulting .CSV file is the same. Five fields are populated with data from the extraction:

- **Obj-Class**   Type of object being extracted
- **Common-Name**   User name
- **Display-Name**   Name displayed for the user
- **Home-Server**   Name of the home server
- **Comment**   Miscellaneous information

You can modify the values in this file or delete certain entries to suit your needs, although a comma must always indicate the separation of one field from the next field. The use of the comma delimiter lets the value of each field vary. For example, the Display Name field can be John Doe or John Dodenhoff, and the comma delimiter ensures that the names are not cut off at the wrong places. Additionally, if commas will be in the data itself—for example "Doe, John"—the data field will need to be embedded in quotes.

Extracting Exchange Server Directories   You can extract recipient information from an existing Exchange Server. This technique can be useful if you want to export Exchange recipients for use on another messaging system or to back up your recipient list, in case you ever need to rebuild or upgrade your Exchange Server.

To export your Exchange Directory, choose Directory Export from the Tools menu of Exchange Administrator. This command opens the Directory Export dialog box, shown in Figure 9-10.

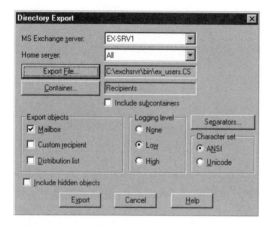

Figure 9-10. *Exporting Exchange Directory information.*

Note Exporting an Exchange Server Directory to a .CSV file is a useful way to create a printable list of the recipient information for your organization in addition to its ability to create mailboxes en masse. Comma-separated value files are a standard file format for many programs and are used to move data between some programs that are otherwise incompatible. The Exchange-created .CSV file can be imported into many other types of applications, such as Microsoft Excel or a database program, and used for other purposes.

The first thing to notice is that you get more control of what information is exported than you do when you extract user lists from Windows NT or NetWare. You can configure the following parameters in this dialog box:

- **MS Exchange Server** This field represents the name of the Exchange Server that will actually perform the export of recipient information. The default selection is the server to which you are currently connected, but the drop-down menu provides a list all Exchange Servers on the site.

- **Home server** The home server is the server in the site that contains the recipient information you want to export. All is selected by default, meaning that recipient information will be exported from all servers in the site.

- **Export file** This field specifies the name of the .CSV file to which the exported information should be saved.

- **Container**   This field specifies the container from which information should be exported. The default choice is the Recipients container, which exists on all servers.
- **Include subcontainers**   When this option is selected, any containers within the specified container are also exported.
- **Export objects**   You can designate which types of recipient objects should be included in the export. You can choose from among all available types of recipients except public folders.
- **Logging level**   Use this option to specify whether a log of the export should be created and whether that log should have low or high detail.
- **Separators**   Use this button to specify what character should be used to separate the values in your export file. By default, this option is set to use a comma.
- **Character set**   You can choose to use either ANSI or Unicode as the character set for your exported file. This choice largely depends on the system to which you will import the information.
- **Include hidden objects**   Recipients can be hidden from the Global Address book so that users do not have direct access to them. Select this option if you want to include hidden objects in the export.

Note   You can also extract information from other sources, such as employee databases. All you have to do is make sure that you save the information to a .CSV file in a format that an Exchange Server can use for an import. If you need more information on this procedure, consult your product documentation.

Real World   The Import Header Tool
The *Microsoft BackOffice Resource Kit, Second Edition* (1998) from Microsoft Press can be quite valuable to you in administering Exchange Server. Each Resource Kit contains technical material compiled by the Microsoft product teams, as well as a CD-ROM that contains valuable administrative tools. The Resource Kit includes several volumes that cover the BackOffice suite of products. The software tools are also available for download from Microsoft's Web site at *ftp.microsoft.com/bussys/backoffice/reskit*.

The Resource Kit also includes a tool called Import Header (HEADER.EXE) that allows you to create .CSV file templates. When you export information from an existing Exchange Server by choosing Directory Export from the Tools menu of Administrator, by default, only certain recipient attributes are exported. If you want to export other attributes, you must create a .CSV file template that defines those attributes.

When you run the Import Header tool, it lists all the attributes available to be exported. After you select the attributes, the Import Header tool creates a .CSV file template. This template is a blank .CSV file with the names of the attributes to export at the beginning. When you choose Directory Export from the Tools menu of Exchange Administrator, designate this file as the one to which you want to export, and all the chosen attributes will be exported.

Importing Directories into Exchange Server   No matter how you create the .CSV file for importing users, the import procedure is the same. To begin an import, choose Directory Import from the Tools menu of Exchange Administrator. This command opens the Directory Import dialog box, shown in Figure 9-11.

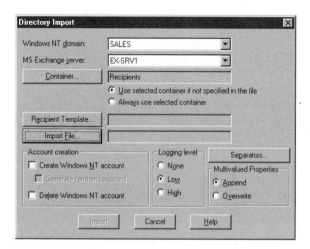

Figure 9-11.   *Importing Directory information into Exchange Server.*

As you can see, this dialog box is quite similar to the Directory Export dialog box (refer to Figure 9-10). You can configure the following in this dialog box:

- **Windows NT domain**   Use this menu to choose the domain in which Windows NT user accounts should be created if you choose to create user accounts along with the new mailboxes. That selection is made in the Account Creation section of the dialog box.

- **MS Exchange Server**   Use this menu to select the Exchange Server in the site on which the new mailboxes will be created.

- **Container**   Designate the container in which the new mailboxes will be placed. You can also specify whether to use the indicated container or containers specified in the import file.

- **Recipient template**   Use this option to specify a recipient template to use when importing recipients. A template is a recipient object that you create to serve as a model for the new recipients to be created during the import. Information configured for the template is included automatically in newly created recipients. (Templates, which can be very useful for ensuring that mailboxes are consistent, are discussed later in this chapter.)

- **Import file**   Designate the .CSV file from which to import user accounts.

- **Account creation**   Use this section to specify whether to create new Windows NT user accounts at the same time new mailboxes are created. If you choose to do so, accounts will be created in the domain specified in the Windows NT Domain field. If you choose to create new user accounts, you can also specify that a random password be assigned to each new account. Finally, you can specify that mailboxes deleted during the import have their associated Windows NT accounts deleted as well. You should create new user accounts only after conferring with your local Windows NT administrator.

- **Logging level**   Specify whether a log should be created during the import process. This log contains details about the process for later review.

- **Separators**   If your import file uses a character other than a comma to separate values, you can specify that character.

- **Multivalued properties**   Some properties of recipients can have multiple values. Use this option to specify whether existing values of such properties are overwritten or appended. An example of a multivalued property is the e-mail addresses of a mailbox. Each mailbox can have multiple e-mail addresses associated with it, such as X.400, SMTP, and MS Mail.

Configuring Mailbox Properties

No matter which method you use to create mailboxes, you configure them the same way — by using the new mailbox object's property sheets. If you create a mailbox by using User Manager For Domains or Exchange Administrator, you can access all these property sheets at the time of creation. If you create mailboxes by importing directory listings, you can access the property sheets only after the mailboxes have been created. To do so, select any mailbox in Exchange Administrator and then choose Properties from the File menu. This section covers the property sheets in detail. The security property sheet, which is used to configure advanced security for a user, is discussed in Chapter 15.

General Property Sheet

The General property sheet, shown in Figure 9-12, is where you configure basic user information. The first name, middle initial, and last name that you enter are used to generate a display name and alias name, according to the Auto Naming rules that you set up in Exchange Administrator. The display name is the name of the recipient as it appears in the Exchange Administrator window. The alias name can be used as an alternate means of addressing the recipient in messages. You can use the Primary Windows NT Account button to change the NT user account with which the mailbox is associated. The rest of the information on this property sheet is used to further identify the recipient. All this information, save for the Windows NT account information, is available to users when they browse the Global Address List.

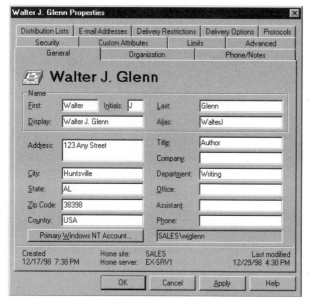

Figure 9-12. *Assigning user information on the General property sheet.*

Organization Property Sheet

The Organization property sheet, shown in Figure 9-13, is used to configure additional information about the user's position in the company. You can use this sheet to specify a user's manager and a list of people who report directly to the user. Click either Modify button to display a list of recipients in the organization. All the information configured on this property sheet is also available in the Global Address List.

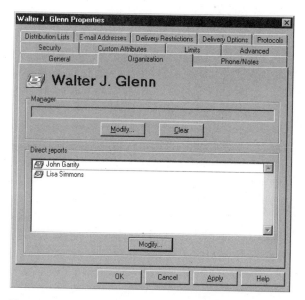

Figure 9-13. *Describing a user's position in the organization by using the Organization property sheet.*

Phone/Notes Property Sheet

The Phone/Notes property sheet, shown in Figure 9-14, lets you configure additional information for a user. It also has a place for you to enter notes about the user. The information on this sheet is available in the Global Address List.

Distribution Lists Property Sheet

The Distribution Lists property sheet, shown in Figure 9-15, lists the distribution lists to which the mailbox currently belongs. You can add or remove distribution lists by clicking the Modify button and then making choices from available lists. Not only can you manage a distribution list from a mailbox's properties, but you can manage a distribution list from the distribution list's properties. For more information on distribution lists, see "Using Distribution Lists" later in this chapter.

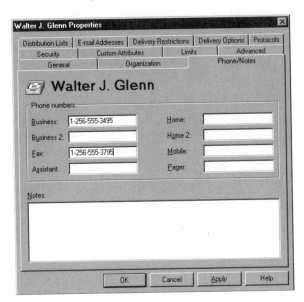

Figure 9-14. *Configuring additional information on the Phone/Notes property sheet.*

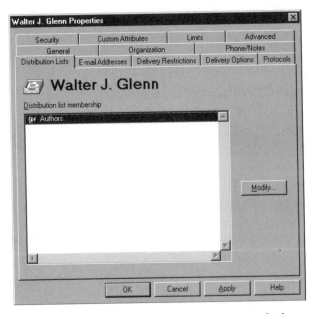

Figure 9-15. *Viewing the distribution lists to which a mailbox belongs.*

E-Mail Addresses Property Sheet

The E-mail Addresses property sheet, shown in Figure 9-16, lets you configure how the mailbox is addressed from different types of messaging systems.

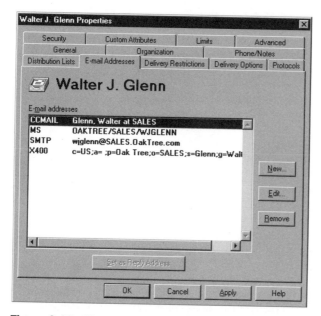

Figure 9-16. *Viewing e-mail addresses for a mailbox.*

When you create a mailbox, four types of addresses are configured automatically by default: cc:Mail, MS Mail, SMTP, and X.400. You can add, remove, or edit addresses as you please. A mailbox can have multiple addresses for a single type. For example, a mailbox for the Web site administrator, Jane Doe, may have *jdoe@company.com* and *webmaster@company.com* as two SMTP addresses. These two addresses will send mail to the same mailbox.

Note   You can change addresses manually for each mailbox. You can also change addressing configuration of the address spaces at the site using the Site Addressing object and have those changes flow down to individual mailboxes. Address spaces are discussed in detail in Chapter 10.

Delivery Restrictions Property Sheet

The Delivery Restrictions property sheet, shown in Figure 9-17, allows you to restrict messages coming into the selected mailbox. By default, all messages are

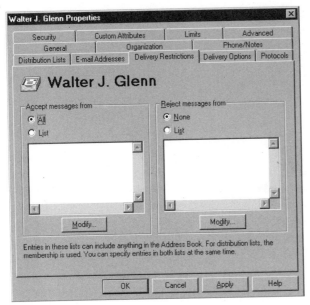

Figure 9-17. *Designating which recipients can and cannot send mail to a mailbox.*

accepted and no messages are rejected. Acceptance and rejection lists are maintained individually. You can specify that messages be accepted only from designated senders and that messages from certain senders be rejected. Click the Modify button below either the Accept or Reject list to add users from the Global Address List. You can add any recipients listed in the organization's directory.

Delivery Options Property Sheet

The Delivery Options property sheet, shown in Figure 9-18, allows you to assign certain types of access—called *delegate access*—to the mailbox to Exchange users other than the primary user.

The first type of delegate access is called Send On Behalf Of permission. You can grant this permission to any recipient in the Exchange Directory by clicking the Modify button below the Give Send On Behalf Of Permission To list. Users included in this list can send messages as though those messages came from the selected mailbox. Any messages sent include the names of both the primary mailbox user and the user who actually sent the message. This permission might be used by an assistant who needs to send a message from a manager who is out of the office.

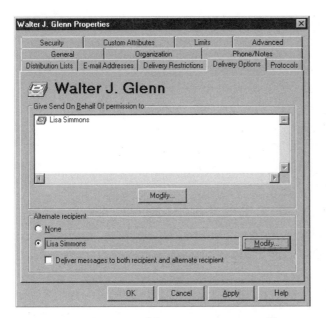

Figure 9-18. *Assigning delegate access to a mailbox.*

Note Send On Behalf Of permission can also be helpful in troubleshooting. If you assign yourself, as administrator, this permission, you can send test messages from any recipient in the organization. This practice can be a great way of testing connections from remote servers. We recommend that you use test mailboxes created for this purpose and not actual user mailboxes. Many users would consider having extended access into their e-mail an intrusion.

The other thing that you can do on the Delivery Options property sheet is assign an alternate recipient for a mailbox. Any messages sent to the mailbox are routed to the mailbox of the designated alternate recipient. As a further option, you can specify that messages be sent both to the primary mailbox and to the alternate recipient. Exchange will deliver a separate reference to the message to all mailboxes listed on this page, so deleting the message from one mailbox does not cause it to be deleted from another mailbox.

Users have the capability of assigning the Send On Behalf Of permission for their own mailboxes from within Outlook. Users also have the ability to specify an alternate recipient from within Outlook. For more information on this topic, see Chapter 19.

Another type of delegate access in Exchange is called Send As permission. This permission is a powerful form of delegate access that can be assigned only by an administrator. The Send As permission is discussed in Chapter 15.

Protocols Property Sheet

The Protocols property sheet, shown in Figure 9-19, allows you to enable or disable individual Internet protocols for the selected mailbox. The columns show whether each protocol is enabled for the selected mailbox, whether the protocol is enabled for the server on which the mailbox is located, and how settings are applied for the protocol. The protocols that you can configure include HTTP (Web), IMAP4 (Mail), NNTP (News), and POP3 (Mail).

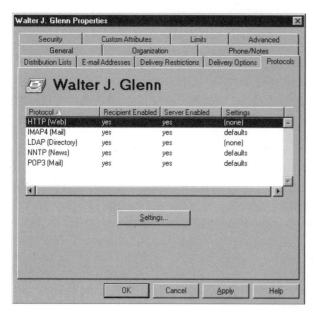

Figure 9-19. *Configuring Internet protocols for a mailbox.*

The LDAP (Directory) protocol is included in this list, but it cannot be configured at the level of the individual mailbox. It is included on this property sheet so that you can easily determine whether it is enabled on the server to which the selected mailbox belongs.

You will learn more about Internet protocols and how to configure them for sites, servers, and mailboxes in Chapter 14.

Custom Attributes Property Sheet

The Custom Attributes property sheet, shown in Figure 9-20, lets you enter information about a mailbox in 10 custom fields. These fields can be used for any information that you need to include that isn't available on the other property sheets. All of these fields are available to users in the Global Address List. By default, these fields are labeled Custom Attribute 1 through Custom Attribute 10, but they can be customized to suit your needs. For information on how to customize the Custom Attribute fields, see Chapter 10.

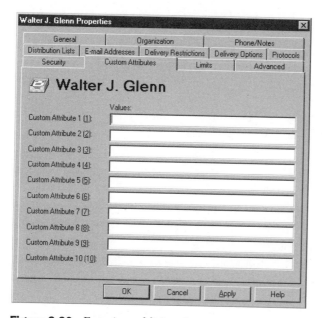

Figure 9-20. *Entering additional recipient information by using Custom Attribute fields.*

Limits Property Sheet

The Limits property sheet, shown in Figure 9-21, lets you assign limits on how the selected mailbox handles messages. These limits are discussed in the following sections.

Deleted Item Retention Time   Exchange Server 5.5 includes a new feature that gives users a certain amount of time to recover items that have been deleted from their Deleted Items folder. When a user deletes a message using

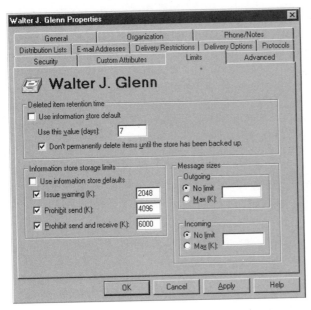

Figure 9-21. *Setting messaging limits for a mailbox.*

a client application such as Microsoft Outlook, that message is placed in the Deleted Items folder. When a user deletes the item from the Deleted Items folder, it is then actually removed from the user's personal folders. However, the deleted item is not actually deleted from the Exchange Information Store. Instead, the message is marked as hidden and is kept for a specified amount of time. During that period, the user can use the client application to recover the item. Note that the ability to recover deleted items requires using Outlook 8.03 or later.

A default retention time is configured for the Information Store of each Exchange site. You can use this default value or override it with a different value for the selected mailbox. If you choose to override the value, you can also specify that deleted messages not be permanently removed until the Information Store has been backed up.

For more information on setting messaging limits for sites and servers, see Chapter 10. For more information on backing up Information Stores, see Chapter 21.

Information Store Storage Limits Often, users send and save huge attachments or are just negligent about cleaning out their mailboxes. Both of these situations can consume a great deal of disk space on your server. Fortunately, administrators can set any of three storage limits on a mailbox:

- **Issue warning**   This limit specifies a size, in kilobytes, that a mailbox can reach before a warning is issued to the user to clean out the mailbox.

- **Prohibit send**   This limit specifies a size, in kilobytes, that a mailbox can reach before the user is prohibited from sending any new mail. This prohibition ends as soon as the user clears enough space to fall back within the limit.

- **Prohibit send and receive**   This limit specifies a size, in kilobytes, that a mailbox can reach before the user is prohibited from sending, receiving, or even editing any mail. The only action that a user can take is deleting messages. This prohibition ends as soon as the user clears enough space to fall back within the limit. To clear enough space, a user must delete items from his or her mailbox and then empty the Deleted Items folder. When a user sends a message to a recipient who is prohibited from receiving any new messages, a nondelivery report is generated and returned to the sending user. Prohibiting the sending and receiving of mail is a pretty strong measure for an administrator to take. We recommend that you implement this solution only if you experience continued problems that you cannot otherwise resolve.

Real World   Cleaning Mailboxes

The best way to govern the size of user mailboxes is to set general Information Store storage limits at the site and server levels and to occasionally set limits at the mailbox level, as necessary. Sometimes, however, this is not feasible. You may not want to set strong limits, or the mailbox may grow out of hand before you have the chance to set limits. In such a case, you have another option: You can clean the mailbox yourself.

You clean a mailbox by selecting the mailbox in Exchange Administrator and then choosing Clean Mailbox from the Tools menu. This command displays the dialog box shown in Figure 9-22. This dialog box allows you to enter various criteria governing messages that you want to remove from the mailbox. After you select the types of messages that you want to remove, you can choose to delete them immediately or move them to the Deleted Items folder.

You should use the Clean Mailbox tool only as a last resort. Limits and kind messages to users are more effective in the long run. Keep in mind that a user's mailbox is a private area. If you invade that private area, you run the risk of alienating users by causing them to lose trust in your messaging system.

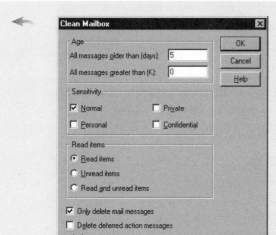

Figure 9-22. *The Clean Mailbox dialog box.*

All these limits can be set for an entire site or server as well. Settings made at the mailbox level override any settings made at the site or server level. For more information on setting storage limits for sites and servers, see Chapter 10.

Message Sizes The last type of limit that you can configure on the Limits property sheet involves message sizes (refer back to Figure 9-21). You can set a limit on the size of messages that can be transferred out of or into a particular mailbox. Limits on outgoing and incoming messages are set individually. If a message exceeds the limit, the message is not sent or received, and the sender of the message receives a nondelivery report.

> **Note** Setting general storage limits for an entire site or server at the same time is much more efficient than setting them for each individual user. Setting limits for a particular mailbox is one way of dealing with users who need to send large messages or users who simply let the junk accumulate.

Advanced Property Sheet

You can use the Advanced property sheet, shown in Figure 9-23, to configure all the options that the Exchange team at Microsoft decided didn't fit on other property sheets.

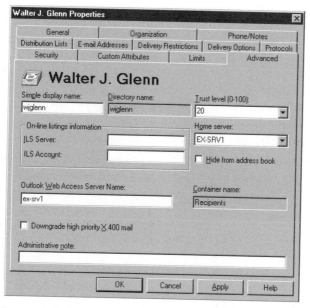

Figure 9-23. *Configuring advanced mailbox options.*

The parameters that you can configure on the Advanced property sheet include the following:

- **Simple display name**   The simple display name is an alternate name for the mailbox. It appears when, for some reason, the full display name cannot. This situation often occurs when multiple language versions of Exchange Administrator are used on the same network.

- **Directory name**   The directory name is the name of the mailbox object as it appears in the Exchange Directory Information Tree (DIT). You can change this name only while creating the mailbox. After a mailbox has been created, this option is no longer available.

- **Trust level**   The trust level determines whether a recipient is included when directories are synchronized between Exchange and a foreign messaging system. Trust levels range from 0 to 100 and are set for both recipients and directory synchronization requestors. If a recipient's trust level is equal to or less than the trust level of the requestor, the recipient is synchronized. For more information on directory synchronization, see Chapter 12.

- **Home server**   This setting specifies the server on which the current mailbox is stored. Selecting a different server is one way of moving a mailbox between servers. Other ways to move mailboxes are discussed later in this chapter.

- **Online listings information**   If you use Microsoft NetMeeting in your organization, this option is for you. NetMeeting allows users to collaborate on documents by using audio, video, and a shared whiteboard. Use the ILS Server and Account fields to set up your Internet Locator Service (ILS). When this information is configured, users can contact and set up meetings with the user of this mailbox. For more information on using NetMeeting in your organization, see *The Official Microsoft NetMeeting Book* (1998) by Bob Summers from Microsoft Press.

- **Hide from address book**   By default, all recipients except public folders are visible to users via the Global Address List. You can use this option to hide a mailbox from that list. The mailbox will still be able to receive mail; it just will not be included in Address Book Views.

- **Outlook Web Access (OWA) server name**   Typically, the OWA server for an Information Store is set at the server level, and all recipients configured on that Exchange Server use the server-level settings. You can, however, designate a different OWA server for an individual mailbox. For more information on using Outlook Web Access, see Chapter 14.

- **Container name**   Multiple Recipient containers can be created on a single server. When you create a mailbox, you can specify the Recipient container in which it will be stored. After the mailbox has been created, this option is no longer available.

- **Downgrade high-priority X.400 mail**   If this option is selected, the current mailbox cannot send high-priority messages to X.400 systems. If a high-priority message is sent, it will be downgraded to normal priority automatically.

- **Administrative note**   An administrative note is a convenient place for you to enter free-form text about a mailbox. This note is visible only on this property sheet. Most objects in Exchange Server allow you to make administrative notes.

Moving Mailboxes

You might want to move a mailbox to a different server for any of several reasons. Perhaps you want to balance the load by splitting up an increasing number of mailboxes on one server and moving them to different servers. Or you might have just installed a powerful new server and want to consolidate mail-boxes located on disparate servers.

Whatever your reason for moving a mailbox, Exchange Administrator provides two convenient ways for you to do so. There is one catch, however: You can use these simple techniques only to move mailboxes between servers in the same site. These techniques do not allow you to move mailboxes to different containers on the same server or between servers in different sites.

Note If you want to move recipients between servers in different sites or to a new Recipient container, use the Directory Import and Export features discussed earlier in this chapter.

The first way to move a mailbox to a different server in the same site is a way that you saw earlier in this chapter. On a mailbox object's Advanced property sheet is a configuration item called Home Server (refer to Figure 9-23). If you choose a different server from this drop-down list, the mailbox is moved to that server.

The second way to move mailboxes between servers on a site is even easier and allows you to move many mailboxes at the same time. In Exchange Administrator, select the mailboxes that you want to move from the Global Address List or a Recipient container. Then choose Move Mailbox from the Tools menu to open the Move Mailbox dialog box, shown in Figure 9-24. Use this dialog box to find the server to which you want to move the mailboxes.

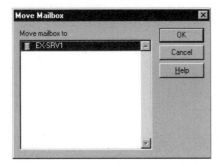

Figure 9-24. *Moving mailboxes between servers on a site.*

Note The Move Mailbox command moves large groups of mailboxes at the same time and fairly quickly. You can also use this command to move mailboxes even if those mailboxes' users are currently online.

If you recall, Exchange uses single-instance storage during normal operations to ensure that only one copy of a particular message ever needs to be stored in the Information Store. Pointers to that message are placed in recipients' mailboxes if that message is sent to multiple recipients. This means that a 1MB message sent to 50 recipients consumes only 1MB of disk space in the Information Store. If a message is not available on the server to which a mailbox is being moved, the message is moved along with the mailbox. For this reason, the amount of space required for individual mailboxes on the new server may be larger than that required on the previous server.

Using Custom Recipients

Custom recipients are objects that serve as pointers to resources outside an Exchange organization. You can think of a custom recipient as an alias that contains an address for that outside resource and rules for handling the transmission of messages. Whenever a user sends a message to a custom recipient, the message is forwarded to the appropriate foreign messaging system. Custom recipients have many of the same attributes as mailboxes and can be viewed in the GAL or site Recipient containers.

Creating Custom Recipients

Custom recipients can be created only with Exchange Administrator. To create a custom recipient, choose New Custom Recipient from the File menu. This command opens the New E-Mail Address dialog box, shown in Figure 9-25. You must select the type of foreign system on which the custom recipient resides, which helps construct an address space that will be used in routing messages to the appropriate external gateway. When you finish, click OK.

Figure 9-25. *Selecting an e-mail address type for a new custom recipient.*

After you choose the appropriate address type, you are asked to enter the actual e-mail address of the recipient, as shown in Figure 9-26. Enter this address according to the specific format of the address type that you've chosen. After you make this entry and click OK, the custom recipient is created. If an appropriate gateway to the foreign system has been configured, users can send messages to the new custom recipient immediately. For more information on configuring Exchange to communicate with foreign messaging systems, see Chapter 12.

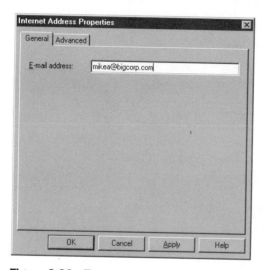

Figure 9-26. *Entering an e-mail address for a new custom recipient.*

Configuring Custom Recipients' Properties

Just like all other objects in Exchange, custom recipients are configured by means of property sheets. The property sheets are displayed immediately after you create a custom recipient and can be opened any time thereafter in the normal manner. Most of the property sheets for custom recipient objects are identical to those for mailbox objects. The biggest difference is that the custom recipient has no Delivery Options or Limits property sheet. Of the remaining property sheets, only two differ in any way: General and Advanced. For that reason, only those two sheets are covered in this section. For details on any of the other sheets, refer to the section of this chapter on configuring mailboxes.

General Property Sheet

The custom recipient's General property sheet, shown in Figure 9-27, differs from the mailbox General property sheet in only one way. Instead of a Primary Windows NT Account field, it has an e-mail field. This field contains the full e-mail address of the recipient, including the e-mail address type (SMTP in

Figure 9-27) and the user's address on the foreign system. You can change this address by clicking on E-mail.

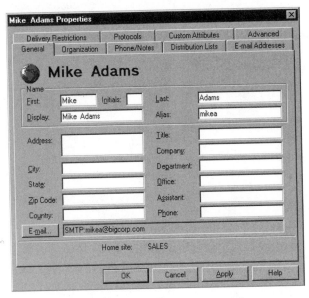

Figure 9-27. *Viewing General properties of a custom recipient.*

Advanced Property Sheet

The custom recipient's Advanced property sheet, shown in Figure 9-28, is different from its mailbox counterpart in several ways:

- There is no Home Server field. Instead, you can designate the Recipient container in which the custom recipient object resides.
- You can configure the maximum size of messages that can be sent to the custom recipient. This option is located on the Limits property sheet for mailboxes.
- You can choose whether to allow rich-text format (RTF) messages to be sent to the custom recipient. Many foreign messaging systems do not support this format.
- You can associate a primary Windows NT account with the custom recipient. The Windows NT account designated on this property sheet will act as a manager for the custom recipient. This manager can then use the custom recipient to send messages. This association provides much the same benefit as the Send As permission.
- There is no X.400 option.
- You cannot assign an Outlook Web server.

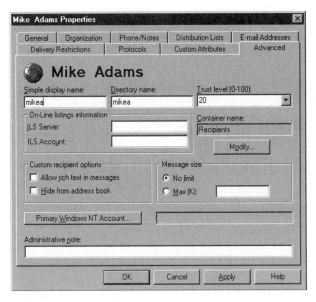

Figure 9-28. *Viewing advanced properties for a custom recipient.*

Using Distribution Lists

A *distribution list* is a special kind of recipient object that is used to reference multiple other recipients. A distribution list can contain any other type of recipient—even other distribution lists. When a message is sent to the distribution list, the list is expanded, and the message is sent to each member of the list individually. Distribution lists can be viewed in the GAL and in site Recipient containers.

Creating Distribution Lists

Creating a new distribution list, which you can do only from Exchange Administrator, is easy. Choose New Distribution List from the File menu. This command opens the property sheets for the new distribution list, as shown in Figure 9-29.

Your first task in creating the distribution list is naming it. You need to provide a display name, which shows up in the GAL, and an alias name, which can be used to address messages to the list. In large organizations, the names of distribution lists should be thought out carefully. A large GAL will be the best camouflage for a distribution list if it does not have a name that users can identify

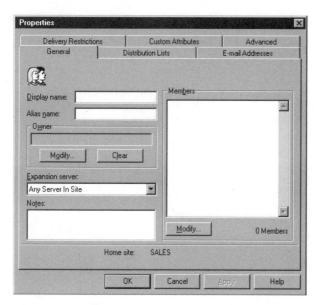

Figure 9-29. *Creating a distribution list.*

easily. The use of alias names was covered earlier in this chapter in the discussion of mailboxes.

The next thing that you need to do is specify an owner for the list. The owner of a list is given permission to modify the list's membership. By default, the administrator who creates the list is the owner, but you can designate as owner any mailbox, distribution list, or custom recipient in the GAL. If you give ownership to another user, that user can use an Exchange client or Outlook to modify the list's membership and does not need access to Exchange Administrator. You can relieve yourself of a great deal of work by specifying owners for distribution lists. As distribution lists grow larger, they can consume a considerable amount of management time.

Your next step is adding members to the list. To do so, click the Modify button below the Members list box. This button opens a view of the GAL that allows you to select recipients — whether custom recipients, mailboxes, or other distribution lists — to include, as shown in Figure 9-30. After you choose the list members, click OK to add them to the distribution list.

The final thing that you may want to do when you create a list is designate a specific expansion server. Remember that whenever a message is sent to a list, the list must be expanded so that the message can be sent to each member of the list. The Message Transfer Agent Service of a single Exchange Server performs this expansion. The default choice is Any Server In Site (Figure 9-29). This choice

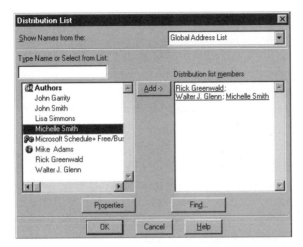

Figure 9-30. *Adding members to a distribution list.*

means that the home server of the user sending the message always expands the list. You can also designate a specific server in the site to handle expanding the list. The choice of a dedicated expansion server is a good one if you have a large distribution list. In this case, expansion could consume a great amount of server resources, which can compromise performance for busy servers. Often, sites have dedicated expansion servers.

When you finish, click OK to create the list. The new distribution list should be available for use almost immediately.

Real World   Using Delivery Restrictions on Distribution Lists
Even though the Delivery Restrictions property sheet for distribution lists is identical to the Delivery Restrictions property sheet for mailboxes, delivery restrictions are often much more useful for distribution lists. In large organizations, DLs can grow quite large, sometimes holding thousands of users. Because of the possibility of misuse, it is not usually a good idea to provide general access to DLs this large. Imagine the increase in traffic if your users send messages to thousands of users every time their kids sell candy bars or every time they find a particularly good joke. Placing delivery restrictions on large DLs allows you to limit access to the lists to a few select, responsible users.

Another potential risk is that somebody from the Internet could e-mail your whole company using a DL's SMTP address. Imagine what your job would be like the day an "anonymous" person e-mailed malicious information to your whole company.

Configuring Distribution List Properties

You can configure other property sheets for a distribution list either when you create the list or after you create it. The General property sheet was covered in the previous section on creating distribution lists. Most of the other property sheets are identical to the Mailbox property sheets of the same name, so refer to the mailbox section of this chapter for details on those property sheets. Note that some of the property sheets found on a mailbox recipient simply don't exist for a distribution list.

The only property sheet that does differ is the Advanced property sheet, shown in Figure 9-31. This sheet holds several configuration items that are familiar to you, such as display name, trust level, and message limits.

Figure 9-31. *Viewing advanced properties for a distribution list.*

You can configure several options that are particular to distribution lists:

- **Report to distribution list owner** If you enable this option, notification is sent to the owner of the list whenever an error occurs during the delivery of a message to the list or to one of its members. Note that this option is unavailable if the distribution list has not been assigned an owner.

- **Report to message originator** If you enable this option, error notifications are also sent to the user who sent a message to the list.

- **Allow out-of-office messages to originator**   Users of Exchange clients can configure rules that automatically reply to messages received while the users are away from their offices. When this option is enabled, users who send messages to DLs can receive those automatic out-of-office messages from members of the list. For particularly large DLs, it's best not to allow out-of-office messages to be delivered, because of the excess network traffic they generate. For more information on configuring rules in a client application, see Chapter 19.
- **Hide from address book**   If you enable this option, the DL is not visible in the GAL.
- **Hide membership from address book**   If you enable this option, users cannot view the membership of the DL by using the GAL.

Using Templates

A *template* is a recipient object that is used as a model for creating other recipient objects of that type. Every recipient type except public folders can serve as a template.

To create a template, create a recipient object as you normally would. Enter any information that you want to use in the model. If, for example, you are creating a mailbox template to use for new employees, you might enter all the organizational, phone, and address information for your company.

> **Note**   When you create a recipient to use as a template, you probably will want to hide the recipient from the address book using the template's Advanced property sheet. This way, users won't be able to view it in the GAL. You can always choose to view hidden recipients in Exchange Administrator, so you will be able to see it. You should also name your template in such a way that it is both easy to find and easy to distinguish from regular recipients.

You can use a template in two ways. The first way is to specify it as a recipient template during a directory import, which allows you to create a batch of new recipients that have common information.

You can also use a template to create an individual recipient. To do so, select the template in Exchange Administrator and then choose Duplicate from the File menu. A set of property sheets for the new recipient object opens, including all the information in the template except for certain names (such as the display, alias, and directory names).

Managing Recipients

As your organization and the number of recipients in it grows, it can become quite time-consuming to scroll through lists of recipients looking for the ones you need. Fortunately, Exchange Administrator can help.

Filtering Recipients

The first option that you might try if you are looking for certain types of recipients is to use the View menu to filter the recipient objects that are displayed in Exchange Administrator. You can use this technique no matter what Recipient container you are viewing at the time. You have a couple of filtering options:

- **Filter by recipient type**   You can choose to view, for example, only public folders or only custom recipients. Filtering your recipient view can be useful if you are looking for a specific recipient and the list based on recipient type is not very long or if you need to select all the recipients of a certain type. You can also choose to view recipients of all types at the same time, of course.

- **Specify whether to view hidden recipients**   This option can eliminate many entries from the display and is also a great way to view all recipients except public folders and other recipients that may be hidden.

Finding Recipients

Exchange Administrator provides a recipient search tool that allows for more sophisticated searching criteria than is available from the View menu. You open this tool by choosing Find Recipients from the Tools menu. This command opens the Find Recipients window, shown in Figure 9-32.

You can use this tool to search for only one Recipient container at a time. The default choice is the Recipients container for the site, but you can select another container by clicking the Container button.

As you see in Figure 9-32, you can use many common attributes to search for recipients, such as the different names for the object and some organizational information. By clicking Custom, you can also search using any of the 10 custom attributes covered earlier in this chapter.

After you select your criteria, click Find Now to display the results of the search. The results are actual recipient objects. You can open these objects' property sheets or perform certain other administrative functions from this dialog box.

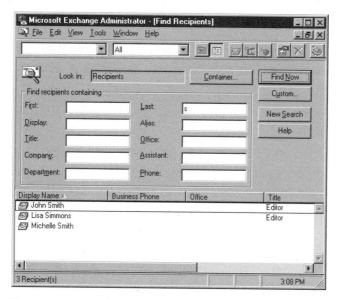

Figure 9-32. *Finding recipients in Exchange Administrator.*

Real World **Using the Find Recipients Tool**

The Find Recipients tool is one of the most useful tools in Exchange Administrator. You might want to use it regularly to manage recipients. Using Find Recipients is much handier than using the simple filtering choices of the GAL or other Recipient containers, and it's often quicker than drilling down through the hierarchical structure of Address Book Views.

Using Address Book Views

Address Book Views are a clever feature of Exchange Server that allows you to group recipients in the GAL according to attributes. Essentially, Address Book Views allow you to add a hierarchical structure to the otherwise flat view provided by the GAL.

Figure 9-33 shows an example of an Address Book View. The view, named Location, groups recipients first by country, then by state, and finally by city. The recipient, Walter J. Glenn, is in Huntsville, which is in AL (Alabama), which is in the United States.

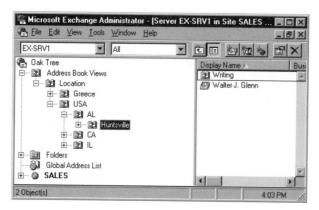

Figure 9-33. *Looking at the hierarchical structure of an Address Book View.*

Address Book Views can be quite useful in large or complex organizations. Users can open these views in client applications and find information on recipients quickly. Administrators can use the views in Exchange Administrator to help organize recipients. After you find a recipient in an Address Book View, you can manage it the same way that you manage recipients displayed in other containers: by opening its property sheets. Views are updated on a 30-minute cycle.

To create an Address Book View, choose New Other Address Book View from the File menu of Exchange Administrator. This command opens a set of Address Book View property sheets, as shown in Figure 9-34.

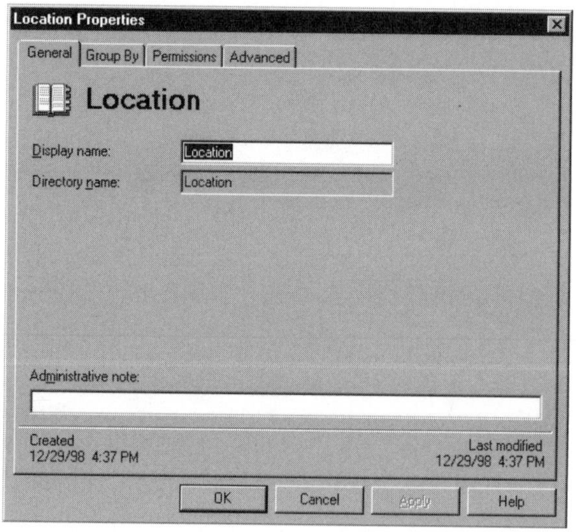

Figure 9-34. *Creating an Address Book View.*

After you enter a display name and directory name, switch to the Group By property sheet, shown in Figure 9-35. This property sheet allows you to define the hierarchical structure of the new view. Choose the top level of your hierarchy from the Group Items By drop-down list, and choose subsequent levels from the Then By drop-down lists.

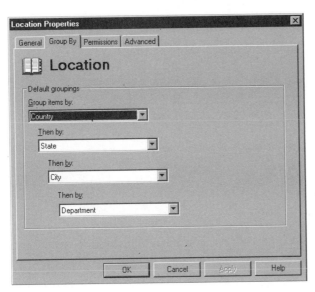

Figure 9-35. *Defining the hierarchy of your Address Book View.*

The attributes by which you can group recipients are as follows: city, company, country, any of the custom attributes that you have defined, department, home server, site, state, and title.

After you define the hierarchy, switch to the Advanced property sheet, shown in Figure 9-36. You need to make a few choices on this property sheet. The first choice is whether to promote entries to parent containers. If you choose this option and if your hierarchy is at least two levels deep, recipients are displayed in all levels that they match. John Smith, for example, would appear in the Los Angeles container, the CA container, and the USA container. If you do not choose the option to promote entries to parent containers, recipients appear only at the bottom level that they match.

The second parameter that you can configure on the Advanced property sheet is whether the view should be available in the client address book. Disable this option if you are creating a view that is for administrative purposes only; enable it if you want users on your network to have access to the view.

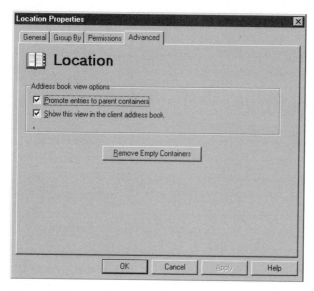

Figure 9-36. *Configuring Advanced properties of an Address Book View.*

Finally, the Remove Empty Containers button removes from the view any containers in the hierarchy that have no recipients in them. This option can be useful in a large organization.

Summary

This chapter discussed how to work with recipients: the destination of all Exchange interactions. You have learned that there are four basic types of recipients in Exchange Server 5.5: mailboxes, distribution lists, custom recipients, and public folders.

Mailboxes are private server-based storage areas for user messages. Mailboxes can be created using either User Manager For Domains or Exchange Administrator. When you create a new Windows NT user account in User Manager For Domains, you automatically are given the opportunity to create a corresponding mailbox. In Exchange Administrator, you can create new mailboxes individually or by importing .CSV files containing lists that have been extracted from Windows NT, NetWare, or another Exchange Server.

Distribution lists can contain any other type of recipient, including other distribution lists. When a message is sent to a distribution list, that list is expanded and the message is sent to each of the list's members. Distribution lists can be created only in Exchange Administrator. Custom recipients are essentially aliases that are used to send messages to users outside the Exchange organization. They are created using Exchange Administrator and configured in much the same way as mailboxes.

Address Book Views are used to group recipients according to different Directory information. Address Book Views are used in Exchange Administrator to provide easier administration of recipients and are used by Exchange clients to generate address books.

With the understanding of the information in this chapter, you are now ready to move on to other topics involved in the deployment of Exchange Server 5.5.

Chapter 10
Managing Sites and Servers

Now that you have installed Microsoft Exchange Server 5.5 and created some recipients, you are ready to explore the ways in which you can manage an Exchange site.

In this chapter, we start looking at the objects that are used to manage an Exchange site and its servers. We examine the configuration objects in the Exchange Administrator as well as how those configuration objects are used to manage Exchange, and we learn how the four core Exchange components cooperate to enable messaging activities. Objects in Exchange are the center of its management, and once you learn the function of each of those objects, you'll find that managing Exchange becomes trouble-free. The discussion of Exchange management continues in Chapter 11, which explains how to manage multiple sites in an organization.

The Hierarchy of an Organization

The Exchange hierarchy consists of an organization object at the top level that contains one or more sites, each of which contains one or more servers. The organization object also contains the Address Book Views, Folders, and Global Address List containers. The hierarchical model is an essential element of managing Exchange sites.

Administration of an Exchange system can be configured to reflect the same hierarchical model that Exchange uses. For example, administrators can be granted global administrative permissions for all objects within the organization. Administrators can be granted administrative permissions for some sites but not for others. Furthermore, administrators can be granted several different levels of permission. This hierarchical administrative model makes Exchange an enterprise-capable system, facilitating the unique administrative requirements of business units that together create a single enterprise.

The Organization and Site Containers

Consider the Exchange Administrator window shown in Figure 10-1. In it, you see several familiar objects. The container object at the top is the organization object. In the figure, the organization represents a fictitious company named Oak Tree. You can view the property sheets for this object, but the only parameter that you can configure is the display name. The organization object is the top-level container that contains and organizes all the other objects in the Exchange system.

Figure 10-1. *Viewing the Exchange hierarchy.*

Note The organization object has a Permissions property sheet, which is shown as a tab in the Property Sheets dialog box. The Permissions property sheet exists for many of the objects in Exchange. The Permissions property sheet allows you to grant users various levels of rights to administer and use the objects in Exchange. By default, the Permissions property sheet is not displayed for all objects in Exchange Administrator. You can enable the Permissions property sheet to be displayed for all objects using the Options command on the Tools menu, as discussed in Chapter 8. (Permissions are discussed in Chapter 15, which covers Exchange security in detail.)

Below the Organization container are several other container objects. Address Book Views and the Global Address List containers, which work together to provide various configured views of Exchange recipients, were discussed in Chapter 9. The Folders container, which contains the public folder objects but not their contents, is reviewed in Chapter 13. The last object in the container pane is the Site container. In Figure 10-1, the Site container is named SALES. This site represents the sales department of Oak Tree. You can view property sheets for the Site container, but you can change only the display name. If this organization had more than one site, a Site container would be displayed for each in the Exchange Administrator container pane.

> **Note**   You can change the display names of the organization and site objects, but the changes affect only how those names appear in Exchange Administrator; they do not affect actual organization and site directory names. In fact, after an organization or site is created, its directory name cannot be changed.

The Configuration Container

Figure 10-2 shows the same hierarchy as Figure 10-1, but the Site container has been expanded. Notice that the Site container holds only two objects: Configuration, which holds all the configurable elements of a site, and Recipients, which contains the recipients for the site.

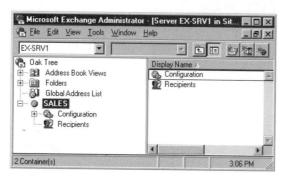

Figure 10-2. *Looking inside the Site container.*

You can also view property sheets for the Configuration container. However, in the Configuration container, you can configure parameters other than just the display name. The Service Account Password property sheet, shown in Figure 10-3, allows you to change the password for the Site Services account used on the site. It is recommended that you restart your server whenever you change the Site Services account password.

You might want to make a Site Service account password change for a couple of good reasons. One reason is security. The Site Service account is a Windows NT user account like any other, but it has extended administrative capabilities within both Exchange and Windows NT, so you may want to change the password on a regular basis.

The second reason that you may need to change the Site Service account password has to do with enabling different sites to communicate. Intersite communication sometimes involves more than one Windows NT domain. The Site Service account can be the same account, or it can be a pair of identically named NT user accounts in different domains that have the same passwords. Further details on intersite communication are discussed in Chapter 11.

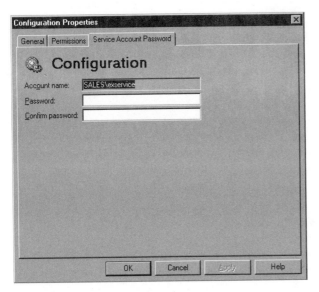

Figure 10-3. *Changing the Site Services account password.*

The Service Account Password property sheet allows you to change the password used by Exchange services to log on under the Site Services account. However, this property sheet does not change the password that is configured within the User Manager For Domains. Whenever you change the Site Service account password, you need to make the change both here and in the User Manager For Domains to ensure that they are synchronized. If you decide to change the Site Service account password, you need to change it on the Service Account Password property sheet first. Then you should change the password for the actual Site Service account's associated Windows NT domain user account in the User Manager For Domains utility.

Next, look at the expanded Configuration container, shown in Figure 10-4. Many configuration objects are utilized in Exchange Server 5.5. Each object in the Configuration container contents is used to manage different factors related to the Exchange site.

Add-Ins

The Add-Ins container, shown in Figure 10-5, holds objects that refer to dynamic link libraries (.DLL files). These .DLL files are components of Exchange Server that support various services, such as the Internet Mail Service and Microsoft Mail Connector. The purpose of the Add-Ins container is simply to hold the extensions of applications and services for Exchange Server. Day-to-day administrative work within Exchange has little to do with added components, because they rarely change after the initial installation. In addition, these components

Figure 10-4. *Looking inside the Configuration container.*

exploit Exchange's internal administrative capabilities, enabling their administration to remain with the standard administrative areas of Exchange.

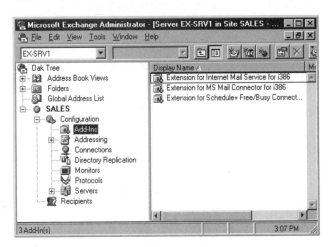

Figure 10-5. *Looking inside the Add-Ins container.*

Note For more information on add-ins for Exchange Server 5.5, consult the *Exchange Server 5.5 Resource Guide* volume of the *Microsoft BackOffice 4.5 Resource Kit* (1999) from Microsoft Press.

Addressing

The Addressing container, shown in Figure 10-6, holds three subcontainers: Details Templates, E-Mail Address Generators, and One-Off Address Templates. Each of these objects allows you to control the dialog boxes that display recipient information to Exchange clients.

Figure 10-6. *Looking inside the Addressing container.*

Details Templates   When someone uses an Exchange client to open an address book, the client builds that address book by using information in the Global Address List. By default, users can view most of the information about a recipient, including name, address, organizational information, and custom attributes.

Details templates are sets of instructions that determine how to display the dialog boxes that the client opens to display this recipient information. When the details template is changed, the entire set of objects relating to that template is affected. The Details Templates container, shown in Figure 10-7, holds all the details templates that can be modified to create custom dialog boxes for all recipient types. The details templates options are:

- **Custom recipient**   This option lists the pointers to those recipients that exist outside the Exchange system.
- **Distribution list**   This option lists the single addresses associated with a group of recipients, facilitating sending messages to user workgroups.
- **Exchange send options**   These options display the dialog box shown to users when they send a message.
- **Mailbox**   This option shows the recipient type that points to the Exchange repository assigned to a single user account.
- **Mailbox agent**   This option displays the dialog box shown for capabilities of a mailbox repository.
- **Public folder**   This option shows the views for the shared repositories of information in the Public Information Stores of the various servers.
- **Search dialog**   This option displays the dialog box shown to users when they are searching for recipients.

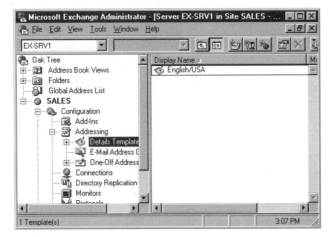

Figure 10-7. *Looking inside the Details Templates container.*

You can modify a particular template simply by opening its property sheet. In Figure 10-8, the standard mailbox template is being modified. All the objects in the window are elements that appear in the client's dialog box. For each element, you can set the X and Y coordinates for the top-left corner as well as the width and height. As you might surmise, modifying templates can be a tedious process. Modifying templates can also be a great way to add custom fields or remove an existing field you want to hide from view.

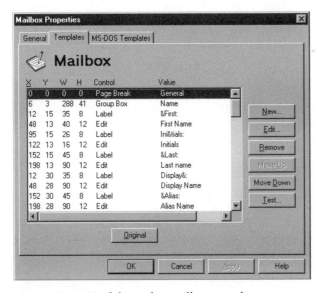

Figure 10-8. *Modifying the mailbox template.*

Real World   **Keep It Simple**

Some Exchange systems must be set up to be as simple as possible for users. In a school system, for example, young students would not be able to understand all of the capabilities that Exchange Server offers. They need fewer options, rather than more, in order to guide them to the correct selections. Exchange Server offers the capability to restrict options through the Details Templates and can make this type of system work effectively.

In this fictitious school system, the most common functions are sending mail and searching for recipients. The Send options and the Search dialog templates can be modified to simplify the way students perform these operations. Extra fields and options can be removed from the dialog box shown to the students to streamline these functions. The result is a smoothly running system with fewer questions and errors by students.

Occasionally, a user wants to send a message to a recipient that is not in the Global Address List or in any of the user's personal address books, such as an Internet user for whom no custom recipient has been configured. This situation is known as *one-off addressing*, and when it occurs, the user's client opens a dialog box that prompts the user to enter the e-mail address. You can use a one-off address template to modify this dialog box. The process is much the same as modifying the details templates. For additional information on one-off addressing, see Chapter 12.

The One-Off Address Templates container holds the following external messaging systems templates:

- **cc:Mail**   Lotus cc:Mail and cc:Mail-compatible systems use these external addresses.

- **Internet**   Internet or Simple Message Transport Protocol (SMTP) compatible systems use these messaging addresses.

- **MacMail**   Apple uses this external messaging address.

- **Microsoft Mail**   MS Mail and MS Mail gateway use these external messaging addresses.

- **X.400**   X.400-compatible systems use this external messaging address.

E-Mail Address Generators   When your Exchange site is connected to a foreign messaging system, addresses are generated for each of your recipients so that users on the foreign system can send messages to users on your system.

These addresses are generated by .DLL files called *proxy generators* because they generate proxy addresses. The .DLL files are represented by objects in the E-Mail Address Generators container. Like the objects in the Add-Ins container, these objects don't require much administration.

Connections

The Connections container holds any objects representing any connectors that have been configured for that particular Exchange site to other sites or to foreign messaging systems. Connectors exist only at the site level because the communication within an Exchange site is automatic and does not require connectors to be created between servers. For more information on configuring connections between Exchange sites, see Chapter 11. For more information on configuring connectors to foreign systems, see Chapter 12.

Directory Replication

In Exchange 5.5, the Directory is a database that stores all the objects that are used to configure Exchange Server. The Directory is seen in the Exchange Administrator as the hierarchy of objects. Each server within a site contains the entire Directory hierarchy and the associated capabilities required to administer that particular site. To manage any individual site, the Administrator must connect to a server within that site.

That database exists on every Exchange Server in an organization, according to what is known as a *multimaster replication model*. That term means that no master copy of the Directory exists. Each instance of the Directory on each server is identical once Directory replication has occurred. If you make a change in the Directory while connected to a specific server, those changes are replicated to all servers throughout the organization.

Directory replication occurs automatically between servers within a single site. You don't need to configure anything. When servers participate in different sites, however, Directory replication takes place only over special Directory Replication connectors that you must configure manually. The Directory Replication container, shown in Figure 10-9, is where Directory Replication connectors are stored. For more information on setting up Directory Replication connectors, see Chapter 11.

Monitors

The Monitors container, shown in Figure 10-10, holds two types of monitor that you can configure to keep tabs on Exchange: service monitors and link monitors (which are discussed in greater detail in Chapter 22). The purpose of these monitors is as follows.

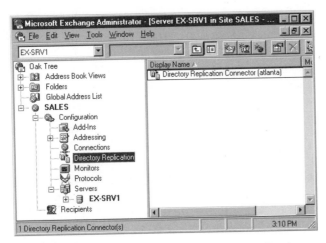

Figure 10-9. *Looking inside the Directory Replication container.*

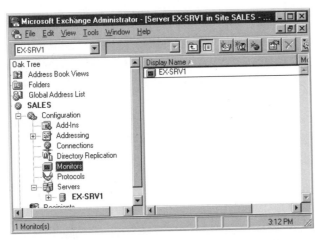

Figure 10-10. *Looking inside the Monitors container.*

- **System monitors**   These monitors keep watch over specified services on a certain Exchange Server. Should any of those services stop, you can specify that the system monitor take a range of actions, from notifying an administrator to restarting the server.

- **Link monitors**   These monitors keep watch over a specific messaging connector—either one used to connect two sites or one used to connect a site to a foreign system. Link monitors periodically send test messages over those connectors and monitor the progress of those messages. Should a connector fail, the link monitor can notify an administrator.

Protocols

The Protocols container is used to configure the site-level attributes of the various Internet protocols that Exchange Server supports. Each site can be enabled for any particular Internet protocol. In addition, servers within the site should be enabled for the Internet protocol. This configuration method not only reflects the hierarchy, it also can facilitate the dedication of individual servers for Internet accessibility, thus distributing services in a custom configuration for the Exchange system.

The types of protocols that are held in this container are:

- **POP3**   Post Office Protocol version 3
- **NNTP**   Network News Transport Protocol
- **LDAP**   Lightweight Directory Access Protocol
- **IMAP4**   Internet Mail Access Protocol version 4

Servers

The Servers container holds configuration objects for each of the Exchange Servers on a site. You can't configure any parameter within this container's property sheets except a display name. However, if you expand the container, you'll find an object for each server on the site, as shown in Figure 10-11. Two servers are configured on the SALES site of the Oak Tree organization: *EX-SRV1* and *ED-EX1*. Notice also that when the Servers container is selected, all servers configured in the site are shown in the content pane along with the version of Exchange Server that the server is running.

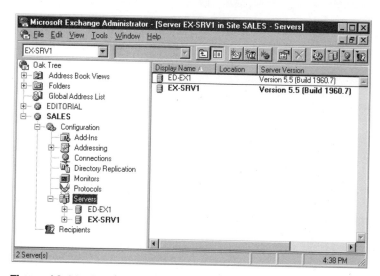

Figure 10-11. *Looking inside the Servers container.*

As you can see, each server object contains other objects, which are used to configure specific functions on that server. The *Server Recipients* object contains the recipients whose mailboxes have been associated with that particular server.

The *Protocols* object contains the Internet protocol configuration objects that have been enabled for the server. These protocols are the same as the ones contained within the site-level Protocols container: POP3, IMAP4, LDAP, and NNTP.

The *Directory Synchronization* object is used for external systems directory synchronization with Microsoft Mail; it is discussed in Chapter 12. The rest of the objects in the Servers container deal directly with the core Exchange components and are discussed a bit later in this chapter.

In addition to containing configuration objects, each *Server* object itself has property sheets that hold valuable configuration parameters. The next few sections detail the property sheets of the server EX-SRV1.

General   The General property sheet, shown in Figure 10-12, has only one parameter that you can configure: server location. Server locations, which are a way of logically grouping servers within a site, allow clients to access the contents of public folders in your organization more efficiently. Note that the General property sheet also shows the version and build of Exchange Server currently installed on the server, which can assist you in upgrading, applying service packs, planning, and troubleshooting.

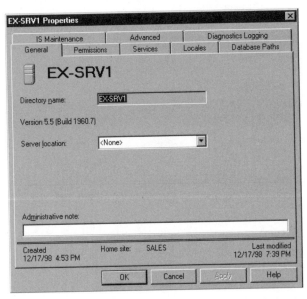

Figure 10-12. *Configuring server location on the General property sheet.*

Services   Earlier in this chapter, you learned that a server monitor watches specified services on a server. The Services property sheet allows you to configure which services a new server monitor watches by default when you create it.

Locales   Certain languages and locales view different information, such as currency values, in different formats. The Locales property sheet, shown in Figure 10-13, allows you to install support for locales on a server. By default, a single locale — typically English depending on the version purchased — is the only locale installed, but you can install support for additional locales. Multiple locales can be installed at the same time.

Figure 10-13. *Installing locales on a server.*

Database Paths   The Database Paths property sheet, shown in Figure 10-14, allows you to change the name and location of each of the Exchange databases. Simply select the database that you want to rename or move and then click Modify. You can also use this method to move multiple databases simultaneously; simply modify all of the paths you want to change, and click Apply. The Modify action stops the services, moves the database files, and then restarts the services. However, unless you have a very good reason to make a change, it's best to leave database names as they are.

Performance Optimizer can also be used to move databases and provides added functionality as well. Performance Optimizer is a powerful tool that performs

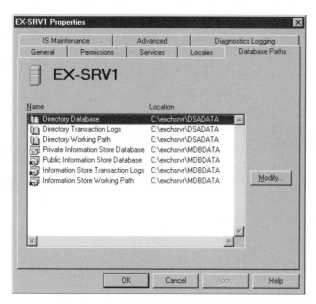

Figure 10-14. *Changing the names and locations of databases.*

tests on your system to determine whether moving various files to different locations will have a positive effect. This tool can also perform multiple moves at the same time. For more information on using Performance Optimizer, see Chapter 7.

IS Maintenance   You can use the IS Maintenance property sheet (Figure 10-15) to set the schedule by which the System Attendant (SA) performs maintenance tasks on the Information Stores. These tasks include deleting items from public folders, cleaning up indexes, and defragmenting Information Stores. By default, the SA performs these tasks between 1:00 and 6:00 every morning. You can change this setting, but it is best to schedule maintenance for the least-busy times for your network. Maintenance tasks can consume valuable server resources that will be needed for other activities in the course of the workday.

Advanced   The Advanced property sheet allows you to enable and disable circular logging. *Circular logging* is a function by which transaction log files are overwritten when they grow to a maximum size. With circular logging enabled, only previous log files with uncommitted changes are maintained on the server. The disadvantage of using circular logging is that it prevents you from using certain types of backups; furthermore, because some log files are discarded before backup, you may be unable to fully restore a server by replaying the log files.

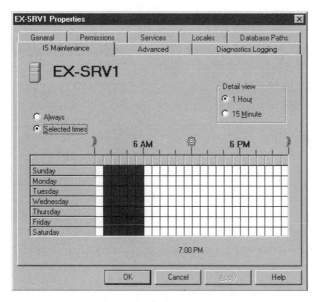

Figure 10-15. *Scheduling IS maintenance.*

For this reason, we strongly suggest that you disable circular logging for all your Exchange Servers. Circular logging is enabled by default.

The Advanced property sheet also allows you to initiate the consistency adjuster, which checks the consistency between the Information Store and the Directory. For more information on using circular logging and the consistency checker, see Chapter 23.

Diagnostic Logging Many objects, including the *Server* object, allow you to enable diagnostic logging. *Diagnostic logging* gathers detailed information about the operation of the object. This information is written to the Windows NT Server Event Log and can be viewed through the Windows NT Event Viewer. This technique and other monitoring techniques are covered in Chapter 22.

Managing Core Components

Four core Exchange components exist on every Exchange Server:

- Directory Service
- Information Store
- Message Transfer Agent
- System Attendant

These services communicate with one another to provide basic messaging and storage functionality. For example, when an Exchange client sends a message, it is immediately placed within that client's associated server's Information Store. The Information Store Service then consults the Directory Service, which maintains the Global Address List, to discover where that message should go. If the message is destined for another mailbox on the same server, the Information Store Service delivers it to that mailbox. If the message goes to another server, site, or messaging system, it is sent to the Message Transfer Agent. The Message Transfer Agent routes it to the appropriate destination. The System Attendant is responsible for making sure that all goes well in these communications.

It is apparent that the four core components are essential to standard functionality within Exchange. These components reflect the hierarchy of the Directory in that they are available at the site level within the organization or at the server level. To work with the site-level core components, you utilize the site's Configuration container. To work with the server-level core components, you utilize the particular server's container.

Managing the Directory Service

The Directory Service (DS) manages the Directory—the database of the entire Exchange hierarchy and its objects. The DS is also responsible for generating the Global Address List, which is only logical because the DS has access to the list of all the Exchange hierarchy, including recipients. Other Exchange services use the Directory Service to look up the information they need. The DS can be configured at both the site and server levels of the organization.

Configuring the DS at the Site Level

The Configuration container for each site contains a DS Site Configuration object that is used to manage the Directory Service for that site. You manage this service by opening the object's properties.

General The General property sheet, shown in Figure 10-16, allows you to configure several items:

- **Display name** You can change the display name of the object at any time. However, we recommend that you do not change display names for objects unless you have a very good reason for doing so. Changing display names can confuse other administrators and cause the documentation of your organization to become inaccurate.

- **Tombstone lifetime** When you delete an object from the Directory, Exchange Server marks that object with something called a tombstone

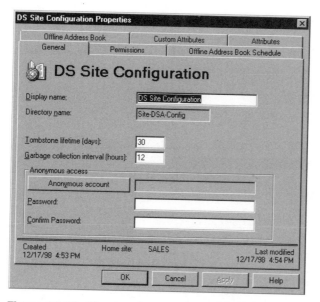

Figure 10-16. *Viewing the properties for the DS Site Configuration object.*

instead of actually deleting the object from the database. When the
Directory replicates to other servers, tombstones are replicated instead of
the *Directory* objects that those tombstones mark. This process ensures
that a *Directory* object is deleted from the Directory of all servers. The
Tombstone lifetime setting governs how long tombstones remain in the
DS. You should set this value to an interval long enough to ensure that
tombstones can be replicated to all servers and across at least one server
backup. For more information on the Directory Replication process, see
Chapter 11.

- **Garbage Collection Interval**   The Garbage Collection Interval represents
the period, in hours, after which the Directory Service removes expired
tombstones.

- **Anonymous access**   When an anonymous user connects to Exchange, that
user is validated through a special Windows NT account created for
anonymous users. You can specify that account and a password to give
anonymous users access to the Exchange Directory of a site.

Offline Address Book   Offline Address Books are used primarily by remote
users who do not have a permanent connection to the Exchange network. These
address books are downloaded while users are connected so that they can access
Directory Information when they are not connected. This procedure allows

users to address and write messages offline. When these users log back on to the network, these message are sent. For more information on working offline, see Chapter 18.

Offline Address Books are generated from a single Recipient container. You designate the containers to generate Offline Address Books for by using the Offline Address Book property sheet, shown in Figure 10-17. For more information on using Recipient containers, see Chapter 9.

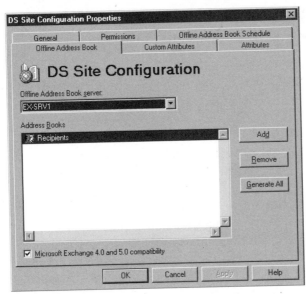

Figure 10-17. *Configuring generation of Offline Address Book.*

By default, the current site's Recipients container is used, but you can select any Recipient container in the organization. If you have more than one book, the client is prompted for which ones to download. You might want to use the Global Address List so that you can give offline users complete addressing information. You can generate an updated Offline Address Book manually at any time by clicking the Generate Offline Address Book Now button. On a multiserver site, you can also designate a specific server to generate the Offline Address Book.

Offline Address Book Schedule   The Offline Address Book Schedule property sheet is a typical scheduling property sheet. (Refer to Figure 10-15 earlier in this chapter for an example.) This property sheet allows you to specify the frequency with which you want to generate updated Offline Address Books. Unless your directory changes frequently, updating address books once a day, which is the default interval, should be enough.

Custom Attributes   You can customize attributes by using the Custom Attributes property sheet, shown in Figure 10-18. Simply change the value of the attribute that you want to customize. When you're done, that new field shows up on the Custom Attributes sheet of every recipient on the site.

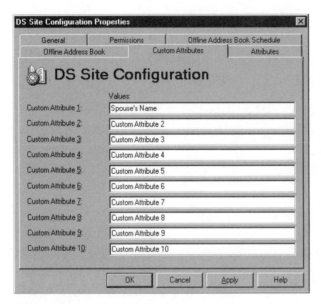

Figure 10-18. *Changing the Custom Attribute field names.*

Attributes   The Attributes property sheet allows you to specify which attributes are displayed to clients that use the Lightweight Directory Access Protocol (LDAP). LDAP is an Internet protocol originally implemented as an open standard for Directory Service access. Exchange uses the LDAP Configuration attributes to allow LDAP clients to be able to access the Exchange Server Directory. For more information on controlling attributes displayed to LDAP clients, see Chapter 14.

Configuring the DS at the Server Level

You configure the Directory Service at the server level by using the *Directory Service* object, which is located in the appropriate server's container. The primary and most common elements of the DS that you can configure at the server level are on the General property sheet, shown in Figure 10-19.

The Update Now button causes the server to send an immediate request for an updated Directory to all other servers on the site. This request is sent automatically within a site every five minutes anyway, but at times, you might need to see the most current view of the complete Directory structure immediately.

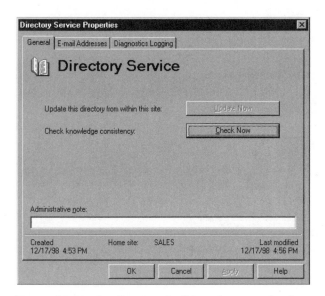

Figure 10-19. *Configuring the DS at the server level.*

The Check Now button causes the server to check for any new servers on the site or any new sites. The Check Now button can be useful if a particular server was down when other servers or sites were added. This check is performed once per day automatically, but the capability to do it yourself can be helpful.

The E-mail Addresses property sheet allows you to designate alternate e-mail addresses for configuration objects and recipients found on an Exchange Server. These e-mail addresses are used to identify objects and recipients to foreign messaging connectors configured in the Exchange organization so that messages from foreign systems can be properly delivered. The following types of e-mail addresses are automatically generated for any object created in Exchange Administrator:

- Lotus cc:Mail
- Microsoft Mail
- SMTP (Internet)
- X.400

You can create, edit, or remove any address type using the E-mail Addresses property sheet. Be sure to exercise caution when removing or editing these addresses. Many objects rely on these addresses to function properly, and changing or removing addresses can cause the system to fail.

Managing the Information Store Service

The Information Store Service provides server-based storage of information. This service actually manages two separate databases: a Private Information Store that contains user mailboxes and a Public Information Store that contains public folders.

Configuring the IS at the Site Level

At the site level, you configure the Information Store service (IS) by using the *Information Store Site Configuration* object, which is located in the Configuration container. The site-level configuration will apply to all servers within a site. At the site level, almost all IS configuration pertains to public folders, which are commonly replicated on multiple, different servers. (For more information, see Chapter 12, which deals exclusively with public folders.)

You can make two general-purpose configuration settings for the Information Store Service at the site level. The first of these settings is located on the General property sheet of the Information Store Site Configuration object, shown in Figure 10-20. The check box labeled Enable Message Tracking causes Exchange Server to create a daily log file that contains the routing information for all messages processed by the Information Store Service. Chapter 22 covers message tracking. For now, just know that for messages processed by the IS in a site, you can turn message tracking on and off on this property sheet.

Figure 10-20. *Enabling message tracking for the Information Store Service.*

The second general setting that you can make at the site level is located on the Storage Warnings property sheet. This property sheet is a typical scheduling sheet, allowing you to specify the thresholds that determine when warnings are issued to users who exceed storage limits on their mailboxes.

Configuring the IS at the Server Level

At the server level, you manage the Information Store Service by using two objects, both of which are located in the container for a specific server. The first of these objects is the *Public Information Store* object, which is used to administer details governing public folders for a server. Configuration of this object is covered in Chapter 12.

The second object — the *Private Information Store* object — is used to administer server-level settings governing mailbox usage for recipients associated with a server. The General property sheet for this object, shown in Figure 10-21, has several parameters that are identical to the parameters that you can configure for individual mailboxes.

Figure 10-21. *Configuring the Private Information Store on a server.*

- Deleted-item recovery time governs how long items deleted from the Deleted Items folder in users' mailboxes on the server are kept by the Information Store Service before being permanently deleted. Until the expiration date, users can retrieve those messages by using Outlook 8.03 or later.

You can also specify that items not be deleted until a server backup has been performed.

- Storage limits set at the server level work the same way as those set for individual mailboxes. You can use these limits to govern how large mailboxes on the server can grow before users must clean them out.

These settings govern all mailboxes on the server that you are currently administering. Any settings made for individual mailboxes override settings made for the server. For more information on recovering deleted items and setting storage limits, see Chapter 9.

The other property sheets for this object mainly concern monitoring various resources of the Private Information Store, although the Public Folder server tab can be used to configure the Public Information Store resources. For this reason, these property sheets are discussed in Chapter 20, which covers monitoring Exchange Servers in detail.

Managing the Message Transfer Agent

The Message Transfer Agent (MTA) is arguably the busiest of the Exchange services. The MTAs primary responsibilities are routing and delivering all messages that leave an Exchange Server and receiving all messages that come in from outside the server. In addition to providing these delivery services, the MTA is responsible for expanding distribution lists and for performing certain types of message translations for foreign environments.

Configuring the MTA at the Site Level

At the site level, you configure the MTA by using the *MTA Site Configuration* object, which is located in the Configuration container for the site. The General property sheet for this object allows you to make only one setting, which specifies whether to enable message tracking for messages processed by the MTA in the site. This basically includes any messages destined for recipients outside the local Information Store or on any distribution list, because the MTA is responsible for expanding distribution lists.

The Messaging Defaults property sheet of the *MTA Site Configuration object,* shown in Figure 10-22, contains parameters that let you fine-tune communications over the MTA. You should leave these values alone until you have a specific need to make changes and fully understand those changes. Changing parameters on this sheet can dramatically affect the overall performance of the network and can cause problems on your network if the changes are made improperly. The following sections present an overview of these parameters.

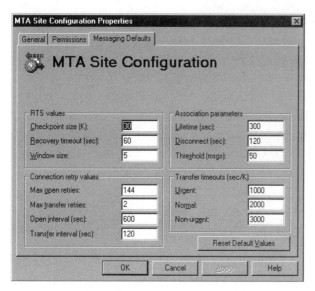

Figure 10-22. *Configuring messaging defaults for a site.*

RTS Values Request to Send (RTS) values govern communications between two MTAs. There are several values that you can configure:

- **Checkpoint size** The checkpoint size determines the amount of critical data, in kilobytes, that can be sent before a checkpoint is inserted into a data stream between two MTAs. A checkpoint, which is inserted by the sending MTA and confirmed by the receiving MTA, indicates the amount of data that has been sent since the previous checkpoint. If the receiving MTA detects that an incomplete transmission has taken place (by comparing the checkpoint value with the amount of data received), it signals the sending MTA to restart the transmission from the last successful checkpoint. You can disable checkpoint logging altogether by entering 0 for the Checkpoint Size value.

- **Recovery timeout** This value specifies the time interval in which a broken connection between two MTAs can be reestablished after a break in transmission before the MTA deletes all checkpointed information. If the checkpointed information is deleted, the transmission must be started over from the beginning.

- **Window size** The window size allows you to specify the number of checkpoints that an MTA can send unacknowledged to a remote MTA.

Association Parameters An association is a logical connection between two systems that is used to transfer messages. Multiple associations can be established over a single existing physical connection. Association parameters govern these logical connections. The parameters that you can configure include the following:

- **Lifetime** The Lifetime value determines the amount of time that the MTA keeps an association open after a message is sent.

- **Disconnect** This value determines the amount of time that an MTA waits for a disconnect request from the remote MTA before terminating an association.

- **Threshold** This value determines the maximum number of messages that can be queued for an association before the MTA opens another association.

Connection Retry Values Connection retry values determine how many times an MTA can try to establish a connection to transfer a particular message. If the MTA cannot establish a connection in the specified number of retries, it sends a nondelivery report (NDR) to the sender of the message. The parameters that you can configure in this section include the following:

- **Max open retries** This value determines the maximum number of times that an MTA tries to open a connection before generating an NDR.

- **Max transfer retries** This value determines the maximum number of times that an MTA tries to transfer a message across an open connection before generating an NDR.

- **Open interval** This value determines the amount of time that an MTA waits before retrying a connection that was unsuccessful.

- **Transfer interval** This value determines the amount of time that an MTA waits before attempting to resend a message over an open connection if the last send attempt was unsuccessful.

You might want to change these parameters to handle an unstable network connection. You will be much better off in the long run if you address the problems that are making the connection unreliable, but getting Exchange to work around the problem in the meantime can be helpful.

Transfer Timeouts Exchange Server handles messages based on their priority. High-priority messages are queued and sent before normal- or low-priority messages. Even NDRs can be generated faster when a high-priority message cannot be sent than when a normal- or low-priority message cannot be sent. This section of the Messaging Defaults property sheet lets you set the amount of time that passes before the MTA generates an NDR for each level of priority.

Configuring the MTA at the Server Level

At the server level, you configure the MTA by using the property sheets of the *Message Transfer Agent* object, which is located in the appropriate Server container. The General property sheet, shown in Figure 10-23, lets you configure several settings:

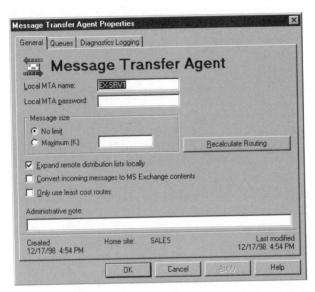

Figure 10-23. *Configuring the MTA at the server level.*

- **Local MTA name and password**   When foreign messaging systems connect to the local MTA, they do so by name. You can change the name of the local MTA in this property sheet. You can also assign an optional password to help prevent unauthorized MTAs from making a connection.

- **Message size**   You can specify the maximum size of messages that can be transferred over the MTA. Messages exceeding this size limit are returned to the sender. This value applies to both incoming and outgoing mail.

- **Recalculate routing**   The MTA is responsible for calculating the routing tables that it uses to determine where to deliver messages. These routing tables are calculated at three distinct times: when you start a server, when you add or reconfigure a connector or gateway (you'll be asked whether you want to do it at this time), and when you click the Recalculate Routing button. Often, you will make several configuration changes in sequence. At such times, it is useful to postpone all recalculation until all changes are made and then recalculate manually.

- **Expand remote distribution lists locally**   A remote distribution list is one that was created on one site but is available on other sites. Typically, expansion lists are expanded on the site where the list was created. If this option is enabled and a user connected to the server sends a distribution list, that list is expanded locally.

- **Convert incoming messages to MS Exchange contents**   When this option is enabled, the MTA converts incoming messages in the X.400 format to the native Exchange MAPI format.

- **Only use least-costly routes**   Often, an MTA has access to different routes over which it can send a message. These routes are typically assigned costs that give bias to certain routes. By default, an MTA attempts the least-costly route first, and if that route is unsuccessful, it moves on to other, more expensive routes. If you select this option, the MTA attempts only the least-costly route. If the attempt is unsuccessful, an NDR is generated.

The other thing that you can do with the MTA at the server level is view any messages that the MTA has queued to be delivered. The MTA on each Exchange Server constructs a separate queue for all other Exchange Servers on the site, as well as queues for the Public and Private Information Stores and connectors to other sites and foreign systems. The Queues property sheet, shown in Figure 10-24, lets you view the messages in each of these queues. This property sheet is a valuable troubleshooting tool that can be used to determine whether an MTA is stuck or if there is a backlog of messages being sent to a particular location. Simply choose the queue that you want to view from the Queue Name drop-down menu, and scroll through the list of messages. You can open the details of any message by double-clicking on it. You can also delete individual messages and change their priority within the queue.

Figure 10-24. *Viewing messages in the MTA's queues.*

Managing the System Attendant

The System Attendant (SA) manages much of what goes on in Exchange 5.5. It is the first of the Exchange services to start, and all other Exchange services depend upon it to start. The SA maintains the routing tables used by the MTA, helps manage encryption in an organization, manages link and server monitors, and maintains message-tracking logs.

Unlike the other core components, which can be configured at both the site and server levels, the SA can be configured only at the server level. You configure the SA by using the property sheets of the *System Attendant* object, which is located in the Servers container.

The General property sheet, shown in Figure 10-25, holds the only parameter that you can configure for the SA: how it handles message tracking log files. By default, the SA is set to remove log files older than seven days. You can change this value or elect not to have the SA delete log files. For more information on message tracking, see Chapter 22.

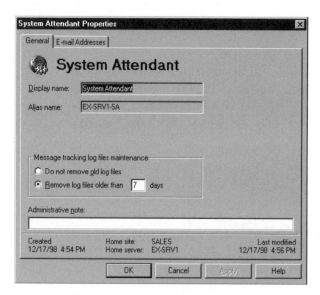

Figure 10-25. *Configuring the System Attendant.*

Summary

Exchange is a powerful and flexible piece of software, and you can shape the way that it operates by adjusting its configuration parameters. In this chapter, you learned many of the activities involved in managing sites and servers. You learned that the Organization object is the topmost Configuration container in Exchange Administrator. The Organization container contains several objects: *Folders, Global Address List, Address Book Views,* and a container for each site in the organization. Each Site container contains two objects by default: the Recipients container for the site and a Configuration container. The Configuration container holds most of the objects used to configure Exchange at the site level. The Configuration container also holds a container named Servers, in which you will find a container for each server configured in the site. Each Server container, in turn, holds objects that allow you to configure services for that server.

There are four core Exchange Server components. Directory Service handles the Exchange hierarchy, also known as the Directory, and assists other services by looking up the location of the objects for them. Information Store service manages the configuration of Information Stores across an entire site and can manage the configuration of the Information Store functions at the server level. Message Transfer Agent manages the movement of messages between recipients that exist on different servers, sites, or messaging systems. System Attendant monitors and manages the functions on the server.

The four core Exchange Server components (DS, IS, MTA, and SA) are each managed at different levels of the Exchange hierarchy. At the site level, core components are configured using the appropriate *Site Configuration* object found in the Configuration container for the site. Each of the core components except for the System Attendant can be configured at the site level and apply to all servers running those services within the site.

At the server level, core components are configured using components found in the appropriate Server container. All of the core components can be managed at the server level. Each server's individual configuration will override that made at the site level. This ability enables customization. The IS is actually managed at the server level using two objects, one for the Private Information Store and one for the Public Information Store.

Chapter 11
Managing Multiple Sites

Within the boundaries of a Microsoft Exchange site, most configuration and communication take place automatically. When you install a new Exchange Server in a site, that server becomes aware of any existing servers. Directory information is replicated to the new server, and messages can be sent to any recipients configured on the new server. None of these tasks requires any extra setup effort on your part.

However, this situation does not apply to communications between sites. In fact, two Exchange sites can exist on the same network and not be aware of each other until you configure the connections between them.

In this chapter, we start reviewing intersite communication within an Exchange system. We will examine server-to-server communication within a single site, how sites communicate with each other, and how to connect to foreign messaging systems, and we will learn how to configure sites and Directory Replication so that their interaction provides a customized messaging system. Exchange Server encompasses a great deal of communication capability, but after looking at the types of communication functions, it is plain to see how Exchange Server can provide a unique messaging system for every enterprise.

Understanding Message Flow in Exchange

The Microsoft Exchange environment can be complicated. As an administrator, you will be well served to learn how messages flow from one place to another in that environment. On a single Exchange Server, the process of communication is relatively simple. Communication in an Exchange system grows more complex as you add servers and sites.

Message Flow on an Exchange Server

In Exchange, the sender of a message is called an *originator,* and the receiver of a message is called a *recipient.* On a single Exchange Server, the flow of messages from originator to recipient is straightforward. When an originator and recipient exist on the same server, the message flow happens as follows:

1. The originator establishes a connection to the Information Store (IS) on the home server and submits a message.

2. When the IS receives the message, it consults the Directory to determine whether the recipient's mailbox exists on the local server, which it does.

3. Because the recipient's mailbox is on the local server, the IS places the message in that mailbox and, if logged onto the system, the recipient will see that a new message is waiting in the Inbox.

Message Flow between Exchange Servers in a Site

When the originator and recipient of a message exist on different Exchange Servers that are within the same site, a level of complexity is added to the message flow, as described in the following sections. Two of the four core Exchange services are responsible for all communication among servers in a site: the Directory Service (DS) and the Message Transfer Agent (MTA).

> **Note**   The other two core Exchange services are the Information Store Service (IS) and the System Attendant (SA). Because it handles the storage of that message at both ends of the transaction, the IS is always involved in a message moving from the originator to the recipient. The SA is always involved in monitoring and managing each Exchange Server.

Directory Service Communications

When a site has only one Exchange Server, all the Directory information for the organization is stored in one place: on that server. When servers are installed into a site, Exchange replicates the Directory information to every server through a multimaster replication model. *Multimaster replication* means that no single master copy of the directory exists; the replicas on all servers are identical.

Within a site, Directory Replication among servers occurs automatically whenever Directory information changes. This replication occurs in the following sequence:

1. When a change is made in the Directory on a server, the DS on the server where the change was made begins a five-minute countdown. Primarily, Exchange provides a default five-minute latency period to allow multiple changes to be made to the Directory, and then the messages can be replicated in a batch. The latency period can be changed in the DS property sheets.

2. When the five minutes, or the custom latency period, are up, the DS notifies every other server's DS within the same site via remote procedure call (RPC) that changes have been made. If RPCs cannot transmit between two Exchange Servers that are configured for Directory Replication, this communication cannot take place.

3. The other servers' Directory Services that receive this notification and do not already have copies of the updated Directory information then request a copy of the changes and update their Directory information.

MTA Communications

The DS handles Directory Replication among servers in a site. The MTA handles all other communication among servers in a site, including messages sent by users and other types of communications, such as link monitor messages and public folder replication messages.

Between two servers in a site, the flow of messages involves a few more steps than when the message simply moves between two mailboxes on the same single server. When an originator sends a message to a recipient on a different Exchange Server in the same site, the message flow occurs as follows:

1. The originator establishes a connection to the IS on its home server and submits the message.

2. When the IS receives this message, it consults the DS to determine whether the recipient exists on the local server.

3. Because the recipient exists on a remote server, the IS passes the message to the MTA.

4. The MTA looks up the recipient's home server in the local Directory and determines the location of the remote server to which the message must be sent.

5. The originating MTA opens an RPC connection with the remote MTA and transfers the message. A direct connection between two MTAs is called an *association*.

6. The remote MTA receives the message and looks up the recipient's home server in the Directory.

7. If the home server is the remote server that just received the message, the remote MTA passes the message to its IS. If the home server is not the remote server that just received the message, the MTA attempts to relay the message to the correct server, as outlined in step 4 of this procedure.

8. The IS looks up the recipient in the Directory to determine whether the recipient resides on the local server. This step may seem superfluous, but remember that Exchange Server 5.5 is an object-based environment. Objects, such as the IS, perform the same actions on a given type of incoming data, regardless of actions already performed by other services or what other services it received the data from. In other words, the IS has no knowledge that the MTA has already determined that the recipient resides on the local server.

9. The IS places the message in the recipient's mailbox and, if the recipient is logged on, the recipient will see that a new message has arrived (Figure 11-1).

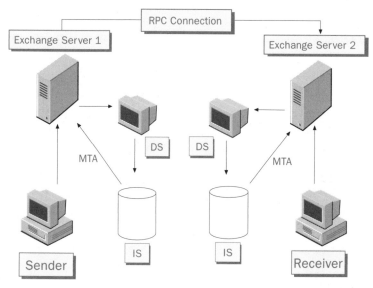

Figure 11-1. *Message path from one server to a second server.*

Message Flow between Sites

Within the boundaries of a site, all connections, message transfer, and Directory Replication happen automatically. This automation makes a single-site organization attractive to administrators because all you really have to do is install Exchange Server 5.5 and let it go about its business. Often, however, you need more than one site in your organization. At such a time, you discover that inter-site communications are different. You must configure and maintain connections between sites yourself.

The standard site connector for Exchange is based on RPC connectivity. An RPC is a session-layer application program interface (API). An RPC is an open standard that can run over multiple, diverse protocols. These protocols include TCP/IP, NetBIOS, IPX/SPX, and Vines. Each of these protocols can run over various physical topologies, both wide area networks (WANs) such as T1, frame relay, and local area networks (LANs) such as Ethernet, token ring, and FDDI. This all boils down to the fact that Exchange runs across multiple network types, and the underlying network infrastructure is not only independent of the Exchange structure, but it can vary between each of the Exchange Servers.

The MTA is responsible for *all* communications between sites. Even the DS must bundle its Directory Replication information into messages and submit it to the MTA for transfer to other sites.

The MTA transfers messages between sites over messaging connectors. *Messaging connectors* are logical connections between sites that you configure using Microsoft Exchange Administrator. These connectors are covered in detail a bit later in this chapter. For now, just be aware that a messaging connector must be configured between two Exchange sites in order for messages to be transferred. When an MTA receives a message that is destined for another site, it routes the message over the appropriate messaging connector to an MTA on the remote site. The MTA on the remote site then delivers the message to its own IS, to the MTA of another server in the site, or even to another site or foreign system. This delivery occurs according to the procedures discussed earlier in this chapter.

Configuring Messaging Connectors

Although the messaging functions within Exchange are independent of the network infrastructure, the messaging connectors are dependent on the network bandwidth available to Exchange. Available bandwidth is different from the total network bandwidth; it is concerned with whatever maximum amount of data can be sent through the network by Exchange, rather than the total amount of data that could be sent through regardless of the originating application. The underlying physical network, as well as the other applications that communicate across the network link, affect which messaging connector should be selected. Each type of connector has strengths and weaknesses in its capabilities in the areas of costing, load balancing, error recovery, speed of throughput, and fault tolerance, which may affect the selection of connector between sites.

Messaging connectors are the logical connections between sites that you create using Exchange Administrator. Four types of messaging connectors can be used to connect Exchange sites in the same organization:

- Site connector
- X.400 connector
- Dynamic RAS connector
- Internet Mail Service

Of these connectors, the site connector and the Dynamic RAS connector can be used only to connect Exchange sites in an organization, which means that they cannot be used to connect to foreign messaging systems. The X.400 connector and the Internet Mail Service can be used to connect an Exchange site to either another Exchange site or a foreign messaging system, or even to another Exchange organization. This chapter covers each type of messaging connector except the Internet Mail Service. Because of the unique and complex uses for the Internet Mail Service, it is reviewed in Chapter 14.

Note You can connect two separate Exchange organizations (as opposed to connecting two Exchange sites) by using the Internet Mail Service or an X.400 connector. However, these connections operate just as a connection to a foreign system would operate. Users can send and receive messages between the organizations, but no Directory Replication or synchronization is possible because the Exchange organizations do not participate in the same Directory. This does not prevent the use of VBScript or third-party tools to create a Directory Synchronization between Exchange organizations via other connectors, however.

Using the Site Connector

The site connector is by far the easiest of the connectors to configure and manage because it was developed to provide an automated connection between sites and because it uses RPC connectivity. Before you configure a site connector, you must make sure that some intersite permissions are set up.

Setting Up Intersite Permissions

The components on each of the Exchange Servers within a site use a common Site Services account to log on to the network and to communicate with one another. Multiple sites may or may not be configured to use the same Site Services account, depending on preferences and security rules in the enterprise. One reason that a site might not use the same Site Services account as another might be the fact that the two sites are in different NT domains and might not have trust relationships set up between them.

There are three ways that you can configure two sites to communicate:

- The two sites can use the same Site Services account. The use of the same Site Services account has no special requirements if the two sites both participate in the same Windows NT domain. If these two sites exist in separate domains, appropriate trust relationships must be configured to allow the use of the same account. Trust relationships are set up through the Windows NT utility User Manager for Domains.

- The two sites can use different Site Services accounts, with each account having administrative permissions on both sites. The Site Services account on each site must be assigned the role of Service Account Admin for the Site and Configuration containers on the other site. Assigning the Service Account Admin role is performed in the Exchange Administrator program. If these two sites exist in separate domains, appropriate trust relationships must be configured to allow the use of different accounts that have administrative permissions in both sites.

- The two sites can use different Site Services accounts, with the site connector on each site configured to use override values that allow local components to log on to the remote site. This option does not require a trust relationship, even though the sites may be in different domains. These override values are configured on the site connector itself.

Creating the Site Connector

After you establish the appropriate cross-site permissions or decide to use override values, you are ready to create the site connector. When you connect two sites, you actually must create a messaging connector in each site. You can think of creating these two messaging connectors as configuring both ends of the connection.

When you create a site connector, Exchange makes configuring both ends a simple task. You can begin the creation from either site, and Exchange Administrator automatically allows you to create both ends of the connector at the same time. This process differs from that of other messaging connectors, because they require you to create each end of the connector separately.

Take the following steps to begin the creation of a site connector:

1. In the Exchange Administrator, choose New.
2. Select Other.
3. Click on the File menu.
4. Select Site Connector. This command opens the New Site Connector dialog box, shown in Figure 11-2.

5. Enter the name of any Exchange Server in the remote site to which you want to connect. The server that you choose will be the one on which the site connector is installed in the other site.

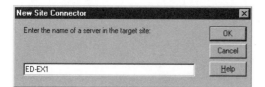

Figure 11-2. *Choosing a server on the remote site.*

Note Even though a messaging connector is configured on a single server, the connector belongs to the entire site. Any user or service on any server on the site can use a messaging connector after it is created. Connectors are also managed at the site level.

When you click OK, Exchange Administrator tries to connect to the remote server. When that connection is made, the property sheets for the new site connector are displayed, ready for configuration.

A site connector is known as both the simplest and fastest connector between Exchange sites (about 20 percent faster than an X.400 connector). In being both fast and simple, however, it loses some of the more desirable configuration aspects that both X.400 and the Internet Mail Service have.

The site connector does allow the administrator to set a cost for the link. The cost is a simple mechanism of determining the priority of one link over another. If a connector has a lower cost, it is preferred over one with a higher cost.

Load balancing is possible if multiple site connectors are created between two separate sites. When an administrator wants two different site connectors to handle all the messaging traffic equally between the sites, the administrator sets up each connector with the same cost.

Fault tolerance is set up by establishing a low cost (the default value of 1 is satisfactory) for the standard connector and an extremely high cost (a value of 100 is recommended) for the backup connector. In this scenario, the high-cost connector is never used except when the other connector fails.

A connector used for fault tolerance should be established over a different network connection. This will prevent Exchange from trying to access and use this connector when the cause of the problem is that the network connection has gone down.

General Property Sheet The General property sheet, shown in Figure 11-3, allows you to configure basic information about the new site connector.

Figure 11-3. *Configuring general properties of the site connector.*

The parameters in this property sheet include:

- **Target site** The target site is the name of the site to which the site connector is configured to connect. This value cannot be changed.

- **Cost** The cost value is used to designate preference for one connector over another when multiple messaging connectors exist between two sites. When determining which connector to route a message to, the MTA always tries the messaging connector with the lowest-cost value first. Cost values range from 1 to 100.

- **Message bridgehead is the local site** By default, any server in the site can use the site connector to send a message to a server in a remote site. You can specify that a bridgehead server be used instead. If a bridgehead server is used, all servers in the site send to the bridgehead server all messages that are destined for a remote site. The bridgehead server then sends the messages over the site connector to the remote site. Bridgehead servers can be particularly useful if two sites are connected over a WAN link. In this case, only the bridgehead server needs to open and maintain connections over the WAN link.

Target Servers Property Sheet The Target Servers property sheet, shown in Figure 11-4, allows you to specify servers in the remote site to which a direct connection can be opened with the site connector. The Target Servers list on the right side of this property sheet shows all remote servers to which a direct

connection can be established. The Site Servers list on the left shows servers
that are not included as target servers. You can move servers between these
two lists by clicking the Add and Remove buttons.

Figure 11-4. *Assigning target servers.*

You can also assign a cost value to each target server. Cost values range from 0
to 100, with 1 being the default value. Lower-cost target servers are always used
before higher-cost target servers. A target server with a cost value of 0 is always
used unless it is unavailable. A target server with a cost value of 100 is never
used unless all other target servers are unavailable.

The target server cost does not relate to the cost of the connector itself. Connector
costs are used by the MTA to determine which connector should be used to
transfer a message in the case that multiple connectors can be used. Target
server costs are used by the MTA to determine the target server to which a message should be transferred, if a particular site connector has multiple target
servers enabled.

> **Note** You don't have to configure a server as a target server for it to receive
> messages from another site. When a server on one site needs to send a mes-
> sage to a server on another site, it opens a direct connection to a target server
> or it forwards the message to a bridgehead server, which then opens a direct
> connection to a target server. When the message has been transferred to the
> target server, the target server can relay the message to any other server in the
> site or even to another site with another messaging connector.

Address Space Property Sheet The Address Space property sheet, shown in Figure 11-5, allows you to create, edit, and delete address spaces associated with the site connector.

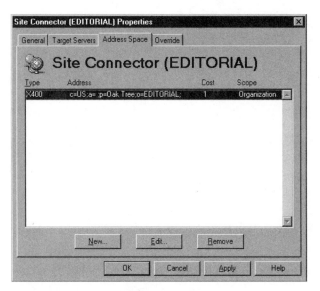

Figure 11-5. *Viewing Address Spaces for a connector.*

The MTA uses Address Spaces to identify the specific connector over which a message should be sent. Notice that an X.400 address space already exists. The MTA is a native X.400 messaging component and uses the X.400 convention even when it routes mail over a site connector. It is important to know that the site connector relies on this X.400 Address Space to deliver messages and that it should not be removed. Address Spaces are covered in more detail in Chapter 12.

Override Property Sheet As mentioned earlier in this chapter, one way to configure intersite access for a site connector is to configure override values. You do so by using the Override property sheet, shown in Figure 11-6.

Enter the name, password, and domain name of the Service Account for the remote site. Use these override values when the Service Account on the local site lacks administrative permissions in the remote site. Override values allow components in the local site to communicate with components on the remote site. The primary benefit of using override values is that trust relationships and cross-site permissions need not be configured.

In general, it is simpler and more efficient to establish trust relationships and cross-site permissions than to use override values. The main reason is that using

Figure 11-6. *Entering override values for the Site Services account.*

trust relationships helps centralize administration. If trust relationships exist and proper administrative privileges have been granted, you can administer different sites from a single location. If trust relationships are not established, you have to log on in the domain in which a remote site exists to be able to administer that site. The capability to use override values is useful when, for reasons of either security or preference, trust relationships are just not possible.

When you finish configuring the information on these property sheets, click OK to create the new site connector. You are immediately given the opportunity to create the corresponding site connector in the other site. The procedure for that configuration is identical to the one you just learned. Remember, however, that this time, you need to enter information from the perspective of the remote site. When the site connector is established in both sites, users can send mail between sites.

Note After you create a messaging connector between two sites, messages can be sent between users in those sites. Users in one site, however, do not have access to Directory information in the other site until you specifically configure a Directory Replication connector between the sites. Directory Replication connectors are discussed later in this chapter. Configuring a Directory Replication connector requires that messages use manual addresses. A manually addressed e-mail is a valid test for each type of connector that is configured before Directory Replication is established. The address format for the e-mail depends entirely on the type of connector.

Using the X.400 Connector

X.400 connectors require more configuration than site connectors. All other things being equal, X.400 connectors also operate roughly 20 percent slower than site connectors do. Using an X.400 connector does have some advantages, however:

- The X.400 connector allows you to configure a connection to any foreign messaging system that is X.400-compliant. X.400 is a standard messaging protocol used by many messaging systems. Because X.400 is a standard, it is very easy to connect to external messaging systems if there are no specific connectors for that system.

- The X.400 connector tends to be more reliable over unstable network connections. This reliability is partially due to better control of the choice of messages that can be transferred over an X.400 connector, when those messages can be transferred, and who can transfer them. Additionally, the X.400 protocol uses a certain amount of bandwidth overhead in order to ensure reliability of the messages. This accounts for the 20 percent difference in performance, but this method can be highly desirable if the network connection is poor or has low available bandwidth, as in many WAN connections. In contrast, the site connector does not allow any type of scheduling or messaging restrictions on the message transfer, and because it relies on RPC connectivity over standard protocol stacks, it does not have additional protocol overhead infringing on its performance.

- The X.400 connector does not require that a trust relationship be configured between domains, as does the site connector.

Two steps are involved in creating an X.400 connector with Exchange Administrator. First, you create an MTA transport stack over which the connector will work. Second, you create the X.400 connector itself. Keep in mind that an MTA transport stack and an X.400 connector must be configured independently in each of the sites that you are connecting.

Creating an MTA Transport Stack

All messaging connectors in Exchange Server 5.5 use MTA transport stacks. The site connector and the Internet Mail Service take care of configuring their own transport stack behind the scenes. X.400 connectors as well as dynamic RAS connectors require that you set up the MTA transport stack yourself.

An MTA Transport Stack, which is configured on a particular Exchange Server, is a set of information about the software and hardware that make up the underlying network. Messaging connectors use the transport stack to know how to format data so that it can be transferred between sites.

> **Note** Transport stacks are used by a particular Exchange Server at the server level only. This configuration differs from the connector or connectors that will use the transport stack. Connectors are used at the site level. Therefore, multiple MTA transport stacks and X.400 connectors can be configured within a site, enabling you to balance the load that messaging connectors place on servers.

MTA transport stacks provide the logical transport conditions over which a connector runs. There are four types of MTA transport stacks, each defined by the type of network hardware or software that you configured: TP0/X.25, TCP/IP, RAS, and TP4/CLNP (Table 11-1).

Table 11-1. Transport Stacks and Associated Connections/Connectors

Transport Stack	Connector	Connection Type
TP0/X.25	Any connectors	Connection using X.25
TCP/IP	Any connector except DRAS	Connection using TCP/IP
RAS	DRAS	Connection over analog lines
TP4/CLNP	Any connector	Connection to a mainframe supporting TP4

No matter which type of MTA transport stack you use, its configuration is nearly identical to the others. Because the TCP/IP MTA transport stack is the most common, it is covered in this section.

You use Exchange Administrator to create MTA transport stacks. From the File menu, choose New Other, then select MTA transport stack to open the New MTA Transport Stack dialog box, shown in Figure 11-7. Use this dialog box to choose the type of transport stack that you want to create and the server on which you want to create it. When you click OK, the property sheets open for the new MTA transport stack.

General Property Sheet The General property sheet, shown in Figure 11-8, is used to change the display name for the MTA transport stack and to configure OSI addressing information. Unless you plan to allow applications other than Exchange Server 5.5 to use the MTA transport stack, you do not need to worry about the OSI addressing values.

If you are interested in learning more about OSI addressing and configuring other applications to use an MTA transport stack, consult the *Microsoft BackOffice 4.5 Resource Kit* (1999), from Microsoft Press.

Connectors Property Sheet The Connectors property sheet, shown in Figure 11-9, lists all the messaging connectors in the site that are configured to use the

Figure 11-7. *Creating an MTA transport stack.*

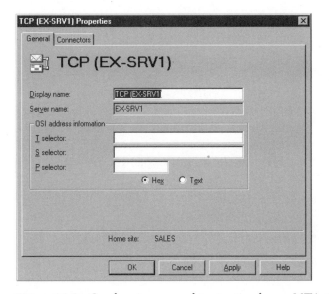

Figure 11-8. *Configuring general properties for an MTA transport stack.*

current MTA transport stack. When you create a stack, this list is blank. As you create new connectors that use the MTA transport stack, those connectors are added to the list.

After you create the MTA transport stack, its configuration object appears in the container of the server on which the transport stack was created.

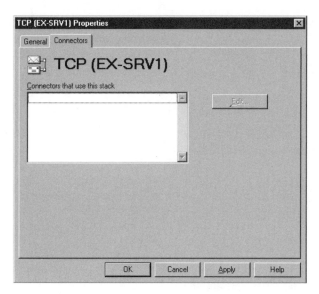

Figure 11-9. *Viewing the connectors that use an MTA transport stack.*

Creating an X.400 Connector

After you create an MTA transport stack for the new X.400 connector to use, you can create the connector itself. In Exchange Administrator, choose New, then choose Other, and then select X.400 Connector from the File menu. This command opens the New X.400 Connector dialog box, shown in Figure 11-10. In this dialog box, select the MTA transport stack that the new connector should use, and then click OK.

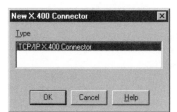

Figure 11-10. *Selecting an MTA transport stack for a new X.400 connector.*

The first thing you notice is that the X.400 connector has considerably more property sheets to configure than does the site connector. Many of the configuration parameters on these property sheets are used to configure the X.400 connector for connection to a foreign messaging system. Connecting to foreign systems is covered in detail in Chapter 12. Thus, some of the parameters on the

X.400 property sheets are not covered in the following sections, but they are discussed in the next chapter.

General Property Sheet   The General property sheet, shown in Figure 11-11, defines basic naming and connection information for your connector.

Figure 11-11. *Configuring general connection properties for a new X.400 connector.*

You can configure the following parameters on this property sheet:

- **Display name**   The display name is the name of the connector as it appears in Exchange Administrator. Notice no default value appears on this property sheet, as it does on the property sheets of most other configuration objects. Although a default display name is not created, you should create a name that includes the type of connector (X.400) and the sites that you are connecting—for example, *X.400 SITE1 -> SITE2*.

- **Directory name**   This setting is the name of the connector as it appears in the Exchange DIT. When the connector is created, the directory name cannot be changed.

- **Remote MTA name**   This setting is the name of the server on the remote site to which the local MTA will connect.

- **Remote MTA password**   Optionally, you can assign a password to an MTA that prevents unauthorized MTAs from opening an association to it.

If a remote MTA has been assigned such a password, enter it in the Remote MTA Password field.

- **MTA transport stack** This setting is the MTA transport stack that the X.400 connector is currently configured to use. By default, this value is set to the MTA transport stack that you chose when you created the connector. You can change the MTA transport stack at any time.

> **Note** You may have noticed that when you configure an X.400 connector, you must designate a specific server in the remote site to which the X.400 connector will connect. This designation is required because the X.400 connector works only by means of messaging bridgehead servers, as described earlier in this chapter. When you configure an X.400 connector between two sites, one server in each site—the bridgehead server—is responsible for transferring all messages over the connector to the bridgehead server in the other site. Unlike the site connector, a single X.400 connector does not support multiple target servers. However, you can create multiple X.400 connectors to handle the load balancing and fault tolerance.

Schedule Property Sheet The Schedule property sheet, shown in Figure 11-12, can be used to restrict the times at which the X.400 connector may be used. By default, the X.400 connector can be used at all times, and for the most part, you want to leave this value alone. At times, however, you may want to limit connectivity — for example, if you have a very busy network or if you have a scheduled maintenance procedure that would cause problems with transferring messages.

You can set an X.400 connector schedule to one of four values:

- **Remote initiated** This setting allows remote sites to connect to the current site, but it does not allow the local site to initiate a connection. Enabling this setting can be useful if sending outgoing messages immediately is not a big concern, but receiving incoming messages is. This setting is often used when the Selected Times setting on another server is configured to control when delivery occurs.

- **Always** This setting allows connections to be made to and from the site at any time.

- **Never** This setting disables the connector and is useful for bringing the connector down while performing maintenance, testing new connectors, or experimenting with load balancing.

- **Selected times** This setting allows you to define specific times at which the X.400 connector is available. Defining specific times can be useful on a

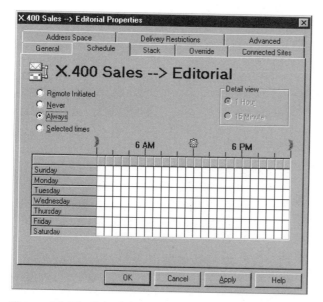

Figure 11-12. *Scheduling the availability of an X.400 connector.*

busy network. If immediate messaging is not a concern, you can schedule messages to be sent only during specific periods, when network traffic is otherwise low. The Selected Times setting is often used when the Remote Initiated setting is used on the other end of a connection. This combination can help ensure that any connection costs are borne only by one side of the connector.

Stack Property Sheet   The Stack property sheet, shown in Figure 11-13, is mostly used for configuring connections to foreign systems. You do need to configure one item on this property sheet, even when you are connecting two Exchange sites. In the Address field, enter either the name or IP address of the remote server to which your X.400 connector will connect.

Connected Sites   The Connected Sites property sheet, shown in Figure 11-14, is used only when you are using an X.400 connector to connect two Exchange sites.

Although messaging between the sites can work if you leave the Connected Sites information blank and configure an address space for the remote site, Exchange Server will not know that it is communicating with another Exchange site unless you specify that fact on this property sheet. If you do not specify it, the

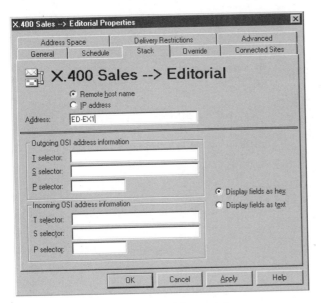

Figure 11-13. *Entering the address of the remote server.*

Figure 11-14. *Letting Exchange Server know that another Exchange site is out there.*

Exchange sites cannot exchange Directory information or allow public folder access between sites. Click New to display a dialog box in which you can enter the name of the remote site to which you are connecting. When you add a connected site, an address space for that site is generated.

Delivery Restrictions   The Delivery Restrictions property sheet, shown in Figure 11-15, allows you to specify which users can and cannot send messages over the X.400 connector.

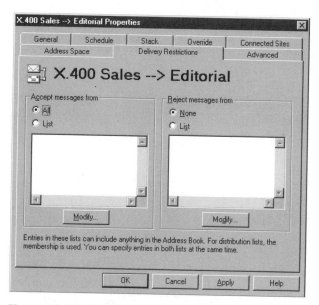

Figure 11-15. *Restricting use of an X.400 connector on a per-user basis.*

You control users' messaging capabilities in either of two ways:

- You can allow all users, except for those whom you specifically disallow, to transfer messages over the X.400 connector. This option is represented on the left side of the property sheet. By default, all users are allowed to use the connector. To specify users who cannot use the connector, select the List option and then click Modify to select users from the address book.

- You can prevent all users from transferring messages over the X.400 connector except those whom you specifically allow to do so. This option is represented on the right side of the property sheet. By default, no users are disallowed. To change this setting, select the List option, and then click Modify to select users from the address book.

Advanced Property Sheet   The Advanced property sheet, shown in Figure 11-16, is almost completely concerned with connections to foreign systems. You may want to configure one parameter, however, even when you are connecting Exchange sites. You can set the maximum size of messages that can be transferred over the X.400 connector. This setting can be useful if you want to limit network activity over a WAN link or other relatively low-bandwidth connection.

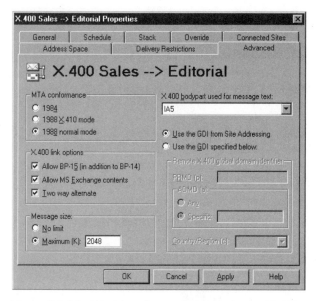

Figure 11-16. *Limiting the message size for an X.400 connector.*

When you finish configuring the property sheets for the connector, Exchange Administrator reminds you that you also need to configure the X.400 connector on the other site. Even though you are reminded, you must explicitly take this action yourself. To do so, use Exchange Administrator to connect to the server on the remote site that you've chosen to function as the bridgehead server. Create an MTA transport stack and X.400 connector on that server, using the procedure that you just learned.

Using the Dynamic RAS Connector

The dynamic RAS connector can be used to connect two Exchange sites between which no permanent network connection exists. As the name implies, the dynamic RAS connector relies on the Windows NT remote access service (RAS) to provide dial-up connectivity between the two sites. Like the site connector, the dynamic RAS connector can be used only to connect two Exchange sites that are part of the same organization.

Before you start creating the dynamic RAS connector, you need to take the following actions:

- Make sure that RAS is configured on the server on which you plan to create the dynamic RAS connector. You can add RAS to an existing installation of Windows NT by using the Network property sheets for the server, which are available from the Control Panel.

- Make sure that a RAS phone book entry exists for the RAS server that will hold the other end of the dynamic RAS connector.

- Make sure that a user account is configured in the remote site with Send As and Mailbox Owner permissions configured on the Site and Configuration containers. Alternatively, you can use the remote site's Site Services account.

As you do with the X.400 connector, you will have to configure each end of the dynamic RAS connector separately. This configuration involves performing the actions in the preceding list, setting up an MTA transport stack, and configuring the dynamic RAS connector itself.

Creating an MTA Transport Stack for a Dynamic RAS Connector

Creating an MTA transport stack for a dynamic RAS connector is much the same as creating one for an X.400 connector. Choose New Other, and then select MTA Transport Stack from the File menu of Exchange Administrator. This command opens the New MTA Transport Stack dialog box, shown in Figure 11-17. This time, you must choose the RAS MTA Transport Stack option. No other type of MTA transport stack works with the dynamic RAS connector. You must also select the server on which the RAS MTA transport stack should be installed.

Figure 11-17. *Creating an RAS MTA transport stack.*

Next, the property sheets for the new RAS MTA transport stack open, as shown in Figure 11-18.

The General property sheet is used to specify a display name for the new stack and to set an MTA callback number. The MTA callback number, which is

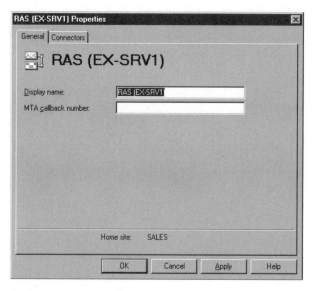

Figure 11-18. *Specifying an MTA callback number.*

optional, can provide some extra security when you use RAS. Whenever the local MTA places a call to a remote MTA, the remote MTA immediately disconnects and calls the local MTA back at the specified number.

> **Note** For the MTA callback number to work, callback security must first be configured for RAS. You can configure callback security by using the Remote Access Admin utility, located in the Administrative Tools (Common) program group on your Windows NT Server.

Creating the Dynamic RAS Connector

After you create the RAS MTA transport stack, you can create the dynamic RAS connector itself. In Exchange Administrator, choose New Other Dynamic RAS Connector from the File menu. This command opens the property sheets for the new Dynamic RAS connector.

General Property Sheet The General property sheet, shown in Figure 11-19, allows you to configure basic information about the dynamic RAS connector.

You can configure the following items:

- **Remote server name** This setting is the name of the server in the remote site to which the dynamic RAS connector will connect. The other end of the dynamic RAS connector must be installed on this server.

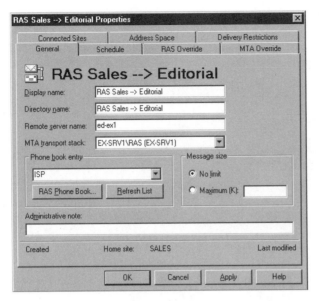

Figure 11-19. *Configuring basic information about the dynamic RAS connector.*

- **Phone book entry**   This setting is the entry in the RAS phone book that the local MTA will use to connect to the remote server.
- **Message size**   You can set a maximum size for messages that can be transferred over the dynamic RAS connector. This setting can be particularly useful because most dial-up connections do not support very high bandwidth.

Schedule Property Sheet   The Schedule property sheet is identical to the Schedule property sheet for the X.400 connector (refer back to Figure 11-12). You can use this property sheet to specify the times at which the dynamic RAS connector is available for use. If the dial-up connection that you are using is also used for other purposes, you may find it useful to schedule activity on the dynamic RAS connector for times when telephone rates are low. Messages that are to be transferred over the connector are queued and sent when the connector is active.

RAS Override Property Sheet   As you recall, one thing that you should do before setting up the dynamic RAS connector is get the name of a user account in the remote site with permissions in the Site and Configuration containers. The RAS Override property sheet, shown in Figure 11-20, is where you specify that account. The local MTA will use this account information to communicate with services in the remote site.

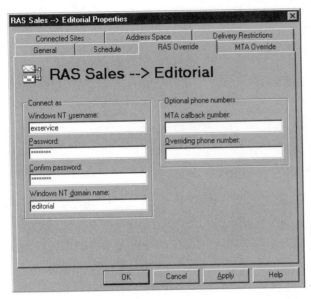

Figure 11-20. *Configuring overriding RAS properties.*

You can also specify an MTA callback number on this property sheet. This callback number overrides any number that you may have entered for the RAS MTA transport stack. Finally, you can use this property sheet to set an overriding phone number that can be used to call the remote server instead of using the phone book entry specified on the General property sheet. Using this overriding phone number is a convenient way of dialing a different phone number without having to edit the RAS phone book.

MTA Override Property Sheet   Chapter 10 covered the site-level configuration of several parameters that determine how the MTA opens associations with other MTAs and transfers data over those associations. The MTA Override property sheet, shown in Figure 11-21, allows you to override the values set at the site level with values set for the current dynamic RAS connector. Because dial-up connections behave much differently than permanent connections, these values can be quite helpful in fine-tuning your MTA's actions.

Connected Sites   The Connected Sites property sheet for the dynamic RAS connector is identical to the Connected Sites property sheet for the X.400 connector. This property sheet is used to specify that the system on the other end of

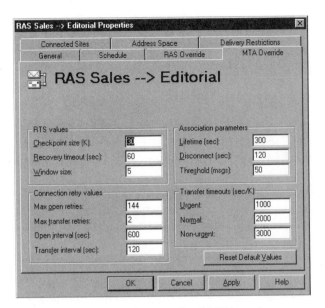

Figure 11-21. *Overriding site-level MTA settings.*

the dynamic RAS connector is another Exchange site. This specification may seem superfluous because dynamic RAS connectors can be used only to connect Exchange sites, but you still must add the remote site to the list of connected sites before full messaging functionality is supported.

Configuring Directory Replication

Understanding Directory Replication is very important for any administrator that has site complexity to his or her organization. The Directory Replication process demonstrates how the Directory information in Exchange flows around an organization.

After you set up a messaging connector between two sites, users can exchange messages but still cannot get to the Directory information for any site but their own. Within a site, Directory Replication between servers happens automatically, according to the multimaster replication model. No such automation occurs between different sites. Until you configure Directory Replication between two sites, each site maintains its own distinct Directory database.

To configure Directory Replication between two sites, you have to create a Directory Replication connector. Directory Replication connectors work on top of existing messaging connectors. For this reason, you must configure one of the types of messaging connectors covered in this chapter before you can create a Directory Replication connector. This discussion covers the actual creation and configuration of the Directory Replication connector. For more information on planning Directory Replication in an organization, please see Chapter 6.

Note Although a Directory Replication connector provides a two-way link between two sites over an existing messaging pathway, the Directory Replication connector does not require that you establish a messaging connector directly between the two sites that you want to connect. A transitive messaging connection will serve just as well. Transitive connections are discussed a bit later in this chapter, in the sidebar titled "Directory Replication Topology."

Creating a Directory Replication connector is easy. From Exchange Administrator, choose New Other, and then select Directory Replication Connector from the File menu. This command opens the New Directory Replication Connector dialog box, shown in Figure 11-22. Select the name of the remote site with which you want to establish Directory Replication and the name of a server in that site. This server hosts the other end of the Directory Replication connector. You can also specify whether the remote site can be reached when an e-mail message is manually addressed to it. If it can be reached, you can elect to create the other end of the Directory Replication connector automatically.

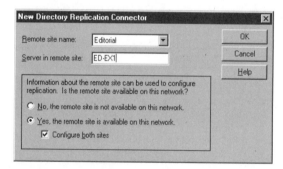

Figure 11-22. *Creating a Directory Replication connector.*

When you click OK, the property sheets open for the new Directory Replication connector. The three property sheets are General, Schedule, and Sites.

General Property Sheet

The General property sheet, shown in Figure 11-23, allows you to configure some basic information for the new Directory Replication connector. You can set a display name and Directory name, as usual. You can also change which servers act as the Directory Replication bridgehead servers in each site.

Remember that Directory Replication occurs between these two specific bridgehead servers — one in each site.

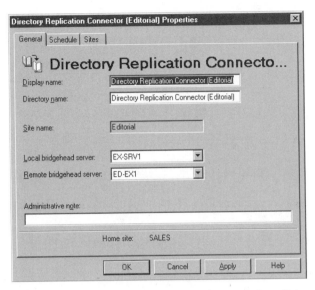

Figure 11-23. *Setting the bridgehead servers for a Directory Replication connector.*

Schedule Property Sheet

The Schedule property sheet is identical to the Scheduling property sheets that you saw earlier in this chapter. Scheduling is very important for a Directory Replication connector. Directory Replication can consume quite a bit of network bandwidth and server resources. You should schedule Directory Replication to occur at times when other network activity is low and when user access to servers is low.

Directory Replication connectors rely on messaging connectors. Thus, any schedule configured for the messaging connectors used by a Directory Replication connector may interfere with the schedule you create for the Directory Replication connector.

Sites Property Sheet

The Sites property sheet, shown in Figure 11-24, shows other sites with which Directory Replication occurs.

Both lists on this property sheet are empty until Directory Replication has successfully occurred at least once. The Inbound Sites list displays all sites from

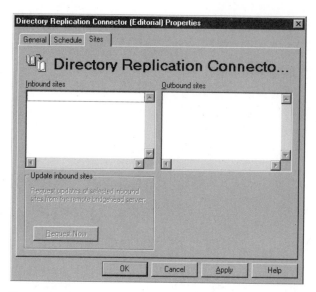

Figure 11-24. *Viewing sites with which replication occurs.*

which the local site receives Directory information through the Directory Replication connector. This list includes the remote site that is directly connected with the Directory Replication connector as well as any sites from which that remote site receives information. You can force a request for updated Directory information from all inbound sites by clicking Request Now.

The Outbound Sites list displays all sites for which the local bridgehead server is configured to replicate Directory information. Each bridgehead server can be configured to replicate information to multiple sites.

After you configure the information for the Directory Replication connector and click OK, you must configure the other end of the connector. If you specified that the other end be configured automatically (refer back to Figure 11-22), that is exactly what happens. You need do nothing further. If you did not specify that the other end be created automatically, such as when you are configuring replication over a dial-up networking connection, you need to connect to the other site with Exchange Administrator and create it yourself, using the procedure that you just learned.

When both ends of the Directory Replication connector have been configured, Directory Replication should occur automatically, according to the schedule that you set. If you set your Directory Replication schedule to Always, you can expect replication to occur within about 15 to 20 minutes, depending upon available bandwidth, number of directory entries, and other variables affecting network connectivity. Once replication occurs, you can see both sites represented within Exchange Administrator, as shown in Figure 11-25.

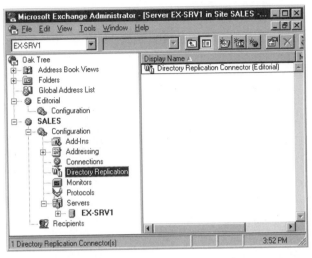

Figure 11-25. *Viewing two sites in Exchange Administrator.*

Exchange uses a utility called the Knowledge Consistency Check (KCC) that can help in managing the intersite Directory Replication. By default, each Exchange Server runs KCC every three hours. KCC performs the following steps when it is run:

1. KCC binds to the local server and discovers the names of the other servers within the local server's site.

2. KCC binds to a remote server in the same site and ensures that the remote server and local server have the same list of server names. If not, KCC synchronizes the Configuration naming contexts in both directions.

3. KCC searches the local server's Directory Replication connectors.

4. For each Directory Replication connector, KCC determines whether there is a corresponding connector in the remote site.

5. KCC then discovers all the connectors in order to build a list of sites.

6. KCC ensures that the replication occurs in both directions between sites.

7. KCC removes Directory Replication that happens with nonexistent servers.

The method that Exchange uses to ensure that conflicts are resolved in the Directory is through the use of update sequence numbers (USNs). Because Exchange uses a multimaster replication model, it is possible that two updates can be made to the same object in the Directory on two different replicas.

When this happens, the Directory uses the USN to determine which change was the most recent.

Real World **Directory Replication Topology**

In an Exchange organization that has more than two sites, Directory Replication is more complicated than in the two-site example discussed in this chapter. Directory Replication connections are transitive. Suppose that you set up a Directory Replication connector between Site 1 and Site 2. Next, suppose that you set up another Directory Replication connector between Site 2 and Site 3. A transitive connection automatically exists between Site 1 and Site 3.

When you set up a multisite organization, it is important that no two sites have more than one Directory Replication pathway between them. Therefore, it is generally best to use a single-line Directory Replication pathway, as shown in Figure 11-26. Notice that the Directory Replication connectors throughout the site form a single pathway throughout all the sites in the organization.

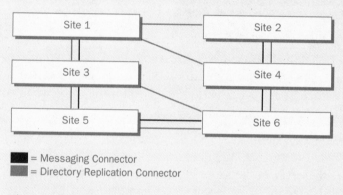

= Messaging Connector
= Directory Replication Connector

Figure 11-26. *Directory Replication pathway.*

Summary

In this chapter, you learned how communications occur between sites in an Exchange organization. Within the boundaries of a single site, most communications happen automatically, with little configuration required on your part. Servers in a site can transfer messages and Directory information between themselves as soon as they are installed. However, between sites, communications are not automatically configured.

Messages are transferred between sites using messaging connectors. Four types of messaging connectors can be used to connect Exchange sites: the site connector, the X.400 connector, the dynamic RAS connector, and the Internet Mail Service. Of these, the site connector and the dynamic RAS connector are used exclusively to connect one Exchange site to another Exchange site in the same organization. The X.400 connector and the Internet Mail Service can connect Exchange sites, but they can also be used to connect Exchange Server 5.5 to foreign messaging systems.

Once a messaging connector is configured between sites, messages may be transferred between the two sites, but no mechanism for sharing Directory information yet exists. The Directory Replication connector allows the servers in different Exchange sites to share Directory information by bundling this Directory information into messages and sending those messages over an existing messaging connector. For this reason, a messaging pathway must exist between two sites before a Directory Replication connector can be configured between them.

Chapter 12
Connecting to Foreign Systems

Exchange Server has the capability to connect to a multitude of messaging systems, including both new systems and legacy versions.

In this chapter, we start connecting to external, or foreign, messaging systems. We explore the reasons for linking to other messaging systems and how to use foreign system connectors to migrate legacy systems to Exchange, and we learn how to establish a comprehensive messaging structure with other enterprises. The combination of Exchange with foreign e-mail systems might seem delicately balanced, but after reviewing the connecting methods, it is obvious how solid Exchange's interconnectivity is for any size organization.

Until this point, we have focused primarily on working within the Microsoft Exchange Server 5.5 environment. You have set up Exchange Servers and sites, and you have configured sites to communicate with one another. You have also learned about much of the basic management that goes on in an Exchange organization. Exchange Server 5.5 is not the only messaging system out there, however. Many types of messaging systems are available today, and you may have to connect your Exchange system to one or more of them. You may, for example, be upgrading from a legacy system or need to establish communications with another company. This chapter covers the basics of connecting Exchange Server 5.5 to other messaging systems, which are referred to as *foreign system*s.

Connecting to Foreign X.400 Systems

X.400 is a messaging standard that can be used by many messaging systems. When an enterprise implements X.400-compliant mail systems, it can support a heterogeneous messaging environment. X.400 uses a strict addressing method that reflects a hierarchical environment. An X.400 address reflects the recipient's position in a messaging hierarchy. For example, the X.400 address for Melissa Craft at MicroAge is g=Melissa;s=Craft;o=Phoenix;p=MicroAge;a=;c=US. Each of these parameters represents a particular X.400 value or hierarchical placement.

"g=" stands for given name, or first name, while "s=" stands for surname or last name. "o=" stands for the X.400 organization but is equivalent to an Exchange site. "p=" represents the Private Management Domain and is equivalent to the Exchange organization. "a=" represents the Administrative Management Domain, and "c=" stands for the country.

Note To find out more about X.400, look at the request for comment number 1330 (RFC 1330). You can find this online at several Web sites, including

http://www.cis.ohio-state.edu/hypertext/information/rfc.html.

In Chapter 11, you learned how to use the X.400 connector to connect two Exchange sites in the same organization. You can also use the X.400 connector to connect Exchange Server 5.5 to any foreign messaging system that supports the X.400 standard.

Real World Using Other Foreign Gateways

Gateways are used in many messaging systems to link dissimilar messaging systems. Exchange Server 5.5 supports many gateways in the form of connectors. The X.400 connector, the Internet Mail Service, the Microsoft Mail connector, the Lotus Notes connector, and the Lotus cc:Mail connector are examples of gateways that are built into Exchange Server 5.5. Other vendors provide a variety of gateways for connecting Exchange Server 5.5 to external, proprietary electronic mail, fax, voicemail, and other systems.

Many connectors are available for Exchange, both offered with the Exchange Server software from Microsoft and offered separately from other vendors. A discussion of every connector that can be used to connect Exchange Server 5.5 to foreign systems is far beyond the scope of this book. For that reason, we limit our discussion to the X.400 connector and the Microsoft Mail connector—the X.400 connector because of the wide acceptance of X.400 as a messaging standard, and the Microsoft Mail connector because its configuration is similar to connectors for other proprietary systems. The Internet Mail Service, which can also be used to link to external messaging systems, is covered in Chapter 14.

If you need to know the specifics of connecting Exchange Server 5.5 to any specific messaging system, first consult the Exchange Server 5.5 product documentation and the *Microsoft 4.5 BackOffice Resource Kit* (1999) available from Microsoft Press.

Creating an X.400 connector to link Exchange Server 5.5 to a foreign X.400 system is the same as creating an X.400 connector to link two Exchange sites, a process that is detailed in Chapter 11.

> **Note** This chapter provides a fairly cursory introduction to connecting to X.400 systems. The material in this chapter should give you the basic understanding that you need to configure a foreign connection, given that the administrator of the foreign system will likely give you most of the specific configuration information. If you need more details on the X.400 standard, consult *Introduction to X.400*, an excellent text by Cemil Betanov (Artech House Telecommunications Library).

Remember that each end of an X.400 connector must be configured separately. This chapter assumes that the foreign system's administrator will appropriately configure the connector in the foreign system. To configure the X.400 connector in Exchange Server 5.5, you first must create an Message Transfer Agent (MTA) transport stack. As you may recall from Chapter 11, the MTA transport stack is a set of information about your network hardware and software configuration. The use of the transport stack allows for a layer of abstraction between the X.400 connector and the network itself.

After you create an MTA transport stack, you must create the X.400 connector itself. To do so, choose New Other, and then select X.400 connector from the File menu in Microsoft Exchange Administrator. Specify the MTA transport stack that you want the new X.400 connector to use. The property sheets for the new connector open, as shown in Figure 12-1.

Figure 12-1. *Creating the X.400 connector.*

Many of the property sheets for the X.400 connector are described in Chapter 11, so this section covers only the ones that pertain to setting up a connection to a foreign system.

Stack Property Sheet

The Stack property sheet, shown in Figure 12-2, is used to specify transport address information about the foreign X.400 system. After you specify the host name or IP address of the foreign MTA, you can provide outgoing Open Systems Interconnection (OSI) addressing information, if necessary. This information may not be required, depending on the foreign system to which you are connecting.

Figure 12-2. *Configuring information about the foreign X.400 system.*

Address Space Property Sheet

Foreign systems typically do not use the same addressing scheme as Exchange Server 5.5. For this reason, the Exchange MTA relies on address spaces to choose foreign gateways over which messages should be sent. An *address space* is the part of an address that designates the system that should receive the message. For example, look at a typical Internet address: *user@company.com*. Everything after the @ sign is the address space. The format of the address space is enough to tell the MTA that the message should be sent via the Internet Mail Service.

The Address Space property sheet, shown in Figure 12-3, allows you to configure an address space for the foreign X.400 system to which you are building a connection. The Exchange MTA compares the destination address of outgoing messages with this address space to determine whether the outgoing messages should be sent over the X.400 connector.

Figure 12-3. *Configuring an address space for the X.400 connector.*

To add an address space, click New. Clicking this button opens the New Address Space dialog box, shown in Figure 12-4, which allows you to specify the type of address space that you want to add. Because you are connecting to a foreign X.400 system, you will want to configure an X.400 address space.

Figure 12-4. *Choosing an address space type.*

After you choose the X.400 address space type, the X.400 Properties dialog box appears, as shown in Figure 12-5. The particular addressing information that needs to be configured for the foreign system should be provided by the administrator of the foreign system. X.400 addresses are case-sensitive and need to be typed in exactly the same format as provided.

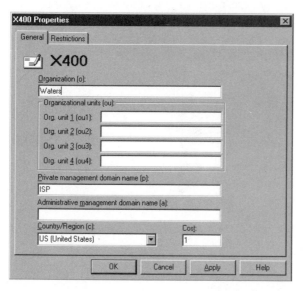

Figure 12-5. *Configuring the new X.400 address space information.*

Advanced Property Sheet

The Advanced property sheet, shown in Figure 12-6, is used to specify options for MTA conformance, links, and message attributes. The settings mostly depend on the specifications of the foreign system to which you are connecting.

The following settings can be configured on the Advanced property sheet:

- **MTA conformance** X.400 standards are periodically published as recommendations. Exchange Server 5.5 supports the two primary recommendations: those issued in 1984 and 1988. New updates have been made to the standard since 1988, but they don't really form a new recommendation. The 1988 recommendation itself has two versions: normal mode and X.410 mode. The default setting is 1988 normal mode, and you can expect it to work with most foreign X.400 systems.

- **Allow BP-15 (in addition to BP-14)** The Body Part 15 (BP-15) standard is part of the 1988 X.400 recommendation and supports several advanced messaging features, such as the encoding of binary attachments. The Body Part 14 (BP-14) standard is part of the older 1984 X.400 recommendation,

Figure 12-6. *Configuring advanced X.400 properties.*

which supports fewer features. If you do not select the Allow BP-15 option, only the BP-14 standard is used.

- **Allow MS Exchange contents** Microsoft Exchange supports the use of Extended MAPI-compliant clients, which in turn support such features as rich text format. Make sure that any foreign X.400 system to which you are connecting supports such features before you allow them to be transferred.

- **Two-way alternate** The two-way alternate specification is an X.400 standard in which two connected X.400 systems take turns transmitting and receiving information. If the foreign system to which you are connecting supports this option, enabling it can greatly improve transmission speed.

- **X.400 bodypart used for message text** This option specifies how message text should be formatted. Unless you are communicating with foreign systems that use foreign-language applications, leave this value at its default setting: International Alphabet 5 (IA5).

- **Use the GDI** The global domain identifier (GDI) is a section of the X.400 address space of the target system. The GDI is used to prevent message loops that can occur with outgoing messages. The administrator of the foreign X.400 system will let you know if you need to modify these values.

Connecting to Microsoft Mail Systems

The Microsoft Mail connector, provided by Exchange Server 5.5, enables messaging connectivity and Directory Synchronization between Exchange Server 5.5 and Microsoft Mail for PC Networks. The Microsoft Mail connector can be used over LAN, asynchronous, or X.25 connections. Microsoft Mail has a considerable history and has optional gateways to external messaging systems. Exchange Server can connect to an existing MS Mail system and utilize the existing gateways. The MS Mail connector was created to seamlessly integrate with MS Mail so that in a case where an MS Mail system is being migrated to Exchange, messaging migration is transparent to the users.

Configuring the Microsoft Mail connector is fairly straightforward, but before you learn how to configure it, you should spend a little time learning how it works.

Understanding the Microsoft Mail Connector

Microsoft Mail is a passive shared-file messaging system, meaning that it uses a centralized post office composed of shared folders on a network server. Each recipient on the Microsoft Mail system is given access to one of these folders. When one user sends mail to another, the client application formats the message and saves it to the recipient's shared folder. The recipient's client application regularly checks that folder to see whether any new messages have arrived.

When configuring the MS Mail connector, a shadow MS Mail post office is created on the Exchange Server. This means that the MS Mail system you are connecting to sees the Exchange Server as just another MS Mail system. It reduces the amount of effort needed to configure the connection, because no additional software is needed for MS Mail. The server where the MS Mail connector is created will add a service to NT that emulates the MS Mail EXTERNAL.EXE application. This application, and now the new NT service, moves messages between post offices. The NT service will move the messages between the shadow post office and the MS Mail system for which it is configured. (Figure 12-7)

Using the store-and-forward concept, Microsoft Mail uses the concept of downstream and upstream post offices. These are directional concepts for mail forwarding through intermediary post offices. If you configure a downstream post office, you select an indirect connection type and name the directly connected post office that would forward the mail through.

As you know, Exchange Server 5.5 is an active client/server messaging system. The Microsoft Mail connector enables the transfer of messages between these two

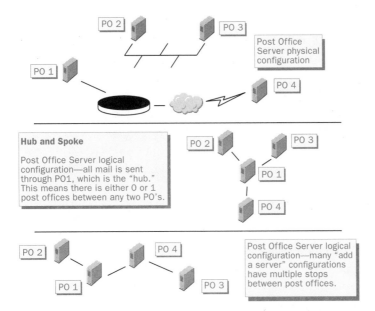

Figure 12-7. *MS Mail post office configurations.*

widely different types of systems. The Microsoft Mail connector has three components, which are necessary for Exchange's seamless integration with MS Mail. Each component provides a function that is similarly provided by an MS Mail system. For example, the Mail Connector Post Office is a "shadow" of a Microsoft Mail post office. The Mail Connector Interchange provides the same function as the EXTERNAL.EXE executable in Microsoft Mail. Finally, the Mail Connector (PC) MTA provides the message-transfer capabilities of a dedicated MS Mail MTA. These are the actual functions provided by these three components:

- **Mail Connector Post Office**   The Mail Connector Post Office serves as a temporary storage area for messages that are being transferred between Exchange Server 5.5 and a Microsoft Mail post office. The Mail Connector Post Office does not contain any actual recipient mailboxes; therefore, it is often referred to as a *shadow post office.*

- **Mail Connector Interchange**   The Mail Connector Interchange is a Windows NT service that provides routing of messages between Exchange Server 5.5 and the Mail Connector Post Office.

- **Mail Connector (PC) MTA**   The Mail Connector (PC) MTA is a Windows NT service that provides routing of messages between the Mail Connector Post Office on the Exchange Server and one actual Microsoft Mail post office. Only one Microsoft Mail connector can be configured on any given

Exchange Server, but each Microsoft Mail connector can connect to multiple actual Microsoft Mail post offices using separate Mail Connector (PC) MTAs for each MS Mail post office. One Mail Connector (PC) MTA exists on the Exchange Server for each post office to which the Microsoft Mail connector connects.

Whenever a message is sent from a user on a Microsoft Mail post office to a recipient on an Exchange Server, each of these three components is involved in the transfer. The Mail Connector (PC) MTA receives the message and places it in a queue in the Mail Connector Post Office. The Mail Connector Interchange polls the Mail Connector Post Office at regular intervals. When a message is present, the Mail Connector Interchange retrieves the message, converts it to Exchange format, and places it in the Exchange Server MTA's queue. The Exchange Server MTA routes the message to the Exchange recipient. When a message is sent from Exchange Server 5.5 to a Microsoft Mail post office, the same process is used but in reverse.

Configuring the Microsoft Mail Connector

The Microsoft Mail connector can be configured to work over a LAN connection or over a remote access service (RAS) asynchronous or X.25 connection. Only one Microsoft Mail connector can be configured on any given Exchange Server, but each connector can connect to multiple Microsoft Mail post offices.

You use Exchange Administrator to configure the Microsoft Mail connector. First, however, you must install the connector itself. If you installed Exchange Server 5.5 using the typical installation type, you are all set; the Microsoft Mail connector is already installed. Otherwise, you need to run Exchange Server 5.5 Setup again to add the Microsoft Mail connector to the installation.

Real World **Configuring a Microsoft Mail Post Office to Connect to Exchange**
On the other side of the system, the Microsoft Mail post office will need to be configured to "see" the new shadow post office on the Exchange Server. To configure this post office, you will follow these basic steps:

1. Open the ADMIN.EXE program and log in as an administrator.
2. Use the arrow keys to select the External Admin menu, and then press Enter.
3. Select the Create menu, and then press Enter.
4. The Enter Network Name prompt appears. You need to type the MS Mail network name that was configured for the shadow post office on Exchange here, and then press Enter.

5. The Enter Post Office Name prompt appears. Place the post office name created for the shadow post office on Exchange here, and then press Enter.

6. The Select Route Type prompt appears. Select Direct because you will not be routing mail through another MS Mail post office to get to the shadow post office. Then press Enter.

7. The Direct Connection Via prompt appears. Select how that connection will occur, and press Enter.

8. At the Create? prompt, select Yes, and press Enter. You can then press Escape until you are asked to quit and exit the program.

When the Microsoft Mail connector is installed, its configuration object appears in the Connections container for the appropriate site in Exchange Administrator, as shown in Figure 12-8. This container holds the configuration objects for each Microsoft Mail connector installed on the site. You configure a Microsoft Mail connector by using its property sheets, which you open in the usual manner.

Figure 12-8. *Viewing the connectors for a site.*

Interchange Property Sheet

Unlike most of the other objects that you configure, the Microsoft Mail connector opens to the Interchange property sheet instead of the General property sheet. The reason for this is that you must select an administrator's mailbox before configuring any other parameters on the connector. The Interchange property sheet, shown in Figure 12-9, basically lets you specify how the Microsoft Mail connector moves information between Exchange Server 5.5 and the Microsoft Mail post office.

Figure 12-9. *Configuring Interchange properties for the MS Mail connector.*

You can configure the following parameters on the Interchange property sheet:

- **Administrator's Mailbox**   The recipient designated in the Administrator's Mailbox field receives any delivery status messages associated with the connector, including any nondelivery reports (NDRs). You must configure an Exchange mailbox in this field before you can configure other parameters for the connector.

- **Primary Language For Clients**   Use the Primary Language For Clients drop-down menu to specify the primary language that the Microsoft Mail clients will use. The default language is English.

- **Maximize MS Mail 3.X Compatibility**   Microsoft Mail 3.X supports only the earliest versions of Object Linking and Embedding (OLE), the Microsoft standard for allowing applications to call the functions of other applications. An example of OLE functionality is embedding a fully functional Microsoft Excel spreadsheet in an e-mail message. When the Maximize MS Mail 3.X Compatibility option is enabled, the Microsoft Mail connector creates two versions of each OLE object — one using the older standards and the other using newer standards. Maximizing compatibility allows clients using Microsoft Mail 3.X to view OLE objects, but it can double the size of any message that uses OLE.

- **Enable Message Tracking**   When the Enable Message Tracking option is enabled, you can use the message-tracking utility in Exchange Administrator to track messages transferred between Exchange Server 5.5 and the Microsoft Mail post office. The message tracking utility is covered in Chapter 22.

- **MS Mail Connector (AppleTalk) MTA**   A version of Microsoft Mail is available for AppleTalk networks. Click this button to access configuration details for that MTA. For more information on using Microsoft Mail (AppleTalk), consult your product documentation.

General Property Sheet

The General property sheet, shown in Figure 12-10, is used to configure the size limit of messages that can be transferred via the Microsoft Mail connector. The Computer Name field shows the Exchange Server on which the Microsoft Mail connector is installed. This value cannot be changed.

Figure 12-10. *Setting a message size limit on the General property sheet.*

Connections Property Sheet

You use the Connections property sheet, shown in Figure 12-11, to set up the list of Microsoft Mail post offices that the Microsoft Mail connector will service. At first, the only post office listed is the Mail Connector Post Office, the shadow post office that is maintained on the Exchange Server.

To add a post office to the list, click Create. Clicking this button opens the Create Connection dialog box, shown in Figure 12-12. This dialog box allows you to configure the name and path of the Microsoft Mail post office to which you want to connect. In addition, the dialog box allows you to specify the type of connection: LAN, async, indirect, or X.25. By default, the Microsoft Mail

Figure 12-11. *Viewing the MS Mail post offices serviced by the MS Mail connector.*

connector attempts to deliver a message to the post office three times before generating an NDR. You can change this value by changing the setting in the Connection Attempts field.

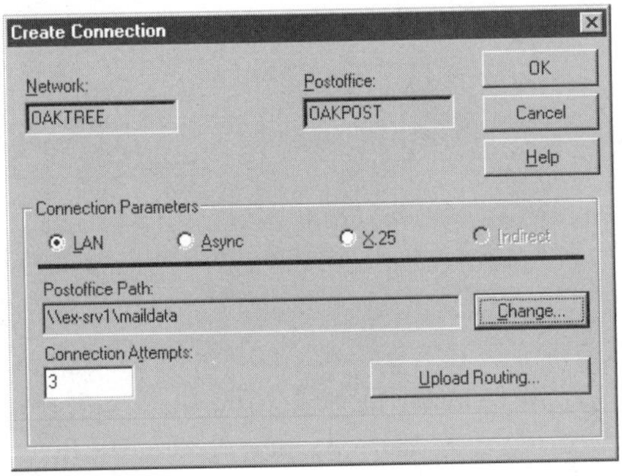

Figure 12-12. *Creating the connection to an MS Mail post office.*

Connector MTAs Property Sheet

The Connector MTAs property sheet, shown in Figure 12-13, is used to create a connector MTA to transfer messages between the shadow post office and the

Microsoft Mail post office. You must create one connector MTA for each Microsoft Mail post office to which you want to connect.

Figure 12-13. *Creating a connector MTA.*

To create a new connector MTA, click New. Clicking this button opens the New MS Mail Connector (PC) MTA Service dialog box, shown in Figure 12-14.

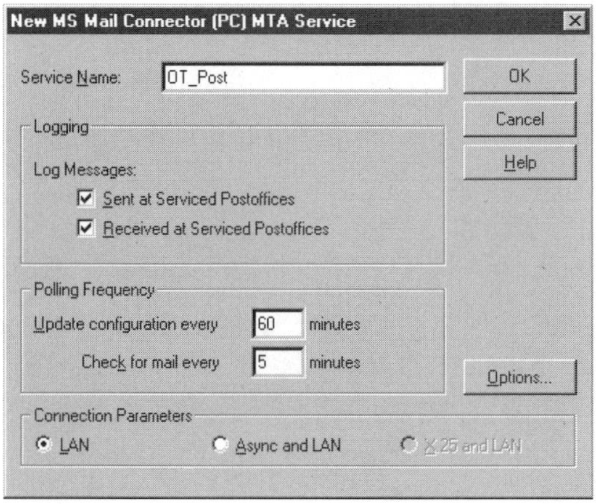

Figure 12-14. *Configuring the connector MTA Service.*

You can configure several parameters in this dialog box:

- **Service Name**   The Service Name is the name of the new Connector MTA service that you are creating. You should use a name that designates the Microsoft Mail post office that the connector MTA will service.

- **Log Messages**   You can elect to create a log of messages transferred over the new connector MTA. You can individually log sent and received messages. This option can be valuable when you are setting up an MTA for the first time and want to make sure that the connection is working as it should. This option can also be valuable in troubleshooting the connector or in gauging the connector's performance.

- **Polling Frequency**   This option has two settings. The Check For Mail Every field specifies how often the MTA should check for new messages in the shadow post office. The Update Configuration Every field specifies how often the MTA checks for changes to information that you configure using the Options button, as shown in Figure 12-15. This information includes:

  - **Maximum LAN Message Size**   This value represents the maximum size, in kilobytes (KB), that can be transferred over the MTA via a LAN connection.

  - **Free Disk Space**   You can elect to have all transfers to and from the shadow post office stop automatically when the available free disk space on your MS Mail post office reaches a specified level. When the shadow post office closes, new messages cannot be sent until free disk space falls back within specified levels.

  - **NetBIOS Notification**   When the NetBIOS Notification option is enabled, MS Mail users can be notified of new messages via a pop-up window.

  - **Disable Mailer**   The Disable Mailer option prevents the MTA from transferring messages between the Microsoft Mail post office and the shadow post office.

  - **Disable Mail Dispatch**   The Disable Mail Dispatch option stops the MTA from distributing any Directory-Synchronization messages. Directory Synchronization is covered later in this chapter.

  - **Startup**   The Startup option specifies whether MTA service starts automatically or must be started manually by an administrator.

- **Connection Parameters**   Use the Connection Parameters setting to specify whether the MTA should connect over LAN, async, or X.25. This setting overrides any setting made for the Microsoft Mail connector itself on the Connections property sheet.

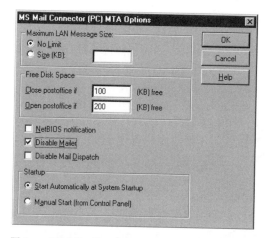

Figure 12-15. *Configuring optional connection parameters for the connector MTA.*

Local Postoffice Property Sheet

The Local Postoffice property sheet, shown in Figure 12-16, is used to configure the Mail Connector Post Office, or the shadow post office. You can set the name of the network (by default the Exchange organization), the name of the post office itself, and a logon password, if you are using RAS to connect. If you change any information on this property sheet, you must click the Regenerate button to rebuild the list of MS Mail addresses for the site.

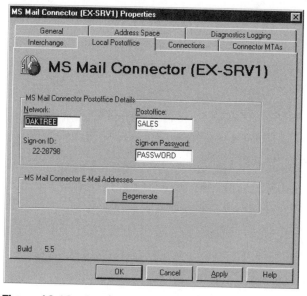

Figure 12-16. *Configuring the shadow post office on the Exchange Server.*

After you configure the information on these property sheets, the Exchange side of the configuration for the Microsoft Mail connector is complete. All you have to do is start the new MTA service and your shadow post office will be on line and ready to go. The new service will be identifiable in the Services Control Panel applet by whatever name you gave the service on the connector MTA's property sheet. Your next step is to go to the Microsoft Mail post offices to which you configured connections and set up external post office entries for the shadow post office. The next step in setting up the MS Mail connector is to send a test e-mail from both the MS Mail and Exchange sides of your mail system.

Configuring Directory Synchronization

After you create the Microsoft Mail connector and configure your Microsoft Mail post offices, message transfer between your Exchange organization and your Microsoft Mail system is enabled. Something is still missing, however. Although users can send messages between systems, users on one system have no access to the Directory information of the other system. Instead, they are required to know each MS Mail address for the recipient (from each side because the Exchange Server acts as a shadow MS Mail post office), and they must specifically address e-mail. To solve this problem, you must configure Directory Synchronization between the two messaging systems.

Note Don't get Directory Synchronization confused with Directory Replication. *Directory Replication* is the replication of the Exchange Directory between Exchange Servers. *Directory synchronization* is the Synchronization of Directory information between an Exchange Server and a foreign messaging system.

Microsoft Mail native Directory Synchronization is exceptionally complex because of MS Mail's file-based systems. MS Mail uses a program called DISPATCH.EXE, which is usually run on a separate machine, along with the EXTERNAL.EXE program. Dispatch, in turn, launches a program called NSDA. NSDA further launches REQMAIN and SRVMAIN. This cascade of programs is confusing; however, it is used for specific reasons. The External program gives the ability to connect to external post offices as configured for that MS Mail post office. Dispatch schedules the connections to those external post offices for Directory Synchronization. NSDA handles Directory Synchronization by running REQMAIN to request the main Directory from the other post office and SRVMAIN to send the local directory to the other post office.

Note Remember that MS Mail was initially written in the mid 1980s, when systems performed Dirsync and had external 33MHz 80286 chips with MS-DOS and 1MB of RAM. A process that seems overly complex now was the only way to get the job done without a minicomputer.

In a Microsoft Mail messaging environment, each Microsoft Mail post office maintains a directory of information about the recipients whose mailboxes exist in that post office. When a network has multiple post offices, a process called Dirsync synchronizes the Directory information between post offices. On the Microsoft Mail network, one post office is set up as a Dirsync server. All other post offices are set up as Dirsync requestors. Three timed events used by the NSDA program, called T1, T2, and T3, govern the synchronization of directory information between the Dirsync requestors and the Dirsync server. Here's how the process works:

1. At the T1 event, every Dirsync requestor on the network sends any changes made to its current Directory information to the Dirsync server. The T1 event fires on all post offices.

2. At the T2 event, the Dirsync server starts a process called DISPATCH.EXE, which in turn starts other processes that combine the Directory information from all Dirsync requestors and the Dirsync server into a Global Address List. The Dirsync server then sends that list back to the Dirsync requestors. The T2 event fires only on the Dirsync server post office.

3. At the T3 event, each Dirsync requestor rebuilds its own Global Address List, based on the new Directory information from the Dirsync server. After these three events occur, all post offices on the network use a common address list. The T3 event fires on all post offices.

When you set up the Microsoft Mail connector, a shadow post office called the Mail Connector Post Office is created on the Exchange Server. This shadow post office can be configured to act as either a Dirsync server or a Dirsync requestor. Unless you are building a new Dirsync system and want to use Exchange Server 5.5 as the Dirsync server, you should set up Exchange Server 5.5 as a Dirsync requestor on your current system.

Real World   Preparing for Directory Synchronization

In the pages of a book such as this one, configuring Directory Synchronization between Exchange Server 5.5 and an existing Microsoft Mail network can seem to be a fairly easy task—and in theory, it is. In the real world, however, things don't always go so smoothly. Often, existing Microsoft Mail networks are unplanned, undocumented beasts that slowly grow over the years in such a way that nobody has a clear idea of how they are set up.

Whether you are implementing a coexisting Exchange organization and Microsoft Mail network or planning a migration, take the time to thoroughly document and clean up your existing Microsoft Mail network. This effort will make it much easier to configure, maintain, and troubleshoot message transport and Directory Synchronization. The following are a few suggestions to get you started.

- Document the current Microsoft Mail network. Identify all the existing post offices, including the users of those post offices.

- Document the current Directory Synchronization topology. Where is the Dirsync server? Which post offices are requestors?

- Have users clean up their existing Microsoft Mail post offices if you plan to migrate messages to Exchange Server 5.5.

- Resolve any outstanding problems on the Microsoft Mail network, ensuring that Directory Synchronization works correctly, before you configure the Microsoft Mail connector in Exchange Server 5.5.

Real World   Configuring Exchange Server 5.5 as a Dirsync Requestor
Setting up Exchange Server 5.5 as a Dirsync requestor is quite simple. In Exchange Administrator, choose New Other Dirsync Requestor command from the File menu. This command opens the New Requestor dialog box, shown in Figure 12-17. This dialog box lists the available Dirsync servers on the network.

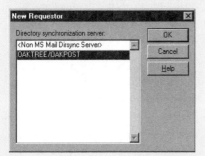

Figure 12-17. *Creating a new Dirsync requestor.*

Remember that even though you can have only one Dirsync server on a given Microsoft Mail network, you can have several Microsoft Mail networks on a given physical network. Select the server for which you want to create a requestor, and click OK. The property sheets for the new Dirsync requestor open.

General Property Sheet   The General property sheet, shown in Figure 12-18, allows you to define basic properties about the new Dirsync requestor.

On this property sheet you can configure the following parameters:

- **Name**   This setting is the name of the new Dirsync requestor. You should use a name that indicates the server on which the requestor is installed and the name of the Microsoft Mail network — for example, *server_name (dirsync) network_name*.

Figure 12-18. *Configuring the General properties of the new Dirsync requestor.*

- **Append To Imported Users' Display Name**   When this option is selected, the requestor name is added after each custom recipient that is created by the Dirsync process. This can be very useful in identifying recipients created by a specific requestor.

- **Dirsync Address**   This option specifies the custom recipient that receives Directory Synchronization messages. By default, the Dirsync Address is set to a hidden administrator's mailbox, $SYSTEM, on the Dirsync server.

- **Address Types**   Use the Address Types section to specify which address types the new Dirsync requestor will submit to the Dirsync server during synchronization.

- **Requestor Language**   Use the Requestor Language option to specify the language version used by the Dirsync requestor. The Dirsync server uses this information in formatting the address lists that it sends back to the requestor.

- **Server**   Use the Server drop-down menu to specify the Exchange Server on the site that will act as the Dirsync requestor. The default selection is the server to which Exchange Administrator was connected when you created the requestor.

Import Container Property Sheet   The Import Container property sheet, shown in Figure 12-19, is used to define the Recipient container on the Dirsync requestor where addresses that are imported from the Dirsync server should be stored. This option is available only while you are creating the requestor; after the requestor is created, you cannot change the Recipient container. You can also specify a trust level to be assigned to any new recipients that are generated and placed in this container, a process that is explained in the following section.

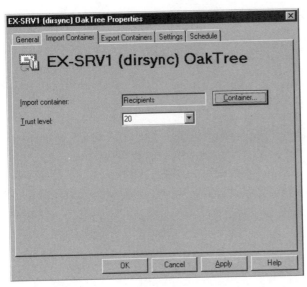

Figure 12-19. *Specifying an Import container for the Dirsync requestor.*

Export Containers Property Sheet   The Export Containers property sheet, shown in Figure 12-20, specifies the Recipient container whose recipients should be exported to the Dirsync server during the T1 event. Available Recipient containers are shown in the list on the left side of the property sheet. Selected Export containers are shown in the list on the right side of the property sheet. You can move containers between these two lists by clicking the Add and Remove buttons. You can also set a trust level for the recipient export. During synchronization, only recipients whose trust level is equal to or below the trust level of the requestor are exported to the Dirsync server.

Settings Property Sheet   The Settings property sheet, shown in Figure 12-21, is used to specify various settings that govern the new Dirsync requestor.

You can alter these settings on this property sheet:

- **Dirsync Password**   You can set a password on a Dirsync server to prevent unauthorized access to the system. If such a password is in effect, you must enter the password in the Dirsync Password field.

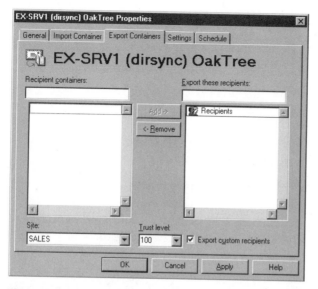

Figure 12-20. *Configuring the Export containers for the Dirsync requestor.*

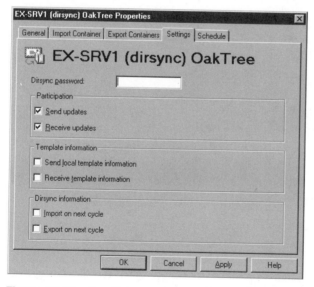

Figure 12-21. *Specifying settings in the new Dirsync requestor.*

- **Participation** You can specify individually whether the Dirsync requestor sends updated Directory information to the Dirsync server, receives updated information, or both. This feature can be useful if you have a great deal of Directory information being transferred. You can actually set up separate Exchange Servers to receive and send Directory information.

- **Template Information**   If your Microsoft Mail post offices use address templates, you can use these options to import Microsoft Mail templates and export Exchange Server 5.5 templates. Templates allow users of one system to manually enter the addresses of the users on the other system on an ad hoc basis when they create new messages.

- **Dirsync Information**   Use these options to force the Dirsync requestor to perform both an import and an export of every address available on the Dirsync server during the next T1 and T3 events. Select these options for the first time your new requestor enters the Dirsync cycle.

The final property sheet you will need to configure is the Schedule property sheet. Two Dirsync events, T1 and T3, are important for every Dirsync requestor. The Schedule property sheet allows you to configure the time at which the T1 event is fired. The T1 event is when the requestor sends updates to the Dirsync server. By default, this happens once each night. You do not need to configure a schedule for the T3 event for an Exchange Server 5.5 Dirsync requestor because updates are dynamically committed to the Directory as soon as they reach the requestor.

When you finish configuring these property sheets, your Exchange Server 5.5 will be set up as a Dirsync requestor. You then need to configure the Dirsync server on the Microsoft Mail network with information about the new requestor. For more information on this procedure, refer to your Microsoft Mail product documentation.

Setting Up Exchange Server 5.5 as a Dirsync Server

Configuring Exchange Server 5.5 as a Dirsync server is even easier than configuring it as a Dirsync requestor. Three steps are involved in configuring Exchange Server 5.5 as a Dirsync server:

1. Use Exchange Administrator to configure a *Dirsync Server* object for the Exchange site.

2. Configure a *Remote Dirsync Requestor* object in Exchange Administrator for each remote Dirsync requestor on the Microsoft Mail network.

3. Configure the remote Dirsync requestors to use the new Dirsync server.

The following sections cover the first two steps of this process. For the third step, refer to your Microsoft Mail product documentation.

Configure a Dirsync Server Object in Exchange Administrator   To configure a Dirsync Server object, choose New Other Dirsync Server from the File menu of Exchange Administrator. This command opens the Dirsync Server property sheets, shown in Figure 12-22.

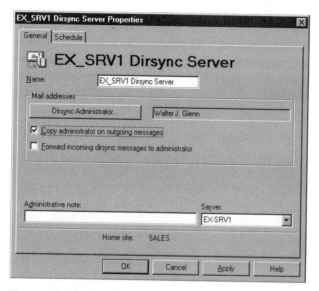

Figure 12-22. *Configuring the Dirsync Server object in Exchange Administrator.*

As you can see, there is much less to configure for the Dirsync server than for the Dirsync requestor. The Schedule property sheet is identical to the Schedule property sheets that you have grown used to by now. The Schedule property sheet is used to define times at which the Dirsync server sends master address list updates to remote Dirsync requestors — otherwise known as the T2 event.

The General property sheet is used to configure several parameters:

- **Name**   This setting is both the display name and the Directory name of the Dirsync server. You should use a name that includes the name of the Exchange Server on which the Dirsync server is being installed.

- **Dirsync Administrator**   Click the Dirsync Administrator button to designate a mailbox to which synchronization status messages should be sent.

- **Copy Administrator On Outgoing Messages**   When this option is selected, all outgoing synchronization messages from the Dirsync server are copied to the Dirsync administrator's mailbox during the T2 event. Enabling this option often results in a large number of messages in the administrator's mailbox, but the messages are useful in troubleshooting problems with synchronization.

- **Forward Incoming Dirsync Messages To Administrator** When this option is selected, all incoming messages from Dirsync requestors are forwarded to the Dirsync administrator's mailbox during the T1 event. Again, this option can be a valuable aid in troubleshooting synchronization problems.

- **Server** Use the Server drop-down menu to select the Exchange Server that will act as a Dirsync server. By default, the server selected is the one to which Exchange Administrator was connected when you created the Dirsync server.

Configure a Remote Dirsync Requestor Object in Exchange Administrator For each remote Dirsync requestor on the Microsoft Mail network that will be serviced by the new Dirsync server, you must configure a Remote Dirsync Requestor object in Exchange Administrator. To create the Remote Dirsync Requestor object, choose New Other, and then select Remote Dirsync Requestor from the File menu of Exchange Administrator.

The process that you use to configure the remote Dirsync requestor is virtually identical to the process that you use to configure Exchange Server 5.5 as a Dirsync requestor, so refer to that section earlier in this chapter for details.

After you create a remote Dirsync Requestor object for each Dirsync requestor on the Microsoft Mail network, remember to configure the actual Dirsync requestors themselves.

Note Setting up a peaceful coexistence between an Exchange organization and a Microsoft Mail network involves more detail than a single chapter can provide. You can find additional valuable information on coexistence and migration issues in *Deploying Exchange Server 5.5* (1998) in the *Notes from the Field Series* from Microsoft Press.

Summary

You have now learned most of what you need to know about setting up Exchange communications. You have installed an Exchange Server, creating a site and an organization in the process. You have examined how communications take place between Exchange Servers on the same site. You have configured various types of messaging connectors between different Exchange sites so that users can transfer messages. You have also configured Directory Replication between sites by using the Directory Replication connector. In this chapter, you also learned how to configure Exchange Server 5.5 to transfer messages and synchronize Directory data with foreign messaging systems.

In the next chapter, you will learn how to configure public folders and public folder replication in an Exchange organization.

Chapter 13
Public Folders

Sharing information is a powerful method of facilitation for workgroups and teams. If that information can be shared in geographically distant locations, it is even more important. Microsoft Exchange Server 5.5 offers that powerful groupware foundation upon which to build through its implementation of public folders.

In this chapter, we start looking at the shared storage architecture of an Exchange Server system. We explore how a user views shared storage and how to implement public folders, and we discover how to implement collaborative applications to create a systematic groupware structure. Exchange Server has many fascinating components, but when you understand the impact of sharing information, the knowledge simply follows how to take advantage of those components all together.

Microsoft Exchange Server 5.5 is a robust messaging system that allows users to exchange electronic messages by using a variety of methods. Chapter 9 covered the creation and management of three of the four basic types of Exchange recipients: mailboxes, distribution lists, and custom recipients. This chapter covers the fourth type of recipient: the public folder.

This chapter describes how public folders are created, managed, replicated, stored, and accessed in an Exchange organization.

Understanding Public Folder Storage

Public folders are wonderful things; they provide centralized storage of virtually any type of document or message and allow controlled access by any user in the organization. Public folders provide the basis of workflow applications for Exchange Server 5.5.

Although most of the administration of Exchange is conducted in the Exchange Administrator application, public folders are somewhat different. The Exchange Administrator can administer the properties (not the content) of any public folder, and the public folder is the only place where the Public Information Store, which contains public folders, is administered. The Exchange client, however, is used when a public folder is created and a user can administer the public folder properties and content. Because public folders are used for workflow applications, and because most users work solely in the Exchange client (Outlook), the administration of public folders was developed to reflect the application with which a user works.

When you create a public folder using an Exchange client, that folder is created in the Public Information Store of a particular Exchange Server, which is often referred to as that folder's home server. Any Exchange Server that has a Public Information Store can host a public folder. In a typical organization, some folders exist on one server, others on another server, and so on. When a user creates a top-level public folder, it is placed in the Public Information Store on that user's home server. When a user creates a lower-level public folder, it is placed in the Public Information Store of that new folder's parent folder. In addition, each individual public folder can be replicated to other servers in the organization. As you can see, this situation can get complicated. Public folders exist on different servers, and some public folders have instances on multiple servers.

To ensure that information about public folders is distributed throughout the Exchange system, the Directory Service maintains a public folder hierarchy, which is a single hierarchical structure that contains information about all the public folders in an organization. This hierarchy is automatically replicated to every server in the organization during normal Directory Replication.

A public folder is considered to have two parts. The first part is the public folder content—the actual messages inside the public folder. The second part is that folder's place in the organization-wide public folder hierarchy. The contents of a public folder exist on a single server, unless you specifically configure the content to be replicated to other servers. The public folder hierarchy, on the other hand, is automatically replicated to every server in the organization during normal Directory Replication.

Real World   Dedicated Public Folder Servers

Some administrators prefer to use dedicated public folder servers. A *dedicated public folder server* is one from which the Privat Information Store has been removed. Dedicated public folder servers are useful in large organizations in which large amounts of public data and frequent access to that data consume a great deal of server resources. To use dedicated public folder servers in your organization, follow these steps:

1. Decide which servers you want to be your dedicated public folder servers.

2. Remove the Private Information Store from your chosen dedicated public folder servers. To do so, simply find the Server container for the appropriate

server in Exchange Administrator and delete the *Private Information Store* configuration object. Be careful deleting the Private Information Store from existing servers; any mailboxes in the store will also be deleted.

3. Remove the *Public Information Store configuration* object from all your organization's servers that will not host public folders. To do so, delete the *Public Information Store* configuration object from the Server container. If the Public Information Store you want to remove already holds public folders, you must make sure that current replicas of those folders exist on other servers before deletion.

4. Run Performance Optimizer on each of the servers on which you have made changes, to optimize the servers' configuration.

When you finish these steps, you are ready to create your public folders.

Creating Public Folders in Microsoft Outlook

You can create public folders only by using an Exchange client — Microsoft Outlook, Microsoft Exchange Client, or Microsoft Outlook Web Client. This section confines its discussion to Microsoft Outlook. The procedure for creating a public folder with other clients is roughly the same.

Figure 13-1 shows the main Microsoft Outlook window, with the folder list displayed and the public folders item expanded.

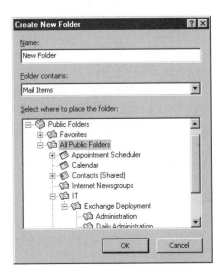

Figure 13-1. *Expanded Public Folders container in Outlook.*

To create a public folder, ensure that the All Public Folders object (or the folder where you want to create it) is selected, choose New, and then select Folder from the File menu. The Create New Folder dialog box opens (Figure 13-2). Enter the name of the public folder that you want to create, select the folder in which it should be created, and click OK. That's all there is to it.

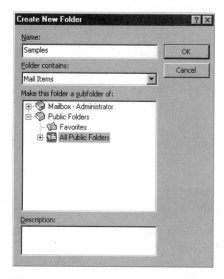

Figure 13-2. *Creating a public folder is as easy as naming it and choosing where it goes.*

Real World   Subscribing to List Services

A list service is similar to a newsgroup, but differs in that it is run completely within e-mail. Each subscriber receives a copy of each other subscriber's comments in his or her own Inbox. As long as your Exchange Server has access to a list service server via Simple Mail Transport Protocol (SMTP), which is offered within the Internet Mail Service, you can subscribe a public folder to mailing lists. To successfully do this, you will need permissions to add a public folder from the Exchange client. You will also need to be assigned the Exchange Permissions Admin role.

In Exchange, each folder acts as a recipient and stores information in the form of messages, just like a mailbox. A public folder has an e-mail address and can be subscribed to a mailing list, just like any other recipient.

First, you need to create the public folder, which must be done from the client (Exchange Client or Microsoft Outlook), following the procedure you have just learned. When the Create New Folder dialog box appears, you should place a name in the top field for the new folder. The second drop-down menu lets you set the type of messages that can be posted in this folder. You can create folders for appointment items, notes, tasks, and mail items. The default item type you see in this box is whatever type of item that can be posted in the parent folder. The bottom portion of the dialog box shows the hierarchy where you can select the location for the folder, which may be necessary if you selected a different folder than the one you wanted to be the parent of the new folder.

Once the folder is created, open Exchange Administrator. Open the Folders container, and select the folder that you just created in the client. Next, press Alt-Enter to see the public folder's property sheets. Select the Permissions tab and add yourself with the Send As permission. Check the SMTP address of the folder on the E-Mail Addresses tab and write it down. Next, select the Advanced tab and clear the Hide From Address Book option.

Go back to the Exchange client, and create a new message to the list service to which the public folder will subscribe. You will need to view the From field of the message box, so select the View menu and click From Field. Place into the From field the e-mail address for the public folder that you wrote down. The list service may include instructions on what to place in the contents of the message. A typical content will be SUBSCRIBE FOLDER, where FOLDER represents the name from which you want responses to the list service to be shown. The list service should respond with a welcome message or a request for a confirmation message.

Now that the public folder is successfully subscribed to the list service, you can hide the public folder from the address book. It was only unhidden to ensure that the e-mail address would be resolved the first time that the list service responded.

Managing Public Folders in Outlook

After you create a public folder, you can configure it in several ways. The management of a public folder occurs in two places: Outlook and Exchange Administrator. Because users can create public folders, it is advantageous to allow them certain managerial responsibilities, which is why part of the management occurs in the client.

When a user creates a public folder, that user automatically becomes the folder's owner. The owner is responsible for the folder's basic design, which includes access permissions, rules, and the association of electronic forms. To perform this management, the user can simply open the property sheets for a particular public folder in Outlook. Public folders can also be managed to a degree from within the Exchange Administrator, but the Outlook option means that the user has a single application with which to be concerned.

General Property Sheet

The General property sheet of a public folder, shown in Figure 13-3, allows you to change the name of a public folder and enter an optional description of that folder. You can also choose the name of an electronic form that should be used to post new items to the folder. By default, the generic Post form is selected. For more information on creating and using electronic forms, see Chapter 24.

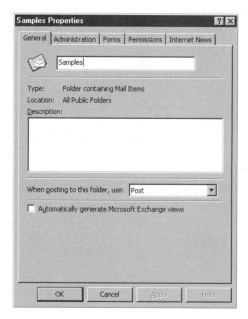

Figure 13-3. *Configuring the General properties of a public folder in Outlook.*

Finally, you can specify that Exchange Client views of the folder be generated automatically. Exchange Client and Outlook process forms in different ways. This option provides compatibility in Exchange Client for folders created in Outlook.

Administration Property Sheet

You use the Administration property sheet, shown in Figure 13-4, to set various parameters governing a public folder's use.

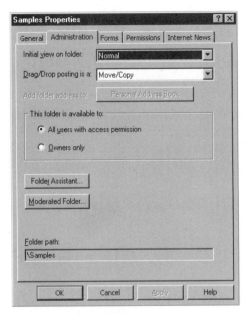

Figure 13-4. *Configuring Administrative properties for a public folder with Outlook.*

The parameters on this property sheet include the following:

- **Initial View On Folder**   This option specifies the initial Outlook view that is used whenever the public folder is opened. Views include the default Normal threaded view as well as views grouped by discussion subject, topic, and poster.

- **Drag/Drop Posting Is A**   This option simply defines what happens when an item is dragged into a public folder. Options include Move/Copy and Forward.

- **This Folder Is Available To**   This selection allows you to specify whether the folder is accessible by anyone who has appropriate permissions or only by folder owners.

- **Folder Assistant**   The Folder Assistant lets you create rules that apply to new items placed in the folder. Rules include such actions as automatically replying to or rejecting messages based on the posting user or subject. For more information on using rules, see Chapter 19.

- **Moderated Folder** A *moderated folder* is one for which newly posted items must be approved by a moderator before being made available to the public. Click this button to configure the folder's moderators. If you choose to use moderated folders, keep in mind that users' posts to the folders will not immediately appear. For this reason, you may want to configure an automatic reply to messages posted to moderated folders, letting users know that the moderator has received their messages.

Forms Property Sheet

The Forms property sheet, shown in Figure 13-5, allows you to specify forms that can be used in conjunction with a public folder. The forms specified on this property sheet make up the choices for the default form specified on the General property sheet (refer back to Figure 13-3). You can also manage any associated form from this property sheet.

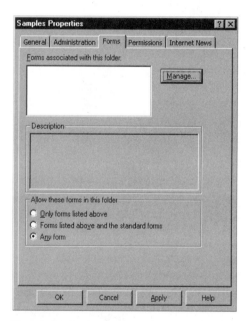

Figure 13-5. *Associating forms with a folder in Outlook.*

Note Much of this section's discussion of folder management in Outlook may seem cursory. This is because much of the discussion revolves around the association of electronic forms with public folders. Part VI of this book (Chapters 23–27) is dedicated to the subject of creating applications in Exchange Server 5.5. The chapters in that part cover the creation, association, and management of forms in detail.

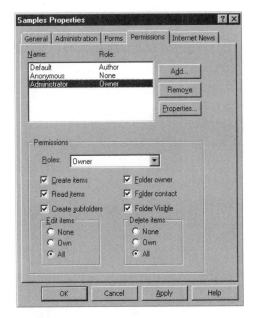

Figure 13-6. *Assigning access permissions to a public folder.*

Permissions Property Sheet

The Permissions property sheet, shown in Figure 13-6, allows you to specify users and their assigned permissions on the current public folder.

Each user can be assigned one of several roles. Each role has a set of associated permissions. The available permissions are as follows:

- **Create Items**   The user can post items in the folder.
- **Read Items**   The user can open any item in the folder.
- **Create Subfolders**   The user can create subfolders within the folder.
- **Edit Items**   The user can edit items in the folder. The None option indicates that a user cannot edit items. The All option indicates that a user can edit any item in the folder. The Own option indicates that the user can edit only items that he or she created.
- **Folder Owner**   The user is granted all permissions in the folder, including the ability to assign permissions.
- **Folder Contact**   The user receives copies of any status messages regarding the folder, including nondelivery reports.
- **Folder Visible**   The user can see the folder in the public folder hierarchy.

- **Delete Items** The user can delete items in the folder. The None option indicates that a user cannot delete items. The All option indicates that a user can delete any item in the folder. The Own option indicates that the user can delete only items that he or she created.

The permissions associated with any given role can be modified. Table 13-1 shows the available roles and the default permissions granted for each role.

Table 13-1. Public Folder Roles and Their Associated Default Permissions

Role	Create	Read	Edit	Delete	Subfolders	Owner	Contact	Visible
Owner	Yes	Yes	All	All	Yes	Yes	Yes	Yes
Publishing editor	Yes	Yes	All	All	Yes	No	No	Yes
Editor	Yes	Yes	All	All	No	No	No	Yes
Publishing author	Yes	Yes	Own	Own	Yes	No	No	Yes
Author	Yes	Yes	Own	Own	No	No	No	Yes
Nonediting author	Yes	Yes	None	Own	No	No	No	Yes
Reviewer	No	Yes	None	None	No	No	No	Yes
Contributor	Yes	No	None	None	No	No	No	Yes
None	No	No	None	None	No	No	No	Yes

The configuration of public folders that we have covered in this section is all accomplished using the Outlook client. The next section covers the configuration of public folders in Exchange Administrator.

Note One other property sheet, the Internet News property sheet, is involved in management of public folders in Outlook. That property sheet is covered in Chapter 14, which discusses publishing public folder content to the Internet.

Managing Public Folders in Exchange Administrator

You manage public folders on three levels within Exchange Administrator. At the site level, you specify general parameters for how a site's information stores handle public folders. At the server level, you specify how the Public Information Store for a server handles public folders. At the level of the public folder itself, you specify properties that govern that folder.

Managing Public Folders at the Site Level

To manage public folders at the site level, you use the *Information Store Site Configuration* object, which is located in the Configuration container of each site. The properties of public folders that you manage at this level govern the behavior of the Information Store Service on every server on the site. You access these properties through the property sheets of the *Information Store Site Configuration* object.

Setting the Public Folder Container for a Site

The General property sheet, shown in Figure 13-7, allows you to specify the Recipient container in which newly created public folders are placed. The default choice is the Recipients container for the site, but you can select any Recipient container. You can also enable message tracking, a feature that allows you to use Exchange Administrator to track any messages sent on a site. This feature is covered in Chapter 20.

Figure 13-7. *Specifying the Recipients container for public folders on a site.*

Creating Top-Level Folders

Top-level folders are those folders at the top of the public folder hierarchy. By default, all users can create top-level public folders. Those folders are placed on the user's public folder server, which typically is that user's home server.

Many administrators prefer to restrict the creation of top-level folders, for a very good reason. All subfolders created within a top-level folder are created on the same server that holds the top-level folder in which they are created. By restricting the creation of top-level folders to specified users, you can ensure that public folders are created only where you want them to be.

The Top Level Folder Creation property sheet, shown in Figure 13-8, lets you specify which users can and cannot create top-level folders.

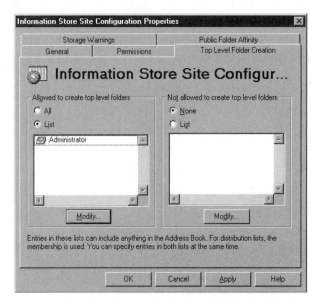

Figure 13-8. *Specifying which users can and cannot create top-level folders.*

This property sheet contains two lists. The list on the left specifies users that can create top-level folders. By default, all users have this permission. If you add even one name to this list, all other users in the site are implicitly prevented from creating top-level folders. The list on the right specifies users that cannot create top-level folders. By default, this list is set to none, meaning that no users are specifically denied the ability to create top-level folders.

Real World   Restricting Top-Level Folder Creation
There is another very good reason to give only a few users permission to create top-level folders: If too many users can create top-level folders, the public folder hierarchy can quickly grow unwieldy. By limiting permission to create top-level folders, you can define organized public folder categories into which new public folders must be placed when users create them.

Note This section does not cover two of the property sheets for the *Information Store Site Configuration* object: Public Folder Affinity and Storage Warnings. The Storage Warnings property sheet is used to set the times at which warnings are sent to users who have exceeded their storage limits. The

Public Folder Affinity property sheet, which points to the places from which you want a public folder to be read, is covered later in this chapter, in the section that discusses how to set up intersite public folder access.

Managing Public Folders at the Server Level

At the server level, you manage the behavior of public folders on a server by using the property sheets for the *Public Information Store* object, which are located within the container for a particular server. Most of these property sheets are used to govern public folder replication (discussed in detail later in this chapter) or to monitor use of public folders (discussed in Chapter 20). Two property sheets, the General property sheet and the Age Limits property sheet, are used for more general purposes in management of public folders.

General Property Sheet

Exchange Server 5.5 supports a welcome new feature called Deleted Item Recovery. When a user deletes a message from a folder, that message is marked as hidden and is actually retained for a certain number of days before being permanently deleted. Within that period, known as *deleted-item retention time*, the user can recover the item. To do so, however, the user must be using Outlook 8.03 or a later version.

You set deleted-item retention time on the General property sheet of the *Public Information Store* object, shown in Figure 13-9. Simply set the number of days that you want to allow for deleted items to be recovered. The default setting is 15. In addition, you can specify that items not be permanently removed from the information store until at least one backup has occurred.

You can also use the General property sheet to set a storage limit for public folders on a server. This storage limit represents a size (in kilobytes) that the public folders on a server can reach before a storage warning is issued to the folders' contacts. You can override the storage limit set at the server level for individual folders, as you see a bit later in the chapter.

Age Limits Property Sheet

Public folders can grow quite large and unmanageable if they are left unchecked. Fortunately, Exchange Server 5.5 allows you to configure a maximum age limit for items in public folders. At the server level, the Age Limits property sheet, shown in Figure 13-10, allows you to configure the maximum age that messages in all public folders on a server can reach before they are removed. By default, no age limit is set. You can override any age limit set at the server level for individual public folders.

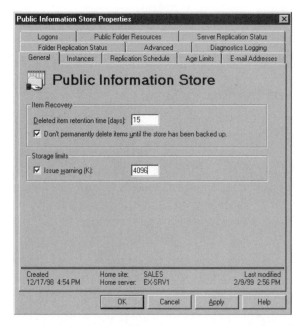

Figure 13-9. *Setting deleted-item retention time and storage limits for a public folder.*

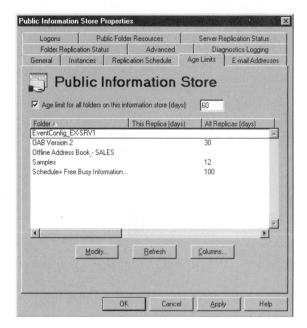

Figure 13-10. *Setting age limits for the public folders on a server.*

Note Although age limits make sense for folders that have time-sensitive data, such as an internal classified ads folder or a newsfeed from the Internet, they should be used with caution because most Exchange users expect to be able to retrieve their data. Public folder age limits work in combination with deleted-item retention time. Suppose that you set a 20-day age limit on your public folders and a 10-day deleted-item retention period. An item is deleted on day 19—one day before it would automatically expire. The deleted-item retention period starts at this point. If the item is recovered within the deleted-item retention period, the age limit for the newly recovered item is reset to add 20 more days.

Managing Public Folders at the Folder Level

Public folders can also be managed in Exchange Administrator on a folder-by-folder basis. Every public folder has a Configuration object within Exchange Administrator. You can find these objects in several places:

- **In the site-level Recipients container in which they were created** By default, public folder objects are created in the Recipients container on a site. Also by default, public folders are hidden from view in the address book. Use the View Hidden command on the View menu of Exchange Administrator to view hidden objects. You will learn how to make a folder visible later in this section.

- **In the Global AddressList** All recipient objects are located in the Global Address List, although the same note about folder visibility in the Recipient container applies to the Global Address List.

- **In the Folders container** The Folders container in Exchange Administrator displays the complete public folder hierarchy for an organization and is probably the easiest place to manage your public folders.

No matter where you manage public folders in Exchange Administrator, you do so by using the property sheets for the public folder object. Some of these property sheets deal only with public folder replication, which is covered later in this chapter. The property sheets that are used for more general public folder management are covered in this section.

General Property Sheet

The General property sheet, shown in Figure 13-11, defines some basic properties of the public folder.

These properties include the following:

- **Public Folder Name** This setting is the name as it appears in Exchange Administrator.

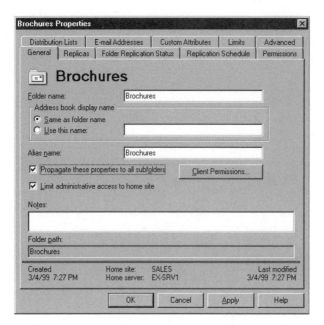

Figure 13-11. *Configuring basic properties for a public folder.*

- **Address Book Display Name** You can also give the public folder a name that will appear in the address book, if you want it to be different from the primary public folder name.

- **Alias Name** The Alias name is used to address messages posted in the folder.

- **Client Permissions** Click this button to define a user's access roles and permissions for the folder. The roles that you can assign by clicking this button are identical to those that you can assign by using the folder's property sheets in Outlook, as discussed earlier in the chapter.

- **Propagate These Properties To All Subfolders** This option is visible only if the currently selected folder contains subfolders. This option is used to force configuration changes made on the current folder to be applied to those subfolders.

- **Limit Administrative Access To Home Site** When this option is enabled, only administrators within the local site can administer the public folder. This option helps prevent the accidental rehoming of the folder to another site. *Rehoming* is the movement of the public folder's home server to a different server. You perform rehoming using the Advanced property sheet, which is discussed later in this chapter.

Limits Property Sheet

The Limits property sheet, shown in Figure 13-12, defines messaging limits for the public folder.

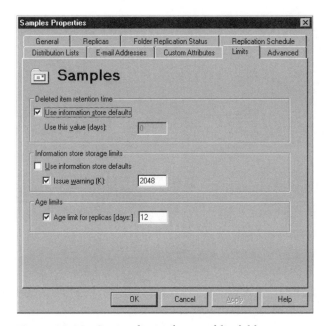

Figure 13-12. *Setting limits for a public folder.*

You can define the following limits on this property sheet:

- **Deleted Item Retention Time**   This setting defines the number of days that deleted messages are retained in the folder before being permanently removed. This setting works the same way that the setting at the server level works, as discussed earlier in the chapter. Any settings made at the public folder level override settings made for the server.

- **Information Store Storage Limits**   You can use the storage limits defined at the server level or override those settings for this particular folder.

- **Age Limits**   You can set the maximum amount of time in days that a message remains in this public folder before it expires.

Advanced Property Sheet

You use the Advanced property sheet, shown in Figure 13-13, to configure several parameters for a public folder.

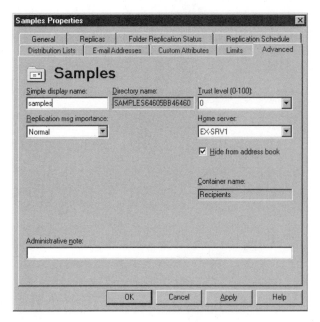

Figure 13-13. *Configuring Advanced properties for a public folder.*

Following are some of the parameters that you can configure:

- **Simple Display Name** If the name of the public folder is long or contains non-ANSI characters, the public folder may be inaccessible from certain computers, clients, or messaging systems. Set a simple display name to be fairly short and to use only universally recognized characters.

- **Directory Name** This setting is the name of the public folder in the Exchange Directory Information Tree (DIT). After a folder is created, the Directory name cannot be changed.

- **Trust Level** The trust level determines whether a public folder is included in Directory Synchronization with foreign messaging systems. If the trust level exceeds the trust level set for the Directory Synchronization requestor, the public folder is not included in synchronization. Directory Synchronization and trust levels are discussed in more detail in Chapter 12.

- **Home Server** No matter how many instances of a public folder exist, each public folder has a home server. The home server plays a part in how public folders are accessed for information when multiple instances exist, as you see later in this chapter. You can rehome a folder simply by choosing a new server from the drop-down menu. The menu contains a list of servers on the site that currently maintain a replica of the public folder.

- **Hide From Address Book**   By default, all public folders are hidden from view in the address book. If you want a public folder to be viewed in the address book, simply clear this option. Mail can still be sent to a hidden folder, but the address must be known.

Setting Up Intersite Public Folder Access

When a user opens a public folder with an Exchange client, the process is fairly simple from the user's point of view. The user browses the public folder hierarchy, opens a particular folder, and views the contents of that folder. Behind the scenes, however, this process is not so simple. Remember that although the public folder hierarchy is present within the Directory of every server in an organization, the content of any given public folder could be anywhere — on a server on the same site as the user, on a server on a different site, or even on multiple servers. Therefore, the client application must have a way of locating the contents of the particular folder that the user selected.

The client searches for the content of a public folder by following these steps:

1. Each client's Private Information Store is configured with the name of an Exchange Server that acts as a public folder server for that client. The first place that the client checks for a public folder's content is its public folder server.

2. The client checks, in random order, any other servers in the same location as the home server. Random-order checking is performed to provide a level of automatic load balancing. Server locations are a way to logically group servers on particularly large sites. You can set a server's location by using the General property sheet of the server's container in Exchange Administrator.

3. The client checks any server to which the client has an existing RPC connection.

4. The client checks, in random order, any remaining servers on the site.

5. After all servers on the site have been checked for the content of the public folder, the client may check servers on other sites if site affinity has been configured between the two sites and if the network supports RPCs. Sites are checked in order of increasing affinity values. When a site is checked, the servers in that site are tried in random order. If multiple sites have the same affinity cost, the servers in those sites are pooled together and tried in random order.

Exchange automatically configures which folder is accessed. The one thing that you need to configure manually is site affinity. By default, no affinity exists among any sites in an organization. This situation can present a problem. Suppose that a public folder exists on one site in an organization. Because the public folder hierarchy is replicated to all servers in the organization, users on other sites can see that the public folder exists. Those users cannot access the folder's content, however, unless an affinity has been manually established between their site and the site on which the public folder exists. Affinity is disabled by default in order to prevent clients from accessing public folder content in remote sites when local replicas exist.

Fortunately, site affinity is relatively easy to configure. You configure site affinity using the Public Folder Affinity property sheet of the *Information Store Site Configuration* object, shown in Figure 13-14. Available sites in the organization appear in the list on the left. Sites to which affinity has been configured appear in the list on the right. You can move sites between the two lists by clicking the Add and Remove buttons. When you establish affinity with a site, you must also set an affinity value. The default value is 1, but you can choose any value between 0 and 100. Sites that have a lower affinity value are always searched before sites that have a higher affinity value. Sites with an affinity value of 100 are used only if all other sites are unavailable.

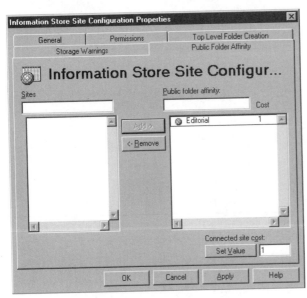

Figure 13-14. *Configuring affinity between sites.*

> **Note** Public folder affinity works in one direction. When you configure affinity with another site, you set it up so that users on the current site can access public folder content on those remote sites. Users on those remote sites cannot access content on the current site until you set up affinity on the remote sites.

Replicating Public Folders

Public folder content is not replicated to other servers automatically. You must set up replication manually, on a per-folder basis. However, you can configure the automatic replication of child folders for which the parent folder is replicated. Each public folder can be configured individually to have replicas on multiple servers.

Public folder replication follows the multimaster replication model, in which every replica of a public folder is considered a master copy. In fact, there is no easy way to distinguish a replica from the original after replication occurs.

Creating Replicas of a Public Folder

After you decide which folders you want to replicate, you manually create and configure the replicas using either of two methods. The first method involves pushing replicas from one server to other servers by using the property sheets of the public folder that you want to replicate. The second method requires pulling replicas of existing folders to a server by using the property sheets of that server's *Public Information Store* object. Both methods are covered in the following sections.

> **Note** "Push" vs. "pull" technology is an interesting debate. Formerly, legacy systems used only pull technology. That is, each computer had to send a request before receiving any information. Then came push technology. In a push system, a configuration or subscription process registers the location of the destination for information. Once that location is set, the information is automatically sent to the destination. The benefit of push technology is its automation. The benefit of pull technology is that it is very useful for troubleshooting connectivity and sending information without a schedule.

Pushing Replicas to Other Servers

You can push a replica of an existing public folder to another server by using the property sheets of the public folder itself. In Exchange Administrator, open the property sheets of the public folder for which you want to create replicas; then switch to the Replicas property sheet, shown in Figure 13-15.

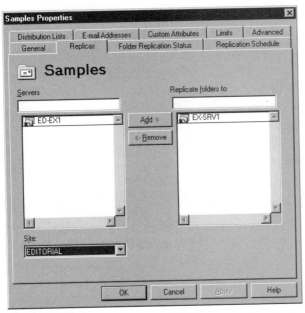

Figure 13-15. *Pushing replicas of a public folder to another server.*

On the left side of this property sheet, you'll find a list of available servers on the selected site. You can change the selected site using the drop-down menu at the bottom of the property sheet. On the right side, you'll find a list of servers to which you want to push a replica of the public folder. Notice that the home server of the public folder is already listed as hosting a replica. Click the Add and Remove buttons to move servers between the two lists. When you click OK, the replicas are created on the selected servers and are included in scheduled public folder replication. If the Propagate These Properties To All Subfolders option is selected on the General property sheet of the public folder, replicas of all subfolders will also be created on the selected servers.

Pulling Replicas from Other Servers

You can also pull replicas of an existing public folder to a server. To do so, open the property sheets of the *Public Information Store* object for the server to which you want to pull replicas. Then switch to the Instances property sheet, shown in Figure 13-16.

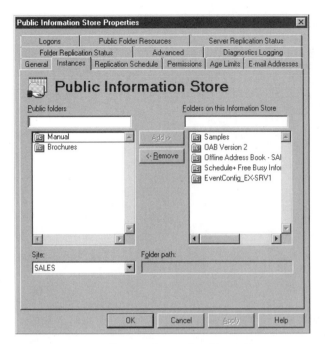

Figure 13-16. *Pulling replicas of public folders to a server.*

The list on the left side of this property sheet displays available public folders on the selected site. The list on the right side shows folders that already exist in the current information store. To create a replica of a remote folder, select the folder from the list of available folders on the left, and then click Add. When you click OK, the replicas are created.

Scheduling Replication

After you create replicas of public folders, you can set up a schedule by which replication will occur. You can configure a single schedule for all folders on a server by using the Replication Schedule property sheet of that server's *Public Information Store* object, shown in Figure 13-17.

The settings that you make on this property sheet govern how often changes in public folders on the server are replicated to other servers. You can configure a different schedule for individual public folders by using the Replication property sheet for the public folder itself. Schedules for folders override schedules set at the server level.

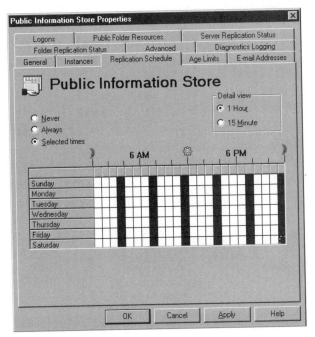

Figure 13-17. *Scheduling replication for the public folders on a server.*

When folders are replicated, there is the possibility of conflicts as users work against different replicas. Exchange has a way to handle replica conflicts intelligently and automatically. First, the Exchange Server allocates revision numbers to all messages posted in a public folder. Using the assigned revision number, the server identifies conflicts as they occur. The server then places both conflicting revisions in the replica for manual resolution and replicates these revisions throughout the Organization.

Summary

You've now learned everything that you need to know to set up a good public folder system in your Exchange organization. You've learned that every public folder consists of two parts: the content of the public folder and that folder's place in the public folder hierarchy. The public folder hierarchy is replicated automatically to every server in the organization. Public folder content is replicated to other servers only when you configure the replication manually. Public folders are created with an Exchange client and are managed through both the client and Exchange Administrator. Client applications find and access the content of a public folder by searching servers within the site in a specific order. Client applications can access public folder content on another site only if affinity has been configured between the two sites. In Chapter 14, you will learn how to configure Exchange Server 5.5 to support various Internet protocols.

Chapter 14
Supporting Internet Protocols

Internet integration is a requirement for many businesses as they move toward electronic commerce. In addition, Internet technology and its accompanying TCP/IP protocol suite now pervade most private networks in the form of intranets. Users now frequently access Internet resources, such as the Web and Internet e-mail, from within their companies' private networks as part of their daily business functions. Many users also use the networking capabilities of the Internet to log on remotely and utilize their companies' network services from a distance.

Microsoft Exchange Server 5.5 provides native support for popular Internet messaging protocols. In this chapter, we explore the integration of the Internet with an Exchange Server system. We look at the protocols used by Internet and intranet technology as well as how those protocols are implemented with Exchange Server, and we learn how to integrate an Exchange Server with Internet messaging and news systems. Exchange Server is a complex, Internet- and intranet-capable system, but with the guiding hand of the Internet Mail Service, it is a straightforward task to configure and connect to the Internet.

Using the Internet Mail Service

The Internet Mail Service (IMS) is a fully functional Simple Mail Transfer Protocol (SMTP) host that is used to transfer messages with other SMTP hosts. SMTP has long been the standard protocol for transferring messages between two hosts over TCP/IP. You configure the Internet Mail Service from within Microsoft Exchange Administrator.

Installing the Internet Mail Service

In Exchange Administrator, you use the Internet Mail Wizard to install the Internet Mail Service. Before installation, however, you must ensure that certain prerequisites are met. These prerequisites include ensuring that TCP/IP is correctly configured on your server, entering your Exchange Server name into your Domain Name System (DNS) database or HOSTS file, and knowing what SMTP addressing scheme your organization uses.

Configuring TCP/IP

The Internet Mail Service runs on top of TCP/IP. The IMS does not require an MTA transport stack, as do some connectors — merely that TCP/IP be correctly configured on the Exchange Server on which the IMS will run. Setting up TCP/IP is relatively simple, and the IMS can run on a server with a continuous (network) or noncontinuous (dial-up) connection. Simply assign your server an IP address and a domain name, which usually is something like *organization_name.com,* and then configure IP services, including host name entries and MX records in DNS. If you are using a dial-up connection, you also need to make sure that the Microsoft Windows NT remote access service (RAS) is installed and that you have a phone-book entry configured for the remote connection.

Configuring DNS

On the Internet (or on any TCP/IP network, for that matter), every device is represented by an IP address — a four-part dotted-decimal notation such as 192.168.0.1. A device with a TCP/IP address is called a *host* and is assigned a host name, which is a character-based name that is easier for humans to recognize and remember than its IP address. The format of the host name is *host@domain.com.* When a host name identifies a resource on a TCP/IP network, computers must translate that host name into an IP address because computers communicate using only IP addresses. This translation is called *name resolution.*

There are two basic methods of name resolution on a TCP/IP network. The first method of resolving host names to IP addresses involves using a file called a HOSTS file. The *HOSTS file* is a single, flat file that simply lists hosts on a network and each host's IP address. To use the IMS with a HOSTS file, you must enter into that file the domain name and IP address of the hosts to which the IMS may need to transfer messages. As you might imagine, this process can be time-consuming.

The second method of resolving host names to IP addresses is more efficient. It involves the *Domain Name System* (DNS), a hierarchical, distributed database of host names and IP addresses. Depending on your situation, you may have a DNS server on your network, or you may rely on the DNS server of your ISP. Either way, you need to make sure that the Exchange Server on which your IMS resides is configured with the address of a valid DNS server. This configuration enables the IMS to resolve the IP addresses of hosts to which it may need to transfer messages.

You are likely to want outside SMTP hosts to be able to transfer messages to the IMS. To enable this capability, you must create two records in the DNS database so that those other hosts can resolve your server's IP address. The first record that you must create is an *address record*, or a *record*. The second record is a Mail Exchanger record, or *MX record*, which is a standard DNS record type used to designate one or more hosts that process mail for an organization or site.

More Info   This chapter provides a simplistic discussion of configuring TCP/IP and DNS, but these topics encompass a monstrous amount of material. If you need more information about using TCP/IP and DNS in the Windows NT environment, see *Running Windows NT Server 4.0* (1996) from Microsoft Press.

Understanding SMTP Addressing

Before you install the IMS on your Exchange Server, you need to know the SMTP addressing convention used in your organization. SMTP addresses follow the convention *recipient@domain,* in which *recipient* is the name of a recipient and *domain* is the fully qualified domain name of the domain in which that recipient exists. A typical SMTP address, therefore, might be *someone@microsoft.com.* Domain names have a hierarchical structure, the levels of which are separated by periods. In the domain *microsoft.com,* for example, *microsoft* is a subdomain of the *com* domain.

The default SMTP addressing structure used by Exchange Server 5.5 is *recipient@site.organization.com.* Many administrators modify this structure to *recipient@organization.com.* Knowing your organization's addressing convention before you install the IMS is a requirement. Most administrators remove the "site." portion of *site.organization.com* because allowing each user to change from site to site would require a new e-mail ID.

Note   You may have the authority to modify the default SMTP addressing for your site. If so, keep in mind that any domain name you decide on must be registered with the appropriate authority and entered into the DNS database as an MX record before your organization can receive messages from other SMTP hosts.

Running the Internet Mail Wizard

After you make sure that your Exchange Server is ready, you install the IMS by using the Internet Mail Wizard. To launch the wizard, choose New Other, then select Internet Mail Service from the File menu of Exchange Administrator. The welcome screen of the Internet Mail Wizard simply informs you of the steps that you will take while you use the wizard. When you click Next, a second welcome screen appears, warning you of the prerequisites for setting up the IMS.

On the next screen of the Internet Mail Wizard, shown in Figure 14-1, you must specify the Exchange Server on which the IMS is to be installed. The default selection is the Exchange Server to which Exchange Administrator was connected when you launched the wizard, but you can specify any other server in the site. This screen also allows you to specify whether you will be using RAS to connect to the Internet. If you specify that the IMS will use RAS, an extra screen is added to the wizard, allowing you to select the RAS phone-book entry that the IMS should use.

> **Note** If at all possible, try to connect to the Internet using a continuous connection. Most users expect that their e-mail will be delivered the moment they click Send. The dial-up method can take awhile to establish a connection before mail is delivered, and there is a greater possibility of errors.

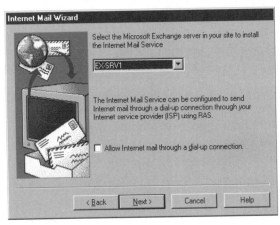

Figure 14-1. *Selecting an Exchange Server on which to install the IMS.*

The wizard screen, shown in Figure 14-2, prompts you whether other host connections to the server should be allowed for the purposes of rerouting messages. You can selectively designate that messages from different hosts be routed to different SMTP hosts or processed by the IMS. You might want to have the IMS process messages coming from one SMTP host, for example, but have messages from mail clients routed somewhere else. It is important to know that any server that is accessible from the Internet with unlimited SMTP connections will enable anyone to send mail via that server. This could lead to misuses such as spam that you would prefer not to happen.

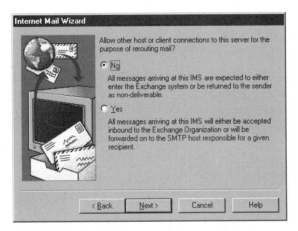

Figure 14-2. *Choosing whether to allow rerouting by the Exchange Server.*

The next dialog box (Figure 14-3) lets you specify how the IMS should route outgoing mail. The default choice is for the IMS to directly transfer messages to destination hosts by looking up those hosts on a DNS server. If you choose this option, you need to have the address of a DNS server configured in the TCP/IP settings for your Exchange Server.

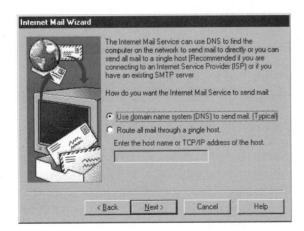

Figure 14-3. *Specifying how the IMS should route messages.*

The other option that you can choose on this screen is for the IMS to route all outgoing messages through a single host. You choose this configuration if you want to transfer all outgoing messages directly to another SMTP host (your ISP's host or your own firewall, for example) and have that host handle the transfer of mail from there. This option is quite useful when you want to hide your mail system from hosts on the Internet for purposes of security or bandwidth use.

The ensuing screen of the Internet Mail Wizard, shown in Figure 14-4, lets you place certain restrictions on outgoing messages. The default setting allows users on your network to send messages to any Internet address, but you can limit the addresses to which mail can be sent. If you choose this option, you have to configure those allowable addresses manually after the Internet Mail Wizard finishes. You learn how later in the chapter, in the section on configuring the Internet Mail Service.

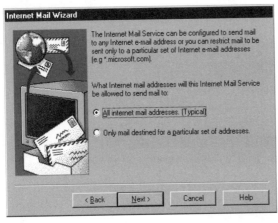

Figure 14-4. *Restricting addresses to which messages can be sent via the IMS.*

After that, you are prompted to define the address space that will be used to generate SMTP addresses for your users. As mentioned earlier in this chapter, the default address space establishes the Internet addressing structure *@site.organization.com.* You can change this value now, or you can change it later using the property sheets of the IMS.

The following IMS dialog box permits you to designate a recipient that is to receive nondelivery reports (NDRs) concerning the IMS. The default choice is to use or create a mailbox called Administrator, but you also define any mailbox or distribution list. This mailbox receives any messages addressed to *postmaster@yourdomain.com* and any e-mail sent to that company with the wrong mailbox address, such as *sales@company.com,* where there is no "sales" mailbox, public folder, or other recipient.

Real World   Sending Nondelivery Reports (NDRs) to Distribution Lists

NDRs are a method of monitoring the success of messaging actions. You can configure nondelivery reports to be sent in reference to the IMS, public folders, intersite messaging connectors, and foreign gateways, to name just a few options. You can specify any recipient, a distribution list, a single mailbox, a public folder, or even a custom recipient to receive NDRs. Several interesting techniques make this capability quite useful.

Some administrators like to set up a distribution list of Exchange administrators and designate that the members of this list receive nondelivery reports. This method is the obvious way to use distribution lists, but it is not the only way. You could also create a distribution list in which you put the mailboxes of certain administrators who have been given the task of dealing with NDRs. You could even create a public folder for NDRs and include that folder in the list. That way, you could keep a log of nondelivery reports and even maintain threaded discussions of them.

On the next screen of the wizard, shown in Figure 14-5, you must enter the password for the Site Services account for the site. Like any other service in Exchange, the IMS must have access to the Site Services account to perform its duties.

Figure 14-5. *Entering the Site Services account password for the IMS.*

When you complete this screen, you are nearly finished installing the IMS. The next, and final, screen of the wizard summarizes what you have configured for Internet connectivity in Exchange. When you click the Finish button, you are informed that the IMS has been installed.

Configuring the Internet Mail Service

After you install the Internet Mail Service, a dialog box will recommend that you run Performance Optimizer. Whenever you add or change a component within Exchange, you should run Performance Optimizer to ensure that performance is optimal for the Exchange users. Whether you choose to do this or not, you can further configure the IMS the way that you configure any other element of Exchange Server 5.5: by using the property sheets of its *Configuration* object in Exchange Administrator. The *Internet Mail Service* object is located in the Connections container for the site, which itself is located in the Configuration container.

When you open the property sheets for the Internet Mail Service, you notice that the Internet Mail property sheet is displayed first, instead of the General property sheet.

Internet Mail Property Sheet

The Internet Mail property sheet, shown in Figure 14-6, is used to configure some basic parameters governing how the IMS handles SMTP messages.

Figure 14-6. *Configuring basic mailing options for the IMS.*

The following parameters can be configured from the property sheet:

- **Administrator's Mailbox**   This setting is the name of the mailbox or distribution list to which nondelivery reports concerning the IMS are sent. By default, this field is set to the recipient that you selected in the Internet Mail Wizard, or it is empty if a recipient was not selected.

- **Notifications** Click this button to open a dialog box that lets you specify the types of nondelivery reports sent to the selected administrator's mailbox. By default, notifications are sent only when multiple matches for a single e-mail address are found. Other types of NDRs are generated when e-mail addresses cannot be found at all, when a destination host cannot be found, when a protocol error occurs, or when a message timeout is exceeded.

- **Attachments (Outbound)** Use this section to specify how outbound messages are encoded. Internet messages are encoded in two formats: MIME and UUENCODE. MIME is a rich, modern format that is widely used. MIME messages can be further formatted as plain text or HTML. UUENCODE (and the BinHex variant) is an older standard that is still used by many POP clients (such as Eudora) and by most Macintosh-based mail clients.

- **Character Sets** Use this section to specify the default character sets used for transferring inbound and outbound messages for both MIME and non-MIME formats.

- **Specify By E-Mail Domain** Click this button to open a dialog box that allows you to specify different character sets, encoding methods, and size limits for different remote e-mail domains. If a specific domain, perhaps a customer or branch office, has custom requirements for character sets or encoding methods, they should be customized here. If you need to restrict messages to a certain domain — perhaps if the domain has a size limit restriction — the message size limit can be adjusted for that domain, and other domains can remain at the standard limits.

- **Clients Support S/MIME Signatures** S/MIME is a secure version of the MIME format that allows messages to be signed and encrypted. Choose this option only if you use clients that support the S/MIME standard. When selected, Outlook clients that receive messages signed or sealed using S/MIME will see an additional attachment to the message containing the signature. When this option is disabled, inbound multipart/signed messages are converted to unsigned MIME messages.

- **Convert Inbound Message To Fixed-Width Font** By default, SMTP hosts send messages in a variable-width font, which can disrupt the layout of plain-text messages in some mail clients. Use this option to convert inbound messages that use variable-width fonts to use fixed-width fonts.

- **Enable Message Tracking** Message tracking is a feature of Exchange Administrator that allows an administrator to track a message's path from originator to recipient. Choose this option to enable message tracking for the IMS. Message tracking is discussed in detail in Chapter 20.

- **Advanced Options**   Click this button to open a dialog box that allows you to configure several advanced options (see Figure 14-7). These advanced options include:

  - **Send Microsoft Exchange Rich-Text Formatting**   By default, users can decide whether to send messages that use rich-text format from within their clients. If you deselect this option, you prevent rich-text formatting from being sent.

  - **Disable Out-Of-Office Responses**   Exchanges can be configured to provide an automatic reply to incoming messages, stating that the user is away from the office. Choose this option to disable that function for messages that your users receive from the Internet. Out-of-office responses can take a network to its knees when users turn the feature on while receiving large amounts of incoming e-mail and if the network link has a small amount of bandwidth available. This situation is exacerbated by upset list service owners when a user subscribes to one or more list services and receives hundreds of e-mails per day. In that case, the list service is flooded with multiple out-of-office replies because each message appears to be from a different recipient, although the response address is the same. And sometimes — depending on the list service configuration — those out-of-office replies are forwarded right back to the sender's e-mail box. Disabling any out-of-office replies to the Internet is usually a benefit to the system.

  - **Disable Automatic Replies To The Internet**   Exchange can be configured to send other types of automated replies. You can prevent that practice by choosing this option. Like disabling out-of-office responses, disabling automatic replies can be beneficial to the Exchange system.

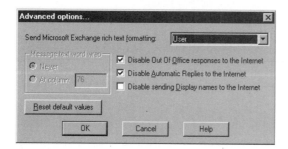

Figure 14-7. *Configuring Advanced Mailing options for the IMS.*

- **Disable Sending Display Names To The Internet**   By default, messages outbound to the Internet include the sender's e-mail address and display name. Choose this option if you want to prevent the display name from being included.

General Property Sheet

The General property sheet, shown in Figure 14-8, has one parameter that you can configure: message size. If you want, enter the maximum size (in kilobytes) for messages that will be transferred over the connector. This limit applies to both incoming and outgoing messages.

Figure 14-8. *Setting message size limits on the General property sheet.*

Dial-up Connections Property Sheet

The Dial-up Connections property sheet, shown in Figure 14-9, is used to configure the connection and scheduling details if the IMS uses RAS. The list of available connections is composed of entries in the RAS phone book. The IMS can be set to use only one phone-book entry at a time. Click the Mail Retrieval and Logon Information buttons to configure scripts and logon information that may be required by the foreign host.

You also use this property sheet to schedule the times during which the IMS can use RAS to transfer messages. By default, the IMS dials the remote host every

Figure 14-9. *Configuring the IMS dialup connection.*

four hours on a daily basis. You can also set the IMS to dial out at a certain time each day or whenever mail is queued to be transferred.

Connections Property Sheet

The Connections property sheet, shown in Figure 14-10, is used to define several parameters that govern message delivery over the IMS.

These parameters include the following:

- **Transfer Mode** Use this section to specify whether the IMS is to be used for inbound messages, outbound messages, both, or neither. You could, for example, designate one server to process inbound messages and one to process outbound messages. Clicking the Advanced button opens a dialog box that allows you to specify the maximum number of messages that can be sent and the maximum number of simultaneous connections to remote hosts that the IMS can maintain.

- **Message Delivery** This section lets you specify whether the IMS should route all outbound messages itself, using a DNS server, or whether it should forward all messages to a single host for delivery. You specified the default setting for this option when you used the Internet Mail Wizard to install the IMS.

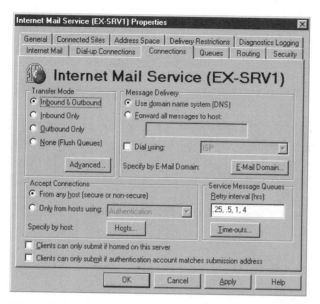

Figure 14-10. *Configuring connection properties for the IMS.*

- **Dial Using**   If you choose to route all messages through a single host, you can specify that a RAS phone-book entry be used to connect to that host.

- **Accept Connections**   This section allows you to configure authentication security for incoming connections. By default, connections from any remote host are accepted. You can specify that connections be accepted only from hosts that use authentication, encryption, or both. Clicking the Hosts button opens a dialog box that allows you to specify (by host name or IP address) the hosts from which you want to accept connections.

- **Service Message Queues**   The Retry Interval field lets you configure the IMS to wait a specified number of hours before retrying a connection to a host to which a previous connection failed. In the Retry Interval field, you can enter a series of numbers separated by commas. The first number determines the time that the IMS waits between the initial connection attempt and a subsequent attempt. The second number defines the interval between the second attempt and a third. The last specified interval is repeated until the connection is made or the specified timeout value has been reached. Click the Time-Outs button to specify the timeout value.

- **Clients Can Only Submit If Homed on This Server**   If this option is selected, clients can submit messages for delivery over the IMS only if they have a mailbox on the server on which the IMS resides.

- **Clients Can Only Submit If Authentication Account Matches Submission Address**   If this option is enabled, clients can submit messages for delivery over the IMS only if their logon account matches the address in the From field of the message.

Routing Property Sheet

The Routing property sheet, shown in Figure 14-11, is used to specify whether incoming messages from SMTP hosts or mail clients should be routed to other SMTP hosts instead of being processed by the IMS. You can selectively designate that messages from different hosts be routed to different SMTP hosts or processed by the IMS. You might want to have the IMS process messages coming from one SMTP host, for example, but have messages from mail clients routed to another SMTP server.

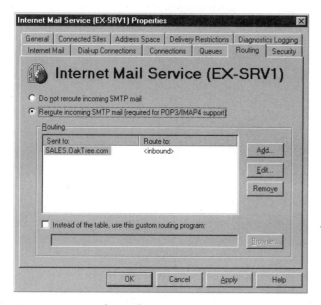

Figure 14-11. *Selectively rerouting inbound SMTP messages.*

If you plan to support POP3 (or IMAP4) clients in your organization (a topic that is discussed later in this chapter), you want to enable rerouting on this property sheet. POP3 clients use SMTP to send messages to the IMS. If the messages are addressed to an external SMTP address (*user@internet_domain.com*), those messages must be processed by the IMS. If the messages are addressed to an internal SMTP address (*user@your_organization.com*), the message must be routed to the Exchange Server.

Security Property Sheet

The Security property sheet, shown in Figure 14-12, is used to configure security on outbound connections to other systems. This list on this property sheet displays any e-mail domains for which security has been configured. At first, only the default entry is shown; that entry defines security on all outbound connections. You can edit the default entry or add an entry for a specific domain.

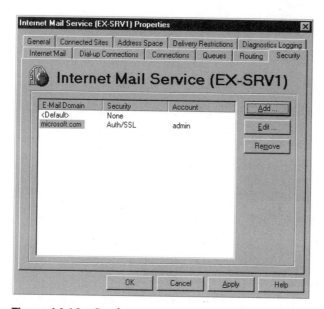

Figure 14-12. *Configuring security on outbound SMTP connections.*

Clicking the Add button opens the Edit E-Mail Domain Security Information dialog box, shown in Figure 14-13. Enter the name of the e-mail domain for which you want to configure security, and specify the type of security that you want to use.

Security options include the following:

- **No Authentication Or Encryption**   When you choose this option, no security is provided for this domain. This option is useful if you want to set one level of security for default connections but exclude certain e-mail domains.

- **SASL/SSL Security**   Choose this option if Simple Authentication and Security Layer (SASL) or Secure Socket Layer (SSL) methods are supported by the remote e-mail domain for which you are configuring security.

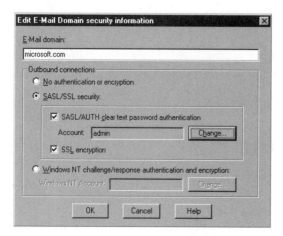

Figure 14-13. *Configuring security for remote e-mail domains.*

- **Windows NT Challenge/Response Authentication And Encryption**
  Choose this option only if the foreign e-mail domain to which you are connecting is also a Windows NT domain. To use this form of security, you need to provide a valid user account and password in the remote domain.

Configuring Advanced Protocol Support

In addition to supporting SMTP through the Internet Mail Service, Exchange Server 5.5 supports the following Internet protocols:

- **POP3 and IMAP4**   Post Office Protocol 3 (POP3) and Internet Message Access Protocol 4 (IMAP4) are message access protocols used to retrieve messages from a server.

- **HTTP**   Hypertext Transfer Protocol (HTTP) is used to transmit information from Web servers to Web browsers.

- **NNTP**   Network News Transport Protocol (NNTP) is used to transmit newsgroup information between Usenet servers and to give newsreader clients access to that information.

- **LDAP**   Lightweight Directory Access Protocol (LDAP) is used by LDAP clients to look up Directory information from LDAP-enabled servers.

This section examines in detail the support that Exchange Server 5.5 provides for each of these protocols. First, however, you learn how to use Exchange Administrator to manage protocols in general.

Managing Protocols

In Exchange Server 5.5, protocols typically are managed at three levels: the site level, the server level, and the mailbox level. If you configure a setting for a protocol at the site level, that setting affects all servers on the site but can be overridden on particular servers. Settings made for protocols at the server level affect all recipients on that server but can be overridden for particular mailboxes. Exceptions to these general rules exist, of course, and are discussed in the sections on the individual protocols.

Each Site container and each Server container in your organization holds a subcontainer called Protocols, as shown in Figure 14-14. You can configure parameters that apply to all protocols on a site by using the property sheets for the Protocols container at the site level. Likewise, you can configure parameters that apply to all protocols on a server by using the property sheets for the Protocols container at the server level.

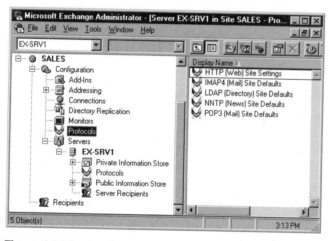

Figure 14-14. *Configuring General protocol properties.*

The property sheets for the Protocols container at each level are virtually identical. The General property sheet doesn't really let you configure anything. The following sections focus on the Connections and MIME Types property sheets.

Connections Property Sheet

The Connections property sheet, shown in Figure 14-15, lets you accept or reject protocol access based on IP address. By default, all connections are accepted. You can specify whether to accept or reject connections from specific clients by clicking New and then entering the client's IP address and the desired action (accept or reject) in the dialog box that appears. Rules in the list are processed in the order in which they appear in the list. Settings that you make at server level override settings that you make at the site level.

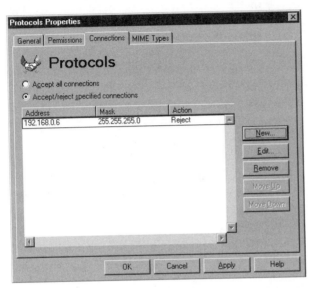

Figure 14-15. *Defining which clients can use protocols.*

MIME Types Property Sheet

The MIME Types property sheet, shown in Figure 14-16, is used to define file extensions for inbound attachments that use the MIME encoding method. You might specify, for example, that all content of the text/plain MIME type is put into a file with a .TXT extension. Most applications register themselves on this list, but you can add, edit, or remove entries manually. Entries are processed in the order in which they appear in the list. You can adjust this order by clicking the Move Up and Move Down buttons.

Configuring Post Office Protocol 3

Post Office Protocol 3 (POP3) is by far the most popular message access protocol used on the Internet today. The POP3 protocol supports the retrieval of messages from server-based inboxes. Any POP3-enabled e-mail client—including Outlook, Outlook Express, and Eudora—can be used to retrieve messages from an Exchange Server 5.5 inbox. POP3 clients cannot access other personal or

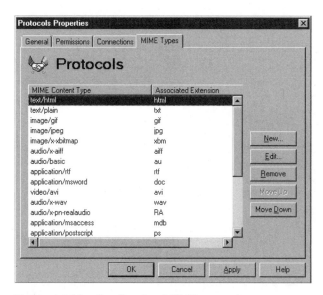

Figure 14-16. *Configuring MIME extensions.*

public server-based folders on the server; neither can they access any scheduling information. POP3 clients are used only for the retrieval of messages from the Inbox. Most POP3 clients use SMTP to send messages.

POP3 is supported by default during a typical installation of Exchange Server 5.5. To enable POP3 message retrieval, however, you need to first configure the protocol in Exchange Administrator. You can configure the POP3 protocol at three levels in Exchange Administrator:

- **Site**   Settings made for the POP3 protocol at the site level represent default settings that are inherited by all servers on the site.

- **Server**   Settings made for the POP3 protocol at the server level override settings made at site level and are inherited by all mailboxes on the server.

- **Mailbox**   Settings made for the POP3 protocol at the mailbox level override settings made at server level. One exception to this rule is that if POP3 support is disabled at the server level, it is disabled for all mailboxes, regardless of settings made at the mailbox level.

Configuring POP3 at Site and Server Levels

At the site and server levels, you configure the POP3 protocol by using the property sheets of the POP3 object in either the site- or server-level Protocols container. The configurations for the levels are essentially identical.

General Property Sheet The General property sheet, shown in Figure 14-17, is used to change the display name of the POP3 object in Exchange Administrator and to enable or disable the protocol at whichever level you are administering: site or server.

Figure 14-17. *Enabling the protocol at site or server level.*

Authentication Property Sheet The Authentication property sheet, shown in Figure 14-18, is used to specify the methods of authentication that POP3 clients use when connecting to the Exchange Server. By default, the client can connect using any supported authentication method. For more information on security and authentication methods, see Chapter 15.

Message Format Property Sheet The Message Format property sheet, shown in Figure 14-19, is used to specify the format to which Exchange Server 5.5 messages are converted when they are retrieved by a POP3 client: MIME or UUENCODE. You can also specify whether you want to support the Exchange rich-text format.

Idle Time-Out Property Sheet The Idle Time-Out property sheet, shown in Figure 14-20, is used to specify the maximum period (in minutes) that a POP3 client can maintain an open, idle connection to the Exchange Server before being forcibly disconnected. The default value is 10 minutes.

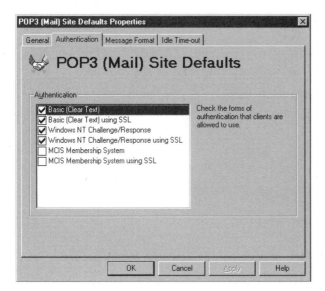

Figure 14-18. *Choosing authentication methods for POP3 clients.*

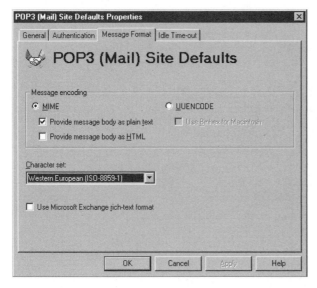

Figure 14-19. *Choosing a message format for POP3 clients.*

Configuring POP3 at Mailbox Level

You can also configure the POP3 protocol for individual mailboxes. To do so, you use the Protocols property sheet of the mailbox in question, as shown in

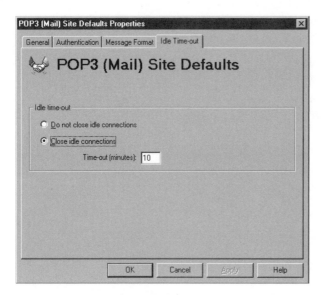

Figure 14-20. *Configuring the maximum time that an idle POP3 client can remain connected.*

Figure 14-21. The list on this property sheet displays installed protocols and specifies whether they are enabled or disabled at the server and mailbox levels. The list also shows any other settings that may have been made for the protocol.

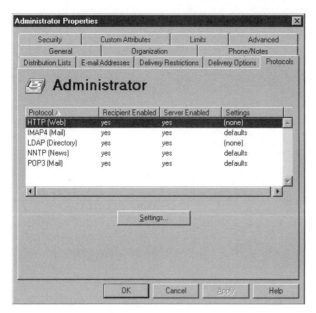

Figure 14-21. *Configuring protocols for a mailbox.*

To edit the settings for a particular protocol, select it from the list and then click Edit. This action opens the Protocol Details dialog box, shown in Figure 14-22. You can specify whether the POP3 protocol should be enabled for this mailbox and whether to use certain server-level default protocol settings or override those settings.

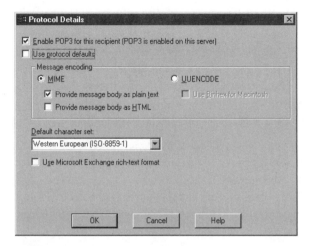

Figure 14-22. *Configuring details for a protocol at mailbox level.*

After you configure the POP3 protocol on the Exchange Server, POP3 clients are ready to retrieve messages. For information on how to set up a POP3 client, see Chapter 17.

Real World   Internet Message Access Protocol 4

Exchange Server 5.5 also supports a message access protocol known as Internet Message Access Protocol 4 (IMAP4). IMAP4—a newer, more powerful message access protocol than POP3—is gaining greater acceptance in the Internet world. IMAP4 offers several powerful advantages over POP3, including the following:

- IMAP4 clients can browse server-based folders, including public and personal folders. IMAP4 clients are not restricted to the inbox, as are POP3 clients.

- IMAP4 clients can manipulate message and folder the structure; moving, deleting, and viewing messages without having to download them from the server. IMAP4 clients can also create new server-based folders.

- Multiple IMAP4 clients can access shared mailboxes simultaneously.

This chapter does not describe how to configure IMAP4, because the process is very similar to configuring POP3. You shouldn't have much problem setting up the IMAP4 protocol.

Configuring Outlook Web Access

By using Outlook Web Access and Hypertext Transfer Protocol (HTTP), Exchange Server 5.5 allows users to access server-based resources with a standard Web browser. Typically, a Web browser contacts a Web server and requests a document that is formatted in Hypertext Markup Language (HTML). The Web server uses the HTTP protocol to transmit this document, and the Web browser displays the document to the user.

Outlook Web Access, a component of Exchange Server 5.5, works in conjunction with the Active Server component of Internet Information Server (IIS), as a sort of liaison between a Web browser and Exchange Server 5.5. To the Web browser, Exchange Server 5.5 appears to be a sophisticated Web site. To Exchange Server 5.5, the Web browser appears to be a fully MAPI-compliant mail client.

Users can use a Web browser to send and receive messages, access public folders, and retrieve Directory information. Users can access the Exchange Server over the company LAN or over the Internet by logging on over a secured connection under a valid user account. Anonymous access is also supported. To log on to an Exchange Server, simply enter the URL for the server in your browser, using the format *http://server_name/Exchange*. When logon occurs, an encrypted and authenticated session is established between the Web browser and the computer running IIS. IIS then logs the user on to the Exchange Server, using Outlook Web Access.

Note When you access an Exchange Server from the Internet, through a firewall or a proxy server, using the Outlook Web Access, you will most likely use a different address than *http:/server_name/Exchange*. Instead, you will probably use the IP address or host name in place of *server_name such as http://mail.company.com/*.

Figure 14-23 shows the main mailbox page of the Web client. You learn more about setting up and using a Web client in Chapter 16.

Note If Exchange Server 5.5 and Internet Information Server are running on the same server, Web clients can be logged on via the Windows NT Challenge/Response authentication method using the Microsoft Internet Explorer Web browser. If Exchange Server 5.5 is on a different computer from Internet Information Server, only basic (clear-text) authentication is supported. However, in either case, SSL will be able to work.

Outlook Web Access is installed by default during a typical installation of Exchange Server 5.5, if an existing installation of Internet Information Server

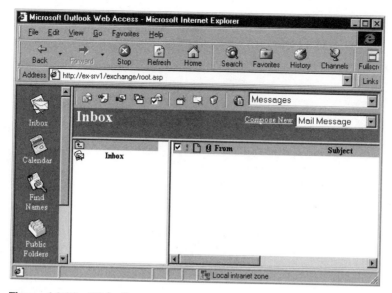

Figure 14-23. *Web clients can perform most of the same tasks as Outlook clients.*

3.0 or later is also found on the server. If you installed IIS after Exchange Server 5.5, you need to add the Outlook Web Access component by using Exchange Server 5.5 Setup.

Outlook Web Access is configured in Exchange Administrator. Unlike other protocols, however, Outlook Web Access can be configured only at the site level. You configure Outlook Web Access by using the property sheets of the HTTP (Web) Site Settings object, located in the site-level Protocols container.

General Property Sheet

The General property sheet, shown in Figure 14-24, is used to enable the protocol for the site and to configure anonymous access. You can give Web users anonymous access so that they can access public folders and Directory information via the Global Address List.

Folder Shortcuts Property Sheet

The Folder Shortcuts property sheet, shown in Figure 14-25, is used to specify the public folders that anonymous users can access (if you choose to allow anonymous access). By default, anonymous users cannot access public folders. You can add a public folder to the list by clicking New and then choosing the public folder that you want to add in the dialog box that opens. To permit

Figure 14-24. *Configuring basic Outlook Web Access properties.*

anonymous access to a public folder, you must also grant the appropriate access permissions to the anonymous user account using the Client Permissions button on the General property sheet for the folder itself. The procedure for granting these permissions is discussed in Chapter 13.

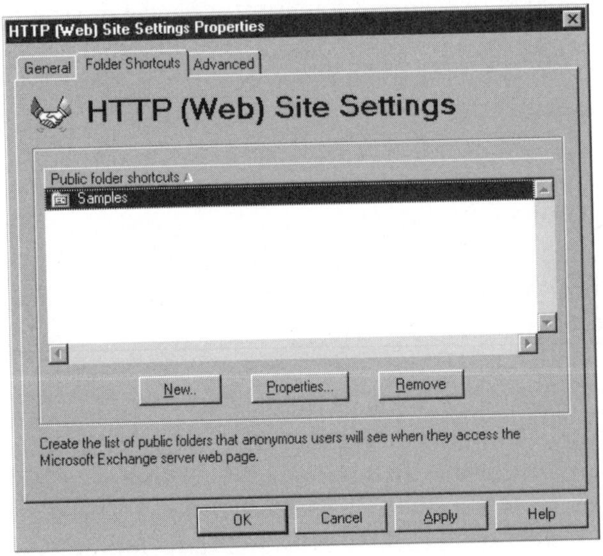

Figure 14-25. *Specifying public folders for anonymous access.*

Advanced Property Sheet

The Advanced property sheet, shown in Figure 14-26, is used to govern how Web clients access the Exchange Directory. Set the number of address book entries that will be shown to a Web client when the address book is opened. By default, only 50 entries are shown. If a search of the address book returns more than 50 entries, the user is instructed to further refine the search.

Figure 14-26. *Limiting the number of address book entries shown to a Web client.*

Configuring Network News Transport Protocol

Support for the Network News Transport Protocol (NNTP) in Exchange Server 5.5 allows the integration of an Exchange organization into the Internet's Usenet newsgroup environment. *Usenet* is a network of distributed discussion forums known as *newsgroups*, in which threaded discussions take place. Tens of thousands of these newsgroups are available on the Internet, on every subject imaginable. These newsgroups are maintained on Usenet servers around the world. Your ISP may maintain a Usenet server of its own.

The administrator of each Usenet server decides which of the available newsgroups is carried on that server and can also create newsgroups. Usenet servers exchange newsgroup information in one of two ways. A server can be configured to push newsgroup information to other servers or to pull information from another server. Either way, this transfer is called a *newsfeed*.

Exchange Server 5.5 can act as a fully functional Usenet server via a component called the Internet News Service. The INS is installed using the Internet News Wizard, which is discussed later in this section. Right after installation, newsreader clients can access any newsgroups on the Exchange Server that are implemented as standard public folders.

You create a newsgroup on an Exchange Server in two ways. The first way is to configure a newsfeed and pull selected newsgroups from another Usenet server. The second way is to use an Exchange client to designate an existing public folder as a newsgroup. Both of these methods are covered in the following sections.

Creating a Newsfeed

You create a newsfeed in Exchange Administrator by using the Newsfeed Configuration Wizard. Before you start creating a newsfeed, however, you have to gather the following information:

- The name of the Usenet site to which you will configure the newsfeed. This name will be a fully qualified domain name, such as *news.isp.com*.
- The names or IP addresses of the Usenet servers on that site.
- The user name and password your Exchange Server will use to log on to the Usenet site. Note that some Usenet sites require validation and others do not.
- The active file of newsgroups available on the Usenet server. You get a chance to download this file during the wizard process, and most ISPs make the list available for download. Otherwise, you must have the list before you begin.

When you have this information, you can launch the Newsfeed Configuration Wizard by choosing New Other Newsfeed from the File menu of Exchange Administrator. The welcome screen of this wizard simply reminds you of the prerequisites for setting up the Internet News Service.

The next screen of the Newsfeed Configuration Wizard, shown in Figure 14-27, asks you to select the Exchange Server on which the newsfeed will be created and the fully qualified domain name (FQDN) of that server. The default selection is the server to which Exchange Administrator was connected when you launched the wizard, but you can select any other server on the site.

Next, you are asked whether you want to create an inbound newsfeed, an outbound newsfeed, or both, as shown in Figure 14-28.

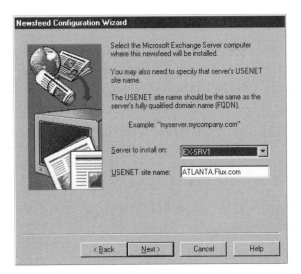

Figure 14-27. *Selecting an Exchange Server on which to install the newsfeed.*

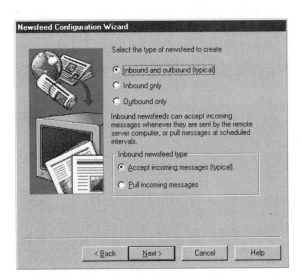

Figure 14-28. *Choosing whether to create an inbound newsfeed, an outbound newsfeed, or both.*

The default setting is to create both, meaning that newsgroups will be pulled from and pushed to the remote Usenet server. If you want to create an inbound newsfeed, you also have to specify whether you want to accept incoming messages—

in which case the remote server pushes messages to the Exchange Server—or whether you want to pull messages from that server. This choice primarily depends on the bandwidth that you can dedicate to the newsfeed and on whether the newsfeed will occur over a dial-up connection. If you are using a dial-up connection or if you want to control the bandwidth used by the newsfeed, you configure a pull newsfeed.

In the next screen of the wizard (Figure 14-29), you are asked whether you want to connect to the Usenet site over your LAN or to use a dial-up connection. If you choose to use a dial-up connection, you also have to enter connection information, including the RAS phone-book entry to use and the user name and password for connecting to the Usenet site.

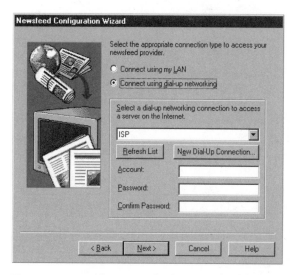

Figure 14-29. *Choosing whether to connect by LAN or dial-up connection.*

Next, you are asked to specify how often the Exchange Server should connect to your newsfeed provider. The default value is 15 minutes.

On the next screen of the Newsfeed Configuration Wizard, you enter the fully qualified domain name of the remote Usenet server. This name usually is something like *news.isp.net*. This information, along with much of the information on the next few screens, is provided to you by the remote Usenet administrator.

Next, you must enter the IP address or host name of the host server on the remote Usenet site, as shown in Figure 14-30. You can also enter the names or addresses of any additional host servers that you want to configure.

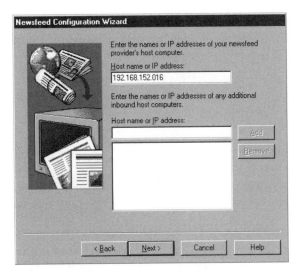

Figure 14-30. *Entering the IP address for the remote server.*

The next screen of the Newsfeed Configuration Wizard, shown in Figure 14-31, lets you enter the user name and password for connecting to the remote Usenet site, if one is required. In the Remote Servers Log In As field, enter the name of a mailbox that your newsfeed provider's servers should use to connect to your Exchange Server. The remote servers will actually log on

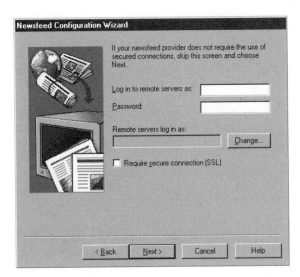

Figure 14-31. *Entering security information for the newsfeed.*

to your domain by using the Windows NT account associated with this mailbox, because Exchange requires NT authentication before a news interchange can occur.

After this step and an informational dialog screen, you are asked for the password to your Site Services account, to verify the installation of the newsfeed. When you provide this password, the newsfeed is created. The wizard requires a few more steps, however.

On the next wizard screen, you are asked to choose a recipient to serve as owner of all of the public folders configured to serve as Internet newsgroups. This parameter is not optional; you must choose a recipient. You can change the owner later.

Next, you are asked to specify where the list of newsgroups on the remote Usenet site is located, as shown in Figure 14-32. This list is known as an *active file*. You have three choices. You can specify an active file on your local hard disk, attempt to download the active file from your newsfeed provider, or elect to exit the wizard and finish the configuration later.

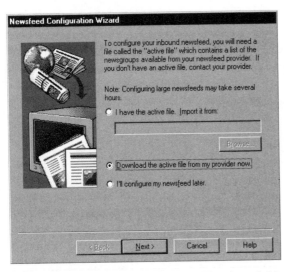

Figure 14-32. *Specifying the active file of available newsgroups.*

When the active file has been loaded, you see a list of newsgroups available on the remote server, as shown in Figure 14-33. Click the Include button, select the newsgroups that you want to receive, and then click Next. The Newsfeed

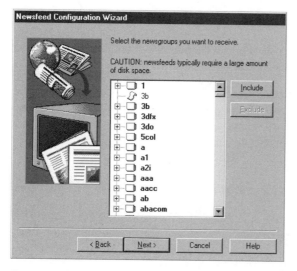

Figure 14-33. *Selecting newsgroups to include in the newsfeed.*

Configuration Wizard creates new public folders for these newsgroups, and the newsfeed configuration is complete.

After you configure the newsfeed, a Newsfeed object is created in the Connections container for the site in Exchange Administrator. You can configure the newsfeed at any time by using the object's property sheets. Most of the property sheets for this object hold the same information that you configured in the Newsfeed Configuration Wizard, so this section does not cover them in detail.

One new parameter, however, is available on the Messages property sheet, shown in Figure 14-34. This property sheet allows you to set size limits on both incoming and outgoing messages.

Real World Don't Get Carried Away with Newsgroups

You'll find that of the tens of thousands of newsgroups that your Usenet provider carries, most are useless to the users of your company. Even the newsgroups that might be useful, however, might generate thousands of new messages per week. When you select newsgroups to pull to your Exchange Server, use caution. Even receiving messages from a few newsgroups every couple of hours can create a great deal of network traffic and use a large amount of your server's resources.

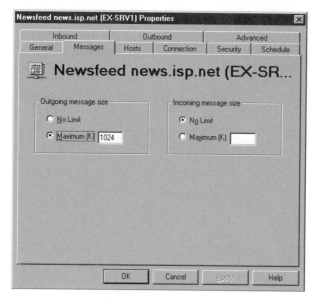

Figure 14-34. *Setting message size limits on the newsfeed.*

Creating a Newsgroup in Outlook

Making a newsgroup out of an existing public folder is a simple process, which you perform using an Exchange client such as Microsoft Outlook. Figure 14-35 shows the main window of Outlook with the *Public Folders* object expanded.

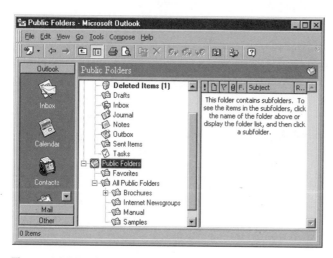

Figure 14-35. *Creating a newsgroup in Outlook.*

Notice the subfolder called Internet Newsgroups. To create a newsgroup, you simply create a new public folder inside the Internet Newsgroups folder. The new newsgroup instantly becomes accessible to newsreader clients. You can also turn an existing public folder into a newsgroup by dragging it into the Internet Newsgroups folder. You can find more information on creating public folders in Chapter 13.

Note If you want to include the newsgroups on your Exchange Server in an outgoing newsfeed, use the Outbound property sheet of the *Newsfeed* object in Exchange Administrator. This property sheet presents a hierarchical list of all available public folders.

Configuring the NNTP Protocol

As you can for the Internet protocols discussed in this chapter, you can configure the NNTP protocol at the site, server, and mailbox levels of Exchange Administrator. At the mailbox level, you use the Protocols property sheet of a particular mailbox to enable or disable NNTP access for the mailbox. At the site and server levels, you use the *NNTP configuration* object, which is available in the Protocols container. Site- and server-level administration are essentially identical processes, so this section covers only site-level property sheets.

The General property sheet, shown in Figure 14-36, is used to enable and disable the NNTP protocol for the site. You can also specify whether clients have NNTP access at site level. If the NNTP protocol is disabled, clients are implicitly denied access anyway. You may want to enable the NNTP protocol for the purpose of establishing newsfeeds but to deny client access.

The Newsfeeds property sheet, shown in Figure 14-37, lists all newsfeeds that are configured on the site. You can open the property sheets of any newsfeed in the list by selecting it and then clicking Properties.

Configuring Lightweight Directory Access Protocol

Lightweight Directory Access Protocol (LDAP) provides a way for LDAP-compliant client applications to access the Directory information of an LDAP-compliant server. LDAP is an open standard that acts as an index of directories. An LDAP client can access multiple LDAP-compliant directories, including the ability to browse the Exchange Directory. Exchange Server 5.5 is LDAP-compliant, thus allowing non-Exchange clients to access the Exchange Directory. LDAP support is often built into POP3 and IMAP4 clients.

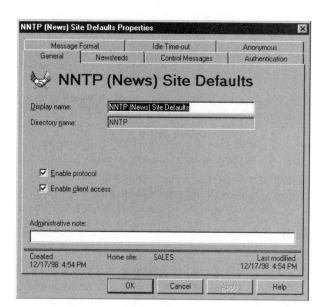

Figure 14-36. *Using the General property sheet to enable or disable NNTP.*

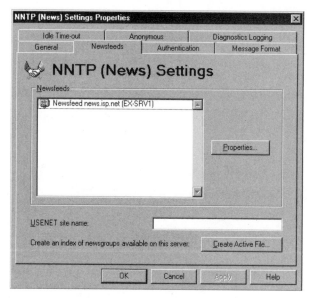

Figure 14-37. *Viewing newsfeeds for a site.*

LDAP is enabled by default during a typical installation of Exchange Server 5.5, meaning that LDAP clients should be able to access Directory information immediately. Unlike other protocols, LDAP cannot be configured at the mailbox level, because it really has nothing to do with individual mailboxes. LDAP can, however, be configured at the site and server levels of Exchange Administrator. Site- and server-level configuration are nearly identical, so this section concentrates on site-level configuration. Remember that settings made at the server level override those made at the site level.

To configure LDAP at the site level, open the property sheets for the *LDAP (Directory) Site Defaults* object, which is located in the Protocols container for the site in Exchange Administrator. Most of the property sheets for the *LDAP* object are the same as the property sheets of the same name for the other protocols. Four property sheets included are:

- **General**   The General property sheet allows you to enable or disable the LDAP protocol at site level.

- **Authentication**   The Authentication property sheet allows you to choose the type of authentication that you want to enable for the protocol.

- **Anonymous**   The Anonymous property sheet allows you to enable or disable anonymous LDAP connections. This option is required for OWA (Outlook Web Access) to work.

- **Idle Time-Out**   The Idle Time-Out property sheet allows you to set the time at which idle connections to an LDAP server are forcibly closed.

One property sheet is unique to the LDAP protocol: the Referrals property sheet. If an LDAP client requests Directory information that is not located in the Exchange Directory, that client can be referred to another LDAP server. Use the Referrals property sheet, shown in Figure 14-38, to specify LDAP servers to which referrals can be made. To add an LDAP server to the referrals list, you must know the DNS and base directory names of the remote server, the port number used to connect to that server, and whether to use SSL to connect.

Summary

In this information-packed chapter, you learned how Exchange Server 5.5 supports several common Internet protocols, including SMTP, POP3, HTTP, NNTP, and LDAP.

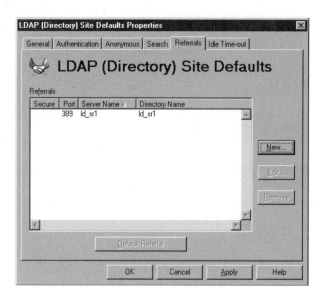

Figure 14-38. *Specifying LDAP servers to which a client can be referred.*

Exchange Server 5.5 supports SMTP through the Internet Mail Service, a Windows NT service that allows an Exchange Server to function as an SMTP server. You install IMS in Exchange Administrator by using the Internet Mail Wizard and configure it by using the *Internet Mail Service* object located in the Connection container in Exchange Administrator.

POP3 and IMAP4 are message access protocols that are used to retrieve messages from server-based mailboxes. POP3 and IMAP4 clients can be used to access Exchange mailboxes over the Internet. Exchange Server 5.5 uses Outlook Web Access and HTTP to allow Web browser access to mailboxes, public folders, and Directory information. NNTP is the protocol used to transfer newsgroup information between Usenet servers; newsreaders also use this protocol to access those servers. Exchange Server 5.5 can act as a fully functional Usenet server. You can configure newsfeeds to other Usenet servers by using the Newsfeed Configuration Wizard in Exchange Administrator. Exchange Server 5.5 also supports Directory access via the LDAP protocol.

Protocols typically are configured at three levels: site, server, and mailbox. Settings made at the site level are inherited by servers on the site. Settings made at the server level override settings made at the site level and are inherited by mailboxes on that server. Settings made at the mailbox level override settings made at the server level. These general rules have two exceptions, however. The first exception is that the LDAP protocol can be configured only at the site and server levels, not at the mailbox level. The second exception is that any protocol disabled at the server level is always disabled for all mailboxes on that server, regardless of settings made at the mailbox level.

In Chapter 15, you will learn about the basic security of Exchange Server 5.5 and how to configure an added level of security known as Exchange Advanced Security.

Chapter 15
Configuring Security

Microsoft Exchange Server 5.5 provides several measures of security. Because of its tight integration with Microsoft Windows NT, Exchange Server 5.5 takes advantage of Windows NT security to allow single-user logon and authentication, cross-domain access, permissions on Exchange resources, and security auditing.

In this chapter we discuss the basic security provided by Microsoft Exchange Server as well as the permissions available to the various roles present in the Exchange Administrator. We also discuss the Advanced Security capabilities provided by Exchange Server 5.5. These capabilities use advanced key technology to provide message signing and encryption.

Understanding Basic Security

Exchange Server 5.5 and Microsoft Windows NT Server are tightly integrated, and Exchange Server 5.5 is designed to take advantage of the Windows NT Server security model. This model boasts several features, including the following:

- **User accounts**   Every user on a Windows NT network has a unique user account. Each user must log on using this account before access to resources on the network is permitted. User accounts and groups of user accounts can be given rights and permissions that provide varying levels of access to resources such as files, directories, and printers. Exchange Server 5.5 objects are also resources to which you can grant rights and permissions. Because they did not have to log in to the system, some users — for example, users connecting to a World Wide Web site that is on Windows NT or a user accessing public folders — may think they are accessing a Windows NT system without using an account. Both of those situations can use a "guest" account to which the user is oblivious. In a later chapter of this book, you will see how a user can connect to public folders without having an account on the network.

- **Domains** A *domain* is a logical grouping of computers, users, and resources on a Windows NT network that share a security database. The *security database* is where user, group, and computer accounts in a domain are defined.

- **Trust relationships** A trust relationship provides a one-way connection between different domains that gives users in one domain permission on resources in another domain. For example, if domain A trusts domain B, users in domain B can be assigned permissions to access resources in domain A. It is also possible to have two one-way trusts so that if domain B also trusts domain A, users in domain A can be assigned permissions to access resources in domain B.

- **Auditing** Windows NT has the capability to record system and application events as well as several security parameters. Exchange Server 5.5 takes advantage of these auditing capabilities, allowing you to track changes in Exchange services and objects as well as errors such as directory access errors.

Exchange Server 5.5 resources are treated much the same as any other resource on a Windows NT network. Users must log on, using a valid user account and password, before they can access mailboxes and other protected information store resources. Administrators must also be granted specific permissions to configure the various objects within Microsoft Exchange Administrator.

 More Info This section provides a brief look at Windows NT security, a topic that could fill volumes. The section assumes that you are familiar with Windows NT security and merely shows you how Exchange Server 5.5 takes advantage of the Windows NT security model. If you need more information on Windows NT security, you might start with *Running Windows NT Server 4.0* (1996) from Microsoft Press.

Assigning Permissions in Exchange Administrator

When you install Exchange Server 5.5, only one account is granted permission to manipulate objects in Exchange Administrator: the account with which you logged on when you performed the installation. If you want other administrators to be able to manage Exchange Server 5.5, you have to specifically grant them administrative permissions. More likely, though, you will want to create user groups to which you assign those permissions and then include specific users in those groups.

You assign permissions to a configuration object by using that object's Permissions property sheet, as shown in Figure 15-1. If you do not see the Permissions property sheet when you open an object, the display of the Permissions property sheet is disabled. You can enable the display using the Options command from the Tools menu of Exchange Administrator. On the Permissions tab of the Options dialog box, select the Show Permissions Page For All Objects option. This procedure is detailed in Chapter 8.

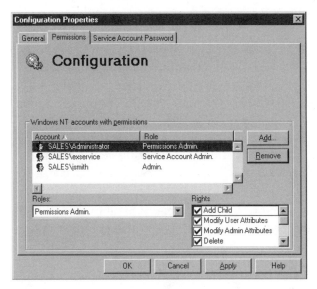

Figure 15-1. *Assigning administrative permissions to an object in Exchange Administrator.*

Users who have permissions on an object are listed on the Permissions property sheet. As you can see, a role is assigned to each user. A *role* is a predefined collection of rights. The following rights can be granted to users for objects in Exchange Administrator:

- **Add Child** This right, available only on container objects, allows a user to create objects inside that container. Assigning the Add Child Right to the Recipients container, for example, allows a user to create new recipients and place them in that container.

- **Modify User Attributes** This right allows a user to modify the attributes of an object that normally are controlled by users. For example, on a mailbox object, user attributes include telephone numbers and addresses. For a distribution list object, membership is considered a user attribute and is assigned to the owner of the list.

- **Modify Admin Attributes**   This right allows a user to modify attributes of an object that normally are controlled by administrators. For example, attributes on a mailbox include the associated Windows NT account, job title, and display name.

- **Delete**   This right allows the user to delete the object on which the right is assigned.

- **Modify Permissions**   This right allows the user to modify permissions on the object. Without this permission, a user can still grant permissions on new mailboxes but cannot modify permissions for existing mailboxes.

- **Send As**   This right allows a user to send mail that contains the object's return address. By default, all users are given the Send As permission on their own mailboxes. This right is also granted to the Site Services account for objects in the Exchange Directory. The Send As right allows server processes, such as the Message Transfer Agent, to send messages to one another. This is different from Send On Behalf Of permissions because the person receiving the message cannot tell that the message has been sent by someone else.

- **Mailbox Owner**   This right allows a user to access a mailbox and to read and delete messages within the mailbox. This right is also granted to the Site Services account for objects in the Exchange Directory so the Directory can send messages.

- **Logon Rights**   This right allows users and services to access the Exchange Directory. Without this right, a user can run Exchange Administrator but cannot connect to a server.

- **Replication**   This right allows replication of Directory information with other servers. The right is granted to the Site Services account so that the Directory Service can perform replication.

- **Search**   If the object is a container, this right allows a user to view the container's contents. This right is effective for restricting access to Address Book View containers.

Note   If you do not see the individual rights listed on the Permissions property sheet, you can make them visible using the Options command from the Tools menu of Exchange Administrator. On the Permissions tab of the Options dialog box, select the Display Rights For Roles On Permissions Page option.

Each predefined role is assigned various rights, as shown in Table 15-1. Any user with the Modify Permissions right can change the rights assigned to an individual user.

Table 15-1. Associations Between Rights and Roles

Right	Admin Role	Permissions Admin Role	Service Account Admin Role	View Only Admin Role	User Role	Send As Role	Search Role
Add Child	X	X	X				
Modify User Attributes	X	X	X		X		
Modify Admin Attributes	X	X	X				
Delete	X	X	X				
Modify Permissions		X	X				
Send As			X		X	X	
Mailbox Owner			X		X		
Logon Rights	X	X	X	X			
Replication			X				
Search							X

As you may have guessed, permissions can be granted for objects at various levels of the Exchange Server 5.5 hierarchy. Permissions granted at one level tend to be inherited by sublevel containers and objects. Three distinct security contexts exist within the Exchange Server hierarchy, however. Permissions granted in one context are not inherited by objects in other contexts. You can think of these contexts as borders that prevent inheritance. These contexts include the following:

- **Organization** Permissions granted to users on the Organization Container object are not inherited by any sublevel objects.

- **Site** Permissions granted to users on the Site Container object are inherited by all objects within the Site container, except for the *Configuration Container* object. Thus, you can grant an administrator permissions on a site for the purposes of connecting to that site with Exchange Administrator and creating recipients. The new administrator will not, however, be able to make any configuration changes in the site.

- **Configuration** Permissions granted to users on the *Configuration Container* object are inherited by objects in the *Configuration* container. Permissions granted on the *Configuration* container allow users to manipulate configuration details for a site, such as connectors, monitors, protocols, and all servers in the site.

Understanding Exchange Advanced Security

In addition to supporting the basic security mechanisms provided by Windows NT Server, Exchange Server 5.5 provides a form of security called Exchange

Advanced Security. Exchange Advanced Security is based on the RSA public-key cryptography system, which allows users to use digital signatures and encryption for increased messaging security. A *digital signature* lets a sender sign a message so that the recipient can verify the message's origin and authenticity. This process is called *signing*. Encryption lets a sender encrypt a message so that only designated recipients can read the message. This process is called *sealing*. Both processes operate using a system of encryption keys.

Using Encryption Keys

Both the signing and sealing processes use encryption keys. *Keys* are security strings of a certain length, measured in bits, used for data encryption. The longer the string, the greater the security provided. There are three basic types of encryption keys.

- **Public Keys** *Public keys* are the public part of a public/private key pair in public key cryptography and are available to everyone on a network. Public keys are stored in the Exchange Directory. Every mailbox on an Exchange Server has two public keys. One public key is part of a signing key pair, and the other is part of a sealing key pair.

- **Private Keys** *Private keys* are the private part of a public/private key pair in public key cryptography and are available only to the user to whom they are assigned. In client applications prior to Outlook 98, private keys were stored in .EPF files on the user's local hard disk; these files are created when Exchange Advanced Security is enabled for a user. In Outlook 98, these keys are stored in the registry in a secure store. Outlook 98 still uses .EPF files when moving a private key from one computer to another computer. Every mailbox on an Exchange Server has two private keys. One private key is part of the signing key pair, and the other is part of the sealing key pair.

- **Secret Keys** The mail client generates *secret keys* during the encryption process, to encrypt actual messages and the contents of attachments. Exchange Server 5.5 supports secret keys based on two standards: Data Encryption Standard (DES), which is based on a 56-bit key and is the standard for the United States government, and CAST (named using the initials of its creators, Carlisle Adams and Stafford Tavares), which is based on variable key lengths ranging from 40 bits to 128 bits. Exchange Server 5.5 supports CAST-40 and CAST-64.

Note The United States government has placed strict controls on the export of encryption algorithms. In fact, these algorithms are classified as munitions. Encryption algorithms that rely on more than a 56-bit string can be exported outside the United States and Canada only if the exporter has a special license exemption. This exemption states that the exporter must include "back-door" capability for law enforcement. As a result, versions of the Key Management Server that support CAST-64 are not shipped outside North America. For more detailed information about exporting encryption algorithms, go to *http://www.lawnotes.com/encrypt.html*

Signing a Message

When Exchange Advanced Security is enabled for a user, that user can sign a message using the mail client. The message itself is not encrypted during the signing process. Signing is merely a way for the message's recipient to verify that the message came from whom it appears to have come from and that the message has not been altered along the way.

During the signing process, a checksum of the message is generated and added to the message. The sender of a message signs the message using his or her own private signing key to encrypt the digital signature (checksum). When the message is sent, it includes the plain-text message, the digital signature, and the sender's signing certificate (which includes the sender's public signing key). The message's recipient uses the sender's public signing key to verify the signature. Once the digital signature has been decrypted using the sender's public signing key, the mail client generates a checksum of the plain-text message to compare to the checksum it decrypted from the digital signature. The message is considered valid if the sender's signing key has not been revoked and if the checksum has not been altered. If the checksums do not match up or if any other problem exists with the message, the recipient is notified, as shown in Figure 15-2.

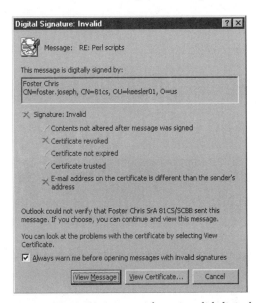

Figure 15-2. *Message with an invalid digital signature.*

Sealing a Message

The sealing process is a bit more complicated than a signing process. When a user seals a message, that user's mail client generates a secret key called a *bulk encryption key*. This bulk encryption key is used to encrypt the message content and any attachments. It is then stored in a lockbox, which is encrypted with the recipient's public sealing key and attached to the message. When the message reaches the recipient, the recipient's private sealing key is used to decrypt the bulk encryption key. The bulk encryption key is then used to decrypt the message and any attachments. If the sealed message is destined for more than one recipient, each recipient's public sealing key is used to generate a different lockbox; however, the message contents and any attachments are encrypted only once.

The reason for using the bulk encryption key to seal the message instead of simply using the public and private sealing keys is speed. The key-pair method of encryption is relatively slow, and sealing large amounts of data can take a long time. Secret key algorithms are much faster, so they are used to encrypt and decrypt the actual message. The sealing key pair is used to securely transmit the secret key.

Note If a message is sent to multiple recipients that use different levels of encryption, the lowest common encryption method is used to seal the message. Suppose that a message is sent to three recipients. One recipient uses CAST-64, one uses CAST-40, and one uses DES. The message is sealed with CAST-40 and sent to all three recipients.

Using Microsoft Exchange Key Management Server

You implement Exchange Advanced Security in an Exchange organization by using a component of Exchange Server 5.5 called Key Management Server, or simply KM Server. KM Server is a Windows NT service that generates public and private encryption keys and acts as a certificate authority (CA) for the network when Exchange Server Service Pack 1 or Service Pack 2 has not been installed.

A *certificate authority* verifies the validity of public keys that have been created for users in the organization through the issuance of certificates. The CA also issues, revokes, and renews certificates. *Certificates* are public keys that have been digitally signed by a trusted authority (the CA) and are used to ensure that public keys have not been tampered with. KM Server uses a certificate format that complies with the X.509 standard.

Real World   Using KM Server with Exchange Server Service Pack 1 and Later
The discussion of the Key Management Server in this chapter is based on its
implementation in the original release of Exchange Server 5.5. With the release
of Service Pack 1 for Exchange Server 5.5, however, a new implementation of
Key Management Server makes some significant changes:

- Microsoft Certificate Server is now used as the certificate authority in an
  Exchange organization. KM Server now acts as the key recovery agent for
  Certificate Server.
- Industry-standard X.509 V3 certificates issued by Certificate Server can
  now be used with S/MIME clients, such as Outlook 98 and Outlook
  Express. Note that KM Server still generates V1 certificates for backward
  compatibility with Outlook 97.
- You can now use KM Server to establish trust relationships with other cer-
  tification authorities by importing root certificates and certificate revocation lists from outside organizations.

In order to use KM Server with Service Pack 1 and later, you must install
Microsoft Certificate Server. Usually, you will install Certificate Server on the
same computer on which KM Server is installed. However, you can install
Certificate Server on a separate computer and use the Certificate Server Web
Client to enable KM Server to communicate with Certificate Server.

If you plan to use KM Server with Exchange Server Service Pack 1 or Service
Pack 2, we strongly recommend that you read the documentation that comes
with the Service Pack.

KM Server provides the following services to an Exchange organization:

- Creates public and private encryption keys. Mail clients create public and
  private signing keys.
- Maintains a revocation list of users for whom Exchange Advanced Security
  has been revoked.
- Generates temporary keys, which are 12-bit security tokens given to users
  when they are enrolled in Exchange Advanced Security. Temporary keys
  allow users to connect to KM Server for the generation of permanent keys.
- Maintains backups of private encryption keys, public signing keys, and the
  revocation list in an encrypted database.

For more information on public-key cryptography, you can go to
http://www.rsa.com/rsalabs/pubs/PKCS/.

Installing Key Management Server

The KM Server component is installed on only one Exchange Server computer in your organization. Using multiple KM Servers in an organization is not currently supported. You install KM Server using the regular Exchange Server 5.5 Setup program. You can install KM Server during the initial installation of Exchange Server 5.5 or at any time afterward by running Setup again and choosing Add/Remove Components in the initial Setup dialog box. The KM Server component is available as an optional subcomponent of the Microsoft Exchange Server component during a custom installation, as shown in Figure 15-3.

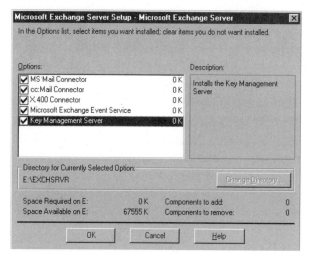

Figure 15-3. *Including Key Management Server during installation.*

Installation of Key Management Server is fairly straightforward, so this section does not cover it step by step. However, you need to be aware of one peculiarity. During installation, you are asked how you want to handle the KM Server password, as shown in Figure 15-4.

The KM Server Service acts as a normal Windows NT service, except that it requires a password to start. You can elect to handle this password in either of two ways:

- **Setup can show you the password so that you can write it down.** This method requires you to enter the password manually each time the KM Server Service starts. Writing the password down can be a security risk your organization is not willing to take. Normally, writing down any password, especially one that is as sensitive as the KM password, is not recommended!

- **Setup can write the password to floppy disk.** If you choose this method, the KM Server Service can be started only if that floppy disk is in the A: drive on the KM Server computer. If you choose this option, you need two blank, formatted floppy disks. One disk is used as a backup. One of the primary

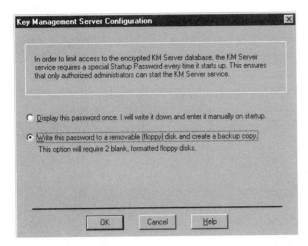

Figure 15-4. *Setting up the KM Server password.*

benefits of using the floppy disk method is that you are able to start the KM Server remotely as long as the floppy disk is in the A: drive of the KM Server computer. However, using this method requires that you keep your KM Server and password disks in a secure location. Otherwise, anyone would be able to stop and start the service. Physical security is important with all your network servers, but it is especially true with the Key Management Server.

When Setup finishes, you must start the KM Server Service manually, by double-clicking the Services icon in the Windows Control Panel. Find the Microsoft Exchange Key Management Server Service, start it, and then provide the password or floppy disk. You can also set the service to start automatically, but you will still need to provide the password each time the service starts. If your password is stored on floppy disk, you can simply leave the disk in the A: drive and the service should be able to start automatically. As noted earlier in this chapter, however, leaving the password disk in the drive can present security issues.

That's all there is to installing and starting Key Management Server. You will need to change your BIOS so that your system does not boot from Drive A:.

Note One common problem occurs for administrators who choose to write their passwords down. When the KM Service is started automatically, it will not prompt you for the password; instead, you may receive a message reading "Error 2140: An internal Windows NT error occurred." To remedy this problem, you can enter the password in the Startup Parameters field in the Services applet in Control Panel. When the service starts, however, the password is deleted from the field. Thus, you will have to enter it each time the service starts. For this reason, it is best to just manually start the service if you choose to write your password down instead of using floppy disks.

Installing Key Management Server on Other Sites

After you install KM Server, Exchange Advanced Security is available to all sites in your organization. You can also administer Exchange Advanced Security for the entire organization by using Exchange Administrator. You can perform this administration only when you are connected to a server in the site in which the KM Server is installed. To administer the KM Server from remote sites, you have to install certain KM Server components in those remote sites. Fortunately, Exchange Server 5.5 makes this process fairly easy. Simply run Exchange Server 5.5 Setup on an Exchange Server in the remote site and install KM Server the same way you installed it in the original site. Setup automatically detects the existing KM Server in the organization and installs only the components necessary for remote administration.

Real World   Things Take Time

When you install the KM Server administration components in additional sites, Setup uses the Directory on the local Exchange Server to determine whether a KM Server already exists in the organization. If you attempt to install these components in additional sites before Directory Replication occurs throughout the organization, Setup determines that no other KM Server exists and performs a full installation. This situation can create authentication and encryption errors on your network.

Configuring Key Management Server

When KM Server installation is finished, two new configuration objects are added to the Exchange Directory: the *CA* object, which is used to enroll users in Exchange Advanced Security, and the *Site Encryption Configuration* object, which is used to configure security settings for a site. In addition, Exchange Advanced Security can be configured on individual mailboxes.

Using the *Site Encryption Configuration* Object   The *Site Encryption Configuration* object is used to configure Exchange Advanced Security defaults for an entire site. The *Site Encryption Configuration* object is located in the Configurations container of the site that you want to configure.

The General and Permissions property sheets contain nothing that you haven't seen before. The Algorithms property sheet, shown in Figure 15-5, allows you to specify the encryption algorithm and message format used by clients on your site.

You can configure three parameters on this property sheet:

- **Preferred Microsoft Exchange 4.0 and 5.0 Encryption Algorithms**   As discussed earlier in this chapter, Exchange Server 5.5 supports three encryption

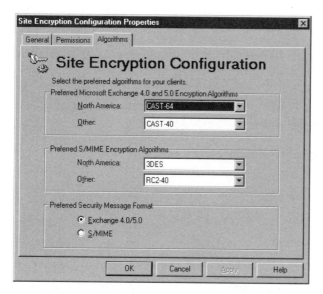

Figure 15-5. *Choosing a security method for your site.*

algorithms: CAST-40, CAST-64, and DES. For North American clients, you can select any of these three algorithms. For clients outside North America, export restrictions limit your choice to CAST-40.

- **Preferred S/MIME Encryption Algorithms**   S/MIME adds security to messages encoded using the MIME format. Five S/MIME algorithms are supported: DES, 3DES, RC2-40, RC2-64, and RC2-128. Only RC2-40 can be used outside the United States and Canada. This option is available only if your system supports S/MIME.

- **Preferred Security Message Format**   Use this option to specify whether you want to use the Exchange 4.0/5.0 or the S/MIME security format. This option is available only if your system supports S/MIME.

Using the *CA* Object   The *CA* object is used to enroll users in Exchange Advanced Security and to set administrative properties for KM Server itself. You can find the *CA* object in the Configuration container in Exchange Administrator. When you open this object, you are asked for a password. The default password is *password*, but you can change it using the Administrators property sheet of the *CA* object itself, as you learn later in this section. You are asked for the password every time you perform an Exchange Advanced Security function in Exchange Administrator. Fortunately, the password dialog box that appears allows you to specify that Exchange Server 5.5 automatically remembers the password for up to five minutes after you enter it.

The Administrators property sheet for the *CA* object, shown in Figure 15-6, is used to grant administrative permissions for KM Server. When KM Server is installed, only the user account with which you were logged on during installation has any administrative permissions. You can add administrators to and remove administrators from the list, and each administrator can change his or her own password. As you see in the discussion of the Passwords property sheet later in this chapter, it is important that individual KM administrators be able to set their own passwords.

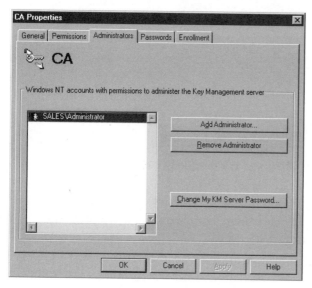

Figure 15-6. *Granting administrative permissions for KM Server.*

The Passwords property sheet of the *CA* object, shown in Figure 15-7, is used to set certain policies for administering KM Server. You can require that certain administrative functions require the authorization of more than one KM administrator. The settings in Figure 15-7, for example, require that the passwords of three KM administrators be provided before a user's security keys are revoked. You cannot specify a required number of passwords that is greater than the number of administrators configured on the Administrators property sheet.

The Enrollment property sheet of the *CA* object, shown in Figure 15-8, allows you to bulk-enroll new users in Exchange Advanced Security. You can also enroll users individually using the Security property sheet of the user's mailbox. Individual enrollment is covered later in this chapter. Bulk enrollment is performed simultaneously on all of the users in a specified Recipient container.

When a user is enrolled in Exchange Advanced Security, a temporary key is generated, and this key must be given to the user. The temporary key is used by that

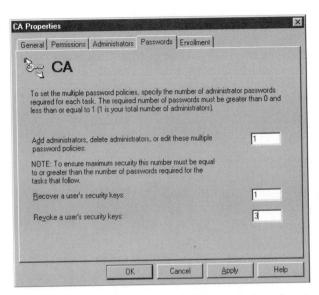

Figure 15-7. *Requiring multiple passwords for administrative tasks.*

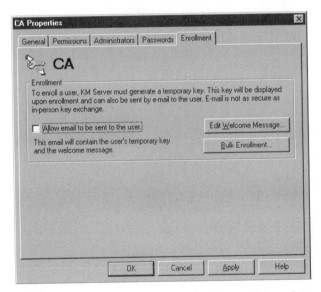

Figure 15-8. *Enrolling users in Exchange Advanced Security by bulk.*

user's mail client to establish an initial connection to KM Server. During the initial connection, KM Server generates the user's permanent key pair.

The temporary key can be distributed by e-mail or in person. Personal distribution is much more secure and is usually done by having users pick up their tokens in person. Sending the key out by e-mail does not guarantee that the intended recipient is the one who receives it. Anyone who reads the e-mail has the key. If you want to allow distribution by e-mail, you must choose the Allow E-Mail To Be Sent To The User option on the Enrollment property sheet. Click Edit Welcome Message to customize the message that is sent to users along with the temporary keys.

To begin the bulk enrollment process, click Bulk Enrollment. This action opens the Bulk Enroll Users In Advanced Security dialog box, shown in Figure 15-9.

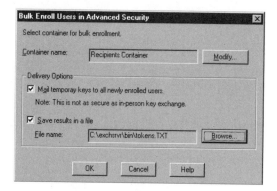

Figure 15-9. *Selecting users to enroll in Exchange Advanced Security.*

In this dialog box, select the Recipient container that includes the recipients you want to enroll. You also need to specify how to distribute the temporary keys to the users. You can choose to e-mail those keys or to save the keys in a file so that you can distribute the keys in person. Even if you choose to e-mail the keys to users, you can still choose to save the keys to a file as a useful precaution against accidentally lost or deleted e-mail messages. When you click OK in this dialog box, the users are enrolled and the keys are sent and/or saved immediately.

Real World   **Sending E-Mail without the Temporary Keys**

When you perform bulk enrollment, you can specify that e-mail be sent but prevent the actual temporary key from being sent with the e-mail. This method can be a great way to tell users, via e-mail, that they have been enrolled in Exchange Advanced Security and that they need to contact you in person to get their temporary keys. To do so, follow these steps in the Enrollment property sheet:

1. Choose the Allow E-Mail To Be Sent To The User option.

2. Click Edit Welcome Message to display the welcome message. The temporary key is included in the message, using the %TOKEN% variable.

3. Remove the %TOKEN% variable from the message. The temporary key will not be sent. You can further customize the message in whatever way you want.

4. Click Bulk Enrollment in the Enrollment property sheet. This opens the Bulk Enroll Users In Advanced Security dialog box.

5. Select the Recipient container that includes the recipients that you want to enroll.

6. Choose both the Send E-Mail and Save To File options.

7. Click OK to enroll your users and send them their customized welcome messages.

Using the Mailbox Object You can perform certain Exchange Advanced Security administrative functions on a per-user basis using the Security property sheet of a user's mailbox. The Security property sheet, shown in Figure 15-10, allows you to view certificate information for the user, to enroll the user in Exchange Advanced Security, and to revoke and recover security keys.

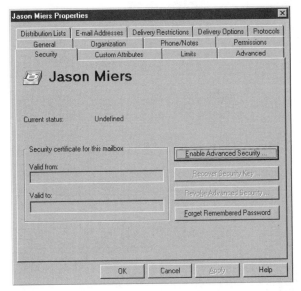

Figure 15-10. *Managing Exchange Advanced Security for a single user.*

You can enroll a user in Exchange Advanced Security by clicking Enable Advanced Security. In the dialog box that appears, you are given the choice of whether to send the user's temporary key by e-mail. Whether or not you send the key via e-mail, the temporary key is displayed so that you can write it down or cut and paste it to another application.

Occasionally, you may need to revoke a user's security keys, such as when that user leaves your organization. To do so, simply click the Revoke Advanced Security button on the Security property sheet for the user's mailbox.

Revoked users are placed in a revocation list that is maintained by KM Server. Users for whom Exchange Advanced Security has been revoked are kept in the revocation list until they are marked for deletion, which by default is about 18 months from when Exchange Advanced Security was first enabled. Within that time, you can recover Exchange Advanced Security for a user by clicking Recover Security Key. You can also use the Recover Security Key option to recover keys when users lose their temporary keys before you set up Exchange Advanced Security on the client, when users lose their Exchange Advanced Security passwords on their client, and when users corrupt or remove the local security file from their client.

It is important to keep the keys because the items they "signed" during the time the key was valid may be important later in time. For example, if an expense report was "signed" six months ago, it may still be needed for consolidation at the end of the year.

Configuring Exchange Advanced Security on the Client

When a user is enrolled in Exchange Advanced Security, that user can activate Exchange Advanced Security using the mail client. This section explains how to perform this activation in Microsoft Outlook.

Outlook 97

To begin, launch Microsoft Outlook 97 and log on under the user account of a mailbox for which Exchange Advanced Security has been enabled. Choose Options from the Tools menu of the Outlook main window to display the Security property sheet, shown in Figure 15-11. You use this property sheet to set up Exchange Advanced Security.

Next, click Set Up Advanced Security to open the Set Up Advanced Security dialog box, shown in Figure 15-12.

In the Token field, enter the temporary key that was generated by KM Server. You must also enter and confirm an Exchange Advanced Security password. This password is required whenever you generate or try to open a signed or sealed message. Outlook 97 automatically generates the Security File path. When you click OK, your request for Exchange Advanced Security is sent to KM Server. You should receive a new message from the System Attendant fairly quickly, stating that the request has been processed.

Outlook 98/2000

Setting up Advanced Security in Outlook 98 and Outlook 2000 is different from the process for Outlook 97. As mentioned earlier in this chapter, Outlook 98 does not utilize an .EPF file to store the public and private keys. The public keys are stored in a certificate; the private keys are stored in a secure store within the Registry. Figure

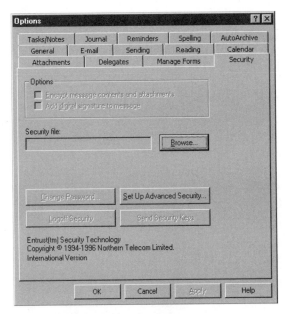

Figure 15-11. *Setting up Exchange Advanced Security in Outlook 97.*

Figure 15-12. *Entering your security information into Outlook 97.*

15-13 shows the Security tab for Outlook 98. The top portion of the tab deals with securing messages; the lower portion of the tab deals with digital certificates.

Let's look at the top portion first. This portion identifies the default security setting. Figure 15-13 shows that this client is using Exchange Security as the default security setting. The sdc5 in parentheses is the name of the keyset being utilized. Clicking Change Settings brings up the Change Security Settings dialog box shown in Figure 15-14.

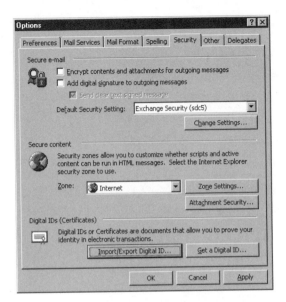

Figure 15-13. *Security tab for Outlook 98.*

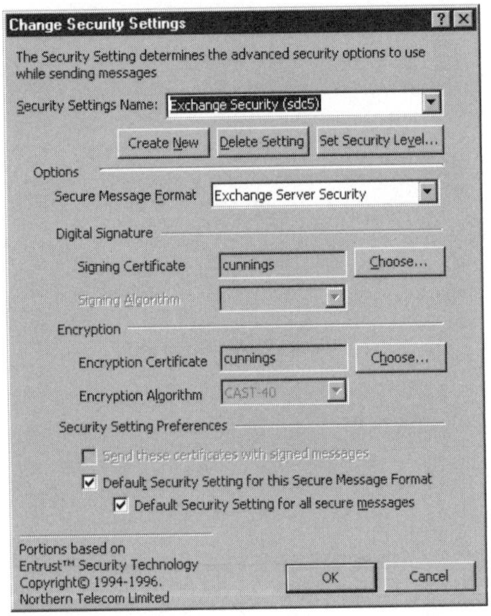

Figure 15-14. *Change Security Settings dialog box for Outlook 98.*

Within the Change Security Settings dialog box, you have the option of selecting the format for secure messages as well as the location for the signing certificate and the encryption certificate. The two formats available for securing messages include Exchange Server Security and S/MIME. S/MIME is available if your Exchange Server 5.5 utilizes Service Pack 1 or later.

Let's go back and look at the lower portion of Outlook 98's Security tab (Figure 15-13). This portion includes an option that allows you to import or export a digital certificate. Figure 15-15 shows that the user is importing an .EPF file from an earlier version of the Exchange client. The .EPF file already exists on the user's system, so simply pointing Outlook 98 to its location is sufficient. You must also type in the password that was set up when the .EPF file was generated as well as a name for the keyset. Outlook 2000 works in the same manner as Outlook 98, even though the screens look slightly different.

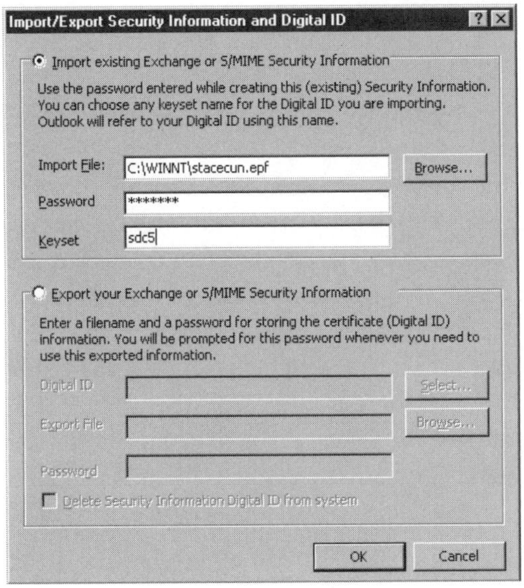

Figure 15-15. *Preparing to import an .EPF file into Outlook 98.*

Also included in the lower portion is an option called Get A Digital ID. This option is used when you do not have a digital certificate to import but want to activate Advanced Security in Outlook 98 or Outlook 2000. Figure 15-16 shows the two choices available when this option is selected in Outlook 2000. To activate security based On The Key Management Server, select Set Up Security For Me On The Exchange Server.

Summary

In this chapter, you learned how Exchange Server 5.5 takes advantage of the Windows NT Server security model, and you learned about Exchange Advanced Security. Exchange Server 5.5 behaves much like any other resource on a Windows NT network. You can grant administrative and user permissions to objects in the Directory by using the Permissions property page for that object.

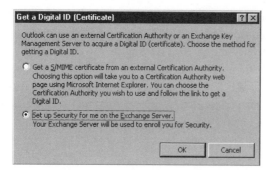

Figure 15-16. *Get a Digital ID dialog box in Outlook 2000.*

Exchange Advanced Security is provided by the Key Management Server component of Exchange Server 5.5. KM Server (without SP 1) is a Windows NT service that acts as a certificate authority for the organization. KM Server generates and maintains encryption keys for users in the organization and creates certificates, which help validate public keys after they have been created. Users in an Exchange organization can digitally sign and seal messages to other users. Signing is a process that allows the recipient of a message to verify the authenticity of a message. Sealing is a process that encrypts the message so that only designated recipients can read it. The signing process relies on the use of public/private signing key pairs. The sealing process relies on the use of a public/private sealing key pair and a secret key generated by the client.

In Exchange Administrator, you administer KM Server by using two new objects that are installed during KM Server installation: the *CA* object, which is used to enroll users in Exchange Advanced Security, and the *Site Encryption Configuration* object, which is used to configure security settings for a site. In addition, Exchange Advanced Security can be configured on individual mailboxes. Using the *CA* object, you can add and remove KM Server administrators, assign multiple-password policies, and bulk-enroll users in Exchange Advanced Security. Using the Security property sheet of an individual's mailbox object, you can enroll that individual in Exchange Advanced Security as well as revoke and recover security keys. After users have been enrolled in Exchange Advanced Security, you complete Setup by entering the temporary-key information into the mail client. The version of the client you use dictates the method of entering the security data into the client.

Throughout this part of the book, you have learned about the deployment of Exchange Server 5.5. In Part IV, you will begin to learn how Exchange clients are deployed in an Exchange organization. Chapter 16 begins with an overview of the clients available for use with Exchange Server 5.5.

Part IV
Deployment of Exchange Clients

Chapter 16
Overview of Exchange Clients

Up to this point, we have focused on the server portion of the Exchange environment because this book is primarily about Microsoft Exchange Server 5.5. But a server does not operate in a void; clients must be attached to the server to complete the picture.

This is the first of four chapters that examine the functionality of the various clients that can be used with Exchange. The chapter briefly discusses the seven main types of clients that you may find in your Exchange environment:

- Microsoft Outlook in a variety of service options
- Microsoft Outlook Express
- Microsoft Outlook Web Access
- Exchange Client
- Microsoft Schedule+
- Microsoft Windows messaging client
- Standard Internet mail clients

Each of these can be used as a client in an Exchange environment, but each has a different set of functions. Because the focus of this book is Exchange Server 5.5, and because each of these clients has a wide range of functionality and features, we do not describe each client in depth. Instead, this chapter simply introduces the major types of Exchange client software. Later chapters explore the areas in which one of these clients, Microsoft Outlook 98, can be used in conjunction with Exchange to implement solutions.

Microsoft Outlook 2000

Microsoft Outlook 2000 is the latest version of Outlook. Outlook 2000 is a component of Office 2000, so it will become widely used as organizations upgrade to this newest version of the popular office suite. Outlook 2000 is included in all five Office 2000 packages: Microsoft Office 2000 Small Business, Microsoft Office 2000 Standard, Microsoft Office 2000 Professional, Microsoft Office 2000 Premium, and Microsoft Office 2000 Developer. Figure 16-1 shows an example of the Inbox in Outlook 2000.

Figure 16-1. *The Outlook 2000 client.*

As you can see, the appearance isn't much different from that of Outlook 98. However, several new features are included in Outlook 2000, including the ability to:

- Publish your personal or team calendar as a Web page using a single command
- Use the Capabilities tab on a Contact item to track and view dynamically all activity related to a contact such as e-mail, appointments, and tasks
- Use Mail Merge to manage mass mailings for e-mail, fax, and print distribution for all of your contacts or for only those selected based on information contained within a set of contact fields

- Support not only POP3 and SMTP but also IMAP4, LDAP, NNTP, S/MIME, HTML Mail, vCard, and iCalendar
- Use the Shortcut Bar to create a shortcut for any file, Web page, or folder
- Use Outlook Today to customize an overview of your e-mail, calendar, and task information in a single location for those times to provide a quick look at the events for the day

You can make the customized Outlook Today view the default screen for Outlook 2000, as shown in Figure 16-2.

Figure 16-2. *Customizing the view of Outlook Today.*

Microsoft Outlook 98

Outlook 98 is currently the most widely used client for Exchange Server 5.5. Outlook 98 comes bundled with Exchange Server 5.5. The Outlook client was available for free to all for a short time, and it is still a free upgrade for users of

Outlook 97. Outlook 98 can be downloaded from *http://officeupdate. microsoft.com* as long as you are a licensed user of any version of Microsoft Office or Exchange Server.

The Outlook products were introduced as Exchange clients with Exchange 5.0. Outlook combines the functionality that was previously contained in both Exchange Client and Schedule+ (both of which are described later in this chapter) to deliver a complete messaging, scheduling, and contact management solution. Outlook clients can also work with public folders to share information.

In addition to providing all the functionality that formerly required both Schedule+ and Exchange Client, Outlook supports add-ins. *Add-ins* are additional program modules that, as their name implies, can be seamlessly added to the Outlook environment to extend the functionality of the product. The Schedule+ add-in, for example, provides compatibility between Schedule+ and the Outlook calendar. The capability to use add-ins makes Outlook a strategic product for Microsoft because third-party developers can use Outlook as an application development platform. An example of a third-party add-in is Pretty Good Privacy (PGP). This add-in allows the user to send encrypted and signed messages using the PGP protocol. (Don't confuse PGP with the Advanced Security discussed in the last chapter. PGP does not use the Key Management Server for its functionality.) PGP is mainly used for Internet Mail and not Corporate Workgroup Mail. Figure 16-3 shows the basic Outlook 98 client.

Outlook 98 (as well as Outlook 2000) can be used with the following service options, each of which provides a different set of features for use in different circumstances:

- **Corporate or Workgroup (CW)** The Corporate or Workgroup Service option is designed for use over a local area network (LAN) with Exchange Server, Microsoft Mail, or another third-party, LAN-based mail system such as cc:Mail or Lotus Notes. CW provides the complete set of Outlook features. In CW mode, Outlook 98 provides all the features that are available in the other modes and more. Depending on the mail server you are using the client machine does not need to have a personal folder, or *.PST file, in order to operate with this service option, because the messages are stored on the server. However, if users want to maintain a *.PST file, they are free to do so. Users must be aware that the *.PST file exists only on their hard drives; it is their responsibility to ensure it is backed up properly to avoid losing mail if the *.PST file

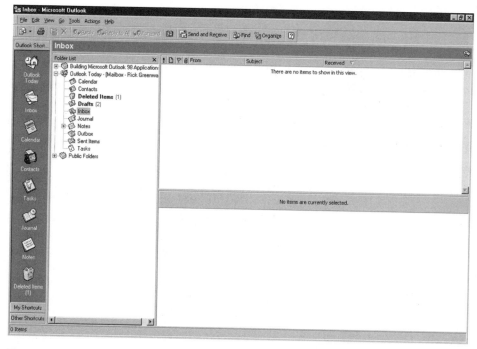

Figure 16-3. *The basic Outlook 98 client.*

becomes unusable. Another important item about *.PST files is that they are not, by default, protected from prying eyes. However, there is an option for users to password-protect files if they so desire.

- **Internet Mail Only (IMO)**   The Internet Mail Only Service option makes Outlook act as an Internet mail client. In this mode, an Outlook 98 user dials in to any server that supports POP3, SMTP, or IMAP4 clients to access mail. Some of the functionality of Outlook, such as the use of voting buttons, is unavailable in this mode. A client machine must have a personal folder, or *.PST file, in order to store messages.

- **Stand-alone Information Manager with No E-Mail**   When you choose to use Outlook 98 in this mode, Outlook acts as a stand-alone personal Information Manager in which you can use its contact, task, and schedule management features. You cannot send or receive mail when Outlook 98 operates in this mode. Even though the client machine is not utilized for mail, it must have a personal folder, or *.PST file, in order to store information used by the other features.

Normally, Outlook 98 is installed with the capability to operate with one of these service options. The Outlook installation program determines which service option of Outlook 98 reproduces the functionality to which you are accustomed. If the Outlook 98 installation procedure detects a previous installation of Outlook 97, the procedure assumes that you want the same set of Outlook features and installs Outlook 98 with the same service option that is present in the existing Outlook 97 setup.

You can change the service option after Outlook 98 has been installed, but you may have to install additional components to make the service option operational.

You will learn how to install Outlook 98 in Chapter 17, how to use Outlook 98 with multiple user profiles and offline in Chapter 18, and how to use rules in Outlook 98 in Chapter 19. In addition, Chapters 23, 24, and 25 discuss using some of the features of Outlook to extend the reach of your Exchange solution. These topics carry over to Outlook 2000 also, so you will be able to accomplish the same tasks using that mail client.

Microsoft Outlook Express

Outlook Express (Figure 16-4) is a subset of the standard Outlook product. It supports only POP3-, SMTP-, and IMAP-based mail, and it does not provide the groupware messaging present in its bigger brother. The program allows you to access mail messages, send mail messages, and read Internet newsgroups, along with providing other functionality such as Lightweight Directory Access Protocol (LDAP). Outlook Express cannot take advantage of most of the collaboration features of an Exchange Server.

Outlook Express is the mail program that comes with Microsoft Internet Explorer, replacing the previous client that was called Internet Mail and News. Outlook Express has also become the default mail reader for Microsoft Windows 98 replacing the product known as Windows Messaging, which is described later in this chapter. Outlook Express provides support for multiple e-mail accounts so they can all be viewed from within one window. Outlook Express also provides the capability for multiple users to have their own individual identities for messages, contacts, and tasks.

Outlook Express provides mail services and some basic rules functionality through the Inbox Assistant, but it cannot create folders on an Exchange Server

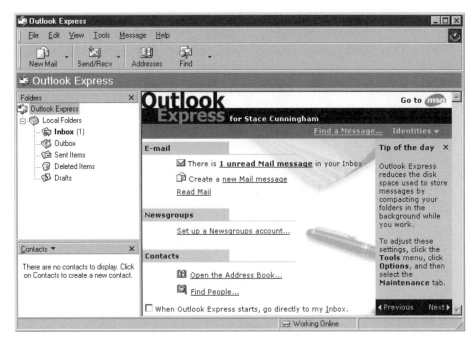

Figure 16-4. *Outlook Express.*

or access any Exchange public folders, unless you are using IMAP4 on your Exchange Server. In addition to reading normal mail messages, Outlook Express can act as a newsreader for Internet newsgroups. Outlook Express can impose some client-side rules for handling incoming mail, but you cannot use it to create server-side rules as you can with the Rules Wizard in the complete Outlook 98 product.

Outlook Web Access

Outlook Web Access (OWA) is a way of accessing mail and scheduling information from an Exchange Server, just as you would from Outlook, through a standard Web browser, such as Microsoft Internet Explorer 3.0 or later and Netscape Navigator 3.0 or later. The version 3 or later browsers are necessary to support the functionality required by HTML 3.2, such as frames, advanced scripting, Secure Sockets Layer (SSL) and Java.

OWA is not a client at all, but a set of Active Server Pages that run in the context of Microsoft's Internet Information Server (IIS), as shown in Figure 16-5. These Active Server Pages use collaboration data objects (CDOs) as an interface to Exchange services. You will learn much more about both Active Server Pages and CDOs in Chapters 26 and 27.

Server Architecture

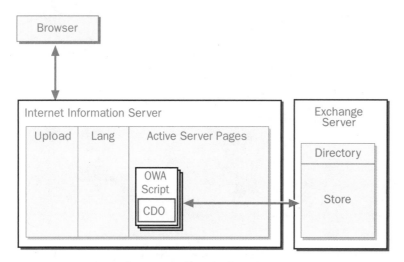

Figure 16-5. *The architecture of Outlook Web Access.*

You can install OWA when you install Exchange Server 5.5. When the Active Server Pages that are used to provide OWA access are installed, a user can access several of the functions available through Outlook, using the browser. Users can have access to functionality for basic e-mail, basic calendar and group scheduling, basic public folders, and collaborative applications (when the forms have been developed with Microsoft Visual InterDev). Some of the items that are *not* available when using OWA are:

- Personal address books (because they are stored on your workstation)
- Spell-checking
- Replied and forwarded flags in list view
- Message flags and Inbox rules
- Three-pane view
- Dragging and dropping to a folder

- Searching for messages
- WordMail and Microsoft Office integration
- Viewing free/busy details
- Task lists and task management
- Exporting to DataLink watch or other devices
- Outlook forms
- Synchronizing local offline folders with server folders
- Access to your .PST file

Outlook Web Access simulates the look and feel of Outlook 98, as shown in Figure 16-6. The universality of the browser client makes OWA an attractive choice in environments that have a widespread mix of clients (such as Windows, Macintosh, and UNIX) and that require a shared messaging client. Outlook Web Access is extremely useful for users, such as information systems staff, who move around to different workstations frequently during the day. They simply check their mail quickly using OWA instead of creating a mail profile on each of the workstations!

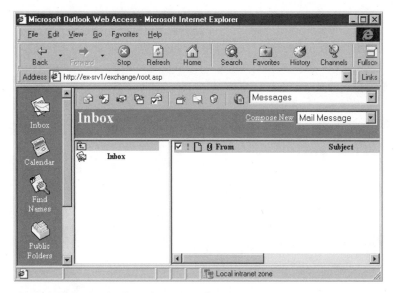

Figure 16-6. *Outlook Web Access client.*

There is no specific integration between Microsoft Office or Internet Explorer and Outlook Web Access, and OWA does not provide any task management capabilities. OWA does allow users to access Exchange public folders and the Exchange Directory.

Exchange Client

Exchange Client, shown in Figure 16-7 on a Windows NT 4.0 machine, delivers many of the functions that are inherent in the Exchange system, such as the capability to access public folders. The Exchange client does not have scheduling capabilities built into it, so it depends on Schedule+ (covered in the following section) to provide this capability.

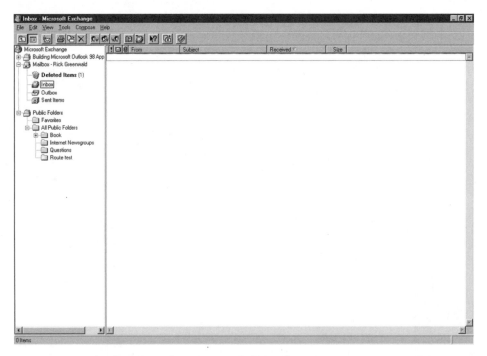

Figure 16-7. *The Exchange client running on Windows NT.*

The Exchange client was the default client for Exchange from the first release of the Exchange product until Exchange Server 5.5 was released. It is available in 32-bit Windows, 16-bit Windows, and Macintosh versions. The Outlook for Macintosh and Outlook for 16-bit Windows versions are not comparable feature for feature to the 32-bit Windows version of Outlook. However, both the Macintosh and 16-bit Windows versions do include e-mail, personal calendaring, tasks lists, and group scheduling. If you have been using Exchange in your environment for a while, you very well might have Exchange Client on some, most, or all of your client machines. Exchange Client is fully supported by Exchange Server 5.5; but it will not be enhanced in subsequent releases of Exchange.

Schedule+

Schedule+ (Figure 16-8) was the default program used for scheduling and contact management for Exchange until Exchange Server 5.5, in which it was replaced by Outlook. Both Schedule+ 1.0 and Schedule+ 7.0 were available in 32-bit Windows, 16-bit Windows, and Macintosh versions. Users moving to Outlook from Schedule+ can import their existing calendar data so nothing is lost in the transition.

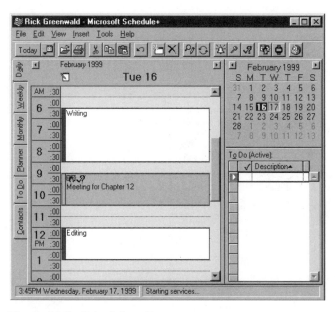

Figure 16-8. *Schedule+ client.*

Schedule+ clients can still be used with Exchange Server 5.5, but Schedule+ will not be enhanced in subsequent releases of Exchange. You can use Schedule+ in an Exchange environment that also includes Outlook users. The two client applications can access the same calendaring information, but Outlook provides some additional functionality such as:

- Journal feature
- Note feature
- Integrated contacts
- Additional views
- Advanced custom view capabilities
- Task delegation
- Advanced printing options
- Public folder with calendars

Windows Messaging

Windows Messaging was the default messaging client included with all versions of Windows until Windows 98. You may not have realized that there was a program with this name on your machine; most users think of it as simply the Inbox. The only way that you would have seen the name of the application was to pay attention to the splash screen that appeared when you double-clicked on the Inbox icon (Figure 16-9).

Figure 16-9. *The splash screen identifying Windows Messaging in Windows NT.*

When you installed the Exchange Client on a machine, the Exchange Client automatically replaced the Windows Messaging client. If you did not have Exchange Client installed on the machine, the Windows Messaging application displayed a simple e-mail client that could not interface with Exchange Server, as shown in Figure 16-10.

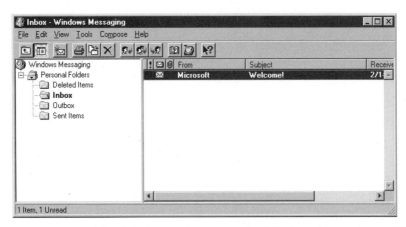

Figure 16-10. *The default e-mail program for Windows Messaging on Windows NT.*

As you see in the figure, the default version of Windows Messaging does not include any of the advanced features that are available in Exchange Client or Outlook, because it could not interface with Exchange Server. You don't see any public folders or the other folders in your normal mailbox that give you access to scheduling capabilities and other features. You have access only to standard mail messages using SMTP or POP3.

In Windows 98, Outlook Express replaced Windows Messaging as the default Windows mail client because it is included with Internet Explorer 4.0 (which is integrated into Windows 98).

Standard Internet Mail Clients

Because Exchange Server 5.5 supports the POP3 Internet mail standard, any e-mail program that can use this protocol can access your Exchange Server. Most popular e-mail clients today can act as POP3 clients.

Real World   POP3 Protocols in Exchange
For generic mail clients to work with Exchange, you have to make sure that the
POP3 service is running on your Exchange Server. You can assign this protocol
in the Protocols container for a site or a server as shown in Figure 16-11, as well
as on the Protocols tab of the property sheet for an individual user, as shown in
Figure 16-12.

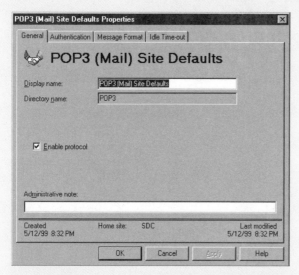

Figure 16-11. *Enabling the POP3 protocol for an Exchange site.*

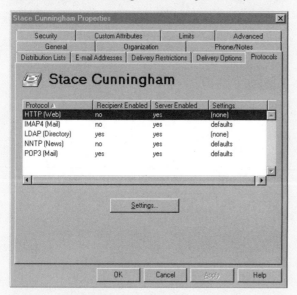

Figure 16-12. *Enabling the POP3 protocol for an Exchange recipient.*

By default, the POP3 protocol and the IMAP4 protocol are enabled when you install Exchange Server 5.5. You can explicitly disable the protocols at two levels of the hierarchy to limit the use of these protocols. For instance, if you want to enable the POP3 protocol for a site, all of the servers in the site automatically support the protocol. If you want to exclude some of the servers in the site from access through the POP3 protocol, you can simply disable it at the site level and enable it for the servers you want to make available.

For more information on POP3 and other Internet protocols, see Chapter 14.

You can use any standard e-mail client to get your messages from Exchange Server 5.5, but you cannot use the advanced scheduling features of Outlook. The IMAP4 protocol is used to access both private and public folders, so a standard Internet e-mail client will allow access to these folders if it supports the IMAP4 protocol. You can configure your Exchange Server as the mail server for a generic e-mail client, just as you would configure any other POP3-compliant server.

You might notice a similarity in the description of Outlook Express, the standard Windows Messaging client, and the use of a standard Internet e-mail client with Exchange. All these clients provide essentially identical functions as Exchange clients because all of them act as simple POP3 mail clients.

Real World   Rules and the Basic Client
You cannot define server-based rules with any POP3 or IMAP4 client, including the standard Windows Messaging client, because the capability to define server-based rules is the exclusive realm of Outlook and the Exchange client. Because many of the rules that you create will be run on the Exchange Server, they will still operate correctly with a standard Internet e-mail client.

Choosing a Client for Exchange

In a philosophical sense, choosing a client for Exchange is easy. Outlook 2000 is the most current version of the Outlook client; it provides the greatest amount of functionality, and it is designated by Microsoft as the official client for Exchange. Outlook 2000 comes bundled with Microsoft Office 2000. If your organization is currently using Office 97, by all means move up to Outlook 98. Outlook 98 is a free upgrade to licensed users of Office 97 that comes with

Exchange Server Service Pack 1 and Service Pack 2. Exchange Client and Schedule+ are supported, but they are no longer being enhanced with new features. Standard Internet e-mail clients miss a great deal of the functionality that Exchange provides, but they are fast enough to be used efficiently over the Internet and are easier to setup for firewall access.

As they say, however, your mileage may vary. You may have a large installed base of Exchange clients, and upgrading them would be a significant administrative task. Some or all of the people in your organization may already have an e-mail program that they like and, rather than go through the pain of change, may choose to forgo the advanced features available with Outlook. Any of these reasons might contribute to a decision to support non-Outlook clients as part of your Exchange environment or to use Outlook Web Access.

You may also have such a widespread mix of client platforms that you need to use the most generic client possible: the Outlook Web Access client. Or you may need to use OWA to service the messaging needs of some of your users and use the complete Outlook product for other users. Client machines can also use standard Internet POP3 and OWA clients to access your Exchange Inbox over the Internet.

Because Outlook 98 is currently the most widely used Exchange client, the following three chapters (and some of the chapters in Part VI) use Outlook 98 as the Exchange client in the examples.

Summary

Exchange Server 5.5 can support a wide variety of clients, including Outlook, Outlook Express, Outlook Web Access, Exchange Client, Schedule+, Windows Messaging clients, and standard Internet e-mail clients. Outlook 98 is currently the most widely used client for Exchange Server 5.5 because it provides the most functionality and is the clear upgrade path for forthcoming Exchange clients. In the future, Outlook 2000 will become the preferred client as organizations upgrade to Office 2000.

Outlook Express is a capable client for Exchange Server 5.5 as long as the POP3 or IMAP4 protocol is enabled on the server. Outlook Web Access is a good client to be used when your organization supports non-Windows-based clients such as UNIX and Macintosh. The HTTP protocol must be enabled on the Exchange Server to take advantage of OWA. The Exchange Client and Schedule+ are still functional alternatives in Exchange environment, although upgrading to an Outlook alternative gives you more functionality. Windows Messaging clients and standard Internet e-mail clients can perform in an Exchange Server environment but are limited in their functionality.

In the next chapter, you will learn how to install Outlook 98 on your client machines, using either the standard installation procedure or a custom installation, from CD-ROM or a shared network disk.

Chapter 17
Installing Exchange Clients

Installation of client software is one of the most repetitive tasks that you face as an administrator. However, this task is required, because a client/server system such as Microsoft Exchange Server 5.5 will not work unless both sides of the equation are in place.

Because this book focuses on Exchange, a broad topic unto itself, space does not permit detailed coverage of installing a client program. This chapter does, however, give you a brief overview of the ways that you can install Microsoft Outlook 98 on your client machines. It explains some of the options in a standard Outlook installation on an individual client and then introduces the Outlook 98 Deployment Kit, which allows you to create a single, customized installation for all your users.

Standard Installation

Outlook 98 comes as part of the installation kit for Exchange Server 5.5. If you have a valid license for any Exchange Server version or for Office 97, you can download Outlook 98 for free from the Microsoft Web site, as described in Chapter 16.

Outlook 98, like most Microsoft programs, is installed with a setup wizard — in this case, a wizard called Active Setup. Active Setup works modularly; it identifies any potential problems, such as insufficient disk drive space, prior to installing any application components. This is very handy when you are installing Outlook 98 across the organization's local area network. The first screen of the Active Setup Wizard prompts you (or the user who is installing Outlook) for some information that the wizard will use to configure the installation. Like all user-friendly wizards, the Active Server Wizard starts with an introduction screen, shown in Figure 17-1.

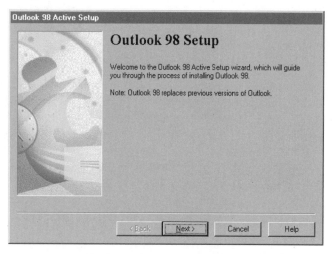

Figure 17-1. *The first screen in the Outlook 98 Active Setup process.*

The subsequent screens of the wizard introduce the license agreement (which the user must accept) and give the installer a choice of three installations: Minimal, which is only Outlook 98 and Microsoft Internet Explorer 4.01; Standard, which also includes Outlook's help function; and Full, which includes many other Outlook add-ons, such as NetMeeting, Outlook Express Newsreader, and additional Outlook enhancements.

> **Note** The Full installation includes everything—all the Office Assistants, all the Personal Information Manager converters, and so on. If you want to install only some of these items, you can go with the Standard Installation and then choose the Add/Remove Programs option in the Control Panel after the install to add selected options.

If you already have an e-mail client installed on the client machine, Active Setup asks whether you want to upgrade the messages, address books, and settings from the existing clients to Outlook. You can select one of the three existing e-mail clients to upgrade, but you must make a choice in the screen shown in Figure 17-2, even if your choice is None Of The Above.

Chapter 16 described the various service options in which Outlook 98 can operate. Active Setup prompts you to choose a service option during installation, although you can change service options after you install the product. Changing the service options of Outlook might involve making a partial reinstallation of the product or some of its components.

If you have Microsoft Schedule+ on the client machine, Active Setup asks whether you want to continue to use it for scheduling or to switch to Outlook 98. Then

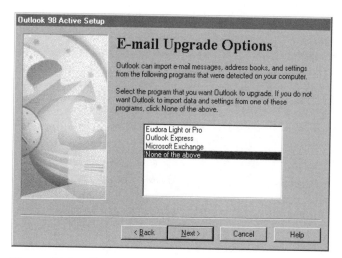

Figure 17-2. *Choosing an upgrade option.*

the final screen of the wizard prompts you for a directory in which to store the Outlook 98 files. After you specify this directory, Active Setup goes to work.

Active Setup performs the following basic steps in installing Outlook 98:

1. Checks to make sure no programs (such as the Microsoft Office Shortcut Bar) that would interfere with the installation are running. If they are, you are prompted to close those programs before proceeding.

2. Copies the files from their source locations to a temporary directory on the target machine. These files have the file extension .CAB.

3. Extracts the compressed files from the .CAB files.

4. Installs Outlook 98 as well as any components that you specified.

5. Prompts you to reboot the machine if some of the installed options require it.

You may wonder why Active Setup is called *active*; it seems to be just a standard installation process. One of the differences comes from its understanding of the way that Microsoft applications work. Many applications share versions of dynamic link libraries (DLLs). As part of the installation process, Active Setup checks to make sure that all the DLLs are the appropriate versions for the product that you are installing. If Active Setup detects some DLLs and they are the appropriate versions, the Active Setup process gives you the option of preserving those DLLs or reinstalling them. Active Setup also allows you to install a product, its components, or upgrades from a CD-ROM or from the Web.

Real World **Keep or Replace?**

Do you choose Door Number 1, which preserves existing DLLs if they are not older than the DLLs that Active Setup will install, or Door Number 2, which performs a clean, fresh installation?

You should choose Door Number 1, for a simple reason. If Active Setup finds other copies of DLLs, the existence of those DLLs almost inevitably means that one or more applications are using those DLLs. But you don't know which DLLs are being used by which applications. It is conceivable, although not probable, that a reinstallation could affect some of those existing applications. Because the software product that you are installing with Active Setup is new to the machine, the safe choice is to leave everything as you found it by accepting the existing DLLs.

The Outlook 98 Deployment Kit

If you are administering a large site, installing Outlook 98 to all of your client machines could be quite a job, especially if you have to do it via *sneak-erware* (actually running from one machine to another with an installation CD-ROM).

You can eliminate the problem of having to go to each individual machine by creating a standard install directory on a shared disk on one of your network servers. All you have to do is copy the Outlook 98 installation disk files to a shared directory and let users know where Outlook is available. Users can then run the Active Setup Wizard to install Outlook 98 on their client machines unless their systems are locked to prevent software installations. In this case, a visit to the individual machine is still required.

Installing Outlook and moving users from an existing mail system (or no mail at all) usually requires a large amount of desktop work, including:

- Installing Outlook
- Configuring profiles
- Testing to ensure all is in order

Often the Outlook installation is also scheduled with a general desktop visit when service packs for existing applications and operating systems are applied. When using NT 4.0 Workstation and even some locked Windows 95 configurations, users may not have the privileges to do their own installations.

The Outlook installation procedure via a shared directory simply changes the distribution medium from a CD-ROM to a shared directory; the actual process of installing Outlook 98 remains the same. However, you may want to create one or more customized installation routines to make it easier for your users to install Outlook and to design customized packages of Outlook options.

Microsoft provides the Outlook 98 Deployment Kit (ODK) to help you create these routines. The Deployment Kit is not available on the Exchange Server 5.5 CDs, but you can get the kit if you are a member of the Microsoft Developers Network (MSDN), a part of the Microsoft Select or Open license program, or a Microsoft Certified Solution Provider. The ODK is a valuable product, so if you have a large number of Outlook installations to perform, you should investigate subscribing to one of these programs.

More Info   You can access the Outlook Deployment Kit documentation from Microsoft's Web site at *http://www.microsoft.com/office*.

With the ODK, you can create installation packages that do not require your users to understand the standard Outlook 98 installation process or the options that it presents. You can also brand the components that are installed with Outlook 98 to meet the specific needs of your users. The result of the ODK is a customized installation kit for Outlook 98. This kit can be stored in a shared network directory or moved to a CD-ROM that you create.

You should think about the type of Outlook 98 installation that you want to create. This planning process includes determining which service options Outlook will use, what Outlook components you want to include, and which bitmaps you want to use to brand your version of Outlook.

The first step in the process is installing the Outlook 98 Deployment Wizard (ODW). You can accomplish this task by running the SETUP.EXE program in the ODK directory of your installation disk and choosing Install Outlook 98 Deployment Wizard. This option installs the program that helps you to create your own Outlook 98 deployment package. The Outlook 98 Deployment Wizard can be installed on any computer that is running Microsoft Windows NT, Microsoft Windows 98, or Microsoft Windows 95 and that has 125MB of available disk space.

After you install the Outlook 98 Deployment Wizard, you can run it from your standard Start menu. The wizard completes its job in five stages:

Stage 1: Gathering information

Stage 2: Specifying Active Setup parameters

Stage 3: Customizing Active Setup

Stage 4: Customizing Outlook 98 Setup options and Internet Explorer

Stage 5: Customizing user settings

The first stage of using the ODW is supplying some basic information about your company and its environment, including the company name, the language used within the company, and the location for the install package that you will create. If you are using a version of the ODK from the MSDN or Select program, the serial number for the ODK is displayed automatically. Other versions may require you to enter the product's serial number from the CD-ROM case.

In the second stage of the ODW, you see a list of the components of Outlook 98, as shown in Figure 17-3. You do not have to install all these components as part of your deployment kit, but it is important that they all be available. The components with green arrows are those in which the latest version is present and fully intact. A yellow caution sign means there has been an update for the component, which should be downloaded. A red "X" means the component is not there.

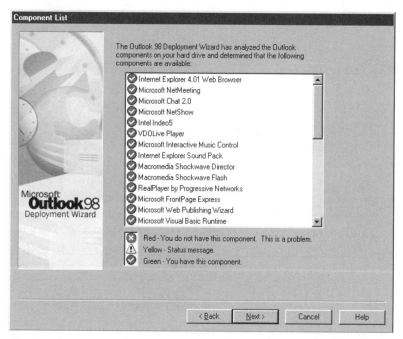

Figure 17-3. *Component list in the Outlook 98 Deployment Wizard.*

You have the option of adding up to 10 additional components as part of your deployment kit. If you want to add any components, the next screen of the ODW, shown in Figure 17-4, allows you to enter the relevant information about additional components. These components can be add-ons for Outlook 98 or any other component that you want to include.

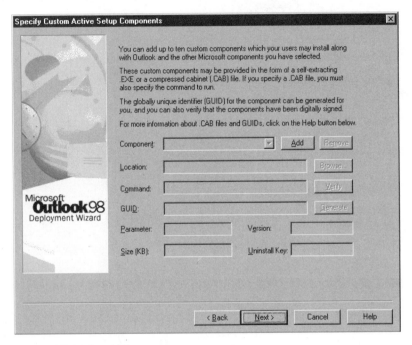

Figure 17-4. *Specifying custom components.*

The next screen of the ODW, shown in Figure 17-5, involves the process of marking the compressed deployment files using a digital certificate. A *digital certificate* is used to sign a file, so that a client can be sure where the file came from and prevent the introduction of malicious files from an unknown source into the system. Digital certificates are beyond the scope of this chapter, but you can find information about this feature in the documentation for the Outlook 98 Deployment Kit and in the ODW's online help system.

The third stage of the ODW, shown in Figure 17-6, allows you to give your own look and feel to the splash screen for a CD-ROM-based installation. You can give the initial screen for the CD-ROM Setup your own title, assign your own bitmaps for the background and menu choices, change the color of the text and the highlighted text, and even change the style for the buttons.

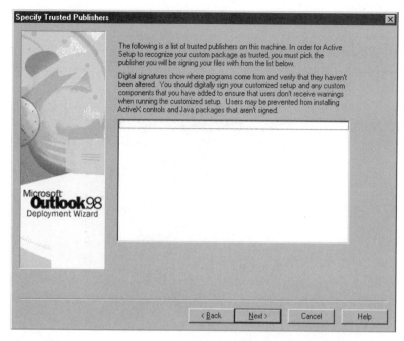

Figure 17-5. *List of trusted publishers on the ODK machine.*

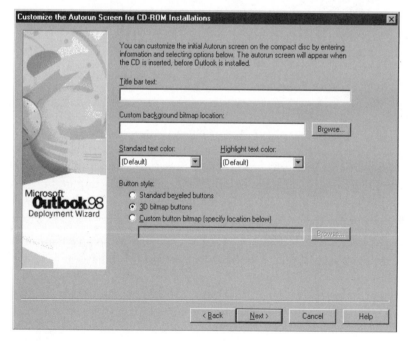

Figure 17-6. *Customizing the Autorun screen.*

The next screen of the ODW, shown in Figure 17-7, lets you set up the installation for silent operation. A *silent install* does not prompt the user during the course of the installation process. In a silent install, you can specify only one installation option, which includes designating the Outlook service option. You can also prevent the installation of Outlook from adding Internet Explorer icons to the desktop, Start menu, and Quick Launch bar on the client machine. If the silent install option is implemented, the settings for the screen shown in Figure 17-6 are irrelevant, because they are not used.

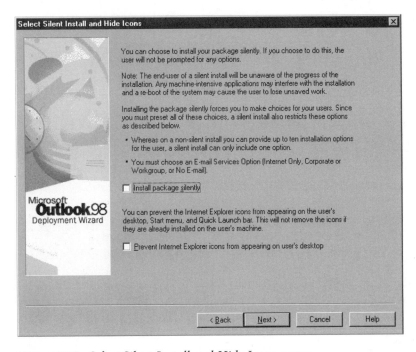

Figure 17-7. *Select Silent Install and Hide Icons screen.*

If you decide not to select a silent install, you can create up to 10 installation options in the next screen in the ODW, shown in Figure 17-8. Each option can contain a different set of components. By default, the wizard includes the three standard install possibilities—Minimal, Standard, and Full—but you can still modify those options by adding or deleting components in the two list boxes at the bottom of the page. Components available for installation include an audio/video/data conferencing tool (Microsoft NetMeeting), a wizard to publish HTML pages (Microsoft Web Publishing Wizard), and many others. You can add an option or delete an existing installation option by clicking the buttons to the right of the option name.

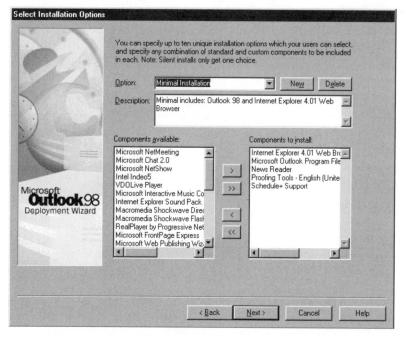

Figure 17-8. *Installation options in the Outlook 98 Deployment Wizard.*

Real World   Custom Installation Packages with Silent Installation
If you chose a silent installation in the screen of the ODW shown in Figure 17-7, the New button, which allows you to add installation specifications, is disabled. Preventing the creation of a new installation package makes sense because a silent installation allows you to select only one installation package.

Although you cannot do anything more than select a single installation option, you can change the name of an installation package and the contents of the package. Therefore, you can, in effect, modify one of the existing packages and eliminate the need to create a custom package from scratch for a silent install.

The next screen of the ODW, shown in Figure 17-9, allows you to specify a version number for the installation package that you are creating. Each time you run the ODW, the version number is incremented automatically, and users are prevented from using any earlier version. The screen also prompts you for a configuration ID—an eight-digit code that explicitly identifies your custom packages.

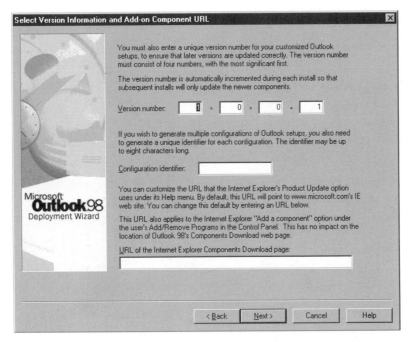

Figure 17-9. *Version information and Add-on Component URL options.*

Normally, new versions of Internet Explorer components are available through a Web page called *Addon95.htm*. If you want to make the components available through a different URL, you can enter that URL in the bottom section in this screen of the wizard. Internet Explorer then accesses that page when a user tries to add new components through the Add/Remove Components option in the Control Panel. If you specify your own Web page for add-ons, you are responsible for designing and maintaining the page. For more information on how to implement this page, refer to the documentation for Internet Explorer.

The last two screens of this stage of the ODW allow you to specify whether the Outlook 98 files are placed in their own folder in the Windows Directory, in the My Programs Directory, or in a directory of your choosing, as shown in Figure 17-10. You can also indicate whether you want to include the Windows Desktop Update in the Outlook installation process, as shown in Figure 17-11.

The fourth stage of the ODW gives you the option of customizing the Outlook 98 and Internet Explorer installations. You have three choices: selecting a service option for Outlook 98; specifying whether you want to allow the new installation of Outlook to support the use of Schedule+; and indicating whether, and how, you want to customize the default appearance of the Outlook bar and the Outlook toolbar. If you did not specify a silent install, you can choose any

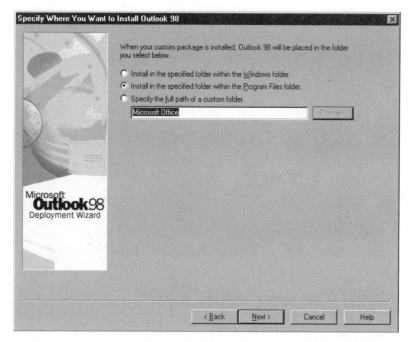

Figure 17-10. *Selecting the location for Outlook 98 installation on the client system.*

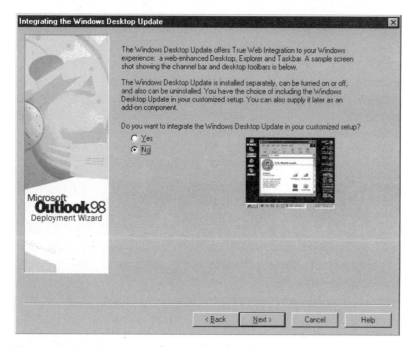

Figure 17-11. *Integrating the Windows Desktop Update screen.*

of the three Outlook 98 service options or allow users to select their own modes, as shown in Figure 17-12. For a silent install, as mentioned earlier in this chapter, you have to specify one of the standard service options.

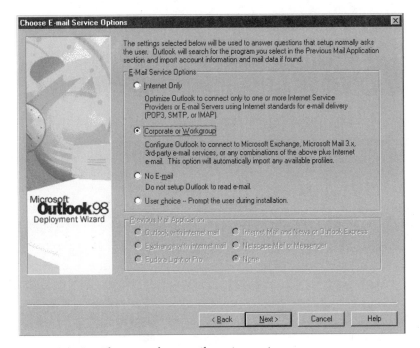

Figure 17-12. *Choosing the e-mail service option.*

As mentioned, you can choose whether to support Schedule+ for group scheduling from the screen shown in Figure 17-13. Outlook 98 natively supports a Calendar option that allows people to share their schedules, invite people to meetings, and use resources, so Schedule+ support may not be necessary for your organization.

The Outlook 98 Deployment Kit documentation covers the ways that you can customize the Outlook toolbars and menus. You can add new options to the menus and toolbars, move existing elements around, and even add new ones. Once designed, the customized toolbars are added using the screen shown in Figure 17-14.

You can also change the appearance and functionality of the Outlook Today page, which is the standard page displayed when Outlook 98 starts. The Outlook Today page displays information in HTML format and is, in a manner of speaking, a home page for Outlook 98. You can modify the Outlook Today page to include a space for breaking news that affects your organization or links to some site-specific utilities and programs.

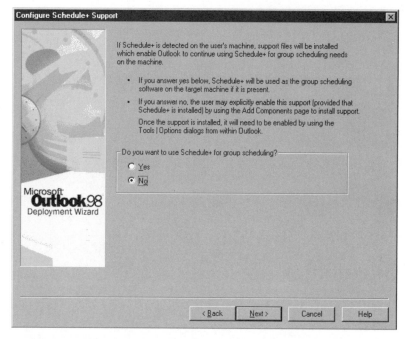

Figure 17-13. *Configuring Schedule+ support for Outlook 98.*

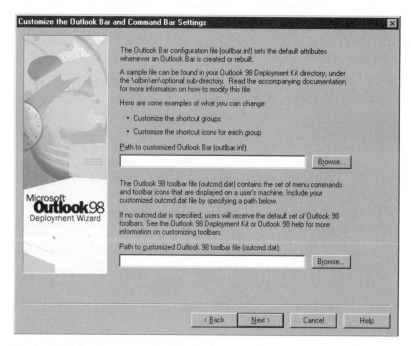

Figure 17-14. *Customize the Outlook Bar and Command Bar Settings screen.*

After the three standard screens in this part of the ODW, you are given the ability to customize the installation of Internet Explorer, as shown in Figure 17-15. This is the same as using the Internet Explorer Administrator's Kit, which is a utility that allows administrators to create a customized installation of Internet Explorer.

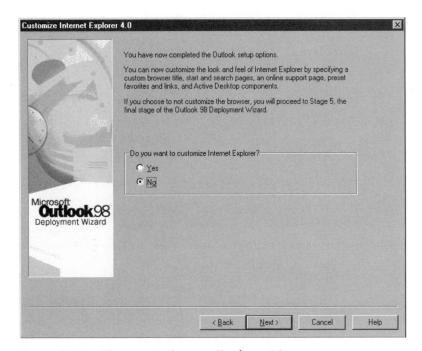

Figure 17-15. *Customizing Internet Explorer 4.0.*

The fifth and final stage of the ODW lets you shape the way that the default options are set for each user who installs this deployment package. You enter most of this information in the screen shown in Figure 17-16.

This screen has an Explorer-type interface in the left panel and a series of configuration options in the right panel. The enormous number of possible customizations available from this screen gives you very fine control of users' eventual use of Outlook and Internet Explorer. The settings that you make in this screen will be the default settings for users, but users can change these settings on their own after installation, under normal circumstances.

Any changes that you make for the help and online support URLs, the Add/Remove Components URL, the Windows title bar, and the default browser channels for the Active Channels bar override any settings that are currently enabled in an existing version of Internet Explorer.

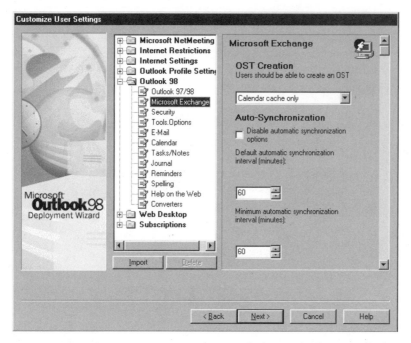

Figure 17-16. *Customizing user settings with the Outlook 98 Deployment Wizard.*

The next screen of the ODW lets you add Registry entries automatically as part of the installation process, as shown in Figure 17-17. The Registry is the central repository of control for a Windows computer; be cautious about adding Registry entries unless you are very familiar with the way that the Registry works. The final screen contains a button labeled Finish. Clicking this button causes the Outlook 98 Deployment Wizard to create all the files necessary for the installation of your own version of Outlook 98. These files are fairly large, so you should make sure that you have at least 120MB of space available on the target disk.

If you are using digital certificates, remember to go back and sign the .CAB files that are created in the Installation Directory.

When the deployment kit is created and tested, all that a user has to do is run the SETUP.EXE program from the CD-ROM or the shared directory where the files created by the ODK reside. If the deployment kit was set up for silent installation, the Setup program shows a splash screen, as a standard install does, but the screen disappears shortly after the installation process begins. At the completion of the installation, the target computer automatically reboots. If the deployment kit was not set up for silent installation, the installation process looks much like a normal Outlook 98 installation but includes the extra components and Setup options that you configured with the ODK.

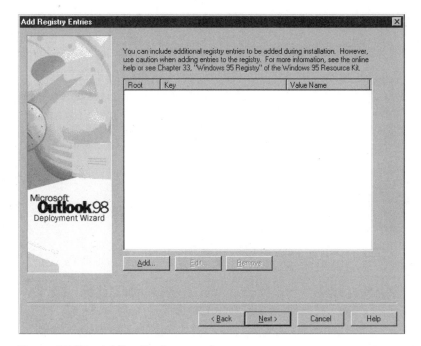

Figure 17-17. *Adding Registry entries.*

You should carefully test your deployment package in your real environment—on machines that are similar to the target machines that will be using the install package. When your testing is complete, your users can install your customized version of Outlook 98 with the deployment kit that you created.

System Policies for Outlook 98

The settings that you specify in the final stage of the ODW are used during the installation process to change the Registry settings on the target computers. You can accomplish the same task by setting up a system policy with the System Policy Editor.

The System Policy Editor allows you to configure many Registry entries for computers and users on a network. By default, the System Policy Editor does not include settings for Outlook clients, but the ODK includes a template with the name OUTLK98.ADM that you can use with the System Policy Editor to assign Outlook-specific Registry settings.

To bring the template into the System Policy Editor, go to the Administrative Tools group of your Windows NT Program Manager and open the System

Policy Editor. After the System Policy Editor starts, choose Policy Template from the Options menu to bring up the Policy Template Options dialog box, and then add the OUTLK98.ADM template to the current list of templates. You can add a template only when no system policies are open in the System Policy Editor.

After you import the template, policy settings for Outlook are part of any policies that you implement for either a computer or a user. The main user policy settings for Outlook are shown in Figure 17-18. When you select a policy at the top of the dialog box, the settings for the policy appear at the bottom of the dialog box.

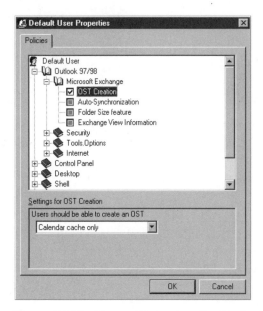

Figure 17-18. *User policy settings for Outlook.*

Using the System Policy Editor has two advantages. One advantage is that the settings in a system policy can be used for both Outlook 98 and Outlook 97. If you have an environment that uses both clients, a system policy can standardize the settings for both varieties of Outlook. Machines that use only Outlook 97 ignore any Registry settings specified in the policy that apply only to Outlook 98.

The other advantage of using a system policy is that by default, machines automatically download the Registry settings contained in the policy whenever they log onto the network. Although users can change the Registry settings manually, the default settings return the next time they log onto the network. You can also set a system policy that prevents users from changing any of the values in the Registry.

This section briefly discussed system policies and the System Policy Editor to make you aware of the extended possibilities that they present. Make sure that you spend some time with the documentation for your Windows NT Server to become more familiar with system policies before you use them in your own environment.

Systems Management Server

Systems Management Server (SMS) is a Microsoft application specifically designed to help administrators address the needs of larger user communities. The ODK contains instructions for creating installation packages and configuration files that can be used by the SMS. The kit also contains a sample Package Definition File (.PDF) that can be used with SMS to distribute the customized version of the client setup executable to the users on your network. The .PDF is a text file that includes the setup parameters necessary to install Outlook 98 using SMS. The contents of the sample .PDF included with the ODK are as follows:

```
[PDF]
Version=1.0
[Package Definition]
Product=Microsoft Outlook 98 8.5
Comment=Microsoft Outlook 98 8.5
WorkstationAccess=UserRead, UserWrite, GuestRead, GuestWrite
SetupVariations=Interactive,Silent
[Interactive Setup]
CommandName=Interactive
CommandLine=setup.exe
UserInputRequired=FALSE
SynchronousSystemExitRequired=TRUE
SystemTask=FALSE
SupportedPlatforms=Windows NT 3.1 (x86), Windows95
[Silent Setup]
CommandName=Silent
CommandLine=setup.exe
UserInputRequired=FALSE
```

```
SynchronousSystemExitRequired=TRUE
SystemTask=FALSE
SupportedPlatforms=Windows NT 3.1 (x86), Windows95
[Setup Package for Sharing]
ShareName=
ShareAccess=UserRead, UserWrite, GuestRead, GuestWrite
[Setup Package for Inventory]
InventoryThisPackage=TRUE
Detection Rule Part 1=File 1
[File 1]
File=outlook.exe
Collect=FALSE
CheckSum=
CRC=0,36112,7590
Date=
Time=
Byte=
Word=
Long=
Token 1=""
Token 2=""
Token 3=""
Token 4=""
[Last Modified]
Date=03-06-98
Time=10:36:52
```

Two steps must be accomplished before distributing Outlook 98 to your client systems. The first step consists of creating a package. The package consists of the .PDF file we discussed and a package source folder. The package source folder contains all of the files necessary for the installation. After the package is created, you must create a job to distribute the package. A job consists of not only the package but also a list of all client systems to which you want the package installed. SMS provides flexibility and granularity so that you install the package only where you want it. For example, you may decide to install the package only to client systems that meet minimum memory and hard drive parameters and ignore all other systems. The job can also be set to run only after a certain time period and become mandatory after a different time frame.

Summary

The Outlook 98 client is the preferred client for Exchange Server 5.5. During the Active Setup installation process, you can configure Outlook 98 in several ways, including selecting the mode in which Outlook will operate and specifying whether to install a minimal, standard, or full set of components.

You can create a shared installation, either on a CD-ROM or on a shared network disk, with the Outlook 98 Deployment Kit using the Outlook Deployment Wizard. Your customized deployment can be designed to give the user several installation choices or to perform a silent installation that does not require user intervention.

The ODK comes with a System Policy template that you can use with the System Policy Editor to shape the way that Outlook operates for users. The ODK can also be used in conjunction with Microsoft Systems Management Server to deliver installation packages for use in large user environments.

Outlook 98 is a robust and full-featured product, and a complete description of even some of its capabilities is beyond the scope of this book. However, some situations specifically relate to the use of Exchange Server with Outlook 98; these situations are covered in the next chapter.

Chapter 18
Using Microsoft Outlook 98

At this point in the book, you have learned about the various clients for Microsoft Exchange Server 5.5 and how to install the Microsoft Outlook 98 client. In this chapter, you learn how to use Outlook 98.

Many of the features of Outlook 98 are especially relevant in a book about Exchange Server 5.5. These features include working while disconnected from the Exchange Server and letting more than one user work with a specific computer. These situations involve the interaction of Outlook 98 with Exchange Server; by exploring these options, you learn more about how Exchange interacts with the Outlook 98 client. This chapter concentrates on these two scenarios for using Outlook 98 and Exchange.

Using Outlook 98 Offline

Exchange Server and Outlook 98 form the two ends of a powerful communications system. Most of the time, people communicate while the programs are in direct contact with each other, so the give and take of the process can proceed freely.

But as you'll remember from Chapter 1, communication with messaging systems such as Exchange is *asynchronous*, which means one party can send a message without the other party's being available to receive the message. Even though messages and replies might fly through your Exchange Server environment as rapidly as they do on the telephone, there is no requirement that the recipient be available when a message is sent or that the sender still be on line when the message is received.

More Info If you want to learn more about Outlook 98, read *Running Microsoft Outlook 98* (1998) by Russell Borland, available from Microsoft Press.

This simple fact means that you can also use the Outlook 98 client without being connected to the Exchange Server. You can read messages in the local folders or create messages that will be stored in your Outbox and sent when you reconnect to Exchange. This powerful feature makes users more productive in many situations that are typically thought of as downtime. (For example, you've probably seen people sitting on planes answering their e-mail.)

You can work offline with Outlook 98 without modifying the software in any way. In fact, if you bring up Outlook without being connected to an Exchange Server, the environment looks almost the same. All the folders for your mailbox are displayed in the folder list, and you can create messages as though you were connected. Of course, the Outlook 98 client had to be connected to the Exchange Server at some previous time, and the folders must be marked for synchronization in order for the folder hierarchy to be the same as that you see when you work offline.

By default, however, public folders are not displayed in the folder list. To understand why this is the default, you must learn about a process called *synchronization*.

Synchronizing Your Mailbox

Synchronizing your mailbox is a simple process from a user perspective, but the system has several complex tasks it performs. When Exchange synchronizes the contents of a folder on an Outlook 98 client with the contents of the matching folder on the Exchange Server, the process makes a copy of any messages that exist in only one location and places them in the other location. Exchange also synchronizes messages that have been deleted in one location but not in the other location.

The standard, default folders (Inbox, Outbox, Deleted Items, Calendar, Sent Items, Contacts, Tasks, Drafts, Journal, Notes) in your Outlook mailbox are synchronized for you automatically, as long as you have set up a location in which to store the contents of these folders on your client machine. By default, Outlook works with folders on the Exchange Server. To work when you are disconnected from Exchange, you must set up an offline folder to work with any Exchange folders.

Note If you add any folders in your mailbox, these folders will not be automatically synchronized. You will have to explicitly set up synchronization for them, as described later in this chapter in the section on public folders.

Setting Up Offline Folders

To enable synchronization, you must set up an offline folder for your Outlook client. The offline folder is stored in a file that has the extension .OST. You create an offline folder in either of two ways: implicitly, by enabling offline access, or explicitly, by specifying the creation of the folder.

To enable offline access and implicitly set up an offline folder, choose the Options menu choice from the Tools menu in Outlook, and click on the Mail Services tab, which displays the property sheet shown in Figure 18-1.

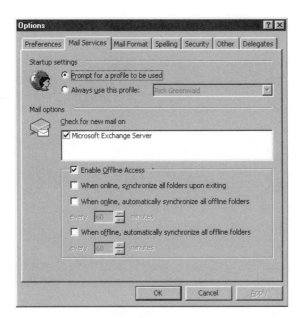

Figure 18-1. *Setting up Outlook to work offline.*

The bottom of this property sheet contains a check box that you can use to enable offline access. When you select this box, Outlook 98 automatically creates a file called OUTLOOK.OST under the root directory of Windows. If you want to have an offline folder with a different filename, you can create the offline folder by choosing the Services menu choice from the Tools menu. Go to the Services property sheet, choose Microsoft Exchange Server, click the Properties button, and click on the Advanced tab. At the bottom of the property sheet is a check box that enables offline access, as shown in Figure 18-2.

Next to the check box is a button labeled Offline Folder File Settings. When you click this button, the dialog box shown in Figure 18-3 appears.

At the top of the dialog box, you see the pathname of an offline file. If the file that contains the offline folder exists, you cannot change its location from this dialog box. The only way that you can set up a different file for the offline folders is to

Figure 18-2. *Advanced tab of Microsoft Exchange Server properties.*

Figure 18-3. *Offline folder settings.*

set up the file before you enable offline access or to explicitly delete the file before entering this dialog box. The default filename is still listed in the File field, but the Browse button next to the field is enabled, and you can edit the value in the field by either explicitly entering a filename or by using the Browse button to search through your existing directories.

Note If you disable offline access after creating an offline folder, the offline folder is not deleted until you explicitly delete it.

When you install Outlook 98, one of the screens in the installation wizard asks whether you travel with this computer, as shown in Figure 18-4. If you choose the Yes option, Outlook sets up an offline folder with the default name in the default location as part of the installation process.

Figure 18-4. *Inbox Setup Wizard asking to set up offline folder.*

Synchronizing Offline Folders Automatically

To set up Outlook 98 for working offline, you must first set up an offline folder. Outlook 98 automatically senses whether the client computer is connected to an Exchange Server when you start the application. You can create messages, delete messages, and perform other standard functions. The next time you start Outlook and connect to an Exchange Server, Outlook and Exchange automatically synchronize the contents of your standard offline folders. Folders set for synchronization in Outlook 98 are identified by a blue mark at the lower left of the folder icons in the folder list, as shown in Figure 18-5. Folders not set for synchronization, such as the Receipts folder shown in the figure, do not have the blue mark.

When you set up an offline folder, you probably noticed the Synchronization options that were part of the Mail Services property sheet. You can use these options to add other types of automatic synchronization for your offline folders. You can choose any of three options for synchronizing the contents of your offline folders:

- **When Online, Synchronize All Folders upon Exiting**   This option is useful if you regularly work offline, because when you choose it, you do not have to remember to explicitly synchronize the contents of your offline folders before you take your machine on a trip. The downside of choosing this option is that logging off Outlook may involve waiting while synchronization occurs.

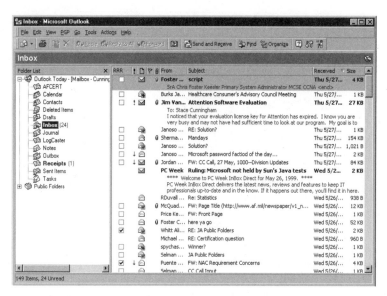

Figure 18-5. *Folders set for synchronization identified in the folder list with a blue mark.*

Note You can stop the Synchronization process by right-clicking on the progress symbol for the synchronization in the Outlook status bar at the bottom of the main Outlook window and then clicking the Cancel button in the shortcut menu.

- **When Online, Automatically Synchronize All Offline Folders** You can keep your offline folders updated by specifying that they should be synchronized on a regular basis. This option includes a field that allows you to specify how frequently this automatic synchronization should occur. Figure 18-6 shows an online synchronization in progress for the Sent Items folder. The synchronization status is indicated in the lower right section of the Outlook window.

- **When Offline, Automatically Synchronize All Offline Folders** At first, this option may be a bit confusing. After all, how can you synchronize offline folders when you are offline? Outlook allows you to use a remote mail dialup connection to send and receive messages — or to synchronize mailboxes — while you are offline. Because transmission over a dial-up connection usually is much slower than it is over a direct connection, choose this option with care.

You can choose one or more of these options, which are automatically implemented until you explicitly turn them off. These options provide other automatic

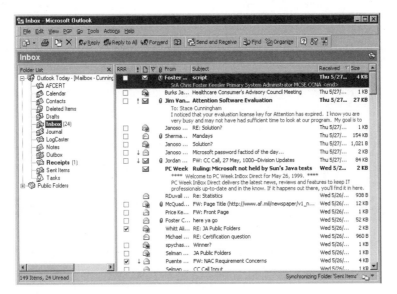

Figure 18-6. *Synchronizing the Sent Items folder.*

synchronization schedules that run in addition to the default synchronization every time you reconnect to Exchange on line.

Synchronizing Offline Folders Manually

Although your offline folders synchronize with the matching folders in Exchange automatically whenever you connect to the Exchange Server, and although you have several other options for automatic synchronization, you might still want to synchronize your offline folders manually from time to time.

When you choose the Synchronize menu choice in the Tools menu, you have three menu options, as shown in Figure 18-7.

You can choose to synchronize all the folders that are enabled for offline operation or to synchronize only the selected folder, if that folder is enabled for offline operation. You also have the option of downloading the address book for your Exchange Server. When you select the menu choice to download the address book, you have some further choices, as shown in Figure 18-8.

Because a Global Address Book can be very large, you can download only the changes that have been made in the address book since you last downloaded the address book. By downloading only the changes, rather than the entire address book, you significantly reduce the time that the download takes. You can also

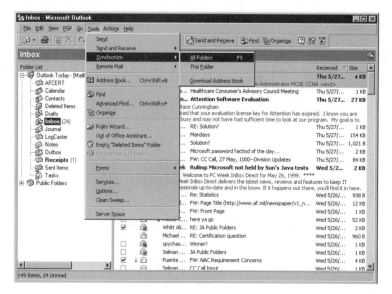

Figure 18-7. *Synchronize choices from the Tools menu.*

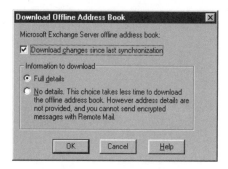

Figure 18-8. *Download address book changes.*

improve the speed of the download by not downloading the full details of the address book. As the dialog box notes, however, this partial download prevents you from sending encrypted messages through remote mail, because the digital IDs for the address book are not downloaded.

Real World   When Synchronization Doesn't Work
Despite the fact that you configured everything correctly on your Outlook 98 client, at times your folders may not synchronize automatically when you reconnect. If Outlook determines that you have a slow connection, it automatically stops synchronization from occurring. You can still synchronize either all folders

or a specific folder by choosing Synchronize from the Tools menu, selecting the appropriate menu item shown in Figure 18-7 earlier in the chapter. It is possible that other errors may stop synchronization from happening. A Synchronization Log file, as shown in Figure 18-9, is always placed in the Deleted Items folder of the offline folders. You should check this log for error codes that may help you solve synchronization problems.

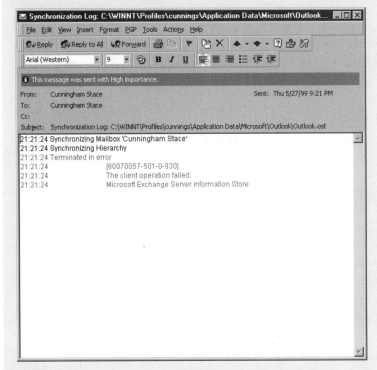

Figure 18-9. *Synchronization log displaying that an error occurred.*

Disabling Offline Use for Your Mailbox

Whenever you enable your Outlook 98 client for offline use, you automatically enable the standard folders in your mailbox for offline use. The only way to disable offline use of your mailbox folders is to disable offline use for your Outlook client. You can disable offline use by choosing either Services or Options from the Tools menu of Outlook 98.

To disable offline access through the Services dialog box, choose Microsoft Exchange Server, click the Properties button, and click on the Advanced tab to display the dialog box shown in Figure 18-2 earlier in this chapter. Then clear the Enable Offline Use check box.

To disable offline access through the Options dialog box, click on the Mail Services tab in the Options dialog box, uncheck the check box labeled Enable Offline Access, shown in Figure 18-1 earlier in this chapter, and then click the Apply or OK button.

These two methods have the same effect. You are no longer able to use Outlook 98 with the contents of any of your Exchange-based folders if you are not connected to an Exchange Server. If you open Outlook with offline access disabled while you are not connected to an Exchange Server, you receive a message that Outlook could not open your default e-mail folders, and Outlook opens with your default file system instead.

Synchronizing Public Folders

As mentioned earlier in this chapter, the standard mailbox folders are automatically enabled for offline access. You can check this capability by displaying the property sheet for one of the folders in the mailbox, such as your Inbox. One of the tabs in the property sheet is labeled Synchronization. However, if you display the property sheet for a public folder, you do not see the Synchronization tab, because public folders, by default, are not enabled for offline access. Public folders typically contain large amounts of information that would clog your client machine. In addition, there are some issues involving multiple users changing the contents of public folders. (See the "Real World" sidebar later in this section.)

You can, however, easily enable a public folder for offline access. Simply make the public folder a Favorite by moving it to the Favorites list in the Public Folders container of the folder list. You can make this change by dragging the folder into the Favorites folder or by choosing the Folder menu choice from the main File menu and choosing Add To Favorites. When you drag a public folder to the Favorites folder, the folder in the Favorites container has the same name as the original public folder. When you choose Add To Favorites, you see the dialog box shown in Figure 18-10.

This expanded list of options allows you to give the folder in the Favorites list a different name and to specify whether the hierarchy of subfolders should be moved with and maintained in the folder as new subfolders are added to the main Favorites folder. When you add a folder to the Favorites list by dragging the folder, only that folder is added to the list.

By designating a public folder as a Favorite, you do not move it from its established place in the public folder hierarchy; you are simply adding the folder to

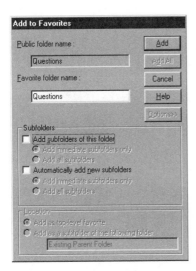

Figure 18-10. *Adding a public folder to the Favorites list.*

your list of Favorites. When a public folder is in the Favorites list, the property sheet for the folder contains a Synchronization tab. You can remove a folder from the Favorites list by selecting it in the list and then deleting it or by making the corresponding choice from the Folders menu.

Real World   Public Folder Synchronization Conflicts
Conflicts can arise if more than one person is using and modifying the items in a public folder offline. If you change an item in a public folder while you are offline, when you synchronize that folder, Exchange checks the timestamp on the existing version of the item. If the timestamp for the item is later than the original timestamp on the item you have changed, it means that someone else changed the contents of the folder item since you last downloaded it. If this type of conflict occurs, you receive a message that includes copies of all conflicting versions of the item. It is up to you to resolve the conflict by combining all the versions of an item into a single version and then clicking the Keep This Item button or clicking the Keep All button to keep all versions of the message, as shown in Figure 18-11.

Describing this procedure is much simpler than implementing it. A user may find it difficult to decide whether to keep an existing item or overwrite it, and the wrong decision could have negative results. For this reason, you should place controls on who is allowed to download and modify public folders through the standard Exchange security system.

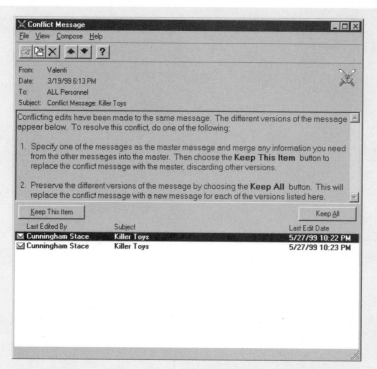

Figure 18-11. *Conflict message allowing a choice of fix actions.*

Shaping Synchronization

After you enable offline access for your Outlook client, you can shape the way that each folder uses the Synchronization process with Exchange. If a folder is enabled for offline use, the property sheet for the folder contains a Synchronization tab, as shown in Figure 18-12.

You can prevent a folder from being available by choosing the radio buttons at the top of the tab. By default, a public folder that has been added to the Favorites list is enabled only for online access, so you must explicitly change this setting if you want to enable synchronization for the folder. When you indicate that a folder is available for online or offline access, you have the option of creating a filter for the Synchronization process. Click the Filter button in the Synchronization tab to display a dialog box that allows you to define filtering conditions, as shown in Figure 18-13.

This dialog box has several tabs that allow you to define a complex condition. After you set up a filter, Outlook uses the conditions described in the filter to

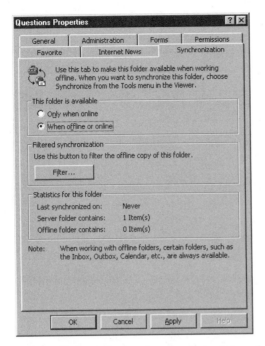

Figure 18-12. *The Synchronization tab in a folder property sheet.*

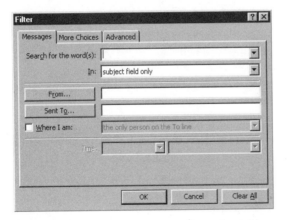

Figure 18-13. *Synchronization filters for folders.*

control which messages are synchronized between the Outlook client and the corresponding folders in Exchange. Keep in mind that these limits are imposed on all future synchronization attempts but have no effect on any messages that currently reside in the offline message store.

Adding filtering to synchronization is an enormously useful tool for getting all the benefits of offline access without incurring the excessive overhead caused by synchronizing less important messages. You could create a filter that disables synchronization for any messages that have large file attachments, for example, or you could synchronize only those messages that have been received from your boss. You have to be careful to remember when you have synchronization filters on. In an offline folder, there is no indication that the messages presented in the folder are not the complete set of messages stored in the matching Exchange folder.

Deciding Whether to Copy or Synchronize

Synchronization is no more than a sophisticated way to automatically copy messages between folders on the Exchange Server and the offline storage file on an Outlook 98 client. For inboxes, outboxes, and other folders in your mailbox, synchronization works well. But should you use the process for public folders?

Public folders, as you learn in many places throughout this book, can serve a wide variety of purposes. A public folder can be a simple repository of static information, such as a library, or a dynamically changing discussion group. You can copy the contents of a public folder to your mailbox simply by dragging the folder into the Mailbox container in your Outlook folder list. When should you copy and when should you synchronize the contents of a public folder?

The longer you have the contents of a public folder away from the Exchange Server, the more changes you make in the contents of the folder and the more people who are doing the same thing. In this situation, it's more likely that conflicting versions of the messages will crop up. Although public folders do have a way to detect conflicts, as described earlier, to use this mechanism to catch conflicts, you have to resolve all conflicts manually.

You should carefully analyze how a public folder is intended to be used offline. If the contents of the folder are meant only to be read, you probably will find that a simple copy operation works well. If you want to make changes in the contents of a public folder, you should seriously consider preventing later conflicts by applying filters to the Synchronization process so that you modify only the messages that are unlikely to be modified by other users.

Enabling Multiple Users with Outlook 98

In one specific situation, the capabilities of Outlook 98 and the capabilities of Exchange work in conjunction. Outlook is a client, and Exchange is a server.

When an Outlook client is connected to an Exchange Server, the client is representing a single user. But in some situations, the same Outlook client can be used to support multiple users at different times. This section of the chapter explores the scenarios in which this situation can occur.

Outlook Profiles, Exchange Mailboxes, and Windows NT

Before you learn how to implement multiple users with Outlook, you need to understand the differences between an Outlook profile and an Exchange mailbox as well as how both of these entities interact with Microsoft Windows NT accounts.

Most Exchange mailboxes are associated with at least one Windows NT user. Part of the process of creating an Exchange mailbox is identifying the Windows NT account that is associated with the mailbox.

A *profile* is a client-side configuration. An Outlook profile is a set of information services configured for a particular user or purpose. The Exchange Server Information Service in a profile includes a reference to an associated Exchange Server mailbox. Whenever a user starts Outlook, he or she uses the information in an Outlook profile to establish a connection with a particular Exchange mailbox, which is in turn associated with a particular Windows NT account.

Normally, each client machine has a single, default Outlook 98 profile. When a user starts Outlook on that machine, the default profile is used to determine which Exchange mailbox will be used as the server side of the environment. If a user is starting Outlook for the first time or is on a machine that does not have a profile, he or she is prompted to create a profile before fully logging on to the associated Exchange Server.

If you want to see the attributes of the profile that is currently being used by your Outlook client, choose Services from the Tools menu of Outlook 98 to display the dialog box shown in Figure 18-14.

Sometimes additional requirements cannot be addressed by a single profile on an Outlook client. The following section discusses situations in which something other than this default configuration is used.

Multiple Profiles with Outlook 98

For several reasons, you might want to use more than one Outlook profile. Perhaps you are using Outlook on a machine that you share with other

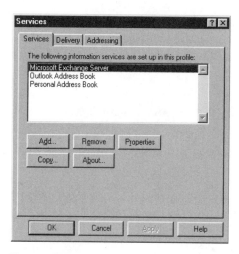

Figure 18-14. *Viewing a profile from within Outlook 98.*

users, so you would want separate profiles to reflect the various mailboxes and configuration information for each user. You might also be using a machine in different circumstances (such as in the office and on the road), so you would want to be able to select a different profile based on your current situation.

> **Note** The following description of creating a profile is based on the Windows *9X* platform. Creating a profile for a Windows NT machine involves essentially the same process except that each NT user has his or her own operating system profile that contains the user's Outlook profile.

When you first log on to Outlook 98, you are prompted to create a profile, which is used as the default profile. To create an additional profile, you go to the Control Panel for the client computer. In the Control Panel, double-click on the Mail icon to display a dialog box, as shown in Figure 18-15.

This dialog box looks very similar to the dialog box available in Outlook 98 under the Services menu choice in the Tools menu. The one big difference is that this dialog box has a Show Profiles button. Clicking this button will bring up a list of the profiles on the machine, as shown in Figure 18-16.

To add a new profile, simply click the Add button, which calls up the Inbox Setup Wizard. The Inbox Setup Wizard prompts you for the values needed for a profile, which include the name of the target Exchange Server and the mailbox

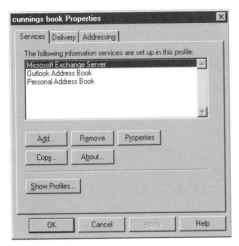

Figure 18-15. *Outlook 98 Properties displayed from the Mail icon in Control Panel.*

Figure 18-16. *A list of mail profiles.*

that the profile will use on that server as well as the location of your personal address book. The Inbox Setup Wizard also asks if you are going to be using this machine while traveling—and if so, it will set up an offline folder. You can also delete or modify existing profiles from this dialog box.

At the bottom of the dialog box, you can specify a user profile to be used as the default profile for this client machine. When you use the default settings,

Outlook uses the default profile to connect to an Exchange Server. The use of a default profile can be somewhat cumbersome because it requires you to go to the Control Panel and display the Mail dialog box every time a user wants to use a different profile.

You can set up Outlook so that you are prompted for a profile every time you start Outlook, as shown in Figure 18-17.

Figure 18-17. *Selecting a profile when starting Outlook 98.*

To enable this feature, choose Options from the Tools menu to display the property sheet shown in Figure 18-18.

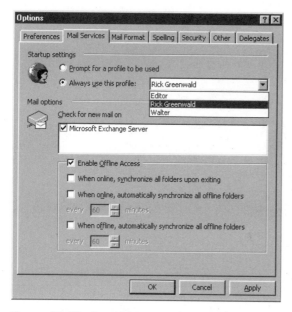

Figure 18-18. *Specifying a startup profile in Outlook 98.*

The Mail Services tab of the property sheet contains a set of two radio buttons. The bottom radio button, which is selected by default, indicates that Outlook should use a specific profile by default. You can indicate any profile as the default profile; the setting that you make in this tab overrides any setting that you made in the Mail dialog box.

The top radio button tells Outlook to prompt you for a profile every time you start the program. If you choose this option, a little dialog box appears every time you start Outlook. The default choice in the dialog box is to use the selected profile as the default profile in Outlook, but you have the option to select a different profile.

Access to Different Mailboxes on Exchange

The Outlook profile described in the preceding section includes client-side configuration information. But remember that Outlook is the client portion of a client/server system. You still need the appropriate user privileges to access the server side of the equation in Exchange.

Exchange security is based on Windows NT user accounts. Before an Outlook client can even access an Exchange Server, the user must log onto a network and establish a connection as a Windows NT domain user. If you will use a different Windows NT username with each profile, you can use multiple Outlook profiles that access different Exchange mailboxes.

Figure 18-19 illustrates this concept by showing that a user gets connected to an Exchange mailbox only after logging on to a Windows NT network with the username with privileges to that mailbox. The connection to the mailbox runs

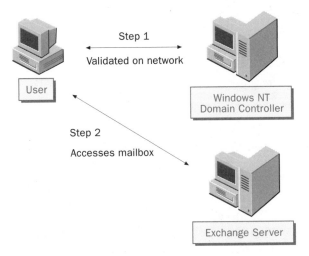

Figure 18-19. *User validates on NT network before being granted access to the users mailbox on the Exchange Server.*

through a specific Windows NT user. In some situations, you may want to access different Exchange mailboxes while using the same Windows NT username. For example, you may want a receptionist to open the mailbox of another receptionist that has called in sick for the day.

When you create a mailbox in Exchange, you are allowed to associate only one Windows NT user with it. When the mailbox is created, you can give permission to other Windows NT users to access the mailbox. You can grant this permission from Microsoft Exchange Administrator by displaying the property sheet for a user on the Exchange Server and then clicking on the Permissions tab, shown in Figure 18-20.

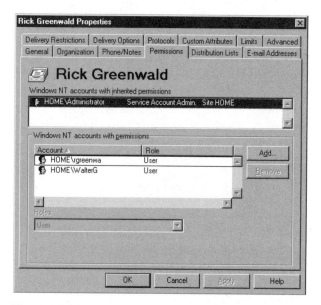

Figure 18-20. *Granting permissions to other Windows NT accounts.*

When you click the Add button, you see a list of Windows NT users and groups. You can select one or more of these entities and then click the OK button to grant them access to the mailbox. You can also delete accounts from the list, but you can never delete from the Permissions tab the Windows NT account that you initially designated as the primary Windows NT account for the mailbox. To delete the primary Windows NT account, you must change the account shown in the Primary Windows NT Account dialog box on the General tab of the mailbox. If the Permissions tab is not available on user mailboxes, you will need to enable it by selecting the Options choice on the Tools menu. After the Options dialog window opens, select the Permissions tab and click in the box located to the left of Show Permissions Page For All Objects, as shown in Figure 18-21.

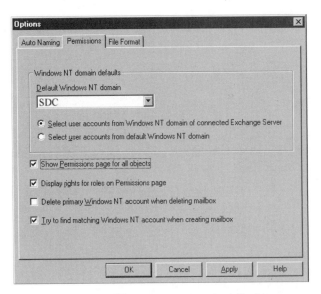

Figure 18-21. *Enabling permissions for all objects.*

You can also allow other users to see any of the folders in your mailbox by granting them permission through the standard properties sheet for a folder in Outlook. If users have permission for a specific folder or if their Windows NT accounts have been granted permissions on the mailbox, they can choose Other User's Folders from the Open menu of the main File menu to open the folder. They can also add the mailbox to their profile by adding the mailbox from the Advanced tab of the Microsoft Exchange Server Properties window. They simply click the Add button in the top portion of the Advanced tab (refer back to Figure 18-2) and select the mailbox they want added.

Users Granting Access to Their Own Mailboxes

In the previous section, the administrator controls access to another user's mailbox using the Exchange Administrator. Using Outlook, users can grant privileges without the need to contact the administrator. This is done by selecting the folder (such as Calendar), selecting properties (right mouse click), and then adding the appropriate user using the Permissions tab, as show in Figure 18-22.

Once the privileges have been assigned to the other user, that user can now access this new information by choosing File, then Open, and then Other User's Folder in Microsoft Outlook.

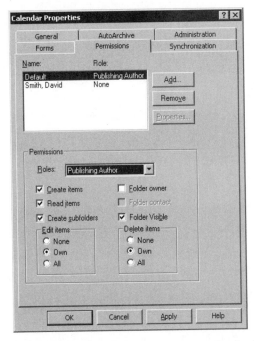

Figure 18-22. *Granting Access using Outlook.*

Roving Users

The discussion in the preceding section concerns a situation in which more than one user accesses the same machine. A *roving user* is a slightly different situation, in which one user does not have a fixed physical location and may consequently be logging on from many machines. You could set up a user profile for this user on each of the machines, but this solution may be impractical. You can address this situation by creating a roaming user profile.

> **Note** In Windows NT parlance, these users have *roaming profiles*. In the language of Exchange, these users have *roving profiles*.

The configuration information for a roving user is stored on a shared disk on a network server, so this information can be accessed from any machine that can connect to the network. When you set up a roving user profile on your

Windows NT machine, client machines that log on to the network with that profile look on the shared disk for configuration information. The common access to the storage of a roaming profile eliminates the need to have this profile stored on many machines. For more information about setting up a shared user profile on Windows NT and various clients, refer to the documentation for those products.

Summary

Outlook is a full-featured client application that can be used in conjunction with Exchange Server, even when the client machine is not directly connected to an Exchange Server. A single Outlook client can support many users, and a single user can roam to different machines and use Outlook on each of those machines to check his or her mail.

The last topic to cover in our brief overview of Outlook 98 is the use of rules, which can shape the way that users interact with their messages. Rules are covered in the next, and final, chapter of this section.

Chapter 19
Rules and Policies

The Microsoft Exchange 5.5 environment is an incredibly powerful tool for sharing information — so powerful, in fact, that you and your users may be overwhelmed by the amount of information it can handle. However, you can create rules and limits to help control the flow of information to Exchange users.

You can control the flow of messages in an Exchange system in two ways. One way is to apply rules, which are defined through an Outlook client and implemented with Exchange Server 5.5. The other way to shape message flow through the Exchange system is to define some of the properties of the Exchange user mailboxes. You will learn about both methods in this chapter.

Limiting Messages with Exchange

Two basic mailbox properties shape message flow for a recipient: Delivery Restrictions and Limits. The Delivery Restrictions property sheet, shown in Figure 19-1, lets you specify whether you want to accept or reject messages from an individual or a distribution list.

You can specify the recipients whose messages will be accepted and the recipients whose messages will be rejected. The default values for these properties are to accept messages from all recipients and to reject messages from no recipients. These two properties work together in some ways. As soon as you specify any recipients from whom to accept mail, Exchange automatically rejects mail from all unlisted recipients. You can identify any recipient in the Address Book for either of the restrictions — individuals or distribution lists.

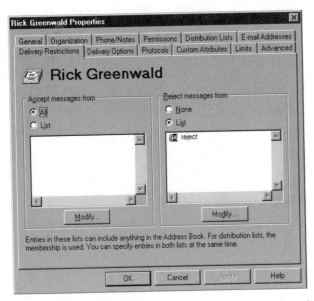

Figure 19-1. *The Delivery Restrictions property sheet for a mailbox.*

Real World   General Rules

You can use distribution lists to enforce general rules for implementing restrictions for a group of users. Suppose that you want all the members of a particular department to reject messages from all the members of another department. You could create a distribution list that would contain all the members of the soon-to-be-rejected department. Then you would specify that list in the Reject Messages From list box of the Delivery Restrictions property sheet for all the members of the receiving department. If someone transferred out of the rejected department, you would merely take that person's name off the distribution list to accept his or her mail again. You can also use the message-size limits of a distribution list, as discussed later in this chapter, to implement restrictions for a group of recipients.

You can set another type of restriction for mail messages by using some of the attributes of the Limits property sheet for a mailbox (Figure 19-2). In the bottom-right corner of the Limits property sheet, you can limit the size of outgoing or incoming messages. The restrictions can be as broad as the Delivery Restrictions discussed earlier in this section; any message, regardless of sender, will be rejected if it is too large.

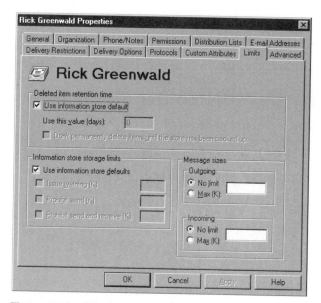

Figure 19-2. *The limits property sheet for an Exchange recipient.*

You can also set a size limit for the delivery of messages to members of a distribution list. The Advanced property sheet for a distribution list, shown in Figure 19-3, has an option that allows you to limit the size of messages that are delivered to the members of a distribution list.

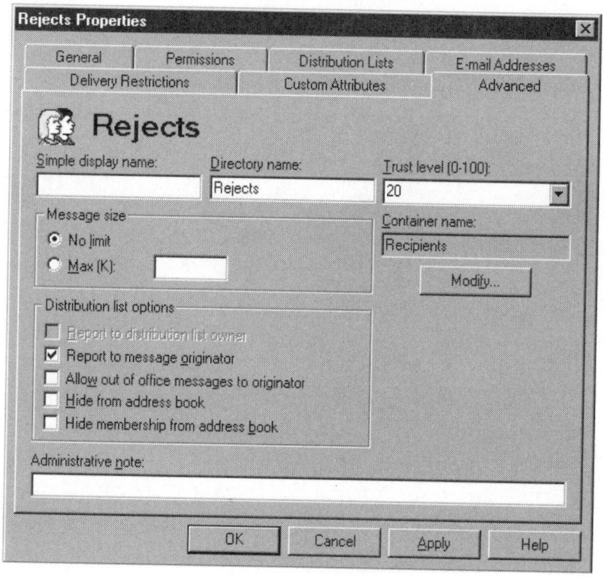

Figure 19-3. *The advanced property sheet for a distribution list.*

If a message is rejected because of a delivery or size restriction, the sender receives a simple message. The message, which is sent from the System Administrator, recaps some of the information in the undeliverable message and states, "A restriction in the system prevented delivery of the message." This message may seem so general as to be merely a useless annoyance. But your system restrictions are a vital part of your overall security scheme for your Exchange environment. If the message gave more specific information, it might allow a malicious sender to figure out ways to get around the restriction.

The Delivery Restrictions and Limits property sheets are available for individual mailboxes and distribution lists but not for public folders. You can easily get around this restriction by making a public folder a member of a distribution list and then setting either of these properties for the list. You could also make it more difficult to send large messages directly to the public folder by taking it out of the Global Address List, as shown in Figure 19-4.

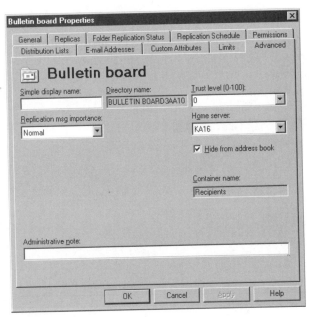

Figure 19-4. *Hiding a public folder from the Global Address List.*

These restrictions are fairly broad; all messages for a particular user or all messages over a certain size are rejected. At times, however, you may want to implement a more subtle type of rule. You can define these rules in the Exchange Outlook client.

Real World   **Sharing Exchange Restrictions**

If the restrictions that you define in Exchange are both broad and limited, why would you use them instead of implementing the same restriction with an Outlook rule? The one advantage of using Exchange restrictions is that they are properties of an Exchange recipient, which means that you can create restrictions for a recipient and use that recipient as the template for defining other recipients. The restrictions are automatically copied to the new recipient when it is created.

Limiting Messages with Outlook Rules

The Outlook client for Exchange allows an Outlook user to implement a much more flexible set of rules for handling messages. In its basic form, an Outlook rule consists of one or more conditions that are evaluated as a whole to return a single Boolean value: True or False. If the conditions evaluate to True, the Outlook rule specifies one or more actions to be taken. If the conditions evaluate to False, the actions are ignored. Although rules can be described in simple terms, the many choices for conditions and actions provide an enormous amount of flexibility.

Defining Outlook Rules

Although all Outlook rules are implemented the same way, Outlook allows you to define rules in several ways. You can use the Rules Wizard, the Organize tool, or the Out of Office Assistant to create specifications that affect the way that messages are handled.

Rules Wizard

The Rules Wizard was introduced in Outlook 97 as an upgrade to the Inbox Assistant and the Out of Office Assistant. This wizard is a beautiful tool, providing great flexibility and an easy-to-use interface. The Rules Wizard is a choice on the Tools menu in the main Outlook menu bar. Five main dialog boxes walk you through the creation of a rule, and an initial screen helps you manage your rules.

Note   You can use the Rules Wizard to assign rules for every potential recipient, from an individual's Inbox to a public folder. You specify the recipient as part of the rule, so it doesn't make any difference which particular container in your Outlook Directory panel is selected when you call up the Rules Wizard.

Management Screen The initial screen of the Rules Wizard, shown in Figure 19-5, helps you manage any rules that you create. The top panel lists the rules that you have already defined. A check box appears to the left of each existing rule, indicating whether a particular rule is currently enabled. The buttons to the right of the top list allow you to create new rules or to copy, modify, rename, or delete an existing rule. You can also change the order in which existing rules are applied to messages.

Figure 19-5. *The initial management screen of the Rules Wizard.*

At the bottom of the first screen of the Rules Wizard is a description of the selected rule. The description is in plain English, and some of the text may be underlined. The underlined text acts as a hyperlink for entities in rules that have more complex values — such as a list of potential junk-mail senders or a link to a page that allows you to define the content of a message to be delivered as part of a rule.

Below the description are buttons that allow you to exit the Rules Wizard by clicking the OK button, to cancel the work that you have done by clicking the Cancel button, or to display options by clicking the button labeled Options. These options are described at the end of the section discussing the Rules Wizard in more detail, because they will make more sense to you when you are familiar with how the Rules Wizard works.

The main purpose of the Rules Wizard is to help you to define rules by answering some basic questions about your rule. You can start the process of defining a rule by clicking the New button to create a new rule or the Modify button to change an existing rule. When you click one of these buttons, the Rules Wizard prompts you for the properties of your rule and displays the current settings for an existing rule.

Type Screen   The first question to ask when creating a rule is what type of rule to create. The type screen of the Rules Wizard, shown in Figure 19-6, may look familiar.

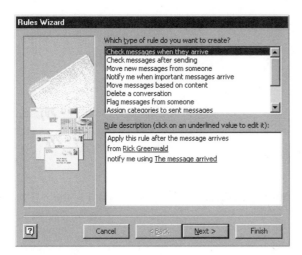

Figure 19-6. *The type of rule screen of the Rules Wizard.*

At the top of the screen is a list of the available times when the rule can be imposed. At the bottom of the screen is a description that further explains the rule. This description may include hyperlinks that allow you to define more information associated with the rule.

You have many choices for rule timings, just as you have many choices for the rest of the screens in the Rules Wizard. Due to scope limitations, this chapter does not attempt to cover all the choices for any of the screens in the Rules Wizard; instead, it describes the general purpose of each screen and the choices each screen contains.

> **Note**   Some of the hyperlinks allow you to define directly the values for which subsequent pages in the Rules Wizard prompt you. If you choose to use these hyperlinks to define these values, the values show up on later screens of the Rules Wizard.

The four buttons at the bottom of the screen allow you to move through the pages of the Rules Wizard and give you the option of canceling any rule definition or modification. The Finish button allows you to finish the definition of a rule immediately, accepting all remaining default values for the undefined properties of a rule. The final screen of the Rules Wizard prompts you for a name for the rule; if you complete the definition of a new rule by simply clicking the Finish button, the rule will have a default name assigned by the wizard.

Real World   One Rule, Two Events
You can select a single event to trigger a rule. If you want a rule to be enforced at more than one time, you can create a copy of the rule from the Rules Wizard management screen and then modify the time when the rule is enforced.

Conditions Screen   The next question about a rule is the conditions under which the rule is imposed. The conditions screen of the Rules Wizard, shown in Figure 19-7, is a little bit different from the first screen of the creation portion of the wizard but similar to all the other screens.

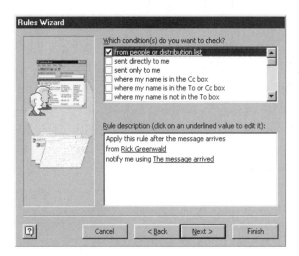

Figure 19-7. *The conditions screen of the Rules Wizard.*

The top list box displays a check box to the left of each option. You can specify one or more conditions for each rule that you define. As you select a condition, the text for the condition is added to the description box at the bottom of the screen. Some of the conditions include hyperlinks to help you define other groups of values. When you define one or more values for a hyperlink, the displayed text changes from a description of the hyperlink to the actual values for the link, and the color of the values that replace the link change. This display convention not only helps you understand the rule, it also reminds you about what you have to define for a rule. You must indicate values for each of the hyperlinks in the description of a rule; otherwise, the rule won't make sense.

Although the hyperlinks appear in the top list box, you can use them only to define values in the description box at the bottom of the screen.

If you want to impose a rule on messages that contain a particular value, for example, you have to specify that value. If you do not indicate a value, the rule will not make sense, because it will be imposed on all messages.

When you specify multiple conditions for a rule, a message must satisfy all the conditions in order to impose the rule. The descriptive text for the rule links conditions with the word *and* to indicate this all-or-none state. If you want to impose a rule for messages that meet one of several conditions, you must define separate rules with separate conditions, which you can easily do by clicking the Copy button of the management screen.

Actions Screen   The next question about a rule is, what actions are to be taken when a message meets the conditions for a rule? The actions screen of the Rules Wizard, shown in Figure 19-8, is very similar to the preceding screen.

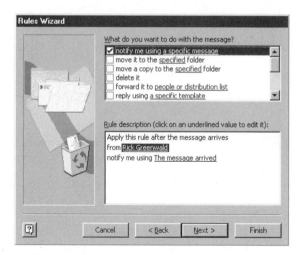

Figure 19-8. *The actions screen of the Rules Wizard.*

You can choose one or more actions to be taken by checking the boxes preceding those actions. When an action is selected, the text for that action is added to the rule description at the bottom of the screen. The hyperlinks for actions vary from the hyperlinks for the preceding screens. Some of these hyperlinks, such as those that link to a specific message or reply by using a specific template, give you a wider range of definition options.

One action deserves special mention. The last action listed specifies that the rule will halt the processing of further rules for the current event. This action fulfills the same purpose as an Exit statement in a function or subroutine. Because you may define many rules for a particular user, you always want the option to exit the rule process without checking for any more conditions. The option to discontinue further processing of rules is also available in the first dialog box for the Rules Wizard.

Exceptions Screen   The next question about a rule relates to the conditions under which the actions proposed in this rule are not executed. The exceptions screen of the Rules Wizard, shown in Figure 19-9, may seem to be a bit redundant. After all, you can specify the conditions that trigger the actions for a rule. Why set the conditions, only to be given the opportunity to override them later in the rule definition process?

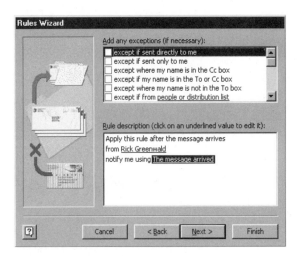

Figure 19-9. *The exceptions screen of the Rules Wizard.*

Defining exceptions to a condition can be a useful productivity feature. It is entirely possible that you want a rule to apply to a particular condition most of the time but not all of the time. Suppose that your boss loves to send his entire group long messages that have nothing to do with you. You could set up a rule that moves messages from your boss to a special folder to await your breathless perusal. Your boss also sends mail directly to you, however, and this mail typically is very important. You could indicate that all messages from your boss normally go to one folder, except for messages that are addressed directly to you. This system would help you separate the wheat from the chaff in terms of communications from your superior. If you are one of those strictly logical types who don't believe in granting any exceptions, you can simply click the Next button to move to the next dialog box.

Identification Screen   The last question about a rule relates to how this rule will be identified. The identification screen of the Rules Wizard, shown in Figure 19-10, prompts you for a name for the rule that you just defined or modified.

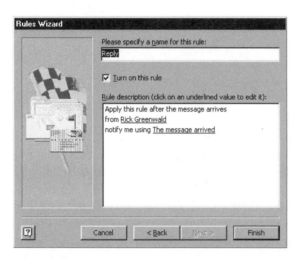

Figure 19-10. *The identification screen of the Rules Wizard.*

You are not required to give a rule a name, because Outlook will assign a default name for you, but you are strongly advised to do so because a name will make managing the rule much easier.

When you finish defining a rule by giving it a name, you can safely click the Finish button to add the rule. When you finish a rule, the Rules Wizard automatically checks the rule for errors and warnings. An error may occur if you forgot to specify values for one of the hyperlinks indicated for the rule. A warning might indicate that a rule could interfere with the operation of another rule. If you left out a required part of a rule, the Rules Wizard will not let you continue until you either specify a value or cancel out of the definition or modification of the rule.

Once the rule is fully defined, Outlook will inform you as to whether a rule is enforced on the server or on the client. This final screen of the Rules Wizard also includes a check box that lets you specify whether a particular rule is enabled. By default, this check box is checked. When you successfully define a rule, you return to the first screen of the wizard.

Options The last items to look at in the Rules Wizard are the available options. When you click the Options button at the bottom of the initial dialog box for the Rules Wizard, the Options dialog box appears (Figure 19-11).

Figure 19-11. *The Options dialog box.*

The dialog box provides two main options, along with the ability to have Outlook prompt you explicitly when it converts any Inbox Assistant rules. The first option allows you to indicate whether you want Outlook to automatically send any new or changed rules to your Exchange Server or only when you explicitly tell it to send the updates. All rules are enforced by the Exchange Server. Even rules that require the presence of a client to complete their execution, such as sending an alert to a user, are processed by the Exchange Server. After you define or change a rule, the Rules Wizard automatically sends the updates to the Exchange Server.

Real World   Exceptions to the Rule
You can, of course, run Outlook without being connected to an Exchange Server. If you are running disconnected, you cannot send any rule updates to the server, so the options that apply to this operation do not appear in the Options dialog box.

At times, you may want to delay sending any updates to the Exchange Server until you define more than one rule. The Exchange Server automatically imposes rules on all appropriate messages as soon as the rules are received. If you are defining multiple rules that work in conjunction with one another, such as variations of the same rule, you might not want to send any of the rules to the server until you finish defining all the rules, so as to avert a potential logical inconsistency.

The other option lets you import or export the rules for a particular user. To import rules, you import the file that contains the rules. When you choose to export your rules, you are prompted for the name of a file to hold the rules; this file will have the extension .RWZ. When you export rules, all the rules for the current user are exported. Exporting rules is a great way to save you some work. If you want to have the same rule for many Outlook users, you can define the common rules, export those rules, and then import them for each user.

Imported rules are automatically added to the end of any existing rules for a user. For this reason, it is generally good practice to plan the common rules that you will implement for your users. If a user imports rules after he or she has defined some of his or her own, you will have to deal with two potential management problems:

- The user may have defined a rule with the same name as one of the imported rules. This situation is not a total disaster, because the name is simply an attribute of the rule; the Exchange Server will be able to differentiate between two rules that have the same name.

- The imported rules are initially implemented after any rules that the user defined—a situation that may interfere with their proper operation. If you want all messages from a particular user to be moved to a common public folder, for example, you could create a rule to implement this function, export the rule, and send it to all the relevant users for them to import. Some of these users, however, may have defined rules that would cause other actions to be taken for a message from this user, so the rule, added to the end of the list of rules, would never be implemented.

Real World   Sharing Rules and Limitations

In your organization, you might want to implement the same restrictions for more than one user. You can share rules and restrictions among a group of users, but you have to implement this sharing differently, depending on whether you are defining the restriction on the Exchange Server or in an Outlook client.

If you want to share a delivery restriction for a group of users with another group of users, you could create a distribution list that contains the names of the target users. You would then assign this list to either of the Delivery Restriction options for each of the receiving users, as described earlier in this chapter—one list for users who will have their messages rejected or one for users whose messages will be accepted. If you knew in advance that you wanted to impose this type of restriction, you could create a mailbox with the restriction and use it as a template for creating the other recipients, because the Delivery Restriction and Limits properties are replicated automatically. In fact, if you think that you might want to impose this type of broad restriction, you may want to create dummy mailing lists and assign them to your target mailboxes. If there are no members in a distribution list that is part of a rejection restriction, the list will have no effect.

As an example, you might create a group of new users who want to reject mail from a group of people. You first create a mailing list to hold the names of the people whose mail is to be rejected. You then create an Exchange user with this mailing list as one of the Delivery Restrictions and use it as a template for the new users. Finally, you can add and delete members from this mailing list as the group of new users decides to reject or not reject messages from them.

This type of restriction sharing has the advantage of being dynamic and easy to replicate. The disadvantages of sharing Exchange-defined restrictions is that the restrictions are broad and undifferentiated, and the messages returned to the sender as a result of the rejection are not the most informative messages in the world.

If you want to share rules that you define with Outlook, you can create a set of rules that you want to implement for many users in a new Outlook account. You can then export these rules by clicking the Options button in the Rules Wizard. After you select a file to receive the export, Outlook exports all the defined rules. You can then import these rules for each user who needs to use them. The imported rules are added to the list of existing rules.

This method allows you to define very specific rules in Outlook. Because a user who wants to use these rules must explicitly import them, however, your maintenance burden might increase. Furthermore, because this method simply adds rules to the end of the list of existing rules and doesn't delete other rules that have the same name, it might not be appropriate for rules that change frequently. If the imported rules must be applied early in the rule enforcement cycle, you may find this technique appropriate.

The Rules Wizard is a nice tool, but it is not the only way that you can impose rules for your Outlook clients. The Organize tool is another such method.

Organize Tool

The Organize tool (Figure 19-12) is a new feature of Outlook 98. A toggle switch in the main Outlook toolbar displays and hides the Organize tool. The Organize tool is also available from the Tools menu.

The Organize tool has four tabs. Each tab contains several options for imposing some type of organization on your Outlook environment, including the ability to assign rules or rule-like logic.

The first Organize tab is designed to let you work with folders. The top menu allows you to move selected messages from one folder to another (the same thing you can do by dragging and dropping messages). The bottom menu gives you a simple way to define a rule. When you define a rule through this tab of the

Figure 19-12. *The Organize tool.*

Organize tool, that rule, along with a default name, appears in the standard list of rules displayed in the Rules Wizard. After the rule is added to the list of rules, you can change its position in the list or modify any of the attributes of the rule. You can call the Rules Wizard directly from the menu bar of this tab.

The second Organize tool tab assigns colors to messages, as shown in Figure 19-13. You can also change the formatting of various categories of messages through the Automatic Formatting option shown in Figure 19-14. This function is the same one that you can get by customizing an Outlook view. Because this type of formatting is applied only in the Outlook client and has no interaction with the messages stored in Exchange, you don't need to create a rule for it.

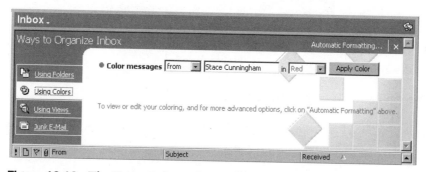

Figure 19-13. *The Using Colors tab of the Organize tool.*

The third Organize tab, shown in Figure 19-15, lets you select or customize a view. No rules are created as a result of any choices on this tab.

The fourth Organize tab, shown in Figure 19-16, lets you assign and work with junk messages and adult-content messages. Junk mail and mail with adult content can be identified in two ways. Exchange can automatically check a message to see whether the content indicates that it might be junk or adult-content mail. If the title of an e-mail message includes the word *sex* several times, for example, the title is a good indication that the mail message contains adult content.

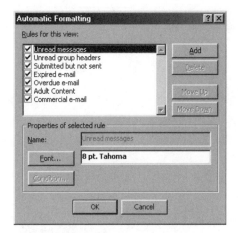

Figure 19-14. *Automatic formatting in the Using Colors tab of the Organize tool.*

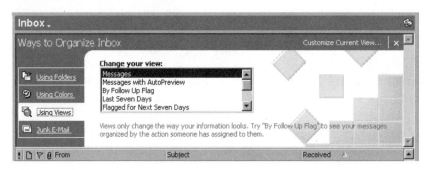

Figure 19-15. *The Using Views tab of the Organize tool.*

Figure 19-16. *The Junk E-Mail tab of the Organize tool.*

Caution As is true of any automatic detection scheme, the process that Exchange uses to identify junk mail or adult-content mail is not perfect. Both types of messages may be able to get by the filtering mechanism, and the filter may occasionally prevent legitimate messages from getting through.

A user can also specifically identify senders who are responsible for sending junk e-mail or messages with adult content to an Outlook user. You can add such a name to either the junk mail or adult-content lists by explicitly entering it in the list, as shown in Figure 19-17, or by right-clicking on a message from the sender and making a choice from the Junk E-Mail menu choices in the pop-up menu shown in Figure 19-18.

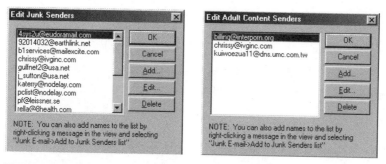

Figure 19-17. *Editing the Junk Senders and Adult Content Senders lists.*

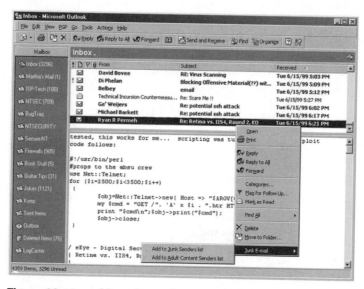

Figure 19-18. *Adding the sender of an e-mail to the Junk E-Mail lists.*

You access the lists shown in Figure 19-17 through the extended Junk E-Mail options in the Organize tool shown in Figure 19-19 or by clicking on the hyperlink for the lists in the Rules Wizard. When a sender is added to either list, Outlook automatically rejects messages from that person.

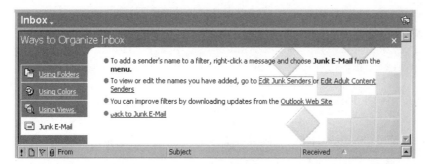

Figure 19-19. *Extended Junk E-Mail options available in the Organize tool.*

The choices on the Junk E-Mail tab let you display junk or adult-content messages in a specific color or move them to a particular folder. You can also use the Rules Wizard to create rules to take specific actions on junk or adult-content mail, according to the filtering program or the identity of the sender.

You can assign specific names to the Junk Senders or Adult Content Senders list, or you can specify an entire domain that is responsible for generating these messages. As soon as you assign any values to either of these lists, you see a new rule called Exception List in the Rules Wizard. As the name implies, this rule gives you a list of senders who are exempted from the Adult Content or Junk Mailers lists, so you could affect all the messages from a particular domain but still allow messages from certain senders to avoid the automatic filtering process. You can also download updated lists of all known junk and adult mailers from the Microsoft Outlook product Web site.

Out of Office Assistant

As you saw earlier in this chapter, you can create rules and toggle them on and off as you please. You can also use the Out of Office Assistant to implement one or more actions based on one of the most common occurrences in the business world: You are not in the office. You can select the Out of Office Assistant menu choice from the Tools menu in Outlook. The first screen of the Out of Office Assistant, shown in Figure 19-20, contains the basic options.

You can specify whether you are in the office, which means that none of the actions assigned in the Assistant are implemented, or whether you are out of the office. If you choose the out-of-office option, you can use the text box to enter a message that will be sent as a reply to each person who sends you a message. The text in the box will be sent only the first time each individual sends you a message. For example, if Ken sends you a message, the Out of Office Assistant replies with the text you put in the box. Next you receive a message from DW, and once

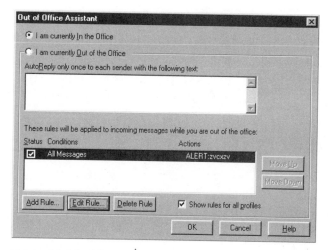

Figure 19-20. *The Out of Office Assistant.*

again the Out of Office Assistant replies with the text you put in the box, because this is the first message received from DW since you enabled the Out of Office Assistant. Two days later, Ken sends you another message; however, the Out of Office Assistant does not forward the text you put in the box, because it knows that it already sent that message to Ken the first time he sent you a message. At the bottom of the screen, you can create rules for the Assistant.

The Edit Rule screen of the Out of Office Assistant, shown in Figure 19-21, contains some of the options that are available in the Rules Wizard. The options available from this screen are sending an alert when the message arrives, deleting the message, moving the message to another folder, copying the message to another folder, forwarding the message to another user, replying with a particular template, and using a custom action defined by the user.

You can click the Advanced button, shown in Figure 19-22, to specify even more detailed conditions for implementing actions with the Assistant. Some of the advanced options include specifying the minimum and maximum message size, the received from and to dates, the importance of the message, and the sensitivity of the message, as well as applying only to items that do not match these conditions.

After you create a rule, it appears in the rules list box at the bottom of the Out of Office Assistant page. You then can edit the rule, turn it on or off, or move it up and down in the list to change when the rule is applied in relation to other rules.

The Out of Office Assistant existed before the Rules Wizard was introduced in Outlook 98. The rules that you define with the Assistant do not appear in the

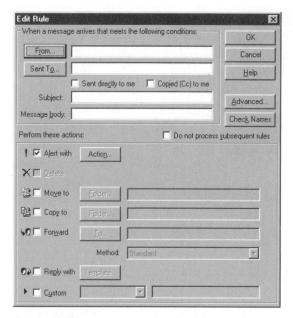

Figure 19-21. *Defining rules with the Out of Office Assistant.*

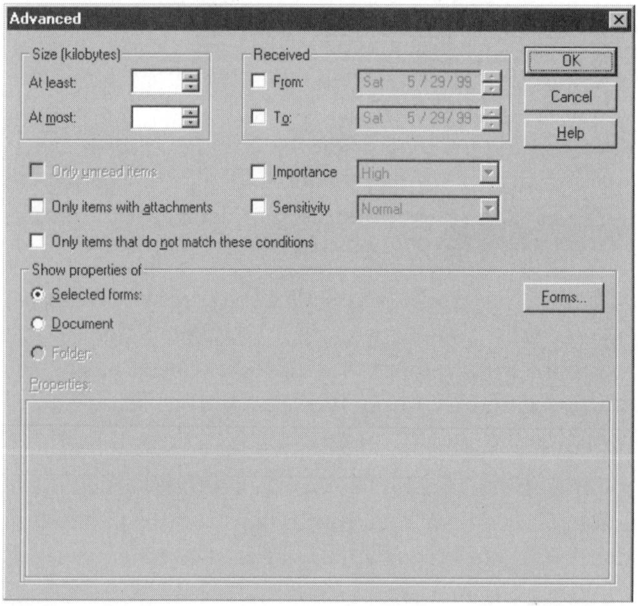

Figure 19-22. *The Advanced dialog box from Out of Office Assistant.*

list of rules in the Rules Wizard. This deficiency is balanced by the ease with which you can turn on a complete set of rules for handling mail when you are not in the office.

Understanding How Rules Are Implemented

After all this talk about rules, you are probably getting curious about how these rules are implemented in your Exchange system. The first and most important thing to realize is that the rules are applied in the order in which they are specified — in the Rules Wizard or in the Out of Office Assistant. The order of rules can have a dramatic effect on the overall logic implemented with multiple rules. For example, if you create a rule specifying that a message is to be deleted if certain conditions are met, that message will not be available for the actions of any subsequent rules. For this reason, you should plan your rules very carefully.

Real World **Test, Test, Test**
You are strongly advised to test your rules before adding them to your list of Outlook rules. You probably want to test a rule by making it perform an action that can be checked, such as moving a message to a designated folder, to ensure that the rule works before you take the more drastic action of having the rule delete a message.

Although rules are defined in your Outlook client, the Exchange Server implements all the rules that it can without involving Outlook. If the action resulting from a particular rule requires user intervention of some kind, the rule is implemented in part on the Outlook client. An example of this type of action is an alert, which must be received by the client. An example of a rule that does not require user intervention is a rule specifying that messages from a particular sender be moved automatically to a public folder. Exchange can, and will, implement this rule all by itself. Exchange's ability to implement rules on its own is an efficient way to work because Exchange takes the specified action as soon as the event that triggers the rule occurs — in this case, the receipt of the message.

Whenever you finish defining a rule in Outlook, the Rules Wizard tells you whether the rule will be implemented on the client side. Client-side rules pose their own problems, for the simple reason that a client may not be available to respond to an action at any particular time. What if a rule specifies that an alert is to be sent to a client, and the client is not connected when the triggering event occurs?

If a rule requires client intervention and the client is not available, Exchange creates a deferred action message (DAM). All DAMs are stored in a hidden folder called a Deferred Action folder (DAF).

If a rule requires any client interaction, the rule is tagged with a client identifier, which is included in the DAM. When an Exchange client logs on, it checks the messages in the DAF to see whether any messages contain the unique identifier for the current profile used by the client. If the client finds a message that matches, it accepts delivery of the message and processes the action indicated in the message.

Real World   Watch Out for Deferred Actions

As the scenario described in this section illustrates, Exchange can easily handle rules that result in deferred actions. A deferred action, however, is always implemented asynchronously; you can never know when, or even whether, the action will be implemented. Keep this fact in mind when you design rules that require client interaction. If you create a rule that alerts a user that a message is waiting for his or her approval, for example, the user may not get that alert for days or weeks — or ever, if that person has left the company. Make sure that any deferred actions are optional or have some type of backup action prescribed for them.

Summary

Your Exchange environment is a terrific tool for encouraging communication, but too much communication can overwhelm a user—a situation that lessens the value of the individual pieces of information. You can use Exchange properties and Outlook rules to help shape the vast flow of communication into a more usable form. Rules are defined through an Outlook client but are implemented with both Exchange and Outlook.

This chapter ends the part of the book on deploying Exchange clients. The next part covers what is probably the single most important topic to you, as an administrator: how to monitor, back up, and tune your Exchange Server.

Part V
Maintenance

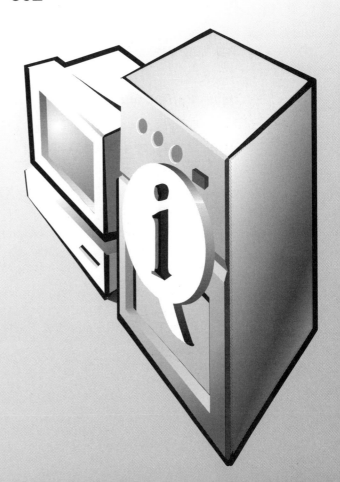

Chapter 20
Monitoring Exchange

One key to running a successful network is keeping a close eye on its operation, especially if you are running a complex system such as a Microsoft Exchange Server 5.5. By keeping close watch over your organization and its components, you can spot potential problems before they occur and quickly respond to the problems that do occur. Monitoring also allows you to identify trends in network use that signal opportunities for optimization and future planning.

This chapter covers many of the tools that you can use to monitor Exchange Server 5.5. Some of these tools, such as Event Viewer and Performance Monitor, are provided by Microsoft Windows NT Server. Other tools, such as server and link monitors, are part of Exchange Server 5.5 itself.

Using the Alerter Service

One simple way to monitor the general state of servers in an Exchange organization is to use the Alerter Service that comes with Windows NT Server. One method of configuring the Alerter Service is by physically going to each server and using the Server applet in the Windows Control Panel. Another method of configuring the Alerter Service for remote servers is by using Server Manager and selecting the remote server you want to configure. No matter which method you choose, you click the Alerts button, as shown in Figure 20-1.

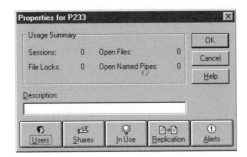

Figure 20-1. *The Alerts button in Server Properties.*

After clicking the Alerts button, you can configure each server to send administrative alerts to multiple recipients, as shown in Figure 20-2. These recipients can include any computers or user accounts that are configured on the network.

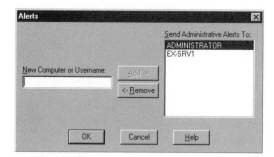

Figure 20-2. *Designating recipient to receive administrative alerts.*

Administrative alerts are sent when certain server events occur. These events include low disk space, security and access problems, and unexpected server shutdown. Figure 20-3 shows an example administrative alert sent when a domain controller for a remote domain cannot be located.

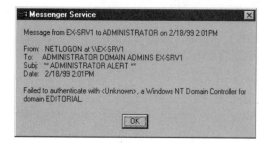

Figure 20-3. *Receiving an administrative alert.*

Note   For alerts to be sent, the Alerter and Messenger Services must be running on the computer creating the alert, and the Messenger Service must be running on the computer receiving the alert. The Alerter Service does not guarantee delivery of the alert, because it does not check with the Messenger Service to see whether or not it was successful. In addition, you must stop and restart both the Alerter and Server Services before alerts can be sent to any new recipients that you add. If you stop the Server Service on a remote computer from Server Manager, remember that you will not be able to restart it with Server Manager, because the remote computer is no longer available in Server Manager.

Using Event Viewer

As you may know, Windows NT Server records many events in its own Event logs. You can view the logs of both local and remote servers by using the Event Viewer utility, which you can find in the Administrative Tools (Common) program group. Windows NT Server maintains three distinct logs:

- **System**   The System log is a record of events that concern components of the system itself, including such events as device driver and network failures.

- **Security**   The Security log is a record of events based on the auditing settings specified in User Manager for Domains.

- **Application**   The Application log is a record of events generated by applications. All Exchange Server 5.5 services write their status information to this log. If you enable diagnostics logging for any Exchange Server 5.5 components, that information is also recorded in the Application log. This log is the most valuable log for monitoring the general health of an Exchange Server. Figure 20-4 shows an entry made when the Internet Mail server could not make a dial-up connection.

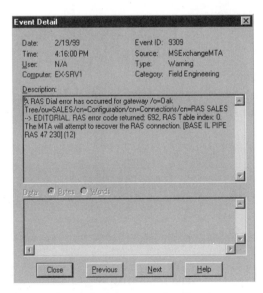

Figure 20-4. *Reviewing an Application event created by Exchange Server 5.5.*

Note Diagnostics logging of Exchange Server 5.5 components generates many entries in the Event Viewer Application log, especially if you have the diagnostics logging level set to Maximum. You should use diagnostics logging only when you are troubleshooting potential problems in specific components, and you should disable it when you are finished. By default, the Application log file is set to a maximum of 512KB. We generally recommend setting this to at least 1MB for general use and even more when using diagnostics logging. By default, each log file overwrites events older than seven days. The default settings for size and overwriting are configurable by changing the Maximum Log Size and Event Log Wrapping options. The Maximum Log Size can be adjusted in 64KB increments.

You can choose from among three Event Log Wrapping options. They are Overwrite Events As Needed, Overwrite Events Older Than "number" Days, and Do Not Overwrite Events (clear log manually). As previously discussed, turning on Diagnostics logging with the level set to Maximum generates a great number of events in the Event log. You want to make sure that you have the wrapping option set correctly for what you are trying to accomplish. For example, if you have it set to overwrite events as needed, you may lose critical information that may have helped you to solve the problem you turned Diagnostics on for in the first place.

If you have a particular log file that you want to save, you have at your disposal three formats in which to save the log. You can save it as a binary Event log file with the .EVT extension, a text file with the .TXT extension, or a comma-delimited text file with the .TXT extension. Binary files with the .EVT extension can be read only with the Event Viewer application; the two text files can be read with your favorite ASCII editor/viewer.

You will encounter five types of events in the three logs, and a unique icon identifies each event type so that you can easily distinguish between the information entries and the error entries. Normally, you will encounter only the first three

Table 20-1. Event Types Displayed in the Event Viewer

Icon	Event	Description
●	Error	A significant problem has occurred, such as an Exchange Server service that may not have started properly.
①	Warning	An event has occurred that is not currently detrimental to the system but may indicate a possible future problem.
❶	Information	A significant event that describes a successful operation has occurred. For example, an Exchange Server service starting successfully may trigger this type of event.
⚷	Audit Success	An audited security access attempt — for example, a successful logon to the system — was successful.
🔒	Audit Failure	An audited security access attempt was not successful. An example is failed access to an audited file or directory.

icons shown in Table 20-1 in relation to Exchange Server. The classification of events is controlled by the applications and system and cannot be configured by the administrators.

Using Diagnostics Logging

All Exchange Server 5.5 services log certain critical events to the Windows NT Server Application log. For certain services, however, you can configure additional levels of diagnostics logging. Diagnostics logging is one of the most useful tools for troubleshooting problems in Exchange Server 5.5.

You can modify the levels of diagnostics logging for all services on a particular Exchange Server by using the Diagnostics Logging property sheet for the server object in Exchange Administrator, as shown in Figure 20-5. On the left side of this property sheet, you'll find a hierarchical view of all the services on the server for which you can enable advanced diagnostics logging. On the right side, you'll find a list of categories that can be logged for the selected service.

Figure 20-5. *Viewing diagnostics logging categories.*

All the major services are represented on this property sheet, including the following:

- **MSExchangeCCMC (Microsoft Exchange cc:Mail Connector)**   Use diagnostics logging on this service to troubleshoot problems with message delivery between Exchange Server 5.5 and a cc:Mail post office.

- **MSExchangeDS (Microsoft Exchange Directory Service)**   Use diagnostics logging on this service to troubleshoot problems resulting from possible Directory inconsistencies and to monitor the progress of Directory Replication.

- **MSExchangeDX (Microsoft Exchange Directory Synchronization Agent)** Use diagnostics logging on this service to troubleshoot problems with Directory Synchronization with foreign mail systems.

- **MSExchangeIMS (Microsoft Exchange Internet Mail Service)**   In previous versions of Exchange Server, this component was named the Internet Mail Connector—hence, the acronym IMS. Use diagnostics logging to troubleshoot problems with the Internet Mail Service.

- **MSExchangeIS (Microsoft Exchange Information Store Service)**   You do not actually enable logging for the Information Store Service as a whole. The MSExchangeIS item expands, allowing you to enable diagnostics logging individually for the Public and Private Information Stores and for the various Internet protocols, as shown in Figure 20-6. Use diagnostics logging on this service to monitor background tasks that occur in Exchange, such as IS maintenance.

Figure 20-6. *Diagnostics Logging tab for components of the Information Store.*

- **MSExchangeMSMI (Microsoft Exchange Microsoft Mail Connector)**   The acronym MSMI stands for Microsoft Mail Interchange. Use diagnostics logging on this service to troubleshoot problems with message delivery between Exchange Server 5.5 and Microsoft Mail post offices.

- **MSExchangeMTA (Microsoft Exchange Message Transfer Agent)** Use diagnostics logging on this service to troubleshoot problems with message delivery and gateway connectivity.

You can also control diagnostics logging by using the server-level objects of the particular service for which you want to log activities. Figure 20-7 shows the Diagnostics Logging property sheet for the *Message Transfer Agent* object, located in the Server container. The categories of information that you can log on this property sheet are identical to those for the MSExchangeMTA service on the Diagnostics Logging property sheet for the server. The Diagnostics Logging property sheet for the individual service provides another way of looking at the same information.

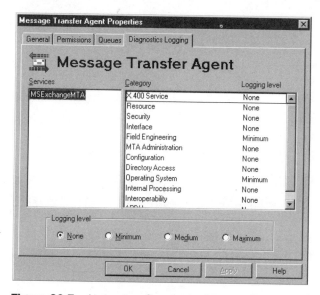

Figure 20-7. *Activating diagnostics logging for a particular service.*

Regardless of where you enable diagnostics logging for a service or which service you choose to log, you can enable four distinct levels of logging. All events that occur in Exchange Server 5.5 are given an event level of 0, 1, 3, or 5. The logging level you set will determine which levels of events are logged:

- **None** Only events with a logging level of 0 are logged. These events include application and system failures.
- **Minimum** All events with a logging level of 1 or lower are logged.
- **Medium** All events with a logging level of 3 or lower are logged.
- **Maximum** All events with a logging level of 5 or lower are logged. All events concerning a particular service are logged. This level can fill an Event log quickly.

Real World   Using High Levels of Diagnostics Logging

Although diagnostics logging can be a very useful tool in some circumstances, at other times it can be more of a hindrance than a help. Enabling high levels of diagnostics logging, such as medium or maximum, can fill up your Event log pretty quickly, often hiding important level 0 events in a flood of trivial events. In addition, many events are logged that may seem like errors but actually are not. These events include the routine errors and timeouts that occur in normal Exchange Server 5.5 operation.

Finally, many events will be logged that are really not documented anywhere in the product literature. Exchange developers often use these undocumented events to perform diagnostics.

Our recommendation is to leave diagnostics logging set to None for general purposes. If you need to troubleshoot malfunctions of particular services, try setting the diagnostics logging level to low or medium for brief periods.

Using Exchange Monitors

Exchange Server 5.5 provides two types of monitors to help you watch over your organization: server monitors and link monitors. *Server monitors* check the status of designated services on a particular Exchange Server. *Link monitors* check the status of a communications link between two servers. Both types of monitors are configured at site level in Microsoft Exchange Administrator.

Using Server Monitors

A server monitor checks designated Windows NT services on a server to detect critical situations. When you create a server monitor, you create it on a particular Exchange Server. By default, it checks on three core Exchange services on the server on which it is installed:

- Directory Service (DS)
- Information Store Service (IS)
- Message Transfer Agent (MTA)

You can add any Windows NT service, including non-Exchange services, to the list of services that a server monitor checks, including services on remote Exchange Servers. A server monitor cannot be configured to monitor the System

Attendant Service of the server on which the monitor is installed because the server monitor itself depends on its own System Attendant to function.

You create a server monitor by choosing New Other, then Server Monitor from the File menu of Exchange Administrator, as shown in Figure 20-8. The following sections describe how to complete the server monitor's property sheets.

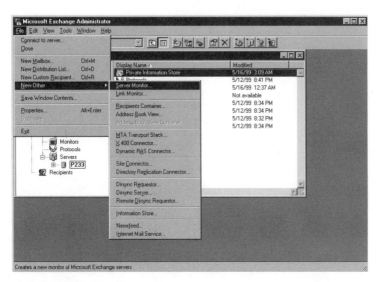

Figure 20-8. *Adding a new server monitor to Exchange Server.*

General Property Sheet

The General property sheet of a server monitor, shown in Figure 20-9, allows you to configure some basic information about the new monitor. Aside from the directory and display names, you can designate the log file to which the server monitor should record its activities.

You also use the General property sheet to set polling intervals for the server monitor. A *polling interval* defines how often the server monitor checks the services that it is monitoring. You can set different polling intervals for normal and critical sites. A normal site is one on which every service is running fine. By default, the server monitor polls normal sites every 15 minutes. If the server monitor detects a problem with a service, the site is escalated to a critical condition. Critical sites are polled every five minutes by default. As you see in the section on the Actions property sheet later in this chapter, the server monitor can take up to three separate actions when a site becomes critical. The polling interval of critical sites is the amount of time the server monitor waits before taking each of these actions.

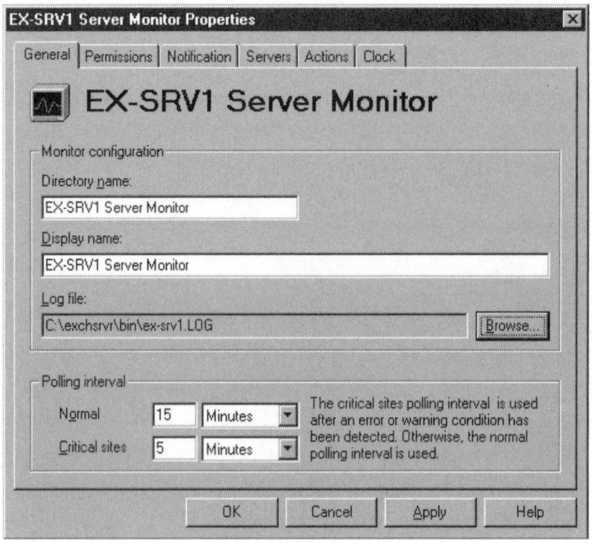

Figure 20-9. *Setting the polling intervals for a server monitor.*

Notification Property Sheet

The Notification property sheet of a server monitor, shown in Figure 20-10, allows you to specify the person to be contacted or process to be launched when a site becomes critical. You can add as many notifications to the list as you like, using the following categories:

Figure 20-10. *Sending notifications of critical server states.*

- **Launch a Process**   Causes an external program to be launched when a site becomes critical. External programs can be useful to, for example, launch a program that sends a notification to a phone or pager number.
- **Mail Message**   Sends an e-mail message about the situation to a designated recipient. Note, however, that if the service in trouble is involved in message delivery, this alert message may not be delivered.
- **Windows NT Alert**   Sends a standard network message about the situation to a designated computer on the network if that computer or user is online. Messages can also be sent to users, provided they are currently logged on to the network.

Regardless of which type of notification you choose, you can specify a delay time for sending the notification. The default delay time is 15 minutes. You can also specify for each recipient whether a notification should be sent during a warning state or only during an alert state.

Servers Property Sheet

The Servers property sheet, shown in Figure 20-11, allows you to designate the servers and services that a server monitor checks. Available servers on the selected site are displayed on the left side of the property sheet. You can change the site using the drop-down menu at the bottom of the property sheet. Servers selected to be monitored are displayed on the right side. Select a server from the Monitored Servers list and then click Services to choose the services on that server that you want to monitor, as shown in Figure 20-12. By default, only the DS, IS, and MTA services are selected for a new server, but you can add any services on the server.

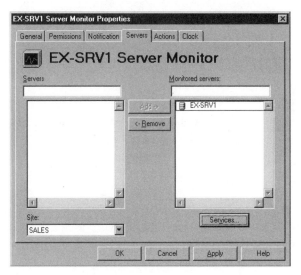

Figure 20-11. *Choosing servers to monitor.*

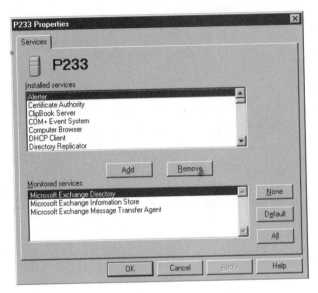

Figure 20-12. *Choosing services to monitor.*

Real World **Modifying Default Monitored Services**

By default, a new server monitor checks only three services on the server on which it is configured: the Directory Service, the Information Store Service, and the Message Transfer Agent. This default also applies to new servers that you add to an existing server monitor. Although adding new services after you create a server monitor is easy enough, you can also change the default services monitored on a per-server basis. To change the default services monitored for a server, follow these steps:

1. Open the properties sheet for the *Server* container object in Exchange Administrator.

2. Switch to the Services property sheet.

3. Select any service or services that you want to add to the default monitored services. You can use either the Ctrl-click or the Shift-click method to select multiple items.

4. Click Add to add the selected services to the list of monitored services.

5. Close the property sheet.

After you perform these steps, any server monitor that you create will monitor the selected services by default. You can restore the original defaults at any time by clicking Default on the Services property sheet.

Actions Property Sheet

The Actions property sheet, shown in Figure 20-13, allows you to specify the actions that the server monitor should take when a service that is being monitored stops responding.

A server monitor can do one of three things when it detects that a monitored service has stopped running: Take No Action, Restart The Service, or Restart The Computer. The server monitor shown in Figure 20-13 is configured to take no action when it first notices that a service has stopped. After a delay equal to one critical polling interval, the server monitor attempts to restart the service. After another such delay, and on all subsequent attempts, the server monitor restarts the computer. This setup is useful because it gives time for notifications to be sent and action to be taken before the server monitor attempts to do anything on its own. If you choose to have the server monitor restart the computer, you can also specify a restart delay (in seconds) and a message to be displayed during the restart delay.

Note Restarting a server can sometimes cause more problems than it solves. Often the inability to start a service is a sign that a more critical malfunction has occurred. Generally, we recommend that you do not have your server monitors attempt to automatically restart servers. It is to your advantage to investigate the reasons that a service may have stopped before resorting to a reboot.

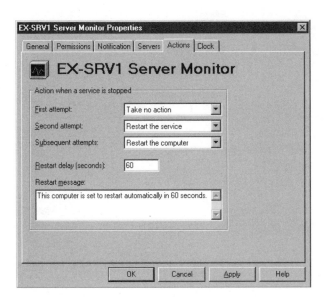

Figure 20-13. *Specifying the actions that a server monitor can take.*

Clock Property Sheet

In an Exchange organization, it is important that the clocks on all your Exchange Servers be synchronized. Although clock synchronization might seem trivial, a server whose date is off by several days can cause such problems as message-delivery failure and improperly deleted items due to incorrect time stamps. Fortunately, you can use server monitors to synchronize the clocks of Exchange Servers.

Use the Clock property sheet of the server monitor, shown in Figure 20-14, to specify the action that the server monitor should take if the clock on one of its monitored servers drifts. You can specify that warning and alert notifications be sent when clocks deviate by a designated amount. For each threshold, you can also specify that the server monitor synchronize the clock on the remote server with its own.

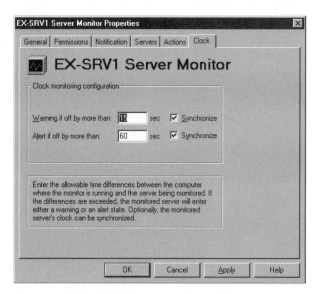

Figure 20-14. *Synchronizing server clocks with a server monitor.*

Using Link Monitors

Link monitors check the communications pathway between a source server and one or more target servers. The source server is the Exchange Server on which you configure the link monitor. Target servers can be other Exchange Servers in the organization or even servers in foreign messaging systems.

For the most part, link monitors work much like server monitors. You can create a new link monitor by choosing New Other, then Link Monitor from the File menu of Exchange Administrator, as shown in Figure 20-15. This command opens a set of property sheets for the new link monitor.

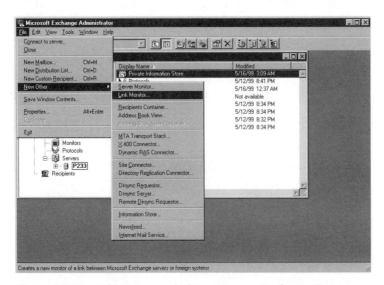

Figure 20-15. *Adding a new link monitor to Exchange Server.*

Much of the configuration of the link monitor is identical to the configuration of the server monitor (covered earlier in this chapter). You set a normal- and critical-site polling interval on the General property sheet of the link monitor just as you do for the server monitor. On a link monitor, polling intervals determine how often test messages are generated and sent to the target servers. Notifications are also set up in an identical fashion for both types of monitors. You use the Servers property sheet to select remote Exchange Servers for which you want to monitor a messaging link.

Notice, however, that unlike the server monitor, the link monitor has no Action property sheet. A link monitor can take no actions when a messaging link fails. Link monitors are used only to send notifications of failed links.

Two property sheets for link monitors do not exist for server monitors: Recipients and Bounce. The Recipients property sheet of a link monitor, shown in Figure 20-16, designates servers in foreign messaging systems or in other Exchange organizations for which the link monitor should check messaging links. You can set up a message to be sent to either an invalid or a valid address on a target server. An invalid address returns a nondelivery report that verifies that the link is operational. Using an invalid address is the easiest way to set up a recipient. You can also send test messages to a valid address. In such a case, the message must be replied to before the link monitor can validate the link. This reply can come from an actual recipient or from a program that is set to reply automatically.

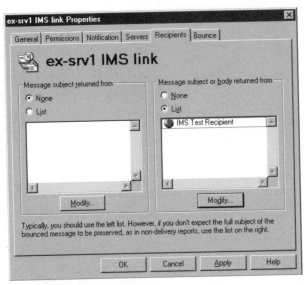

Figure 20-16. *Configuring recipients in foreign messaging systems.*

When you designate a recipient, you must also designate how you expect the message to be returned from that recipient. When the link monitor sends a message to a valid recipient, the message generally is returned with the full Subject field intact. Thus, you usually want to use the list on the left side of the Recipients property sheet to configure valid recipients. When the link monitor sends a message to an invalid recipient, however, the Subject line of the message is not fully preserved, so the link monitor has to rely on the body of the message as well. For this reason, you want to configure invalid recipients by using the list on the right side of the Recipients property sheet. Depending on your situation, you may also have to configure some types of valid recipients by using the list on the right side of the property sheet. You will have to experiment with test messages to make this determination.

The Bounce property sheet of the link monitor, shown in Figure 20-17, specifies the allowable return-trip time, or *bounce time*, for messages that are sent to target servers. By default, the link monitor goes into a warning state after a message has not returned for 30 minutes and an alert state after a message has not returned for 60 minutes. You can use the Notification property sheet of the link monitor to specify which recipients should be notified for warnings and which should be notified for alerts.

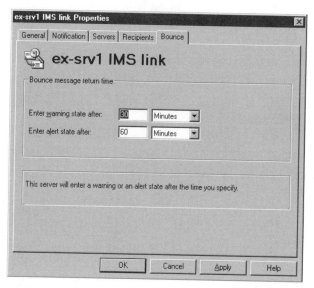

Figure 20-17. *Configuring bounce message return times.*

Starting Monitors

After you create a monitor of either type, a Directory object for it is placed in the Monitors container, which is located in the appropriate site container, as shown in Figure 20-18. Monitors are not automatically started when they are created. You have to start the monitor manually within Exchange Administrator. To do so, simply select the monitor that you want to start, and then choose Start Monitor from the Tools menu. Exchange Administrator must always be open for a monitor to keep running. When you close Exchange Administrator, the monitor stops. If you do close Exchange Administrator with a monitor running, that monitor automatically starts the next time Exchange Administrator launches.

Note Exchange Administrator also provides a command-line parameter that allows you to start a specific monitor. You need to specify the name of the monitor and the site or server on which it is configured. The command format is:

```
Admin /s <server_name>/m[<site_name>]\<monitor_name>\
    <target_server_name>
```

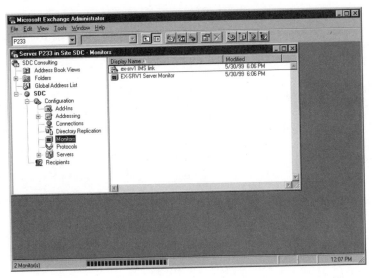

Figure 20-18. *Monitors configured for an Exchange Server site.*

Tracking Messages

Part III of this book covers the property sheets of many Directory objects in Exchange Administrator. If you recall, several of these objects allow you to enable something called *message tracking*. All objects that allow message tracking represent services that are involved in message transfer. The services for which you can enable message tracking include the following:

- **Information Store Service** Message tracking is enabled on the General property sheet of the *Information Store Site Configuration* object, located in the site's Configuration container.

- **Message Transfer Agent** Message tracking is enabled on the General property sheet of the *MTA Site Configuration* object, located in the site's Configuration container.

- **Internet Mail Service** Message tracking is enabled on the Internet Mail property sheet of the *Internet Mail Service* object, located in the site's Connections container.

- **MS Mail Connector** Message tracking is enabled on the Interchange property sheet of the *MS Mail Connector* object, located in the site's Connections container.

- **Lotus cc:Mail Connector**   Message tracking is enabled on the Post Office property sheet of the *Lotus cc:Mail Connector* object, located in the site's Connections container.

When you enable message tracking for a particular service, that service records in its own log file all message transfers in which it is involved. All log files are maintained by the System Attendant Service on each server. When message tracking has been enabled for one or more components, you can track individual messages by using the Message Tracking Center, a component of Exchange Administrator.

Using the Message Tracking Center

You launch the Message Tracking Center (MTC) by choosing Track Message from the Tools menu of Exchange Administrator, as shown in Figure 20-19. This command opens a dialog box that allows you to select an Exchange Server to which to connect. It is best to select the home server of the recipient who sent the message that you want to track.

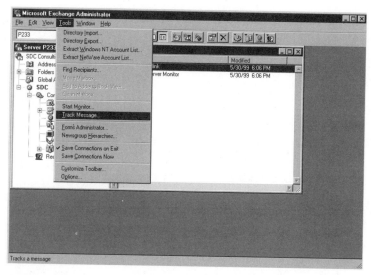

Figure 20-19. *Starting the Message Tracking Center.*

After you connect to a server, the MTC opens and displays the Select Message To Track dialog box, shown in Figure 20-20. Click From or Send To to open a standard address book, from which you can choose the originator or recipient of the message that you want to track in the MTC. You can also specify the number of days back to search for messages. After you enter your criteria, click

Find Now to perform the search. Figure 20-20 shows all messages that were sent by the mailbox administrator in the last two days.

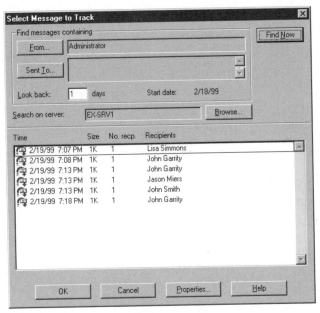

Figure 20-20. *Searching for a message to track in the Message Tracking Center.*

When the messages that meet your criteria are displayed, you can open the property sheet of any message by selecting it and then clicking Properties. Use this method to find the actual message that you want to track. When you find that message, select it and then click OK to return to the MTC main window. Click Track to send the MTC to work tracking the history of the message.

Figure 20-21 shows the MTC main window when tracking is finished. You can select another message to track by clicking Search.

Using Advanced Search

You can perform a more sophisticated search for messages to track by clicking Advanced Search in the main Message Tracking Center window. This action displays a dialog box, shown in Figure 20-22, that lets you search for messages according to three criteria:

- **Sent By Microsoft Exchange Server** This option displays messages sent by Exchange Server 5.5 services. When you choose this option, you can specify the service for which to display messages. Choices include the Directory, Information Store, Message Transfer Agent, and Directory Synchronization

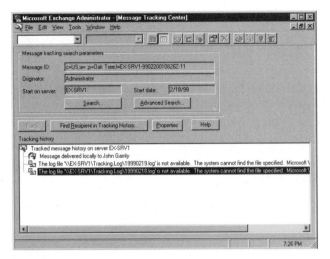

Figure 20-21. *Viewing the history of a message in the Message Tracking Center.*

Services. You can also specify the number of past days to search for these messages.

Figure 20-22. *Advanced Search capabilities of the Message Tracking Center.*

- **Transferred Into This Site**   This option returns you to the Select Message To Track dialog box (refer back to Figure 20-20) and displays all messages that were transferred to the site from any outside source. You can further refine the search by selecting a specific originator or recipient or by selecting the connector over which the message was transferred.

- **By Message ID**   This option allows you to specify a unique message ID by which to search for messages. Every message transferred in an Exchange organization has a unique ID that includes the name of the originating Exchange Server, the date, and a long series of digits. Choosing this option is best when you have one specific message that you want to track, such as a test message that you create. You can find the ID for any message by viewing the properties of a copy of the message in a mail client.

Using Performance Monitor

Performance Monitor is a wonderful tool that comes with Windows NT Server and is available in the Administrative Tools (Common) program group. Performance Monitor graphically charts the performance of hundreds of individual system parameters on a Microsoft Windows NT computer. When Exchange Server 5.5 is installed on a Windows NT Server, several Exchange-specific counters can be charted as well.

How Performance Monitor Works

Although a full discussion of how Performance Monitor works is beyond the scope of this book, this section covers some of its basic concepts. Performance Monitor treats various system components as objects. These objects include such components as Memory, Processor, and Network. Exchange Server 5.5 adds such components as Message Transfer Agent and Directory Service.

Each object in Performance Monitor is broken into many counters, which represent quantifiable characteristics of the object. The *Processor* object, for example, contains one counter named %Processor Time, which measures how much processor time is being used executing non-idle threads. This counter is only one of 10 counters that make up the *Processor* object. A commonly monitored Exchange counter is the Work Queue Length counter of the *Message Transfer Agent* object. This counter measures the number of messages in the MTA's queue that have not yet been delivered. Performance Monitor can monitor multiple counters from different objects simultaneously.

When you first open Performance Monitor, you see a blank screen called a *chart view*, which displays selected counters in real time as a graph. The first thing that you need to do is add some counters. Choose Add To Chart from the Edit menu to open the Add To Chart dialog box, shown in Figure 20-23.

By default, the computer that you monitor is the computer on which you launched Performance Monitor, but you can monitor remote computers as well. In fact, you can even select counters from multiple computers at the same time. In Figure 20-23, the Outbound Messages Total counter of the *MSExchangeMTA* object is being added to the chart view. The resulting chart view, after some time has elapsed, is shown in Figure 20-24.

Don't underestimate the benefit of using Performance Monitor in your Exchange environment. Performance Monitor can be used to collect and analyze data, perform a baseline of your Exchange Servers, and detect problems and provide the proper notification, as well as analyze the problems when they occur. There are

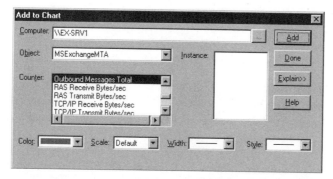

Figure 20-23. *Adding a counter to a Performance Monitor chart.*

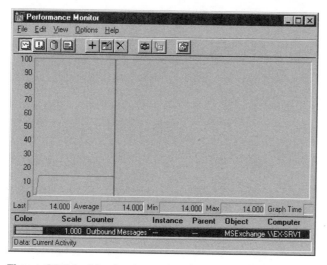

Figure 20-24. *Monitoring an Exchange counter in Performance Monitor.*

several critical areas in which you should use Performance Monitor to watch Exchange Server. These areas are as follows:

- Message Transfer Agent (MTA)
- Information Store (IS)
- System Attendant (SA)
- Directory Store (DS)
- Central Processing Unit (CPU)
- Network
- Disk Input/Output (I/O)
- Memory

Note In order to monitor disk performance you must type **DISKPERF -Y** on each Windows NT system.

Take the time to become familiar with all of the counters Exchange Server provides to Performance Monitor so that you can ensure your Exchange environment runs as smoothly as possible. Also utilize the standard counters that come with Performance Monitor to watch items such as memory, CPU, and Disk I/O.

More Info This section only scratches the surface of Performance Monitor's capabilities. Performance Monitor also logs performance over time and sends alerts. For a complete list of objects and counters installed with Exchange Server 5.5, consult your product documentation.

Preconstructed Chart Views

Exchange Server 5.5 is shipped with several Performance Monitor chart views already constructed for you. These preconstructed views let you monitor several important sets of counters on your Exchange Servers without your having to add all those counters yourself. All these views are available in the Microsoft Exchange program group. You can run multiple views simultaneously.

The following preconstructed chart views come with Exchange Server 5.5:

- **MS Exchange Server Health** This chart displays a summary of the server's CPU use, along with the CPU use of the Directory Service, Message Transfer Agent, and Information Store Service. This chart also displays the number of memory pages used per second on the server, which is one way of monitoring the amount of memory used. This chart is updated every second.

- **MS Exchange Server History** This chart gives you a general idea about server performance. The chart shows the number of current users on the system and the number of messages waiting in internal queues. This chart is updated every 60 seconds.

- **MS Exchange Server IMS Queues** This chart shows the current number of inbound and outbound messages in the Internet Mail Service queue. This chart is updated every second.

- **MS Exchange Server IMS Statistics** This chart, which is updated every 30 seconds, shows the total number of inbound and outbound messages sent through the IMS queue.

- **MS Exchange Server IMS Traffic** This chart displays a continuously updated summary of incoming and outgoing messages over the IMS. The chart also displays the total number of inbound and outbound connections.

- **MS Exchange Server Load**   This chart provides a detailed look at the load on an Exchange Server. The chart tracks the number of messages submitted to the Public and Private Information Stores, the number of address-book queries per second, and the number of Directory queries and Replication updates per second. This chart is updated every 10 seconds.

- **MS Exchange Server Queues**   This chart shows the total current number of messages in the MTA work queue as well as the Public and Private Information Stores' send and receive queues. This chart is updated every 10 seconds.

- **MS Exchange Server Users**   This chart shows how many users are currently connected to the Exchange Server. This chart is updated every 10 seconds.

Using SNMP and the MADMAN MIB

Simple Network Management Protocol (SNMP) is a standard, unsecure communication protocol used to collect information from devices on a TCP/IP network. SNMP was developed in the Internet community to monitor activity on network devices such as routers and bridges. Since then, SNMP acceptance and support have grown. Many devices, including computers running Windows NT, can now be monitored with SNMP.

How SNMP Works

SNMP has a small command set and maintains a centralized database of management information. An SNMP system has three parts:

- **SNMP Agent**   The SNMP Agent is the device on a network that is being monitored. This device is typically a computer that has the SNMP Agent software installed. Windows NT includes SNMP Agent software in the form of the Microsoft SNMP Service, which you install by using the Services property sheet of the Network applet in the Windows NT Control Panel.

- **SNMP Management System**   The SNMP Management System is the component that does the actual monitoring in an SNMP environment. Windows NT does not provide an SNMP Management System. Third-party SNMP Management Systems include Hewlett-Packard's OpenView and IBM's NetView.

- **Management Information Base**   The Management Information Base (MIB) is a centralized database of all the values that can be monitored for all the devices in an SNMP system. Different MIBs are provided for monitoring different types of devices and systems. Windows NT comes with four MIBs: Internet MIB II, LAN Manager MIB II, DHCP MIB, and WINS MIB. These four MIBs allow the remote monitoring and management of most components of Windows NT.

Exchange Server 5.5 and the MADMAN MIB

Exchange Server 5.5 includes a special MIB that you can use to enable an SNMP Management System that manages many Exchange Server 5.5 functions. This MIB is based on a standardized MIB named the Mail and Directory Management (MADMAN) MIB, which is detailed in Internet Request for Comments (RFC) 1566. Microsoft's implementation of the MADMAN MIB meets all the specifications of the standard and adds a few touches of its own. The Exchange MADMAN MIB works by converting the Performance Monitor counters for the MTA and IMS objects to MIBs, using utilities provided with the Windows NT Resource Kit.

> **More Info**   Despite its name, Simple Network Management Protocol is not so simple to use. This section offers only a glimpse of it so that you will know that it is available. If you are interested in deploying SNMP in your Exchange organization, consult *Microsoft BackOffice 4.5 Resource Kit* (1999) and *Microsoft Windows NT Server 4.0 Resource Kit* (1996), both from Microsoft Press.

Summary

In this chapter, you learned that monitoring your network is crucial in spotting problems before they grow too large. You also learned about many of the tools used to monitor Exchange Server 5.5.

The Alerter Service can be used to send administrative alerts from a server to other computers and users on the network. The Windows NT Event Viewer is used to view system and application events logged by Windows NT Server and any running applications. The Event Viewer should be your primary tool in making sure that a server is running smoothly. Exchange Server 5.5 automatically logs all critical events to the Windows NT Application log. In addition, you can use Exchange Administrator to configure higher levels of diagnostics logging for each of the services in Exchange.

Exchange Server 5.5 also provides two monitors used in keeping tabs on your Exchange organization: the server monitor and the link monitor. The server monitor is used to monitor designated Windows NT services on one or more Exchange Servers. Should a service fail, the server monitor can send notification alerts, attempt to restart the service, and even restart the computer. A link monitor is used to monitor the messaging link between two servers by sending periodic test messages. Should a link fail, the link monitor can send alert messages to designated users or computers.

The Message Tracking Center in Exchange Administrator can be used to track the path of a message through all services for which message tracking has been enabled. Performance Monitor is a Windows NT utility that graphically charts the performance of hundreds of individual system parameters on a Microsoft Windows NT computer. When Exchange Server 5.5 is installed on a Windows NT Server, several Exchange-specific counters can be charted as well. Simple Network Management Protocol (SNMP) is a standard communication protocol used to collect information from devices on a TCP/IP network. Exchange Server 5.5 supports the use of SNMP through the MADMAN Management Information Base.

In Chapter 21, you will learn how information is stored and logged on an Exchange Server. You will also learn various methods for backing up and restoring Exchange Servers.

Chapter 21
Backup and Recovery

One key to keeping a reliable network going is planning for what must be done when a piece of that network fails. Nothing is more important than a good backup in ensuring that you can recover from failure. This chapter examines the procedures for backing up and restoring a Microsoft Exchange Server 5.5 server.

Deciding What You Should Back Up

A great deal of information makes up an Exchange Server. Much of this information resides in the Exchange databases of user messages, public messages, and Directory Information. Some configuration information is stored in the Microsoft Windows NT Registry; some is stored in various places in the Exchange Server installation path. This section covers the information that you need to include when you back up an Exchange Server.

Databases

Most of the information in Exchange Server 5.5—including user messages, Directory Information, and configuration information—is stored in several databases. An Exchange Server computer has three core databases:

- **PRIV.EDB**   The Private Information Store database, PRIV.EDB, holds user mailboxes and messages. By default, this database is located in the \EXCH-SRVR\MDBDATA\ folder.

- **PUB.EDB**   The Public Information Store database, PUB.EDB, holds messages posted to public folders. By default, this database is located in the \EXCHSRVR\MDBDATA\ folder.

- **DIR.EDB**   The Directory database, DIR.EDB, holds configuration information regarding the organization. Configuration information includes all the objects in Microsoft Exchange Administrator that are used to configure the various Exchange services. By default, this database is located in the \EXCHSRVR\DSADATA\ folder.

In addition to these core databases, several optional databases might be available on any given Exchange Server. These optional databases represent various services that may be installed on a server, such as a Dirsync or KM Server database.

Transaction Logs

All databases in Exchange Server 5.5 rely on Microsoft Joint Engine Technology (JET) 3.0, which is an advanced database engine that uses Transaction log files to maximize the efficiency and durability of databases. Whenever a transaction occurs on an Exchange Server, the responsible service first records the transaction in a Transaction log. Using Transaction logs allows for faster completion of the transaction than if the service had to immediately commit the transaction to a database because the Transaction log structure is much simpler than the database structure. Transactions are written to the database at a later time, when system processes are idle.

Transaction logs are the primary storage areas for new transactions. One Transaction log exists for the Directory Service, and one exists for the Information Store Service. The DS Transaction log file, called EDB.LOG, resides in the \EXCHSRVR\DSADATA Directory. The IS Transaction log file, also called EDB.LOG, resides in the \EXCHSRVR\MDBDATA Directory.

Data is written to these log files sequentially as transactions occur. Regular database maintenance routines commit changes in the logs to the actual databases later. The most current state of either Exchange service is the service database *plus* the current log file. Therefore, Transaction logs are an essential part of the backup routine.

Checkpoint files are used to keep track of transactions that are committed to the database from a Transaction log. Using checkpoint files ensures that transactions cannot be committed to a database more than once. Checkpoint files are named EDB.CHK and reside in the same directories as their log files and databases.

Log files are always exactly 5MB. When a log file fills (reaches 5MB), it is renamed, and a new log file is created. Old, renamed log files are called *previous logs*. Previous logs are named sequentially, using the format EDB*xxxxx*.LOG, in which each *x* represents a hexadecimal number. Previous logs are stored in the same directories as their current-log-file counterparts.

Note   The fact that a log file is converted to a previous log file does not mean that all the transactions in the log file have been committed. It is not unusual, therefore, to have previous log files that contain uncommitted transactions.

During an online backup of an Exchange Server, previous log files that are fully committed are purged. Previous log files can still consume a good deal of disk space. Exchange Server 5.5 provides a feature called *circular logging* that can help prevent that waste of disk space. When circular logging is enabled, only previous log files with uncommitted changes are maintained on the server. This can significantly reduce the amount of hard disk space that is required for your Exchange Server, compared with keeping all Transaction logs until a backup is completed. The disadvantage of using circular logging is that it prevents you from using differential or incremental backups (discussed later in this chapter). Also, because some log files are discarded before backup, you may be unable to fully restore a server by replaying the log files. For this reason, you should disable circular logging for all your Exchange Servers. Circular logging is enabled by default, as shown in Figure 21-1, but you can disable it on the Advanced property sheet of the *Server* object in Exchange Administrator. You may want to turn on circular logging when importing a large amount of data and performing a full backup. However, you must remember to disable it afterward and do a full backup.

> **Note** Although the Windows NT Backup system is adequate to back up the database from a single Exchange Server, most administrators require a more robust backup system. Third-party backup applications may be required when there are multiple servers, when faster performance is needed, or when a disaster recovery plan requires extended restore features.

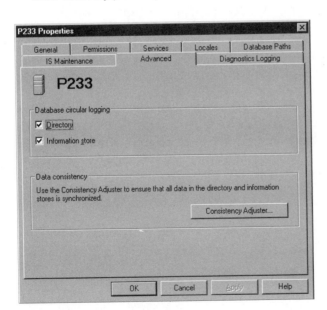

Figure 21-1. *Circular logging on the Directory and Information Store.*

Other Items to Back Up

In addition to Exchange databases and Transaction log files, you will want to include several other items when you back up your Exchange Server:

- **Windows NT Registry**   The Windows NT Registry contains a great deal of configuration information relating to Exchange Server 5.5.

- **EXCHSRVR subdirectories**   Many valuable tidbits, including message-tracking data, are located in various places within the EXCHSRVR subdirectories.

- **User information**   Many administrators allow the storage of users' personal folders (.PST files) and address books on the Exchange Server or another network server. Always make sure that information of this sort is included in your backup strategy. When users store personal folders on their local workstations, administrators typically do not back them up. Most backups are performed after hours, when users tend to turn off their workstations and take their laptops away. On top of these issues, the administrator must set up agents on the user's workstations to enable the backup to work.

Understanding How Backups Work

Now that you have learned some of the items that you need to include in a backup, you need some basic information about the backups themselves. This section covers the five basic types of backups that you can perform by using Windows NT Backup. The section also covers the two ways that you can back up an Exchange Server: online and offline.

Types of Backups

You can perform five basic types of backups by using the Windows NT Backup utility (and most other backup utilities). The key difference between these backup types is how each one handles the archive bit in every Windows NT file. When a file is created or modified, the archive bit is set to on, as shown in Figure 21-2. When some types of backups run, the archive bit is set to off, which indicates that the file has been backed up.

Name	Size	Type	Modified	Attributes
EX22te	3,065 KB	Microsoft Word Doc...	6/24/99 9:33 PM	AC
f22xx04 (was 05)	758 KB	Bitmap Image	2/23/99 11:00 PM	AC
f22xx05 (was 04)	318 KB	Bitmap Image	5/30/99 9:40 PM	AC
f22xx06	886 KB	Bitmap Image	2/23/99 11:00 PM	AC

Figure 21-2. *Showing the archive bit is set to on in a newly created Microsoft Word document file.*

The five backup types are as follows:

- **Normal**   During a normal backup, all selected files are backed up, regardless of how their archive bit is set. After the backup, the archive bit is set to off for all files, indicating that those files have been backed up.

- **Copy**   During a copy backup, all selected files are backed up, regardless of how their archive bit is set. After the backup, the archive bit is not changed in any file.

- **Incremental**   During an incremental backup, all files for which the archive bit is on are backed up. After the backup, the archive bit is set to off for all files that were backed up.

- **Differential**   During a differential backup, all files for which the archive bit is on are backed up. After the backup, the archive bit is not changed in any file.

- **Daily**   During a daily backup, all files that changed on the day of the backup are backed up, and the archive bit is not changed in any file.

Backup Strategies

Given the five types of backups covered in the preceding section, most people have three favorite strategies for backing up a server. These strategies start with performing a full backup of the Exchange Server on a regular basis. One continues with full backups daily, another performs an incremental backup every other day of the week, and finally the last does a differential backup every other day of the week. Here's the difference:

- **Full backup**   Every day of the week, complete a full backup of your Microsoft Exchange Server, including Information Store and Directory. If you follow any other backup strategy, you stand the risk of having to restore to a backup that is several days or weeks old. An example of a failure would be if your "Weekly Full Backup" failed in a "Normal plus incremental"; then you would have to restore to the previous week's backups. Money spent on large-capacity backup systems (such as DLTs) is money well spent.

- **Normal plus incremental**   On Sunday of each week, perform a full backup of all the files on the Exchange Server that you have decided need to be backed up. On Monday, perform an incremental backup that backs up all files that have changed since the full backup. On Tuesday, perform another incremental backup that backs up all files that have changed since the last incremental backup on Monday. At the end of the week, you have performed a full backup and six incremental backups. To restore these backups, you need to restore first the full backup and then each incremental backup, in order.

- **Normal plus differential** On Sunday of each week, perform a full backup of all files. On Monday, perform a differential backup that backs up all files that have changed since the full backup. On Tuesday, perform another differential backup that backs up all files that changed since the last full backup, which occurred on Sunday. Each consecutive differential backup backs up all files that have changed since the last full backup. To restore these backups, you need to restore first the full backup and then only the most recent differential backup.

We recommend daily full backups. The incremental method consumes less time at backup because you are backing up only information that changed during the preceding 24 hours. The incremental method increases the time needed to restore, however, because you have to restore every incremental backup. Because the incremental backup relies on every tape to perform a restore, losing a tape can also present a big problem.

The differential method is just the opposite. This method consumes more time at backup because each day you are backing up everything that has changed since the last full backup. Restore time is reduced, however, because you need to restore only two tapes: the full and the most recent differential.

Online and Offline Backups

As mentioned earlier in this chapter, you can back up an Exchange Server either online or offline.

An *online backup* is performed while the services that are being backed up are still running. This method has the obvious advantage of allowing users to send and receive messages while the backup is being performed. Current databases and transactions are included in a full backup. During an incremental or differential backup, only Transaction logs are backed up. The databases don't need to be backed up, because all changes are recorded in the Transaction logs.

The disadvantage of using online backups is that only the core databases are included in the backup. Optional databases, such as the KM Server database, cannot be included in an online backup.

You may be wondering how an online backup can safely back up all transactions, especially since the core Exchange services are still on line and users are still sending and receiving messages. If a transaction occurs for an .EDB that has not been backed up yet, it is processed just as it always is. However, if a transaction occurs for an .EDB that has already been backed up, it is stored in a *patch file* (.PAT). The patch file is used only during an online backup/restore situation, and there is one patch file for each .EDB. The names of the patch files follow the naming convention of their respective .EDB files, PRIV.PAT, PUB.PAT, and DIR.PAT. When the online backup starts, the .PAT file is created in the respective database directory (MDBDATA and DSADATA). As the backup is taking place, entries are placed in the .PAT file as necessary. When the backup is complete, the .PAT files are written to tape and then deleted out of the MDBDATA and DSADATA directories. An *offline backup* is performed while the Exchange services are stopped. The advantage of performing offline backups is that all files can be included in the backup, including optional databases. The main disadvantage is that during an offline backup, users cannot access the Exchange Server. Another disadvantage is that offline backups are not aware of databases and Transaction logs because they operate at the file level only, so committed transactions are not discarded. One good reason to perform an offline backup is to have some extra insurance that the system can be restored quickly if there are problems after a major systems change.

Using Windows NT Backup

You can perform offline backups by using just about any third-party backup software or by copying the appropriate files to another drive. Most NT Backup products are Exchange-aware, allowing you to perform online backups. The Windows NT Backup utility lets you perform both online and offline backups — and it's free. When you install Exchange Server 5.5, an enhanced version of Windows NT Backup is installed; this version supports online server backups. This section briefly explains how to use Windows NT Backup to perform an online backup of an Exchange Server.

Selecting Components to Back Up

You can find Windows NT Backup in the Administrative Tools (Common) program group, assuming that it was included in the Windows NT installation. To run Windows NT Backup. When the program starts, choose Microsoft Exchange from the Operations menu. A dialog box opens, asking you to which Exchange Server you want to connect, as shown in Figure 21-3.

When you select a server and click OK, the Microsoft Exchange Backup window opens. You can use this window to back up one server or all the servers in your organization. For each Exchange Server, you can choose to back up the Directory Service, the Information Store Service, or both.

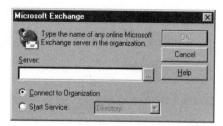

Figure 21-3. *Selecting the Exchange Server to which to connect.*

Figure 21-4 shows both the Microsoft Exchange window and the Drives window. You can use the Drives window to include files from your local server in the backup.

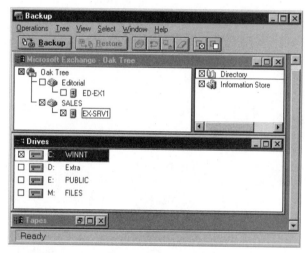

Figure 21-4. *Selecting components to back up.*

Setting Options

After you select all the components that you want to back up, click the Backup button in the toolbar (refer back to Figure 21-4). This action opens the Backup Information dialog box, shown in Figure 21-5.

Depending on what you decided to back up, you may need to configure multiple backup sets. In the example in Figure 21-5, the Information Store Service, Directory Service, and local files of a single server are backed up, thus creating three individual backup sets. You can scroll through the backup sets using the scroll bar in the Backup Set Information section of the dialog box. After you

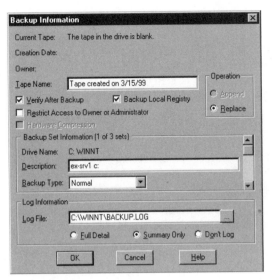

Figure 21-5. *Setting backup options.*

configure your backup sets, click OK to begin the backup. You are informed when the backup is finished or when a new tape is needed.

In this dialog box, you can configure the following settings:

- **Verify After Backup**   Verification of a backup is performed via a file-by-file comparison of the data that is being backed up. Verified backups take longer, but the time is worth it when you are trying to rebuild an Exchange Server. This is why you should always perform a Verify After Backup to ensure the integrity of your backup!

- **Backup Local Registry**   Choose this option if you want to include the local Windows NT Registry in the backup. This option is available only for the local drive backup set.

- **Restrict Access To Owner Or Administrator**   If you choose this option, only the owner (the person who creates the backup) or a member of the local Administrators or Backup Operators groups can restore the tape.

- **Hardware Compression**   Hardware Compression can help fit more information on a single tape. Hardware Compression algorithms are often drive-specific, however. Leaving this option unselected means that you can restore the backup from just about any tape drive.

- **Backup Type**   From this drop-down menu, choose the basic type of backup (normal, incremental, and so on) you want to perform.

Real World Automating Backups

Running a backup routine manually can be tedious, especially when you have a large number of servers to back up on a regular basis. Fortunately, you can use a command-line alternative for running Windows NT Backup: NTBACKUP.EXE. This command supports several command-line switches that allow you to specify the components you want to back up and the backup settings you want to use.

After you create a command that performs the desired backup, save it as a batch file (.BAT), and run it when you need to perform the backup. Or use the command-line utility AT, shown in Figure 21-6, which ships with Windows NT to schedule the .BAT file to be run at specific times. The AT utility works in conjunction with the Scheduler Service so the Scheduler Service must be running in order for AT to function. You can find more information on using NTBACKUP.EXE in your Windows NT product documentation.

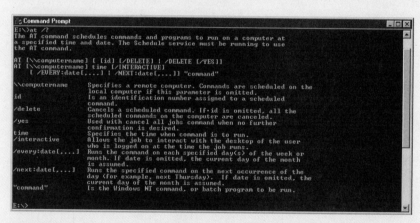

Figure 21-6. *The AT command-line utility has several parameters to configure.*

In addition, the Microsoft Windows NT Resource Kit provides a handy utility called WinAT, shown in Figure 21-7, that is used to schedule programs or batch files to run at specified times and on specified days. WinAT is a graphical version of the AT utility discussed in the last paragraph. You could use WinAT in combination with a batch file to run a full weekly or daily backup schedule. Imagine the convenience of an incremental backup being performed at 2:00 every morning while you are home asleep! You can find WinAT and more information on its use in *Microsoft Windows NT Server 4.5 Resource Kit* (1998), from Microsoft Press.

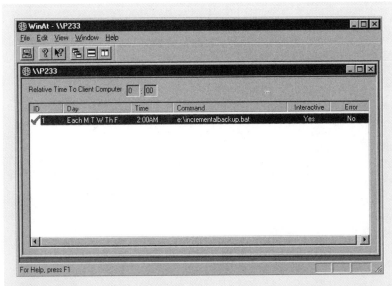

Figure 21-7.   *The WinAT utility, ready to perform an incremental backup using a*
.BAT file.

Restoring Backups

Restoring from an Exchange Server online backup is not a difficult procedure.
First, you have to specify which backup set you want to restore. In Windows
NT Backup, maximize the Tapes window by choosing it from the Window
menu. The Tapes window displays the backup-set information on whatever tape
is in the tape drive, as shown in Figure 21-8.

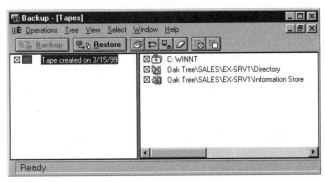

Figure 21-8.   *Choosing backup sets to restore from tape.*

On the tape in this example, you see the three backup sets created in the preceding section. Select the backup sets that you want to restore, and click the

Restore button in the toolbar. This action opens the Restore Information dialog box, shown in Figure 21-9.

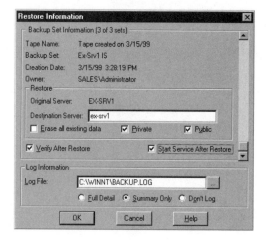

Figure 21-9. *Setting Restore options.*

For each backup set, you can specify whether to erase existing data on the server and whether to verify the data after the Restore operation. If the backup set is an Exchange service, you can also specify whether to start the service automatically after the backup. Finally, if the backup set is the Information Store Service (as it is in Figure 21-9), you can specify whether to restore the Private Information Store, the Public Information Store, or both. After you set your options, click OK to begin the Restore operation.

Note There are several reasons to restore the data from an Exchange Server backup. A user may have deleted something important, or someone may need access to a mailbox when its owner has left the company and the mailbox was deleted too; a slew of other reasons can prompt a data restore request. However, when an Exchange Server has failed and the Windows NT operating system and Exchange files cannot load, more steps are involved. These steps typically require a reinstallation of the Windows NT Server and all the NT service packs, a reinstallation of the Exchange Server software and any Exchange service packs, and finally a restore of the Exchange data.

Real World Using a Recovery Server

The faster and more reliably you can restore your backups, the better. You should therefore test your backups regularly to ensure that they are working as you believe they should. Practicing restoration also puts you in good shape for the real event. You should keep an offline Exchange Server, known as a *recovery server*, running for just this purpose.

Until Exchange 5.5, an administrator was only able to back up and restore the entire Exchange databases and logging files. This was great for a disaster recovery process, but it did not respond to a situation in which a user needed information restored from a specific mailbox. Exchange 5.5 brings this functionality, which reduces the time required for the daily administration of Exchange.

Summary

In this chapter, you learned how to back up and restore an Exchange Server. You learned that the first step in backing up a server is deciding what files you need to back up. These files can include the main Exchange databases (PRIV.EDB, PUB.EDB, and DIR.EDB), as well as existing Transaction logs. You might also elect to back up the local Windows NT Registry, items in the \EXCHSRVR subdirectories, and any server-stored user information.

Once you have decided what to back up, you must decide how to perform the backup. There are five basic types of backups: normal, copy, incremental, differential, and daily. Exchange Server 5.5 supports the use of the normal, incremental, and differential backup types. In addition, you can elect to perform an online backup, in which the Exchange services being backed up are left running, or an offline backup, in which those services are stopped. When you install Exchange Server 5.5, you also install an enhanced version of Windows NT Backup that provides support for online backups.

Performing routine backups of your servers is your primary defense against losing valuable information in the event that something goes wrong with an Exchange Server. However, you will still need to know how to fix those problems that occur. Chapter 22 provides a look at some of the tools you will use in troubleshooting Exchange Server 5.5.

Chapter 22
Troubleshooting Exchange

Nothing is perfect, not your car, your house, or even Exchange Server 5.5. It is no wonder, then, that stores selling car parts and building supplies are successful. Even a stable system like Microsoft Exchange Server 5.5 may break down once in a while. Troubleshooting Exchange Server 5.5 is a skill that you will develop as you solve real problems on your network. One chapter cannot prepare you for all the problems you could face as an Exchange administrator. However, this chapter introduces some of the troubleshooting tools that are available in Exchange Server 5.5 and discusses some places to find more information and help with specific types of Exchange problems.

Using Troubleshooting Tools

When you troubleshoot a system as complex as Exchange Server 5.5, your most valuable tool is your understanding of the system itself. This understanding includes knowledge of how Exchange Server 5.5 works in general and how your organization is set up in particular. Ideally, this book gives you a good understanding of Exchange Server 5.5, and if you took the advice in Chapter 5, you have completely documented your network. With this knowledge in hand, you are ready to find and repair whatever may go wrong in your organization. This section introduces some of the tools that you will use in the process.

Inbox Repair Tool

Not all problems in an Exchange organization occur on an Exchange Server. Many users keep personal folders and offline folders on their client computers. A set of personal folders is stored as a single file with the extension .PST, as shown in Figure 22-1.

Multiple sets of personal folders can be stored on a single client. A set of offline folders is stored as a single file with the extension .OST.

Figure 22-1. *Personal folders stored in a .PST file.*

Like any other type of file, personal and offline folder files can become corrupt. Fortunately, both Exchange Client and Microsoft Outlook provide a tool that helps you repair corrupt personal and offline folder files: the Inbox Repair Tool.

The Inbox Repair Tool (SCANPST.EXE) is installed during a typical installation of Exchange Client or Outlook. The Inbox Repair Tool is available in the System Tools program group on the computer on which Exchange Client is installed. If you use Outlook, the Inbox Repair Tool is installed, but no shortcut is created on the Start menu. You can find the file SCANPST.EXE in the C:\PROGRAM FILES\WINDOWS MESSAGING Directory for Outlook 97 and in the C:\PROGRAM FILES\COMMON FILES Directory for Outlook 98. Note that these are default paths that may be changed during client installation.

When you launch the Inbox Repair Tool, all that you have to do is enter the path and filename of the corrupt file and then click Start. However, before you run the Inbox Repair Tool, you should back up the existing file that you are attempting to repair. The Inbox Repair Tool often discards messages that cannot repair. Without backup, these messages are permanently lost.

The Inbox Repair Tool, shown in Figure 22-2, examines the entire contents of the selected file, discarding messages that cannot be repaired and moving the rest to a specially created Lost And Found folder. When the Inbox Repair Tool finishes running, launch the Exchange Client to access this Lost And Found folder. You should create a new set of personal folders and move any recovered items to these new folders. For more information on using personal folders, see Chapter 18.

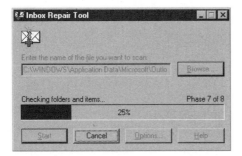

Figure 22-2. *The Inbox Repair Tool scanning a .PST file.*

> **Note**   When all else fails, there is yet another place to turn! Microsoft offers a service to support all of its products, including Exchange Server. The Microsoft support is comprehensive, and the support staff has access to extensive troubleshooting information. When one of your mission-critical servers is down and you have exhausted all other avenues, you should contact Microsoft at *http://support.microsoft.com*.

RPC Ping Utility

Many of the connections among computers in an Exchange organization rely on remote procedure calls (RPCs). Simply put, RPC is a protocol that allows a program on one computer to execute a program on another computer. Exchange Servers in a site rely on RPCs to communicate with one another. Exchange clients connect to Exchange Servers by using RPCs. Likewise, Microsoft Exchange Administrator connects to remote Exchange Servers via RPCs. Often, connectivity problems in an Exchange organization are the result of bad RPC connectivity.

You can use the RPC Ping utility to confirm the RPC connectivity between two systems as well as to make sure that Exchange services are responding to requests from clients and other servers.

RPC Ping has two components: a server component and a client component. You can find both of these components on the Exchange Server 5.5 installation CD-ROM in the \SERVER\SUPPORT\RPCPING Directory.

RPC Ping Server

The server component of RPC Ping is a file named RPINGS.EXE for Intel-based systems, RPINGS_A.EXE for Alpha-based systems, and RPINGS_M.EXE for MIPS-based systems, which you must start on the server before using the client component. To run the server component on Intel-based systems, enter RPINGS.EXE at the command prompt. This command runs the server component using all available protocol sequences, as shown in Figure 22-3. A *protocol sequence* is a routine that allows the return of a ping for a given networking protocol, such as TCP/IP or IPX/SPX. You can also restrict the server component to any single protocol sequence by using the following switches:

- -P IPX/SPX
- -P NAMEDPIPES
- -P NETBIOS
- -P TCPIP
- -P VINES

To exit the RPC server, enter the string @q at the RPC server command prompt.

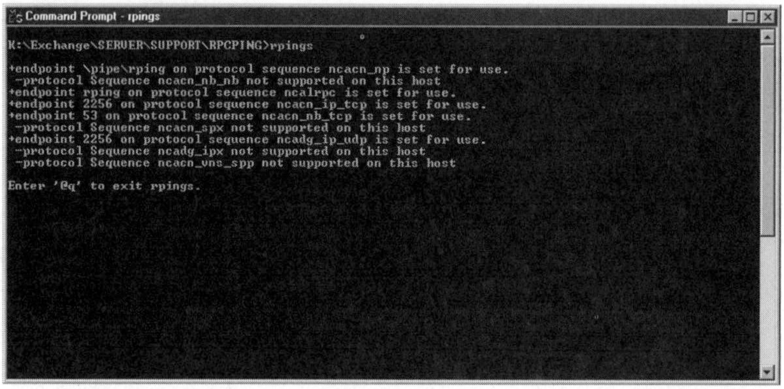

Figure 22-3. *RPINGS running on an Exchange Server.*

RPC Ping Client

After you launch the RPC Ping server on the Exchange Server, you use the RPC Ping client on another computer to test RPC connectivity to that server. There are five versions of the RPC Ping client; the version you use depends on the operating system or the processor on the client:

- **RPINGC32.EXE**   This version is designed to run on computers that use Microsoft Windows 95/98 or Microsoft Windows NT. (Figure 22-4)
- **RPINGC16.EXE**   This version is designed to run on computers that use Windows 3.x.
- **RPINGDOS.EXE**   This version is designed to run on computers that use MS-DOS.
- **RPINGC_A.EXE**   This version is designed to run on Alpha-based systems.
- **RPINGC_M.EXE**   This version is designed to run on MIPS-based systems.

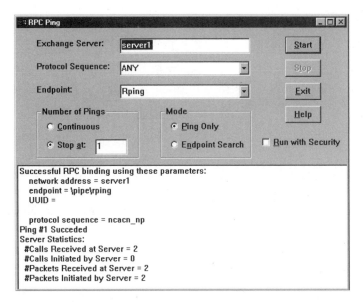

Figure 22-4. *Checking RCP connectivity with RPINGC32.EXE.*

Figure 22-3 shows the main RPINGS.EXE running on the Exchange Server.

You need to set the following parameters before you begin a test:

- **Exchange Server** Specifies the NetBIOS name or IP address (if TCP/IP is used on the network) of the server running the RPC Ping server.

- **Protocol Sequence** Specifies the RPC mechanism that will be used in the test. Options include ANY (all protocol sequences are tested), Named Pipes, IPX/SPX, TCP/IP, NetBIOS, and VINES. The protocol sequence should be set to correspond to the protocol sequence setting on the RPC server.

- **Endpoint** Specifies protocol-specific ports that the RPC client uses to communicate with the server. Choose Rping to collect information about RPC Ping client-to-server communication itself. Choose Store to simulate communications with the Information Store Service on the Exchange Server. Choose Admin to simulate communications with the Directory Service on the Exchange Server.

- **Number of Pings** Specifies whether to ping the server continuously or a certain number of times. This option is available only if you choose Ping Only mode.

- **Mode** Specifies the mode. Ping Only means that the ping is returned directly by the RPC Ping server. End Point Search returns pings from detected endpoints.

- **Run with Security** Verifies authenticated RPCs.

If the RPC Ping from the client is successful with a particular protocol, you want to move that protocol to first in the binding order so that the client system will not have any problems connecting to the Exchange Server. If the RPC Ping is not successful over any protocols, you will need to check for a corrupted RPC.DLL on the client. There are nine RPC*.DLLs for Windows NT clients. All of these files are included in the Windows NT operating system, just as they are for Windows 9x. For DOS and 16-bit Windows clients; the RPC*.DLLs are included with the Exchange Client. If replacing these .DLLs does not fix the problem, you will need to trace the packets between the client system and the Exchange Server. A packet analyzer such as Network Monitor, a Windows NT utility, can be handy in this situation. For information on using Network Monitor to analyze remote procedure calls on a TCP/IP network, see Microsoft Knowledge Base Article Q159298 Analyzing Exchange RPC Traffic Over TCP/IP.

MTA Check Utility

The Message Transfer Agent is responsible for the transfer of all messages outside the Exchange Server. The MTA maintains a separate message queue for each connector or Information Store to which it routes messages. The MTA also creates temporary message queues that are used for processes such as distribution list expansion and message conversion.

All the MTA's message queues are stored in files that have a .DAT extension. These files are located in the \EXCHSRVR\MTADATA Directory on the Exchange Server. These files can become corrupted, just like any other files. Corruption of .DAT files typically happens during an improper shutdown of the MTA, such as in a power failure. Corruption of .DAT files can result in message delivery problems and MTA startup problems.

The MTA Check utility (MTACHECK.EXE) is a command-line tool that attempts to fix all MTA message queues and the messages that those queues contain. The MTA Check utility automatically discards all corrupt messages from the queues, backing up those messages in the \EXCHSRVR\MTADATA\ MTACHECK.OUT Directory.

When the MTA service starts, it automatically runs the MTA Check utility if it is determined that the MTA was not shut down properly. During an automatic check, events are logged to the Windows NT Application log, and an MTACHECK.LOG file is created in the \EXCHSRVR\MTADATA\MTACHECK.OUT Directory.

You can also run the MTA Check utility manually by using the command MTACHECK.EXE. The MTA must not be running to manually use the MTA Check utility. MTACHECK.EXE supports the following command-line options:

- **/F** *<filename>*   Causes the MTA Check utility to log status information to a file with the specified name.

- **/V**   Enables verbose logging and must be used with the /F switch.

- **/RD**   Causes the MTA Check utility to remove all queued Directory Replication messages.

- **/RP**   Causes the MTA Check utility to remove all queued public folder replication messages.

- **/RL**   Causes the MTA Check utility to remove all queued Link Monitor test messages.

If a problem with a queue is encountered, you will see the error in the log as:

```
Queue '241062' required reconstruction

 - corrupted queue file

 69 messages recovered to the queue
```

Other items in the log may consist of the following entry, which reflects a missing file:

```
Object 300596 invalid

 - missing object file

 Object removed from queue '060193'

 MTS-ID: c=US;a= ;p=Lar;l=Seattle0196012020010800000CDE
```

After MTACHECK.EXE completes processing, it will return one of the following messages to show the outcome:

```
Database clean, no errors detected

Database repaired, some data may have been lost

<number> queue(s) required repair out of <percent> detected

<number> object(s) damaged out of <percent> detected

Database has serious errors and cannot be reconstructed.

Some objects missing from the Boot Environment. Please reload the
files from the BOOTENV directory on the install CD.
```

Figure 22-5 shows the results of running MTACHECK.EXE on an Exchange Server.

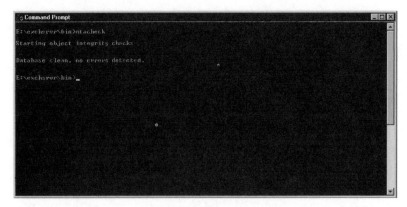

Figure 22-5. *Results of running MTACHECK.EXE on an Exchange Server.*

Information Store Integrity Checker

You use the Information Store Integrity Checker (ISINTEG.EXE) to find and eliminate inaccuracies in the Public and Private Information Store databases, PUB.EDB and PRIV.EDB. You can find ISINTEG.EXE in the \EXCHSRVR\BIN Directory. Before you run ISINTEG.EXE, you must stop the Information Store Service. You can do this using the Services Control Panel applet.

ISINTEG.EXE runs in two modes. The first mode is the test mode and is used only to find and report errors. The second mode allows ISINTEG.EXE to actually fix the errors that it finds. In either mode, ISINTEG.EXE can run 29 tests on your Information Store, as shown in Table 22-1. By default, all available tests are run, but you can run only specific tests, if you want. All test results are logged to one of two files: ISINTEG.PUB (if you are testing the Public Information Store) or ISINTEG.PRI (if you are testing the Private Information Store).

> **Note** The Information Store Integrity Checker is a great tool for troubleshooting. In prior versions of Exchange Server, administrators also used it as a regular maintenance tool. Exchange Server 5.5 is a robust system, and taking the system offline to run the Integrity Checker for maintenance does not add as much value as it did in previous versions.

The following command-line options are available for ISINTEG.EXE:

- **-?**   Displays this list of options.
- **-fix**   Runs ISINTEG.EXE in fix mode, in which the utility can correct table errors, inaccurate cross-reference counts, and unreferenced names.
- **-l** *<filename>*   Specifies a name for the log file other than the default name.

Table 22-1. List of Tests That Can Be Performed from ISINTEG

Name of Test	Description
Aclitemref	Verifies the reference count for items on the Access Control List
Acllist	Examines folders and validates the Access Control Lists
Acllistref	Verifies the Access Control List reference counts
Allacltests	Combines all of the ACL tests (aclitemref, acllist, acllistref)
Allfoldertests	Combines the fldsub, folder, and search tests
Artidx	Verifies the consistency of the NNTP article index
Attach	Verifies the properties for all attachments
Attachref	Verifies the reference counts for attachments
Deleteextracolumns	Deletes all cached indexes
Delfld	Examines deleted folders, validates properties, and accumulates reference counts
Dumpsterref	Combines the msgref and msgoftref tests; also checks the recoverable items count and the size of the recoverable items available for Deleted Item Recovery
Dumpsterprops	Performs the dumpsterref test as well as validates the presence of required columns in the folder table
Fldrcv	Verifies the counts of special system folders, including Restrictions, Categorization, Inbox, Outbox, SentMail, Deleted Items, Finder, Views, Common Views, Schedule, and Shortcuts
Fldsub	Verifies the number of child folders and number of recoverable child folders available for Deleted Item Recovery
Folder	Examines folder tables and message tables; also validates properties for both of these tables
Mailbox	Examines folders, deleted folders, and tables for each mailbox; validates properties and special folders in the folder table and checks their sizes
Message	Examines message tables and verifies message table properties
Morefld	Checks the search links; in the FIX mode, it deletes all of the cached categorization and restriction tables
Msgref	Verifies message reference counts in the messages
Msgsoftref	Verifies message reference count for messages marked for Deleted Item Recovery in the message table
Namedprop	Examines folder, message, and attachment tables as well as validating named properties
Newsfeed	Verifies newsfeed table properties, including permissions
Newsfeedref	Verifies newsfeed reference counts
Oofhist	Verifies Out of Office history information for all of your users
Peruser	Verifies per-user read/unread information
Rcvfld	Cross-checks receive folders with the folder table
Rowcounts	Verifies the number of rows for all tables
Search	Verifies the search links
Timedev	Counts the number of timed events

- **-pri**   Tests the Private Information Store.
- **-pub**   Tests the Public Information Store.
- **-test <*testname*>**   Specifies a particular test that will be performed (refer back to Table 22-1). You can run multiple tests by indicating test names separated by a comma, as in *-test testname1, testname2*.
- **-patch**   Specifies that ISINTEG.EXE be run in patch mode.

Real World   Using ISINTEG.EXE After Offline Restores

Every mailbox and folder in an Information Store has its own globally unique identifier (GUID), which is built by combining that store's base GUID with the particular item's GUID. When you restore an Information Store from backup, the store's base GUID may change. If the base GUID changes, the Directory Service and Information Store Service might accidentally duplicate existing GUIDs when they create new objects. To prevent this duplication, you should always run INSINTEG -PATCH after performing an offline restore. When you perform an online restore, the GUIDs are automatically patched as part of the operation.

ISINTEG -PATCH must be run while the Directory Service is running to allow the utility access to Directory Information. ISINTEG -PATCH checks both the Public and Private Information Stores at the same time. You cannot patch the two stores separately.

Offline Defragmentation Tool

The Public and Private Information Stores on an Exchange Server begin as empty database files. As messages accumulate, the Information Store databases grow. Unfortunately, the databases do not shrink when messages are deleted. Instead, the emptied space is simply marked as available for use during routine garbage collection performed by the Information Store Service. When new messages are stored in the databases, they are written in any available free space before the database increases to hold them. This method of using free space can result in single items actually being broken up and stored in several physical places within the database—a process known as *fragmentation*.

During their scheduled maintenance cycles, the Directory Service and Information Store Service defragment themselves. These services also check for database inconsistencies every time the server is shut down or started. Because of this routine maintenance, fragmentation itself is not much of a problem on an Exchange Server. However, online defragmentation routines do nothing about the sizes of the databases themselves. To compact the databases, you must turn to an offline utility. Exchange Server 5.5 provides an offline defragmentation tool called ESEU-TIL.EXE, which you can use to perform database defragmentation while the Directory Service and Information Store Service are stopped.

You can launch the Offline Defragmentation Tool by entering ESEUTIL.EXE at the command prompt. ESEUTIL.EXE allows you to perform four distinct functions:

- **Defragmentation (/d)**   ESEUTIL.EXE defragments and compacts the database by moving the items in the database into contiguous blocks and removing the free space.

- **Recovery (/r)**   ESEUTIL.EXE can recover a corrupted database by replaying its Transaction logs and checkpoint files. During recovery, ESEUTIL.EXE also removes corrupted files from the database.

- **Integrity (/g)**   ESEUTIL.EXE can check the integrity of a database. Although this function seems similar to that of the ISINTEG.EXE utility, it is not. ISINTEG.EXE is aware of the content of the Information Stores and can check consistency within that content. ESEUTIL.EXE checks the integrity of the database structure itself. Unfortunately, ESEUTIL.EXE can only report structural problems; it cannot repair them.

- **Repair (/r)**   ESEUTIL.EXE attempts to repair the database. Unlike the recovery function, however, the repair function does not cause ESEUTIL.EXE to remove corrupted files or to rebuild the database from logs.

Note   The ESEUTIL.EXE tool is not made to be used as a regular tool for maintenance of your Exchange Servers. You should use this tool only when you are in contact with Microsoft Technical Support.

Finding Help

As an administrator, you sometimes have problems that you cannot solve by yourself. In these circumstances, knowing where to go for help can save your day. Many sources of information on Exchange Server 5.5 are available.

Product Documentation

The product documentation for Exchange Server 5.5 is quite good. Many administrators have never even looked at the product documentation, primarily because they have grown accustomed to shoddy documentation in other products.

The product documentation for Exchange Server 5.5 is in HTML format and is installed with Exchange Server 5.5 during a typical installation. You can access the product documentation, called Books Online, from the Microsoft Exchange program group. Figure 22-6 shows Books Online.

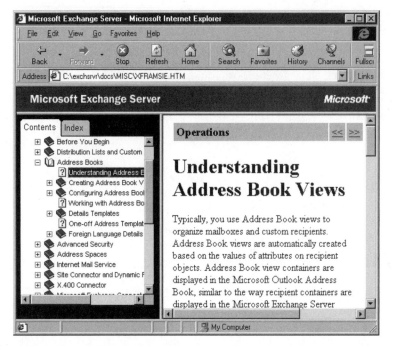

Figure 22-6. *Using the Exchange Server 5.5 product documentation.*

Microsoft BackOffice Resource Kit

Another invaluable resource for any Exchange administrator is *Microsoft Back-Office 4.5 Resource Kit* (1999), from Microsoft Press. The resource kit is a technical reference of all the BackOffice products, including Exchange Server 5.5. The resource kit provides comprehensive technical data detailing the planning, deployment, administration, and troubleshooting of Exchange Server 5.5. The resource kit also contains valuable tools designed to make your life as an Exchange administrator easier. You read about several of these tools in earlier chapters of this book.

Microsoft TechNet

Each month, Microsoft publishes a collection of information and tools called *TechNet*. *TechNet* is a CD-ROM subscription that delivers current information on the evaluation, deployment, and support of all Microsoft products. *TechNet* includes nearly 300,000 pages of information, including the full text of all the Microsoft Resource Kits and the entire Microsoft Knowledge Base. Each month, you also get other CD-ROMs that include useful items such as the following:

- All the published Service Packs for all Microsoft products
- Server and client utilities
- Extras such as the Windows NT 4.0 Option Pack
- Microsoft Seminar Online

TechNet is also now published in a new extended version, *TechNet Plus,* that includes Microsoft software currently in beta testing. Much of the content of *TechNet*, as well as ordering information for the CD-ROM subscription, is available online at *http://technet.microsoft.com*. Further support mechanisms include contacting the local Microsoft office or using Microsoft Support through *http://support.microsoft.com*.

Internet Newsgroups

Internet newsgroups offer the chance to interact with other administrators and to get opinions and ideas about your specific problems. Many newsgroups are available on the Internet. Microsoft maintains a public Usenet server that hosts hundreds of newsgroups on many Microsoft products. The address of this server is *http://msnews.microsoft.com*. Following are a few of the Exchange-specific newsgroups available on this server:

- *microsoft.public.exchange.admin*
- *microsoft.public.exchange.application.conversion*
- *microsoft.public.exchange.applications*
- *microsoft.public.exchange.clients*
- *microsoft.public.exchange.connectivity*
- *microsoft.public.exchange.misc*
- *microsoft.public.exchange.setup*

Hundreds of people, including Microsoft personnel, read and post to these newsgroups daily. These newsgroups are also replicated by many other Usenet servers and may be available through your own Internet service provider's news server.

Summary

In this chapter, you learned about some of the tools that you will use to troubleshoot Exchange Server 5.5.

The Inbox Repair Tool (SCANPST.EXE) is used to repair corrupt personal and offline folder files (.PST and .OST files). The Inbox Repair Tool is installed by default during a typical installation of the Exchange Client.

The RPC Ping utility is used to test RPC connectivity to an Exchange Server. The RPC Ping utility is composed of two parts: the RPC Ping server (RPINGS.EXE, RPINGS_A.EXE, and RPINGS_M.EXE) and the RPC Ping CLIENT (RPINGC32.EXE, RPINGC16.EXE, RPINGC_A.EXE, RPING_M.EXE, and RPINGDOS.EXE). When you launch the RPC server, you can run one of the RPC clients and ping the RPC server to test connectivity.

The MTA Check utility is used to fix corrupt MTA message-queue files (.DAT files). The MTA Check utility is available in the \EXCHSRVR\MTADATA Directory and is launched via the command-line entry MTACHECK.EXE.

The Information Store Integrity Checker tool (ISINTEG.EXE) is used to find and eliminate inaccuracies in the Public and Private Information Store databases: PUB.EDB and PRIV.EDB. You can find ISINTEG.EXE in the \EXCHSRVR\BIN Directory.

The Offline Defragmentation tool (ESEUTIL.EXE) is used to perform four functions on the Exchange databases: defragment, recover, integrity, and repair. You can find ESEUTIL.EXE in the \EXCHSRVR\BIN Directory.

You can find several sources of information on and help with Exchange Server 5.5. The product documentation (Books Online) is installed with Exchange Server 5.5 and is available in the Microsoft Exchange program group. *Microsoft BackOffice 4.5 Resource Kit* provides comprehensive technical data on the planning, deployment, administration, and troubleshooting of Exchange Server 5.5. The resource kit also provides a rich collection of tools for use in administering Exchange Server 5.5. *Microsoft TechNet* is a monthly CD-ROM subscription that includes technical information on all Microsoft products as well as Service Packs, the Microsoft Knowledge Base, and much more. Many Internet newsgroups that concern Exchange Server 5.5 are also available on the Microsoft-run Usenet server *msnews.microsoft.com*.

In this book so far, you have learned a great deal about how Exchange Server 5.5 operates. You have learned how to deploy both Exchange Server 5.5 itself and the clients with which it works. You have also learned about the tools used to monitor, back up, and troubleshoot Exchange Server 5.5. Chapter 23 begins a five-chapter part on how to use the various services provided by Exchange Server 5.5, such as public folders and Active Server Pages, to design your own workflow applications.

Part VI
Creating an Application in Exchange

Chapter 23
Basic Exchange Applications

This final portion of *Exchange 5.5 Companion* explores ways to leverage the inherent power of Microsoft Exchange Server 5.5 by building applications that are based on Exchange.

All these applications are based on a real-life scenario in which two hard-working co-authors, coincidentally called Rick and Walter, are collaborating on a book. They need to include in the loop their faithful editor and others at the company that is publishing their book. You will be creating applications to help Rick and Walter in their collaboration. You could use the basic services of Exchange to help them accomplish many of their tasks, but they want a more customized environment, which you will create for them. Because you will be able to use the applications that you create again and again, it is worth the time and effort to create applications that will help them complete their book.

This chapter examines some easy ways to leverage and extend Exchange via two categories of applications. One of these categories is a simple, "instant" application. The second category requires a little more effort, but it takes advantage of some of the new functionality in Exchange Version 5.5 and Service Pack 1 to easily make a "premixed" application.

An Instant Application

Before you begin to create an instant application, you should step back for a minute and review what an application really is. A client/server application has three components: the data, the application, and the communications between the data and the application. Exchange can work at all three levels of an information system. You can create custom applications by using the features available in Exchange and Outlook to create a collaborative information system almost instantly. Microsoft Exchange provides the data transportation methods (MAPI, SMTP, POP3, WWW) and a place to store the data: public folders.

Building Your First Application

The goal of this initial system is quite straightforward. Rick and Walter must be able to share the chapters that they are working on individually because they review each other's work. For this example, we will use "Rick," "Editor," and "Walter" as the names of the application's users.

To reach the goal of this particular application, you use some of the built-in functionality in Exchange and Outlook. All you have to do is create a small hierarchy of public folders to handle each individual chapter. Perform the following step-by-step instructions for creating this hierarchy:

1. Start Outlook. Expand the Public Folders hierarchy, and select the All Public Folders entry.

2. Choose New from the File menu, and then choose Folder from the submenu, as shown in Figure 23-1. The Create New Folder dialog box appears.

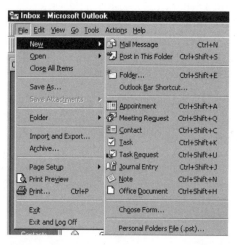

Figure 23-1. *Menu choices for creating a folder.*

3. In the Create New Folder dialog box, enter Book as the name of the folder. Leave the Folder Contains drop-down menu and the navigation tree set to the current defaults, as shown in Figure 23-2. Click OK.

4. The next dialog box asks whether you want to automatically place the folder as a shortcut in the Outlook Bar. Select the check box labeled Don't Prompt Me Again, and then click the No button, to avoid being prompted in the future.

5. Right-click on the new Book public folder and choose Properties from the shortcut menu to display the Book Properties dialog box. For the most part, you want to accept the default properties for the public folder.

Figure 23-2. *The Create New Folder dialog box.*

However, this public folder will be used to pass information between you and your co-author, so you don't want to make the information available to anyone else. Select the Permissions tab of the Book Properties dialog box, shown in Figure 23-3.

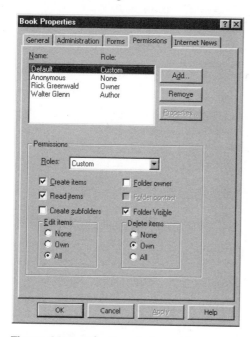

Figure 23-3. *The Permissions tab.*

6. Select the Default name in the Name list box at the top of the tab. In the Permissions section, choose None from the Roles drop-down menu. Clear the Folder Visible check box in the Permissions at the bottom of the tab to prevent other Exchange users from seeing that your public folder exists. You could also just change the Permissions role to None to keep default users from having any access to the folder, even though the folder is still visible.

7. Click the Add button to the right of the Name list box to display the Add Users dialog box, shown in Figure 23-4.

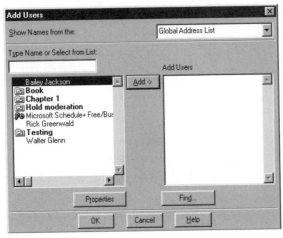

Figure 23-4. *Adding users to the permissions on a public folder.*

8. To make sure that your co-author and editor have access to all the information in the Book public folder, double-click on Walter and Editor (or names you used instead) in the left list box to add them to the right list box. Then click the OK button to return to the Permissions tab of the property sheet.

9. Select the user named Editor in the users list, and change the role to Editor in the Permissions section. The Editor role is a predefined security role with the set of permissions that you see at the bottom of the dialog box. In the Delete Items section, choose the radio button None. Notice that the role for the Editor automatically changes to Custom.

Note One predefined role for your Editor works well for the access you want to allow. The only thing wrong with the permissions assigned to the predefined Editor role is that they include the ability to delete items from the folder. The co-authors are uncomfortable with this option, so you should set up the folder so that they are the only ones allowed to delete items from it.

10. Select the user named Walter in the users list. In the Permissions section, change that user's role to Author. In the Edit Items section, click the All radio button. Because the co-authors, Walter and Rick, trust each other to edit each other's work, you have to change one of the attributes of the default Author role. As you saw with the Editor, when you change any of the attributes of a selected role, the user's role automatically changes to Custom.

11. Click the Apply button to apply the permission changes to the folder. You have created an instant collaboration application by creating a public folder in which the co-authors and their editor can share all the materials for the book while hiding it from other users of your Exchange system. But in the course of writing this book, the co-authors will end up with many pieces of material, including multiple versions of chapters and the graphics used in each chapter. You can automatically use the specifications for the Book public folder in other public folders that will be its children in the public folder hierarchy.

12. With the newly created Book public folder selected, choose New from the File menu and Folder from the subsequent menu to create a new public folder below the Book folder. Name the new folder Chapter 1, and click the OK button at the bottom of the Create New Folder dialog box.

13. Right-click on the new Chapter 1 folder and choose the Properties menu choice from the shortcut menu. Select the Permissions tab. You can see that the permissions you assigned for the Book public folder act as a template for the permissions assigned to all child public folders.

14. Close the Properties dialog box and return to Outlook.

You have now created a collaborative platform that allows the members of the writing team to share a variety of materials.

Benefiting from the Application

Your first Exchange application is really no more than an example of the use of public folders, but it delivers several important benefits:

- It provides a centralized area for sharing all types of information, from versions of documents to bitmaps to mail notes and discussions between the authors and the editors.

- It creates a template for the creation of additional child public folders, which can be used to organize the materials for the entire book.

- It imposes a security model based on existing Exchange users and permissions. You were able to modify the standard security roles to handle the particulars of your situation. Exchange automatically identifies and authenticates all users, so all you had to do was give selected users the permissions they needed.

- It can be included in the automatic replication of public folders within Exchange. For purposes of simplicity, replication was not added to the Book public folder. However, you could easily specify that the contents of the Book public folder and its child folders be automatically replicated to another server within the Exchange organization, such as a server that is closer to your editor.

- It makes the information available as part of the Exchange environment, which means that a wide variety of clients could access the information from anywhere within the Exchange organization.

Your first application is only the beginning. You will be using the public folder structures that you just created in the rest of this section as you learn more ways to extend the reach of Exchange.

Creating a Customized Routing Application

Your second Exchange application is almost as easy to create as your first. You do not have to do any explicit coding or create any objects for this application. This application takes advantage of the server-side events feature of Exchange Server 5.5 and the routing agent in Service Pack 1 that is built on that feature.

The Goal of the Application

Rick and Walter are following a certain procedure as they write the chapters for their book. When one of them finishes a chapter, he sends it to his co-author for review and approval. When the co-author finishes the first edit, he returns the chapter to the original author to accept or disregard the edits. When the original author completes the second round of edits, he sends the chapter off to the editor. This process is a prime example of a workflow process. A *workflow process*, as the name implies, describes the route that a document takes as it makes its way through an organization and the actions that are taken related to the document at each stop.

As you might expect, Rick, Walter, and their editor use Exchange to create this collaborative application. Two new features in Exchange Server 5.5 with Service Pack 1 (SP1) make creating a basic routing application quite simple. The first feature is *server-side scripting*, which was introduced in Exchange 5.5. Server-side scripting allows you to install another service — the Event Service — as part of your Exchange Server. The Event Service is capable of responding to several Exchange events, such as mailing a message or receiving a message. You can write scripts directly to the programming interface of the Event Service.

In SP1, Microsoft delivered a set of *routing objects* that are built on top of the Event Service. These routing objects, as their name implies, were created to implement the type of routing that this application needs. To make things even easier, SP1 includes a Routing Wizard, a Visual Basic program that lets a user easily design a routing path that can be associated with any Exchange folder. The Routing Wizard is a sample program that serves two purposes: implementing a generic type of routing for a folder and providing an example of how to use the Exchange routing objects through Visual Basic.

The end result of all this work by the Exchange team means that you will be able to create your routing application without having to write a single line of code. SP1 even comes with a sample Outlook form that you can use to implement a one-off routing example, so you won't have to create conditional logic for the default event processing provided by the Routing Wizard. All of these components make the routing premixed; you just add a few specifications and serve.

Setting Up the Application

Before you can implement this solution, you have to make sure that a few components of the routing solution are installed as part of Exchange. Modifying Exchange may not be an available option for one reason or another. It is highly recommended that you understand the routing application's functional process, described within the rest of this chapter, before setting up the components needed by it. Before you create your routing application, you have to perform the four procedures described in the following sections.

Make Sure That the Event Service Is Installed

You have the option of installing Exchange Server 5.5 without the Event Service. To find out whether the Event Service is running, open the Control Panel for the Windows NT Server on which you are running Exchange and click on the Services icon. For the Microsoft Exchange Event Service, you should see the status Started, as shown in Figure 23-5. If the Event Service is listed but not running, you can start it by selecting the service and then clicking the Start button in the dialog box.

Note The Event Service will not start if it is on an Exchange Server that is not a public folder server.

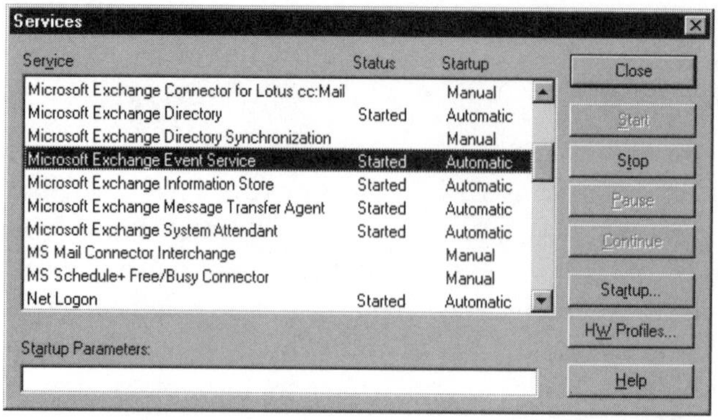

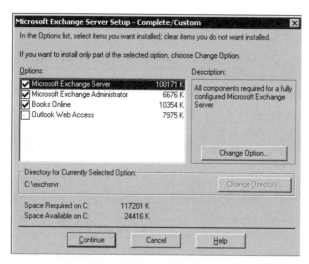

Figure 23-5. *The Microsoft Exchange Event Service running in the Services dialog box of Windows NT.*

If the Event Service is not listed in the Services dialog box, it has not been installed and you need to install it using the Exchange Server 5.5 CD. Once you have started Setup from the CD, click the Add/Remove button. Make sure the Microsoft Exchange Server is highlighted, and click the Change Option button, as shown in Figure 23-6.

Figure 23-6. *Changing the installation options for Exchange Server.*

Place a check mark in the box to the left of Microsoft Exchange Event Service, as shown in Figure 23-7, and click the OK button. Click the OK button again, and enter the password you are prompted for. After the Event Service is installed, be sure to reapply the latest Exchange Server Service Pack to your system.

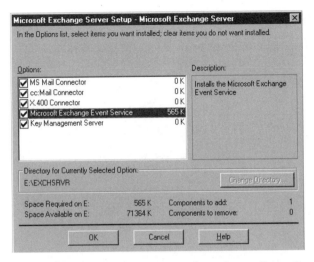

Figure 23-7. *Adding the Microsoft Exchange Event Service to a system.*

Note Because you will be using the Event Service to implement routing, you want to set up the service to start automatically when your Windows NT Server boots up.

Make Sure That You Have Service Pack 1 (or Later) Installed

You can see if you have Service Pack 1 installed by clicking on the About Microsoft Exchange Server menu choice in the Help menu of Exchange Administrator. If the SP is not installed, you will have to install it in order to get the Routing Wizard application described in this chapter. You can get Service Pack 1 by downloading it from the Microsoft Web site at *http://www.microsoft.com/exchange* or by installing it from a CD-ROM, which you can order from Microsoft or which you may have received as part of an MSDN or TechNet subscription.

Make Sure That You Have Permission to Use the Event Service

If you simply installed the Event Service, you may not have permission to use the service. Like all other objects in Exchange, the Event Service has security roles assigned to it.

To assign yourself the appropriate security role, open Microsoft Exchange Administrator. In the navigation panel on the left side of the window, open the Folders container, then the System Folders container, and then the Events Root container. You should see a folder labeled EventConfig_*SERVER*, in which *SERVER* is the name of your Exchange Server, as shown in Figure 23-8.

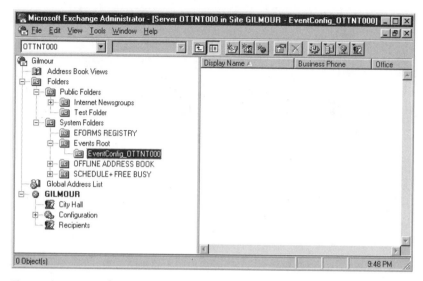

Figure 23-8. *Configuring the Event Service.*

Highlight the EventConfig_*SERVER* folder and select the property sheet for the folder. Click the Client Permissions button on the General tab. If you are not listed as one of the clients who has permission to create items, click the Add button to add your username and then give yourself the appropriate permission, as shown in Figure 23-9.

Install the Routing Wizard

The Microsoft Exchange Routing Wizard must be installed on the Outlook 98 client computer that you will be using to implement routing. The Routing Wizard comes as part of SP1 and later Service Packs, but you have to explicitly install it on any client that you will use to design a route for an application.

In SP1 or later, the Routing Wizard is located in the compressed file called SP1_55SS.EXE. (The format of later Service Packs may include only a single compressed file.) Run this file to decompress it. You will find a file named RWSETUP.EXE in the Directory ENGSERVER\SUPPORT\COLLAB\ SAMPLER\ROUTING and the subdirectory with the name of your client operating system: Win95 or WinNT, which will also have a directory for the different platforms it runs on, Intel and Alpha. (If your system is installed in a language other than English, the first Directory, Eng, will have a different name.) You will find the same file structure on the CD-ROM that accompanies this book.

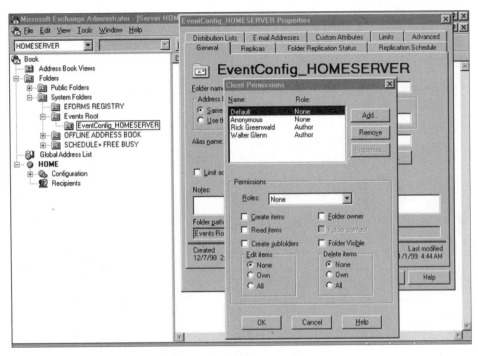

Figure 23-9. *Setting permissions for the Event Service.*

Take the RWSETUP.EXE file to your client machine and run it. The file automatically installs the Microsoft Exchange Routing Wizard as a program. A very small portion of the source code is shown below. This portion of the code is responsible for opening up the address book. (You can also download the entire source code, which includes the forms, for this Visual Basic program from the Microsoft Web site.)

```
'_____ --

' Function: DisplayAddressBook

' Description: Calls up the MAPI Address Book

'_____ --

Function DisplayAddressBook(ByRef objRecipColl As Object, bOneAddress
As Boolean, parentfrm As Form) As Boolean

  On Error GoTo AddressBook_Error

  'Call address book, modal to calling form

  Set objRecipColl = CDOClass.Session.AddressBook( _
```

```
Title:="Choose Recipients", _

oneAddress:=bOneAddress, _

forceResolution:=True, _

recipLists:=1, _

Recipients:=objRecipColl, _

toLabel:="&To", _

ccLabel:="", _

bcclabel:="", _

parentwindow:=parentfrm.hWnd)

DisplayAddressBook = True

Exit Function
```

> **Note** If you try to run this program and get a message about SCRRUN.DLL, you may not have a scripting agent installed on your client. You can fix this situation by visiting the Microsoft Web site at *http://www.microsoft.com/msdownload/vbscript/scripting.asp*, downloading the appropriate version of the scripting agent, and installing it on your client machine. A scripting agent is necessary because it lets you use server-side scripts that run based upon events occurring in folders.

As mentioned in the first paragraph of this section, you need to be running Outlook 98 or later on your client in order to use the routing services for this application. Implementing the following example will be easier if you use the already developed Outlook form that takes advantage of the workflows implemented by the Routing Wizard. You can download this template from the Microsoft Web site at *http://technet.microsoft.com/reg/download/exchange/*, under the name Microsoft Outlook Routing Sample. You can also get the entire source code for the Routing Wizard Visual Basic application on this page, in case you want to examine the underlying code for examples of how you can interact with the Event Service.

> **Note** Both the Outlook template and the source code for the wizard are included on the CD-ROM that accompanies this book.

Sound like a lot of work? You must perform a few steps to implement the new routing feature, but then you can use a wide variety of applications, including workflows, with a minimum of work. The Event Service and the objects that you can build on it allow you to extend Exchange to build collaborative applications.

Creating the Application

You are ready to start creating your first workflow with Exchange, and your first task is to design the workflow. Usually, you want to go through a somewhat formal design process for any application, getting the principals involved to make sure that the application you are creating will meet all their needs. For this simple workflow, Rick, Walter, and their editor have already established a standard process. Rick will write a chapter, send it to Walter for comments, receive the chapter back again to integrate the comments, and then send it on to the editor. All that is left is to implement this process automatically with Exchange. (This particular workflow will be designed for Rick's process, but you could modify the event scripts that it generates to accept submissions from either Rick or Walter.)

Creating the Workflow

The bulk of the work for this application will be creating a workflow process to route the documents, using the Microsoft Exchange Routing Wizard:

1. Choose the Microsoft Exchange Routing Wizard from the Start menu. The first screen of the Routing Wizard, shown in Figure 23-10, introduces the six steps that you perform to create a route that Exchange can use. (You can select the check box at the bottom of the screen if you don't want to see this screen again.) The green square in the left panel indicates where you are in the process of defining a route. The red square in the left panel denotes the finish line for the definition process. Click the Next button to start defining a route.

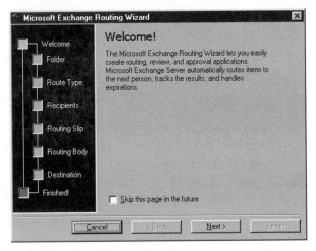

Figure 23-10. *The starting screen of the Microsoft Exchange Routing Wizard.*

2. You are prompted to choose an Exchange profile to use to define the routing. Select your own profile and click the OK button. The Routing Wizard tells you that it is using the profile to actually log on to Exchange. (The wizard uses Collaboration Data Objects, which are described in Chapter 26, to call Exchange services directly from a Visual Basic program.)

3. The next step is selecting a folder in which to install the route. To choose a folder, you must click the Choose Folder button to display the Choose Folder dialog box shown in Figure 23-11. If you created the Book public folder earlier in this chapter, select it as the target folder for the route. Click the Next button to continue.

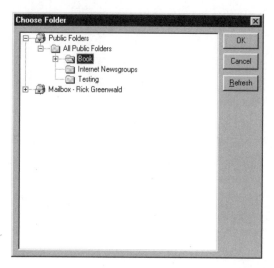

Figure 23-11. *Selecting a folder in the Routing Wizard.*

4. In the next screen of the Routing Wizard, shown in Figure 23-12, you can choose either of two basic routing types: sequential or parallel. The *Sequential Route*, which is listed at the top of the screen, sends the message from one recipient to the next in sequential order. When one recipient finishes with a message, that recipient has the option to approve the message and send it on to the next recipient or stop the workflow process by rejecting it. The other type of route is the *Parallel Route*. In this type of route, the message is sent to all other recipients simultaneously. For this application, you want to leave the Sequential Route selected but change the value in the Number of Recipients field to 3. Click the Next button to continue.

5. In the next screen of the Routing Wizard, you specify each of the three recipients for the route. Three buttons allow you to select each of the recipients.

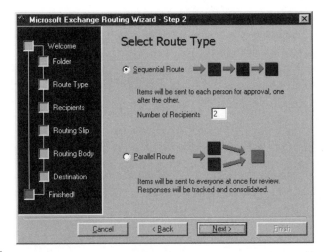

Figure 23-12. *Selecting a route type in the Routing Wizard.*

When you click any of the buttons, you can see by the dialog box shown in Figure 23-13 that you have quite a bit of flexibility in designing how your routing will work.

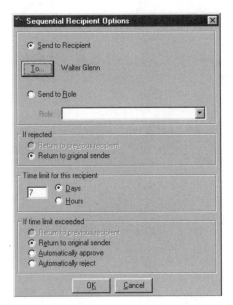

Figure 23-13. *Recipient options for a sequential route.*

You can designate a specific user or a role as the recipient. If this recipient rejects the message for some reason, you can specify whether to send the message back to the preceding recipient or return it to the sender. You can place a time limit for this step in the workflow process in days or hours. You can also indicate the type of action that you want Exchange to take if this step in the process is not completed during the indicated time span. These options allow you to handle a failure in the workflow process in the most appropriate way. Click Next to continue.

Note For this example, you should click the To button for each recipient to select an Exchange user as the recipient and leave all the other values in the Sequential Recipient Options dialog box at their default settings.

After you select Walter Glenn as the first recipient, Rick Greenwald as the second recipient, and the Editor as the third recipient, the Step 3 screen of the Routing Wizard should look like Figure 23-14.

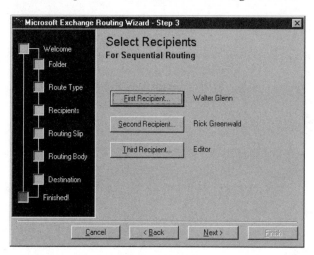

Figure 23-14. *Defining recipients for a route.*

6. In the next screen of the Routing Wizard, shown in Figure 23-15, you implement workflow processes so that you can use them properly over the Web.

If you are using Exchange as part of a client/server environment, there is no additional overhead to include the message—and any attachments that the message might contain—as an attachment to the routing slip that this wizard creates automatically. If you are using Outlook Web Access, however, you may prefer to use a link to indicate the subject of the routing slip. This link allows all the participants in the routing process to go to a specific location on the Web to see the message and any linked attachments.

Figure 23-15. *Defining the routing slip type.*

Because you are implementing this in a standard Exchange client/server environment, you can leave the top radio button selected and click the Next button to continue.

7. In the next screen of the Routing Wizard, you design the message that will be in the body of the routing slip, as shown in Figure 23-16. What you are actually designing with the Routing Wizard at this point is the routing slip: the object that will be routed from one recipient to the next, with the file that you want to route included as an attachment. This screen of the Routing Wizard allows you to add a generic message to the body of the routing slip. Because this workflow will always be used to route chapters to your co-author and editor, you should add a generic message such as the one shown in Figure 23-16. Click the Next button to continue.

8. In the last step of the Routing Wizard, you define a simple action to take when the routing process has been completed successfully. You can select the check box at the top of the screen to send the routed item to another recipient, or even to a public folder, when the workflow process is complete. When you select the recipient for this final report, you can indicate whether that recipient should get the final summary report with the routed item attached or just the final summary report. You should select the check box, click the Choose Recipient button to select Rick Greenwald as the final recipient, and leave the top radio button selected. The screen will look like Figure 23-17 when you complete this process. Click the Next button to continue.

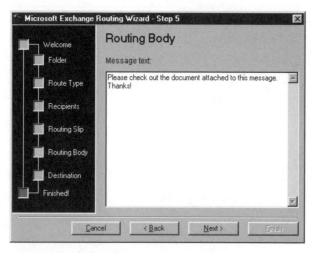

Figure 23-16. *Creating text for the routing slip.*

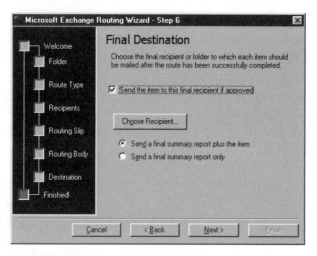

Figure 23-17. *Designating a success action.*

9. With the help of the Routing Wizard, you have finished defining your routing. All you have to do now is click the Finish button to actually generate the routing instruction for Exchange. When the wizard creates the Route Map and installs a Route Agent for the designated folder, you see a success message, as shown in Figure 23-18. Click the OK button to close the Routing Wizard.

Note Did you get a message saying that the Route Map was installed but the Route Agent was not? If so, you probably didn't give yourself the proper security permission for the EventConfig_*SERVER* folder.

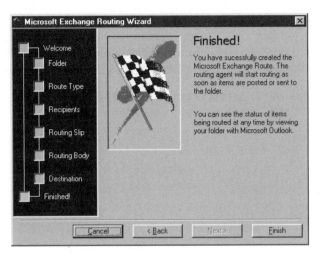

Figure 23-18. *The successful completion of the Routing Wizard.*

You have done almost all the work necessary to implement a workflow process. By answering a few simple questions in the Routing Wizard, you created all the scripts necessary to implement a fairly sophisticated process. As you see in the following section, some of the parameters of an Outlook form can override the workflow process. The Routing Wizard, however, creates the basic routing scripts that the Exchange Event Service uses to implement the workflow process.

Using the Workflow

You can see how the workflow process that you just created works by trying it out.

Workflow Step 1   Open Outlook under the user named Rick. Reduce the size of the Outlook window, and open File Manager next to Outlook. Select a document and drag it over to the Book public folder.

Workflow Step 2   Either log off as Rick and log on as Walter, or go to another machine that is logged on as Walter. When you open the message, as shown in Figure 23-19, you can see in full the same message created by the routing process. The original mail posting is attached to the routing form, and an information line at the top of the page prompts you, as Walter, to respond by clicking one of the buttons at the top of the form.

At the bottom of the message are two URLs that Walter can use to approve or reject this step of the workflow process. These URLs serve the same function as

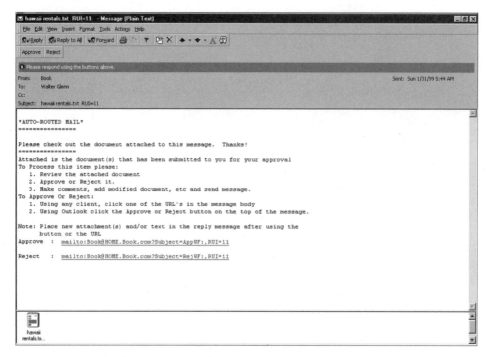

Figure 23-19. *The first message in the workflow process.*

the Approve and Reject buttons but are included in case the recipient is using Outlook Web Access.

Workflow Step 3 Because this procedure is just a test, approve the message by clicking the Approve button. Approving the message gives the choice of sending the message on immediately or adding comments with the response. You should leave the first radio button selected and click the OK button. Click the Send button.

Workflow Step 4 When the response has been sent, the information at the top of the original message changes to indicate that the recipient approved the step and lists the time when the approval occurred. This message remains in the Inbox, so Walter can use it for tracking purposes.

If you go to the Book folder immediately after Walter sends his approval, you can see another message in the folder, with Walter's approval. If you open the message, you see that the attachment is not included with the message. After the Event Service has had a chance to do its work, both of these messages are combined into a single message, which includes some entries in the tracking tab, as shown in Figure 23-20.

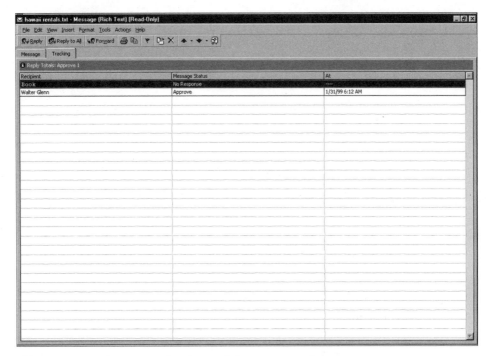

Figure 23-20. *The posting for the workflow process after one step.*

Workflow Step 5   The ball is back in Rick's court because he is the next step in this particular routing process. You can either go to a machine that is logged on as Rick or log off and then log on again as Rick. When you check your Inbox, you have a new message. The preview frame shows the same initial message, as does the complete message when you open it. If you look at either the attached document or the document in the public folder, however, you can see Walter's response to your initial query. In this sense, the routing and the messages associated with it act as the managers of the process, while the subject of the process—the original message—remains in the public folder.

You should edit the response so that you can see the results of another edited response and then approve this step. As was the case with the earlier response, the information message changes as soon as the approval is sent. The Exchange Event Service rolls the new approval into the main post in the folder, as shown in Figure 23-21.

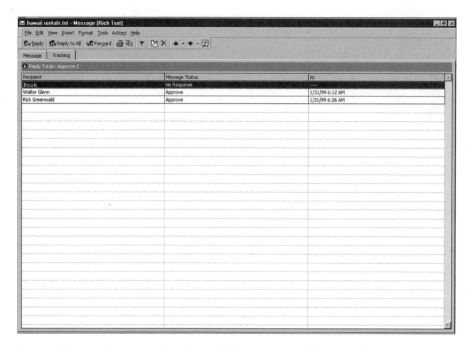

Figure 23-21. *The posting for the workflow process after two steps.*

Workflow Step 6 It's time for the Editor to add an approval to the process. Change to the Editor by moving to a machine logged on as the Editor, or log off and log back in to Outlook again. Once again, you see the message that has been routed into your Inbox. Once again, open the message and approve the workflow.

Workflow Step 7 The workflow process is complete. If you look at the main message in the Book folder, you see that it has changed significantly. The message, shown in Figure 23-22, now has a history of the workflow process in the message, rather than just on the mapping tab.

Workflow Step 8 As a last step in the process, you can log on as Rick and see the completed record of the workflow in his Inbox, as shown in Figure 23-23. This message has a message as an attachment. When you open the attachment, you see the same history of the routing process that you saw in the destination folder in Figure 23-22.

The Routing Wizard made everything happen for you by creating the routing scripts that were used by the Exchange Event Service. You can leverage those same scripts with a different list of recipients by using a simple Outlook form.

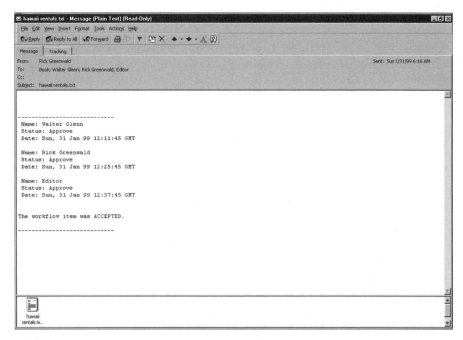

Figure 23-22. *The completed posting for the workflow process.*

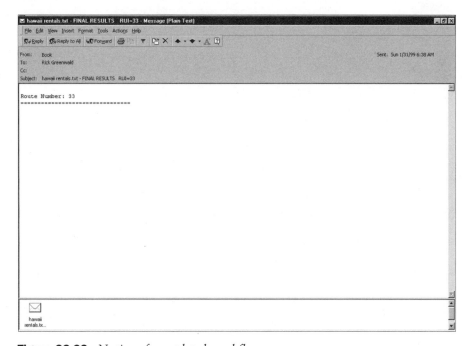

Figure 23-23. *Notice of completed workflow.*

Changing the Recipients of the Workflow

The workflow that you have created works just fine for Rick, but what about Walter? He doesn't want to route his chapters to himself as the first recipient. Fortunately, Walter can use an Outlook form template to implement a workflow with a different set and order of recipients. This form overrides the specific implementation of the workflow and gives Walter what he wants.

The Outlook template in question comes on the CD-ROM that accompanies this book. After you get the form template from the CD-ROM, which is located in the Examples folder within the Chapter 23 folder, install it as a template by following these steps:

1. Copy the file named ARTICLE.OFT to the Outlook Directory, located in the Templates Directory of your Microsoft Office Directory. Typically, this directory is located in the Program Files Directory.

2. Open Outlook, choose Forms from the Tools menu and then choose Design a Form from the submenu. The Design Form dialog box appears, as shown in Figure 23-24, with the Standard Form Library selected.

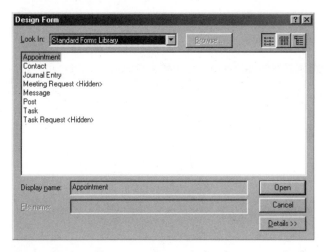

Figure 23-24. *The Design Form dialog box in Outlook.*

3. Choose Templates in File System from the Look In drop-down menu. Select the Article template, and click the Open button.

4. Next, select a folder to house the form. For this example, select the Book folder inside the All Public Folders folder.

5. This template contains macros. Because a macro could contain a virus, Outlook specifically asks whether you want to enable the macros for the

template. This template came from a secure source, so simply click the Enable Macros button. If you don't, the form will not operate properly.

6. The form template, shown in Figure 23-25, is complete in itself, so all you have to do is publish a copy of it to the appropriate folder.

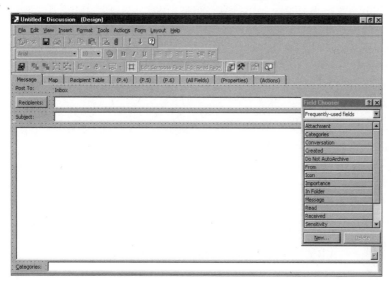

Figure 23-25. *The Outlook form template.*

7. Choose Forms from the Tools menu, and then choose Publish Form As from the subsequent menu.

8. Choose the Book folder from the Look In drop-down menu at the top of the form. Give the form the name Chapter Routing, and click the Publish button.

9. Close the Outlook template form.

You are finished. In a few simple steps, you added a form that can modify the recipients for the original routing plan with the macro code embedded within the template. The last thing to do is test the new routing scenario.

Using the Outlook Routing Form

To understand how your premixed routing application works with the new Outlook form, you have to run it through its paces. This section shows the routing process from the view of all the users in the process. You can achieve the same result by logging onto your machine and Outlook under different user names.

1. Begin by selecting the Book public folder in which you published the Outlook form.

2. Choose New Chapter Routing from the Actions menu, and enter the names of the recipients who will be involved in the workflow. For this limited example, you are sending the form to Walter and then receiving it back for final comments.

3. The order in which the names appear in the To box is the order in which the workflow will be routed. When you finish entering text, click the Post button in the top-left corner of the form.

Note With this Outlook form, you have to specifically attach any documents to the message. This process is unlike the automatic processing of moved documents that occurs with the default routing installed by the Routing Wizard.

You can go through the entire workflow process for Rick and Walter, but the process works in the same manner as the default routing process that you explored earlier in the chapter. The message goes from one recipient to the next; the posting in the folder is updated as participants in the process approve the message; and when the process is complete, a history of the process is posted in the folder and sent to Rick, the originator of the workflow.

With hardly any trouble at all and with no additional coding, you have modified the way that your original workflow process operates, with the help of the Outlook form template, to suit Walter's purposes—all with premixed components. Routing is just one of the ways that you can use the Exchange Event Service.

Benefiting from the Application

This second application produced many benefits at a fairly low cost. Your first workflow application is:

- **Easy to build** The Routing Wizard set up the event scripts on Exchange for one default workflow process, and the Outlook template could be used to implement almost any workflow.

- **Robust** A great deal of functionality is built into the routing process. A message can be routed to a variety of respondents, each respondent can approve or reject the message, and all the information is tracked throughout the process.

This application might provide the exact routing functionality that you need. Even if it doesn't, you can review the set of instructions for the Routing Wizard and the Outlook template to learn how to implement your own routing applications.

Summary

In this chapter, you used a few of Exchange's built-in features to create collaborative applications quickly. These applications are great, but creating them may have whetted your appetite to start designing and implementing applications that address your organization's needs more specifically. In the next few chapters, you will learn how to create your own forms and how to integrate external applications with the services Exchange provides—just as the people who created the Exchange Routing Wizard did.

Chapter 24
Using Customized Forms

In this chapter, you get your first taste of creating a customized component for your collaborative application. You will create a customized form for collecting and sharing information among the members of your writing team. You will use the Microsoft Outlook 98 forms development environment because Outlook is the preferred client for Microsoft Exchange Server 5.5 at this time. By creating your own customized form, you both streamline the way that data is collected and ensure that the data is correct. You shape the generalized functionality of the standard forms used with Exchange to suit the purpose of your application.

This chapter does not provide a comprehensive discussion of creating and using forms; entire books have been written on that topic. The chapter does, however, discuss the basics of form development and gives you an idea of some ways to use customized forms to extend the reach of your Exchange environment.

Understanding the Basics of a Form

The most important thing you need to know about a *form* is that it displays and inputs data. The form and its associated data are collectively known as an *item*.

This simple statement has several implications. First, the form is separate from the data with which it shares an item. Although a close correspondence usually exists between the controls on a form and the fields in the data, a form could have controls that are not associated with data fields, and vice versa. When you create custom forms, you must create both a field and a control to display the contents of the field.

In this sense, a form is the user interface component of an item. A form is made up of *controls*, which are the individual visual interface components. These components can be simple text fields, combo boxes, or complex ActiveX components that have been added to the Outlook development environment.

A form can be stored in one of several places. Often, a form is stored in the same folder as the data with which it is used. Forms can also be stored in common libraries. Individual users can store a form on their own clients because they may need the form to view the data in a folder when they are not connected to an Exchange Server.

If you have been performing the exercises in this book in chapter order, you created a form in Chapter 23. But even if you did not walk through that exercise, you are familiar with forms because you use forms every time you use Exchange. Forms are the user interface to the data in Exchange; they are the basis of all operations that involve user input. Four types of forms come with Outlook 98:

- **Mail forms**   Mail forms are used for mail messages that are sent by a user to another user, distribution list, or folder that is included in the Global Address List. A mail form is an item that is meant to be sent via Exchange's message-transport functionality.

- **Post forms**   A post form is slightly different from a mail form in that it is intended to be posted to a folder rather than sent to an individual recipient. For this reason, post forms generally are used for folder-based applications such as discussion groups.

- **Office document forms**   You can create a form that is based on a Microsoft Office document, such as a Word document or an Excel spreadsheet. These forms act as containers for the functionality embedded in the Office document and handle the interface with the Exchange messaging environment.

- **Built-in forms**   Outlook 98 comes with several prebuilt forms that handle specific tasks, such as creating contact information or scheduling a calendar appointment.

Virtually all forms are created from a starting point called a template. A *template* is an outline of a form that includes the basic functionality of the form. You start with a template and *publish* it (add it to a specific folder or library) as a specific form.

Outlook comes with many templates. As you learned in Chapter 23, you can add custom templates to your Outlook environment. In fact, you can create a template from a form, so any functionality you add to a customized form can immediately become a building block for other forms. As you see in this chapter, you can switch any form used in Outlook from run-time mode to design mode, so you can use any existing Outlook form as the basis for another form.

Building the Application

As Rick and Walter work on their book, they discover that they must write the same information about each chapter each time they submit it to the editing process. They always want to include information such as the chapter number, the chapter title, and the current status of the chapter. In addition, they always want to attach one or more components of the chapter, such as text and screenshots.

Although Rick and Walter are collaborating on the book, they don't always format information the same way, and they sometimes forget to include some of the vital information with their submissions. The form that you create in this chapter standardizes the information submitted with each chapter. This form makes it easy for Rick, Walter, and their editor to quickly see the essential chapter information for each submission made with the form.

Creating a form involves several phases:

1. Opening a form in the design environment
2. Modifying the controls on the form
3. Adding any required logic to the form
4. Testing and publishing the form

Working in the Forms Development Environment

In Chapter 23, you entered the forms development environment long enough to publish a form. You found this form by choosing Forms from the Tools menu, choosing Design A Form from the submenu, and using the forms browser to select and open a form template. The template opened the form as part of the design process. If you remember that a form is the user interface to the data in an item, you might not be surprised to learn that you can switch directly from using a form to designing a form.

To begin working in the design environment for forms, follow these steps:

1. Choose New from the File menu and Mail Message from the submenu to display a new mail message form.
2. Choose Forms from the Tools menu of the Message and then choose Design This Form from the submenu. This command takes you to the forms development environment, shown in Figure 24-1.

In development mode, the mail message form looks much as it does when you are running it, with the same text fields and radio buttons as the run-time version of

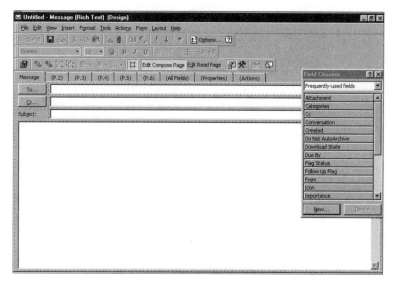

Figure 24-1. *Forms development environment.*

the form. However, a few things are different about the environment in which you design forms.

First, you see a series of tabs along the top of the form. The first tab is named Message; the last three tabs are named (All Fields), (Properties), and (Actions); and the tabs in between are labeled (P.2) to (P.6). Each of these tabs with the default labels of (P.2) to (P.6) represents a potential tab in the form. If a tab is shown with its label in parentheses, the tab will not be part of the form at run time.

The last three tabs in the forms development environment list attributes that relate to the overall form. You do not need to understand these tabs right now, although you will look at one of them later in the chapter.

When the forms development environment first opens, you see a floating window labeled Field Chooser. As described earlier, a field is a structure for holding data. Outlook comes with a series of predefined fields that are used in the standard Outlook forms, and the Field Chooser makes it easy to reuse these field definitions in your own forms. You do not need to use the Field Chooser yet, so close it by clicking the Close button in the top-right corner of that window.

The other features of the forms development environment that you need to know about are the four tools in the last toolbar above the form, shown in

Figure 24-2. These tools display the windows with which they are associated: the Field Chooser window, the Control Toolbox window, the Properties window, and the View Code Window, respectively. You can also display any of these windows by choosing menu commands, but using the handy tools is easier.

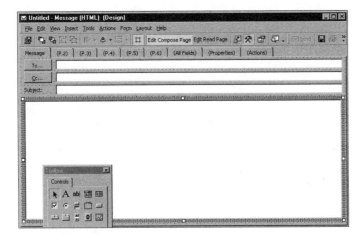

Figure 24-2. *Tools for frequently used windows in the forms development environment.*

Modifying the Form

You start the process of modifying the form by making some room for the fields that you want to add:

1. Select the main text area of the mail message form. Lower the top of the text area by dragging the center-top handle, shown in Figure 24-3. Because the messages to be created with this form will always be used to send chapter materials to a folder, you do not need to provide a specific subject for the message.

2. Delete the text box to the right of the Subject label. Select the Subject label, and then delete it. The form should now look like Figure 24-4, with a large blank area for adding the fields that you need. Now you can add controls and the underlying fields that they will display.

3. Click on the Control Toolbox tool to display the Control Toolbox window. Then click on the Label tool, which is represented by the large letter "A."

4. In the form, create a label by dragging and sizing the label in the area where the Subject label used to be.

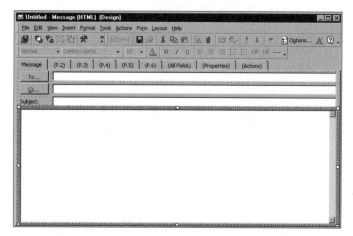

Figure 24-3. *The handles surrounding the text area.*

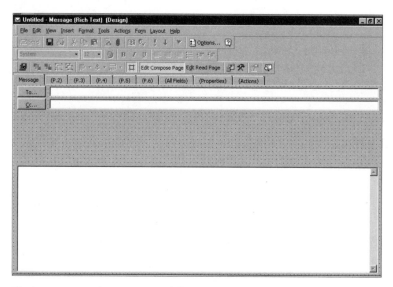

Figure 24-4. *The customized form, ready for your controls.*

5. Right-click on the new label and choose the Properties choice from the shortcut menu. The Properties dialog box appears (Figure 24-5).

6. Change the name of the label to ChapterNumberLabel and the caption for the label to Chapter Number:, then click OK to close the Properties dialog box. Adjust the size of the label to fit neatly around the new caption by highlighting the new label and moving the handles.

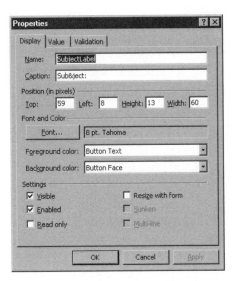

Figure 24-5. *The Properties dialog box.*

7. Click on the TextBox tool (the abl icon) in the Control Toolbox window and create a small text box to the right of ChapterNumberLabel.

8. Right-click on the text box and choose Properties from the shortcut menu. Notice that this time, the Properties dialog box appears with the middle Value tab displayed, rather than the Display tab. A label object does not need to be connected, or *bound*, to an underlying data field, because it is used only for display in a form. A text box control, on the other hand, usually is bound to a field. The Value tab allows you to select a predefined field to associate with this control or to create a new field. You want to create a new field for Chapter Number.

9. Click the New button to display the New Field dialog box, shown in Figure 24-6.

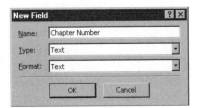

Figure 24-6. *Defining a new field.*

10. Enter Chapter Number as the name of the field and Number as the type of the field, and choose Truncated: 1,235 –1,235 from the Format drop-down menu. Because the book will have fewer than a thousand chapters, you might as well limit the format in the field definition. Click OK.

11. In the Initial Value section of the Value tab, select the check box to set the initial value for the field and enter 1 for the value. Because you will never have a chapter numbered 0, you have to provide an initial value for this field.

12. Switch to the Display tab and name the control ChapterNumber. Click OK. Adjust the size of the text box when you return to the forms development environment.

> **Note** Giving this control a name may seem to be an extra step because you aren't going to reference it anywhere else, so you might wonder why you can't just accept the default name. The reason for naming the control is simple. The default name for a control typically is meaningless—TextBox1, for example. If you ever have to reference this control or any other control in subsequent code or to share this value with another form, you will have no idea what the control relates to if it has a meaningless name. An ounce of documentation, in the form of a meaningful label, saves a pound of frustration when you try to build on your work later.

13. Insert a new label below the Chapter Number label and give it the name ChapterTitleLabel and the caption Chapter Title:, as described in steps 2 and 3.

14. Insert a new text box control to the right of ChapterTitleLabel. Bring up the properties sheet for the new control. Select the Value tab. Click the Choose Field button. Select the Frequently-Used Fields menu choice and the Subject field from the list of frequently used fields, as shown in Figure 24-7. Although earlier you deleted the *control* associated with the Subject field, you still want to use the field with this new control in your form.

15. Switch to the Validation tab and specify that a value be required for this field. Switch to the Display tab and name the field ChapterTitle. Add a new label below ChapterTitleLabel and give it the name StatusLabel and the caption Status:.

16. Click on the ComboBox tool in the Control Toolbox window. If you aren't sure which icon represents the ComboBox tool, you can hold the mouse over each tool to get a tool tip that identifies the icon. Create a combo box to the right of StatusLabel. Display the properties for the combo box by right-clicking on the control and selecting the Properties menu choice.

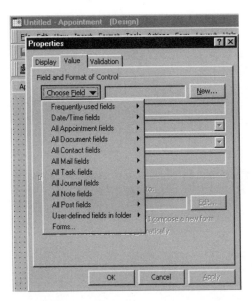

Figure 24-7. *Adding the Subject field from Frequently-Used fields.*

17. Create a new field for the combo box by selecting the Value tab and click-
    ing the New button. Give the new field the name of Chapter Status and a
    type and format of Text. Click OK to return to the Properties dialog box.
    Some of the previously disabled text fields on the Value tab are now avail-
    able, as shown in Figure 24-8.

    > **Note**   Why did we give the field the name ChapterStatus instead of a more
    > direct name, such as Status? An existing Outlook form has a field called
    > Status, and the properties of this field may not be exactly what you need for
    > your customized form.

18. Type the possible values for the combo box in the Possible Values text box,
    separating the values with commas. For this example, type First Draft,
    Editing, Completed.

19. At the bottom of the Value tab select the check box labeled Set The Initial
    Value Of This Field To: and enter First Draft as the initial value. Switch to
    the Validation tab and select the check box labeled A Value Is Required
    For This Field. Switch to the Display tab, name the combo box
    StatusCombo, and click OK.

You have finished adding almost all the controls that you will need for this
form. Adjust the size of the main message window, if necessary, to fit nicely in
the page, as shown in Figure 24-9.

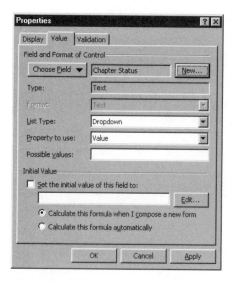

Figure 24-8. *Combo-box properties.*

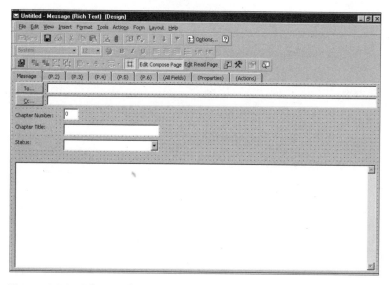

Figure 24-9. *The nearly complete custom form.*

Making the Form Easier to Use

The value of the ChapterNumber field will always be an integer. You can add a spin button control to make it easier to set the value for the field. To add a spin button control and make it work properly with the ChapterNumber control, follow these steps.

1. Click on the SpinButton tool in the Control Toolbox. (This tool is the second from the right in the bottom row, as shown in Figure 24-10.)

Figure 24-10. *The SpinButton control in the Control Toolbox.*

2. Drag the SpinButton control next to the ChapterNumber text box.

3. Display the Properties sheet for the spin button.

4. Associate the value of the SpinButton control with the field that you defined for the text box by selecting the Value tab of the Properties sheet and selecting the ChapterNumber field. (The ChapterNumber field can be found by going to the Choose Field menu and then selecting User Defined Fields in Inbox, as shown in Figure 24-11.)

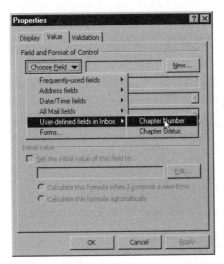

Figure 24-11. *Choosing the ChapterNumber field in the SpinButton control.*

5. Name the spin button SpinChapterNumber. Click OK to set the properties for the new control.

The spin button can now be used to set the value of the ChapterNumber field. Later, when you run the form, you will see the spin button at work. The positioning of the spin control is shown in Figure 24-12.

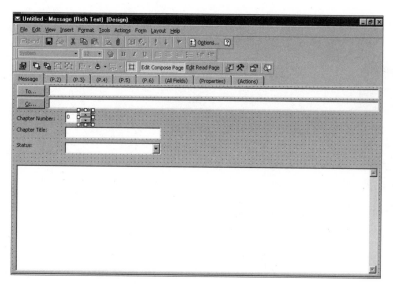

Figure 24-12. *Your custom form with a spin control.*

At this point you have completed only half of the form: the part used to compose a message. You typically create a version of the form to read the data included in the message; however, you can use the compose form for reading as well.

Adding a Read Page

Outlook's creators realized that composing and receiving messages are similar, but not identical, operations. When you compose a message, you typically want to add information to most of the controls in the form. When someone reads the message, that reader has no need to edit the data in the message. In fact, because the data in a message is a separate entity from the form, you normally want to prevent a message's recipient from modifying the data. If a recipient wants to modify the information, he or she typically uses a different type of form, such as a reply form.

For this reason, Outlook's creators gave all the default forms the capability to be two separate types of forms: one for composing a message and one for reading a message. Everything that you have modified in your custom form up to this point has been on the Compose page for the message. Next you must modify the Read page of a form, which you can do by completing the following steps.

Note If you are adding pages to a form, the Read and Compose pages, by default, use the same layout. If you want to create a new page for a form and separate the Read and Compose page layouts, you can make the appropriate choice from the Form menu.

1. Click the Edit Read Page button—in the same toolbar that contains the tools for the Control Toolbox—to see the Read page, shown in Figure 24-13. As you can see, the Read page looks as though it hasn't been affected by any of the modifications that you made on the Compose page, and in fact, it hasn't. The Read page also has a few extra controls to show who sent the message and when it was sent. Changing the layout of the Read page is easy. You want to include all the controls that you added to the Compose page after you make some room for them.

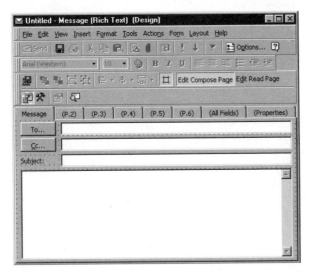

Figure 24-13. *The unmodified Read page for your custom form.*

2. Hold down the Shift key and click on the Subject label, the text box to the right of it, and the main message box.

3. Delete all these controls from the Read page by choosing Clear from the Edit menu. When you take this action, one of the toolbars on the page disappears. Because you have cut the only editable field in the Read page, you don't need a toolbar that controls the formatting of information on the page.

4. Return to the Compose page by clicking the Edit Compose Page button in the toolbar. Select all the new controls that you added to the page, as well as the resized Message field, by dragging the mouse to create a selection box that includes part of each of the controls.

5. Copy the selected controls. Switch to the Read page by clicking Edit Read Page, and paste the copied controls into the page layout. Rearrange the controls so that they fit nicely on the Read page and aren't overlaying any of the existing controls.

6. Display the property sheet for each of the new text box and combo box controls and select the Read Only check box at the bottom of the Display tab, as shown in Figure 24-14. After you have completed each of the text box and combo box controls, return to the form. Even though you did not change the Message field, it is already marked as read only. This is because the Message field is a predefined control with its own rules, one of which is that it is a read-only field.

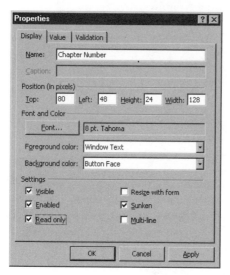

Figure 24-14. *Selecting Read Only for a text box control.*

7. Delete the spin control. You will not be allowing recipients to modify the value of the ChapterNumber field, so the spin control is unnecessary.

You have finished modifying the Read page for your customized message form. The Read page layout should look like Figure 24-15.

Your form now contains all the controls that you need. You could make the form easier to use by adding some features that automatically handle the repetitive functions in the form, such as addressing the form properly. To do so, you must add some simple logic to the form.

Adding Logic to a Form

Your new form is set up to collect the information that a chapter submission form requires, but each author still has to remember to address the form to the right people. This activity is not cumbersome, but you can make it automatic by adding some simple logic to the form and thereby relieving the user of this responsibility.

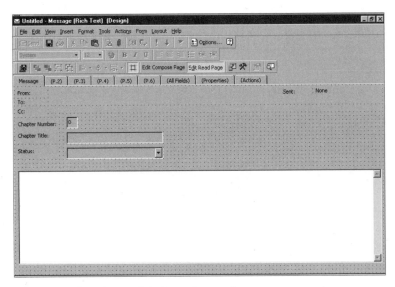

Figure 24-15. *The modified Read page for your custom form.*

You add logic to your form by attaching some simple code to some Outlook events. An event occurs when a specific part of the overall process takes place, and each Outlook message form fires certain events.

You will be using two events in implementing your code. The first is the Open event. As its name implies, the Open event is fired when the form is first opened. You can use the Open event to set the name of the primary recipient for your custom message because all you need to know to set this option is the name of the current user.

The second event is the Send event, which is fired when a message is sent. You will add code for this event to send a copy of the message to the appropriate public folder and to determine whether the message has a Completed status. In terms of our example, if the chapter has gone through its internal editing cycles, you want to copy this message to the editor so that the editor can begin working on the chapter.

You add code for an event by using the Script Editor as described in the following steps.

Script Editor Step 1

Open the Script Editor for the form by clicking the last button in the toolbar that contains the shortcuts (refer back to Figure 24-2).

Script Editor Step 2

Choose Event Handler from the Script menu, which will bring up a list of events.

Script Editor Step 3

Select the Open event and click the Add button. When you return to the Script Editor, you see that it has added the necessary syntax to add logic for the Open event, as shown in Figure 24-16.

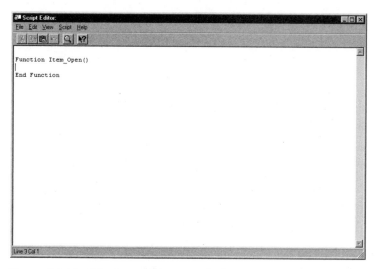

Figure 24-16. *The Script Editor, ready for you to add your code.*

When the form is first opened, you want to determine who opened it. You determine the form's user by querying the CurrentUser property, which resides in the Namespace of your Outlook application in the object hierarchy. The Namespace of your Outlook application acts as a root object for the Outlook object hierarchy. You have to use the Mail Application Programming Interface (MAPI) qualifier to look at the values for the current mail session object of your computer, which is where you can get the CurrentUser property for your environment. If you do not understand the concepts of object hierarchies, don't worry—all you have to do is enter the code listed in the following steps.

Note In the interest of space, this chapter does not provide an extensive explanation of the hierarchical model of objects in Outlook. For more information on the subject, refer to a book dedicated to creating applications with Outlook, such as *Building Applications with Microsoft Outlook 98* (1998), from Microsoft Press.

Script Editor Step 4

Add code to the Script Editor so that the entire script reads as follows:

```
Function Item_Open()
    If Application.GetNameSpace("MAPI").CurrentUser = "Rick Greenwald"
    then
        Item.Recipients.Add("Walter Glenn")
    Else
        Item.Recipients.Add("Rick Greenwald")
    End If
End Function
```

Note The completed code is included on the CD that accompanies this book in a file called OPENCODE.TXT, which is located under the Examples folder in the folder labeled Chapter 24.

You use the *Add* method for the Recipients collection to add a name to the recipients list. Outlook uses the Recipients collection to hold the names of all the recipients. The default location for displaying a recipient in the form is the To control.

Because the sample book has only two co-authors, your code can use a simple If ... Else ... EndIf structure to test for the current user. If the CurrentUser is "Rick Greenwald," the recipient "Walter Glenn" is added to the recipient list. If the CurrentUser is not "Rick Greenwald," the logic assumes the CurrentUser must be Walter Glenn and adds "Rick Greenwald" to the recipient collection.

Script Editor Step 5

To see whether this code works properly, run a form directly from the Outlook development environment. Choose Run This Form from the Form menu. Your form should look like the one shown in Figure 24-17, assuming that you were logged on as the user identified as Rick Greenwald. If you were logged on as any other user, the To control will show Rick Greenwald as the recipient. Close the form to return to the development environment. Click No if you are prompted to save.

Script Editor Step 6

To complete your custom form, you must implement two more logical steps. The first step is to add code that copies the mail message to the public folder that you created for the chapter inside the public folder Book. Chapter 23 covers the creation of these public folders. You implement this code in the Send event for the form because the value in the ChapterNumber field may change repeatedly until the message is sent.

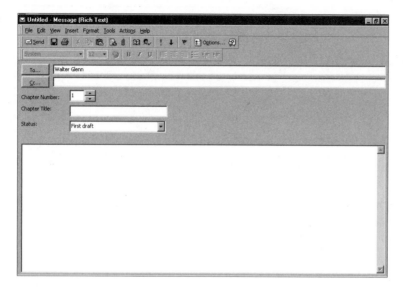

Figure 24-17. *First implementation of logic in your customized form.*

Script Editor Step 7

Open the Script Editor again. Choose Event Handler from the Script menu to bring up a list of events, and then select the Send event. This action adds a code section for the Send event to your script below the Open event handler.

Add the following code to the Send event:

```
ChapNum = Item.GetInspector.ModifiedFormPages("Message").
    Controls("ChapterNumber").Text

Set Myrecipient = Item.Recipients.Add("Chapter " & ChapNum)

Myrecipient.Resolve

Set Myrecipient = Nothing
```

> **Note** The completed code for this event is included on the CD that accompanies this book in a file called OPENCODE.TXT, which is located under the Examples folder in the folder labeled Chapter 24.

This code is similar, in some ways, to the code you entered previously. You use a hierarchy of object names and dot notations to get a value for the ChapterNumber field, although this hierarchy uses the *GetInspector* and *ModifiedFormPages* methods to find the relevant control. You also use the *Item.Recipients.Add* method, although this time you set the return value from the method to a variable in the program.

> **Note** Notice that you used the TEXT property for the *ChapterNumber* control, rather than the VALUE property. Remember that the ChapterNumber field was defined as a numeric value, so you couldn't easily concatenate it with the "Chapter" string. The TEXT property is the text representation of the value in the control.

> **Note** Just as this chapter does not explain the entire hierarchy structure, it does not go into detail about using methods, properties, and the dot notation necessary to indicate the structure of object hierarchies. If you are at all familiar with Visual Basic or VBScript, this type of notation should be old hat to you. If you are not, numerous books on the topic can help you with programming for Exchange or Outlook.

The reason you must capture the return value for the function is that you want to reference the entry in the recipients list in the next line of code. The *Resolve* method, as the name implies, resolves the name of a recipient to the appropriate e-mail address. Normally, Outlook would perform this step for you, but it does not do so instantly. Because the message will be sent as soon as this code completes, you have to force the resolution of the e-mail address so that the message can be sent successfully.

The last line of code sets the value of the variable to *Nothing*, which destroys the variable and frees the memory used for the variable. It is always good programming practice to clean up your variables when you finish using them, to prevent the gradual buildup of memory use.

Script Editor Step 8

The final step in adding logical operations to the form is specifying that a carbon copy of the message be sent to the editor automatically if the status for the chapter submission is Completed. To accomplish this, add the following code in bold to the existing code for the Send event:

```
ChapNum = Item.GetInspector.ModifiedFormPages("Message").
   |Controls("ChapterNumber").Text

Set Myrecipient = Item.Recipients.Add("Chapter " & ChapNum)

Myrecipient.Resolve

Set Myrecipient = Item.Recipients.Add("Rick Greenwald")

Myrecipient.Resolve

If Item.GetInspector.ModifiedFormPages("Message").
   Controls("StatusCombo").Value = "Completed" then
```

```
Set Myrecipient = Item.Recipients.Add("Editor")

Myrecipient.Resolve
```

End If

Set Myrecipient = Nothing

This last bit of code checks to see if the status for the chapter has been set to Completed. If it has, the code adds the editor to the recipient list so that the editor is immediately informed when a chapter is ready for work.

> **Note** You can click the Save button at any time to have Outlook save a copy of your form to the currently selected folder. You can also use the Save As button to save the form in a particular location. Outlook indicates that the saved message is a form by displaying an icon at the start of the form. When you go back and open the item, the form comes up in a run-time version, which you can quickly switch to development mode.

Script Editor Step 9

Because you are now setting the value for the To control automatically, you don't need to allow users to enter their own addressees. It is good programming practice to lock down user choices, where appropriate, to help prevent run-time errors. You can accomplish this objective using the Read Only option. Select the To text box control on the Compose page of your form. Then open the Properties sheet and check the Read Only check box. Just in case either of the co-authors wants to copy someone else on this message, you can leave the CC control available for writing.

You don't need to change the Read page because you have already set the relevant controls on that page to read only. But you should always think about making modifications on the Read page whenever you make changes on the Compose page of a message form.

You are now ready to let your custom form take its first steps out into the world.

Finishing and Publishing the Form

To run your form again to make sure that it works properly, follow these steps:

1. Choose Run This Form from the Form menu to bring up a run-time version of the form.

2. Choose Completed from the Status drop-down menu.

3. Add some relevant information for the Chapter Number and Title.

4. Enter some text in the main message area so that you can easily identify this particular message.

5. Click the Send button to send the mail message.

If you have the ability to log onto Exchange as either the other co-author or as the editor, you can check the inboxes of these users to make sure that the message was delivered.

To make the form widely available to Exchange users, you must publish the form to a folder. When you publish a form to a folder, you are adding the form to a forms library. Forms libraries are a way of organizing forms within Outlook.

You have several choices for the forms library. You can publish a form to your personal forms library, which only you can access. You can also publish a form to a specific public or private folder. When you publish a form to a folder, the form is available to everyone who has access to that folder, and the form is listed in the Actions menu. (Chapter 23 explains how to publish a form to the public Book folder.) The following steps walk you through the process of publishing a form:

1. When you return to the forms development environment, select the Tools menu, then the Form menu, and then the Publish Form As menu choice. You see the Publish Form As dialog box, shown in Figure 24-18.

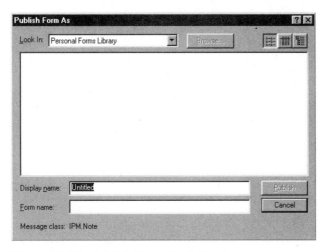

Figure 24-18. *Publish Form As dialog box.*

2. Choose Outlook Folders from the Look In drop-down menu. Click the Browse button to the right of the Look In menu. A tree of all available Outlook folders appears.

3. Expand the Public Folder entry and the All Public Folders entry below it.

4. Select the Book folder, and then click OK.

5. Enter Chapter Submission in the Display Name text box. Notice that the form name and the underlying message class name are automatically filled in with the same value as the display name.

6. Click the Publish button. A message box asks whether you want to select the check box that will include the form with the item (Figure 24-19).

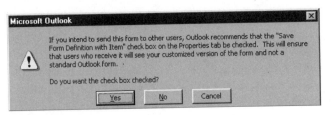

Figure 24-19. *An Outlook warning.*

7. Click the Yes button. (You will explore the meaning of this choice later in this chapter, when you look at some of the properties of the form.)

8. Exit the development environment and save your form when prompted.

You've done it! You have published your first custom form.

You can also save the form as a template, as a text file, or in another format by choosing Save As from the File menu in the development environment. When you save a form as a template, you can use it as the starting point for development of other forms. If you are going to create many forms based on a particular style, creating a template for the group of forms makes sense.

Remember that when you publish a form, you are making the form available to other users as well as registering it to your Outlook environment. If you want to modify the form further, all you have to do is open it and then switch to development mode.

However, your form can also be edited by anyone who has edit privileges on the folder to which you published the form. If you want to prevent this situation, you can set security on the form's design environment by modifying the form's properties.

Setting security on a form's design is easy. Remember the other tabs that were visible in the forms design environment? One of those tabs is labeled (Properties). If you go to the design environment and click on the (Properties) tab, you see the page shown in Figure 24-20.

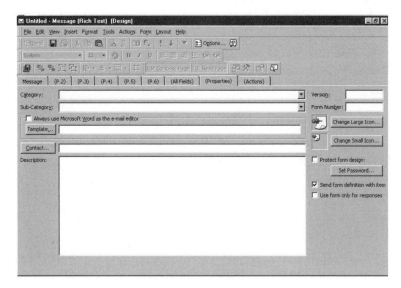

Figure 24-20. *The Form properties page.*

You can select the check box labeled Protect Form Design and then set a password that would be required to enable the form for editing. When you select this check box, it prompts you for a password. A user will have to know this password to be able to edit the form.

You can also give a form a version number and a form number, change the icon that represents the form in a folder, and specify that you want to send a form definition with the item when it is retrieved by a recipient. Because you've already indicated that you want to save the form definition with the item, the check box for this choice is checked.

Including the form with an item is a handy way of making sure that the recipient has the necessary form to view the data in the item. Remember that the form is the container in which the data for the item can be seen. Without a copy of the form, the user will not be able to view the data. To avoid having to install all possible forms on each Outlook desktop, you can simply include the form definition with the data item. In some situations, however, a company doesn't want to allow anything other than pure messages to be transmitted to client machines, because an Outlook form might contain code that could damage a recipient's machine. For these situations, you should not include the form definition with the data item.

You've spent long enough developing your first form; now you're ready to try it out from its new home in a public folder.

Using the Application

Your form is readily available to you through the public Book folder. To use the form from that folder, follow these steps:

1. Select the Book public folder.

2. Choose New Chapter submission from the Actions menu (Figure 24-21).

3. Fill in the message form (Figure 24-22) with relevant data and set the Status to Completed.

4. Send the message.

Figure 24-21. *Your new form listed in the Action menu.*

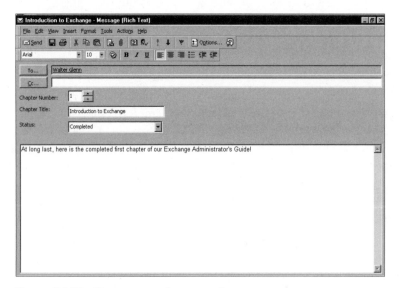

Figure 24-22. *Your custom form running.*

If you are able to log in as one of the other recipients, you can make sure that the mail message was sent correctly. You can also just check to see whether the message arrived in the Chapter 1 public folder.

> **Note**   What if the Chapter 1 public folder has not been created? The *Resolve* function of the *Send* event will fail, so the overall *Send* will also fail. You could add code to check for the existence of the appropriate chapter file and to add a new file if one is not already present, but that task is beyond the scope of this chapter.

Benefiting from the Application

Granted, this particular custom form was a bit simple. However, it served its purpose in that this chapter gave you a taste of the capabilities of custom forms development while demonstrating some concrete benefits.

Your simple custom form delivered several benefits. With a custom form, your application allowed the collection of a standard set of data items for each chapter. This simple specification alone can help facilitate the collaborative process of creating a book or compiling shared information. In addition, by including some code to limit acceptable values for items like the chapter number and to ensure that a specific set of data was always included with the message, your application added a significant amount of integrity to the collaborative process.

Summary

By creating your own customized forms in Outlook, you can create a user interface that addresses your application's specific needs. You can add code to provide logic and validation to your Outlook form, and you can publish your form so that it will appear in the Outlook menu bar as a standard part of the environment.

The Outlook forms you define act as the user interface for your application. Your Exchange Server takes care of the storage and distribution of the data the Outlook forms collect. In this way, Exchange and Outlook make a complete development platform.

This chapter gave you a whirlwind tour of developing forms with Outlook, and the form that you created addressed a particular, personal need. You can address other needs by using forms with Exchange folders. Chapter 25 explores using these two components to create a discussion group application.

Chapter 25
Using Discussion Groups

When you think about collaboration, you can't help but think about the need for discussions with many contributors. In the past, the primary form of discussion involved face-to-face meetings, which consume a large amount of time, especially when participants are in different cities or countries.

Creating and using discussion groups is one way that you can create instant collaboration with Microsoft Exchange Server 5.5. You can shape the functionality of these discussion groups to directly address the needs of your group. This chapter walks you through the creation of a basic discussion group in a public folder and then details how you can extend the reach of this basic application with customized forms and views.

Building the Application

As Rick and Walter work together on writing their book, they realize that they need to expand their circle of collaboration. Although the co-authors interact with each other on a daily basis and frequently correspond with their editor, they often need input from the larger community of Exchange experts. At these times, they have questions that other experts can answer, or they want to discuss issues with a wider audience.

The perfect vehicle for this type of collaboration is a public folder set up as a discussion group. In this chapter, you create a public folder for Rick and Walter to use, and you impersonate them to test the functions of the folder.

The first step in creating this discussion group application is creating a public folder that will act as the home of the discussion group. Following these steps, you can use Microsoft Outlook as a client to create this public folder.

1. In Outlook, choose New from the File menu, and then choose Folder from the subsequent menu. You see the dialog box shown in Figure 25-1.

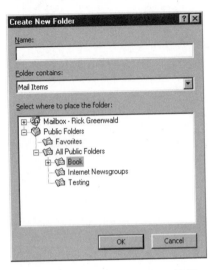

Figure 25-1. *The Create New Folder dialog box.*

2. Enter the name Technical Discussion in the Name text box, and leave Mail Items selected in the Folder Contains drop-down list.

3. In the directory-tree list box, open the Public Folders and All Public Folders, and then select the Book public folder. To create the public folder for your discussion group, click OK.

4. To give the other contributors access to the materials in the folder, you must change the security on the folder. Open Microsoft Exchange Administrator for your Exchange Server.

5. In the organizational hierarchy pane on the left side of the Administrator window, open Folder, Public Folders, and then the Book folder, as shown in Figure 25-2.

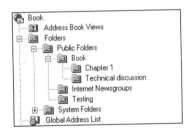

Figure 25-2. *The expanded public folders in Exchange Administrator.*

6. Select the Technical Discussion folder, and click the Properties button in the Administrator toolbar to bring up the Properties sheet for the folder.

7. On the main Properties sheet, click the Client Permissions button. Select the Default user in the Name panel of the Client Permissions page of the Properties sheet.

8. In the Permissions area, choose Author from the Roles drop-down menu to give the default user author privileges. Because you want to encourage widespread use of the discussion folder, you give everyone author privileges to the folder.

> **Note** You could set the security for the folder on the Permissions property sheet for the folder in Outlook, which looks exactly the same as the Client Permissions sheet in Exchange Administrator.

You have finished the initial setup work for your discussion folder. If you have been reading this book in chapter order, you probably remember that this series of actions is just like the actions that you took in Chapter 23 to create a shared public folder. In fact, the public folder that you created has most of the functionality that you need in a discussion group already embedded in it. You can see how this functionality works in the following section.

Testing the Application

You can test this application by making multiple posts to a discussion folder yourself. But to give you a feeling for how the discussion folder really works, this chapter walks you through the use of the folder. If you are following along in your own Exchange environment, you need to use two client machines or keep logging in to Exchange as a different user with a different user profile.

In order to properly demonstrate the discussion folder, you must impersonate the two co-authors or use two of your own user profiles in place of Walter and Rick. To begin the demonstration, log on as Walter to inaugurate the new discussion folder with the first post, then follow these steps:

1. While you are logged in as Walter, select the Technical Discussion folder. Click the New Post In This Folder button at the far left end of the Outlook toolbar.

2. Create a message with the title of First Post and include in the body some text that indicates that this is the first message. If you look in the Technical Discussion folder, you see the new posting.

3. Log off as Walter and log back on as Rick, the other co-author. Go to the Technical Discussion folder and open the message.

4. Click the Post A Reply button in the Outlook toolbar and create a response to Walter's initial posting. Click the Post button in the Outlook toolbar. When you return to the main Outlook window, open the Technical Discussion public folder. You see the two messages displayed, as shown in Figure 25-3, but they may not look the way you expected. The two messages are displayed in the folder to which they were posted, but there is no easy way to determine that one message is actually a response to the other message.

5. The reason for this situation is simple and can be changed through the configuration of the public folder. The entity that you are seeing in the right panel of the main Outlook window is called a *view*. The view provides a high-level look at the contents of a folder. You can modify this view to show the items in the folder in a more appropriate manner.

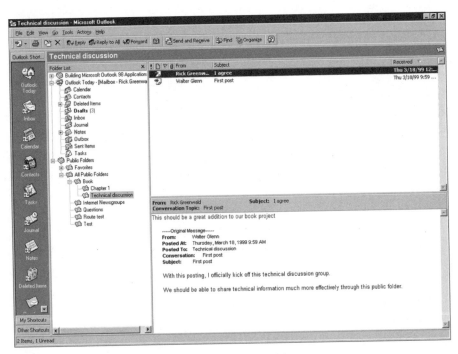

Figure 25-3. *The initial view of the discussion folder.*

6. While you have the Technical Discussion folder selected, choose the View menu from the main Outlook toolbar, select the Current View menu, and finally choose Customize Current View. This command displays the View Summary dialog box, shown in Figure 25-4.

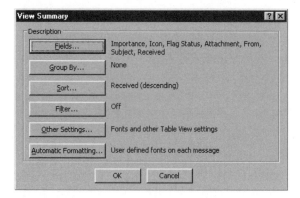

Figure 25-4. *The View Summary dialog box.*

7. Click the Group By button to display the Group By dialog box. In the first (and only enabled) drop-down menu, choose Conversation. This setting specifies that the Conversation field is used to group the postings in the folder.

Note   The Conversation field is a field in the form used for replies in this public folder. The value of the Conversation field is automatically set to the title of the initial posting on a topic. All subsequent replies to the posting keep the same value for the Conversation field, so the Conversation field is ideal for identifying ongoing conversations.

8. Make sure that At Last Viewed is selected in the Expand/Collapse Defaults section. This setting causes Outlook to remember the way that the discussion topics were expanded and collapsed in the view the last time you had the view open.

9. Click OK in the Group By dialog box to return to the View Summary dialog box. Click OK.

   When you return to the main Outlook window, you see that you have made some progress. The postings have been sorted by conversation topic. You can expand or contract a topic by clicking on the plus sign (+) or minus sign (–) to the left of the topic. The postings below the topic still don't look right, however, because there is no visual indication that one posting is a reply to another posting. You can add this feature by modifying the view one more time:

10. Choose the View menu from the main Outlook toolbar, select the Current View menu, and finally choose Customize Current View. This screen should look familiar to you.

11. Click the Sort button and the Sort dialog box appears. Choose Conversation Index from the Sort Items By dialog box. Click OK.

12. Click OK again to close the View Summary window.

Note Unfortunately, the changes that you made in the view apply only to your copy of the view. Other users must modify their own views to see the same arrangement of postings in the folder, although you can set a particular view for a folder as the default view.

In order to set this view as the default view that an Exchange user sees, you must look at the properties of the folder. This is done simply by selecting the File menu, the Folder option, and then the Properties option. In the Folder properties sheet, you then click on the Administration tab. In the top option, Initial View On Folder, click the down arrow and select the view that was just created. Note that this will be the initial view for a user that has never looked at that folder before. Those users who have looked at the folder will have the view they were using previously.

The newly modified view shows the responses grouped by conversation and sorted by conversation index, as shown in Figure 25-5. The *conversation index* is an internal index Exchange maintains to track the level of posted responses. Selecting a value to group by causes the collection of items to be placed under an entry that can be expanded and collapsed, whereas sorting on a value simply causes the items to be indented. The indentation caused by sorting occurs in the first field in the view that contains text, which in this case is the From field.

Note If a conversation contains any unread items, the heading of the conversation is displayed in bold, as an unread item would be, and the number of read and unread items on that topic is displayed after the topic. If all the items in a particular conversation have been read, the topic is displayed in a normal font, followed by the total number of items on the topic.

The view looks just about right. But if you have any experience with technical discussion areas, you know that most of the responses to an initial post can be categorized, so categories would help make the information in the discussion folder more immediately valuable. To add a category to the

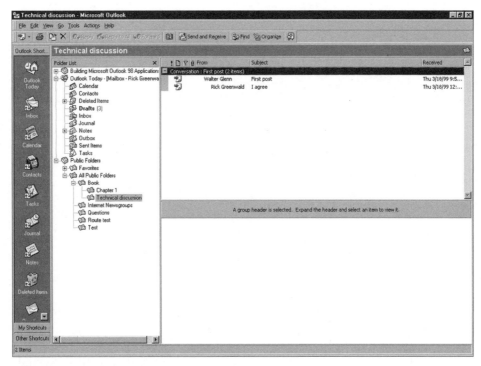

Figure 25-5. *The newly modified view of the Technical Discussion public folder.*

discussion group, you have to create a custom form and modify the way that the folder operates.

Extending the Application

The first step in extending the basic discussion group application is creating a form for posting replies to a conversation. This response form is based on the form that you currently use to post a message to the folder. You will create this form in stages throughout the remainder of this section.

Creating the Reply Form

Follow these steps to create a basic reply form:

1. In Outlook, select the Technical Discussion folder under the All Public Folders container, which is under the Public Folders container.

2. Go to the File menu of the main Outlook toolbar, select New, and choose Post In This Folder.

3. Once the form is opened, go to the Tools menu, choose Forms, and select Design This Form to open the form in design mode.

4. Delete the Categories button and text field at the bottom of the form. Adjust the size of the main message window to make room for the field that you will be adding to the form.

5. Right-click on the Subject text box and choose Properties from the short-cut menu.

6. Select the Read Only check box because replies to a posting in this folder will use the same subject as the original message. To make the subject of this response the same as the subject of the original question, click on the Value tab, select the check box labeled Set The Initial Value Of This Field To, and click Edit.

7. Go to the Field button and select Frequently-Used Fields. Then choose Subject from the list that appears. This will cause "[Subject]" to appear in the text box that shows the initial value. Click OK to return to the Properties window. Click OK to save the changes to the form.

8. Add a label to the form by selecting the label object from the Toolbox and dragging it for sizing between the Subject and the message text box. (If you are unfamiliar with the techniques used to design a form in Outlook 98, refer to Chapter 24 for an overview.)

9. Display the Properties window for the label by right-clicking on the label and selecting the Properties choice. Name the label ResponseTypeLabel, and enter Response Type as the caption. Click OK to return to the design environment, and then adjust the label to fit neatly around the text.

10. Add a combo-box control to the right of the label.

11. Display the Properties window and click the New button to create a new field for the form. Give the field the name ResponseType and click OK.

12. Enter the following list of possible values: Answer, Further Question, Workaround, and Documentation Reference. Set the initial value of the field to Answer by selecting the check box label.

13. Display the Properties window and name the control ResponseTypeCombo. Click OK to return to the design environment.

14. Copy the ResponseType controls and the Message control, and then click Edit Read Page in the toolbar to display the Read page.

15. Delete the Subject controls, the Categories control button and text field, and the original Message control, and then paste the controls that you just copied into the Read page.

16. Set the ResponseType control to Read Only by selecting the Read Only check box in the property sheet.

17. Publish the new form to the Technical Discussion public folder with the name of "Technical response" by going to the Tools menu, selecting Forms, and choosing Publish Form.

18. Exit the form by selecting Close from the File menu.

The Compose page of your modified form should look like Figure 25-6.

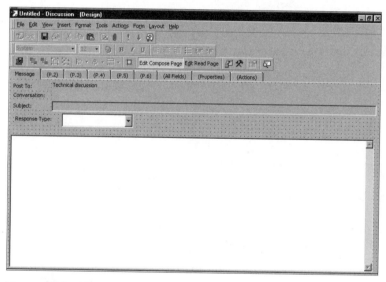

Figure 25-6. *The new version of the form.*

Modifying the Initial Form

The form you just modified works as a response form. You must modify the initial posting form so that it automatically calls this response form instead of the default response form. To do so, follow these steps.

1. Open the form New Post In This Folder. Get into design mode by going to the Tools menu, selecting Forms, and selecting Design This Form. Because you do not need any categories in this post, delete the Categories button and text field. Adjust the Message field so that it takes up the extra space.

2. Go to the Read page for the form. Delete the Categories objects, adjust the size of the Message field, and make both the Message field and the Subject field read-only.

3. Click on the Actions tab for the form. This tab contains a list of the actions a user can perform from the form, as shown in Figure 25-7. Forms include default actions, and you can add your own custom actions, as you will see later in this chapter.

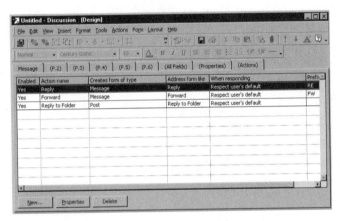

Figure 25-7. *Actions that can be performed using this form.*

4. Double-click on the Reply action to see the Form Action Properties dialog box.

5. Clear the Enabled check box in the Property sheet for the Reply action, and click OK. Follow the same procedure to disable the Forward and Reply To Folder actions.

6. Click the New button at the bottom of the Actions tab. The Form Actions Properties dialog box will appear, as shown in Figure 25-8.

7. Name the new action Technical Response. Choose the Technical Response form that you just created from the Form Name drop-down menu.

8. Choose Include And Indent Original Message Text from the When Responding drop-down menu.

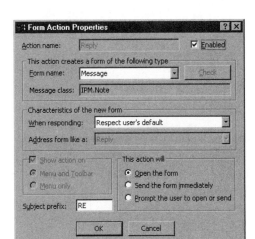

Figure 25-8. *The Forms Actions Properties dialog box.*

9. Choose Reply To Folder from the Address Form Like A drop-down list. At this point, the Form Action Properties dialog box should look like Figure 25-9. Click OK.

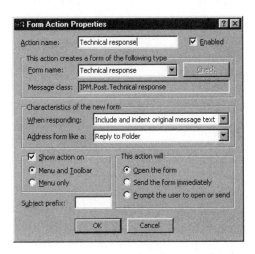

Figure 25-9. *The completed entries for the new Technical Question action.*

10. Publish the new form to the Technical Discussion public folder with the name "Technical Question" by going to the Tools menu, choosing Forms, and selecting Publish Form.

You have successfully added to the Technical Question form an action that automatically calls up the Technical Response form when a user wants to post a response to the form. Adding an action to a form causes a button to appear at the top of the form, which you will see later in the chapter when you use the new form for the first time. This button is correct for the initial Technical Question form, but you must also adjust the actions for the Technical Response form because there may be multiple nested responses.

Adding an Action to the Form

To add an action to the form, follow these steps:

1. You can change the response form by disabling the existing actions and adding a new action, as you did for the form you just modified in the previous section. As previously mentioned, there may be many responses to the Technical Question form, so the Technical Response form must also have the button so that users may respond to other responses, because each Technical Question may have multiple nested response forms, creating a hierarchy for the discussion. Select the Technical Discussion public folder. Select the Tools menu, select Forms, and choose Design A Form. The Design Form window appears.

2. Choose Technical Discussion from the Look In drop-down menu and double-click on the Technical Response form.

3. On the Actions tab, disable the three existing actions, as you did in the preceding section for the Technical Question form.

4. Add a new action called Technical Response, with the same characteristics as the corresponding action in the previously modified Technical Question form.

5. Publish the form to add the new changes to the existing Technical Response form.

Hiding an Action

Only one thing is still amiss in this discussion form. You may have noticed that one of the actions for the Technical Discussion folder was to create a new Technical Response form. This situation makes sense because the form was published to the folder, but it is not what you want. The Technical Response form should be used only in response to a question or another response, so it shouldn't show up in the Actions menu. You can hide the form from an unsuspecting user by following these steps:

1. In the main Outlook window, right-click on the Technical Discussion folder and choose Properties from the shortcut menu, to display the Properties dialog box.

2. Select the Forms tab. Select the Technical Response form and click the Manage button to display the Forms Manager dialog box.

3. Select the Technical Response form and click on the Properties button. The Form Properties dialog box appears (see Figure 25-10).

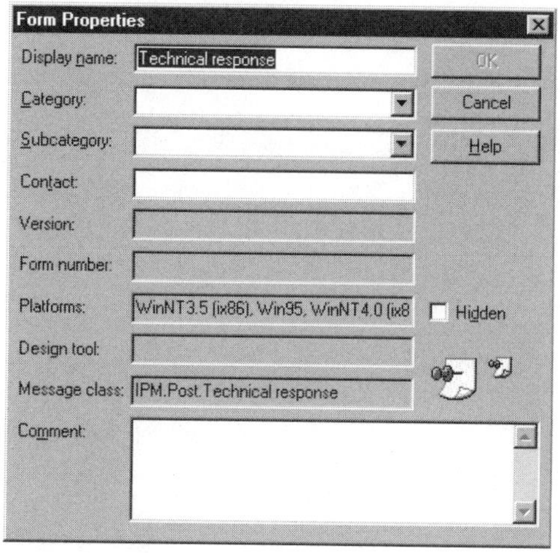

Figure 25-10. *The Forms Properties dialog box.*

4. Select the Hidden check box, and click OK.

5. Close the Form Properties dialog box and return to the Technical Discussion Properties dialog box. Click OK.

If you go back and click on the Actions menu for the form, you see that the only action listed is the New Technical Question action.

Running the New Version of the Application

Now that you have modified the Technical Question form and the Technical Response form to meet your needs, it's time to see the newly modified discussion group at work:

1. Select the Technical Discussion public folder and choose New Technical Question from the Actions menu.

2. Enter a subject that identifies the posting as the first question for the folder and add some text in the body of the message. Click the Post button at the left end of the top toolbar to send the question to the folder.

3. You are returned to the Outlook window. Double-click on the message that you just posted. The form that appears is a little different from the original response form, as shown in Figure 25-11.

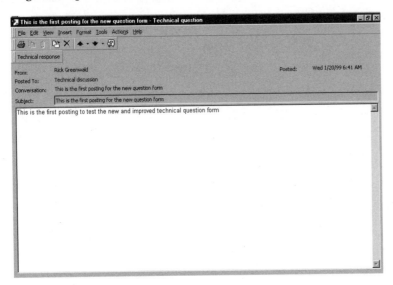

Figure 25-11. *The new Read form for the Technical Question item.*

4. Click on the Technical Response button for the new action to display the new response form, shown in Figure 25-12.

5. Create a suitable response and make sure that the Response Type is set to Answer. Post the response by clicking the Post button on the toolbar.

When you return to the main Outlook window, your response is right where you expected it to be — below the initial question.

By adding your own custom question and response forms to the discussion folder, you have shaped the way that the discussion group is used. As a last extension to your discussion group application, you can create a view that eliminates some of the listings of the postings and allows you to concentrate on the answers and workarounds that appear in the folder:

1. Select the Technical Discussion folder in the folder listing pane. Choose the View menu, select Current View, and choose Define Views. The Define Views dialog box appears, as shown in Figure 25-13. This dialog

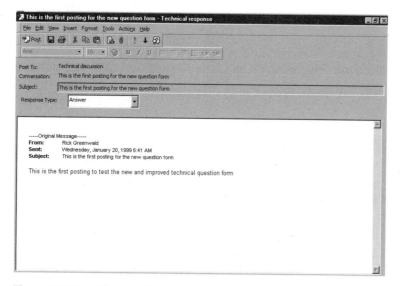

Figure 25-12. *The new Technical Response form.*

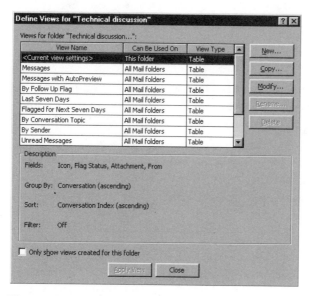

Figure 25-13. *The Define Views dialog box.*

box lists all the views that are currently defined for the folder. When you select a view, a description of the view appears in the bottom half of the dialog box.

2. Because you want to create a new view, click the New button. A dialog box like the one shown in Figure 25-14 is displayed. You are prompted to provide a name for the view and the type of view as well as to specify who is allowed to use the view. Name the new view Answers Only. Choose Table for the type of view and choose the middle radio button so that only you can see the view in this folder. Click OK.

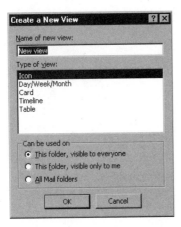

Figure 25-14. *The Create A New View dialog box.*

3. The next window is the same window that you used to modify a view. You want to change the fields, change the way that the view is grouped and sorted, and add a filter to the view. Click the Fields button to bring up the Show Fields dialog box.

4. Remove the Importance, Flag Status, Attachment, and Subject fields from the list on the right. (The Subject for each entry is the same as the conversation topic, so having it repeat in each subsequent message line would be redundant.)

5. Go to the Select Available Fields From drop-down menu and select User-Defined Fields in Folder.

6. Move the ResponseType field to the right list box and click the arrow buttons to position it after the From field. Click OK to return to the View Summary dialog box.

7. Click Group By to bring up the Group By dialog box and choose Conversation as the first Group By item. Click OK.

8. In the View Summary dialog box, click Sort and change the first sort item to Conversation Index. Click OK.

9. In the View Summary dialog box, click Filter to display the Filter dialog box. The Filter dialog box is a little different from the other dialog boxes that you use to define a view. The first tab of the dialog box allows you to apply filtering conditions to the basic message. Because you want to apply a filter to a user-defined field, click on the Advanced tab. The Filter dialog box should look like Figure 25-15.

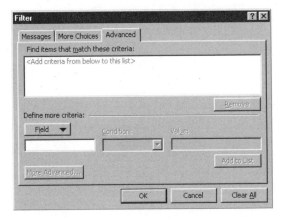

Figure 25-15. *The Advanced tab in the Filter dialog box for a view.*

10. Click Field, select Technical Response form, and then choose ResponseType.

11. Select Is (Exactly) from the Condition drop-down menu and enter Answer into the field. Click Add To List to add your new filtering condition.

12. Add a condition that checks to see whether the ResponseType is exactly equal to Workaround, and add that condition to the filter conditions list by going through the same process as you did to check for the value of Answer. Click OK.

13. Click OK again to return to the Define View dialog box. Select the new view and click the Apply View button to see the view in action. The Technical Discussion folder should look like the folder shown in Figure 25-16.

This view is ideal for the busy co-author who wants to see only the answers, not the entire discussion chain. Because you are the only co-author who fits this description, you specified that this view is available only to you.

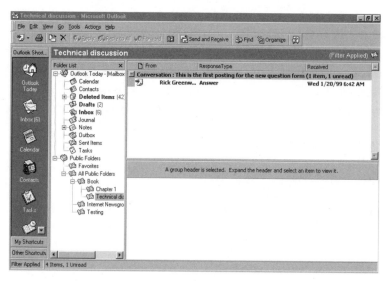

Figure 25-16. *The newly defined Answers view.*

Benefiting from the Application

The Technical Discussion folder that you set up leverages many of Exchange's inherent strengths. First it enables discussion. You easily created an area that encourages free exchange of ideas. Although this chapter focuses on creating a simple, single-site discussion group, keep in mind that replication of public folders — a built-in feature of Exchange — would allow this discussion to span multiple servers and sites in widely separated areas. By creating customized post and response forms, you made sure that each response to an initial technical question includes some basic information about the nature of the response. By streamlining the way that users interact with the forum, you ensure that everyone who uses this forum can work cohesively through the forms you created.

Finally, the Technical Discussion folder presents different views of the same information. You learned in Chapter 24 that the form and its data are separate and distinct parts of an Exchange item. Likewise, a view of the contents of a folder is separate from the items in the folder, so you can easily create views that give you an appropriate summary of the information in the folder. A well-designed view can help you answer questions about the contents of a folder without having to examine each item.

Summary

In this chapter, you learned quite a bit about using the standard tools and functionality in Exchange and Outlook to extend the reach of the Exchange environment. You created a discussion group based on a standard public folder and created response forms to customize the users' interaction with the discussion group to the needs of the application. You also learned how to limit the actions in any form to set up a standardized interaction with the items in the discussion group and how to create your own views to give a more meaningful appearance to the standard listing of items in the folder.

Chapter 26 takes you outside the immediate Exchange environment to create applications that are built with other tools but are still based on the capabilities of Exchange.

Chapter 26
Using Collaboration Data Objects

To this point, you have used the tools and capabilities of Microsoft Exchange Server 5.5 and the Microsoft Outlook client to extend the Exchange environment. It's time to step outside these confines and see how to use the services provided by Exchange from outside the immediate Exchange environment. In this chapter, you use Collaboration Data Objects (CDOs) to build a client application that uses Visual Basic to extend the reach of your Exchange system.

Why would you want to build your own applications instead of using the robust clients that can work with Exchange? As you see in this chapter, you can create applications that are specifically tailored to the issues that you must address and that leverage the power of Visual Basic and Exchange Server. With a single click of a button, one of the authors for whom you are creating applications can submit all the materials for a chapter in a single directory as an attachment; he can also create the public folder that will receive the attachment, if that folder does not already exist.

Understanding Collaboration Data Objects (CDOs)

A CDO is a COM interface to the underlying services provided by Exchange. (COM, which stands for Common Object Model, is defined in the next section.) CDOs were introduced with Exchange Server 5.5, but the role CDOs play was performed, under a different name, in earlier versions of Exchange. Exchange 4.0 included what was called the OLE Messaging library, and Exchange 5.0 had a similar technology called Active Messaging. Both technologies, like CDOs, were types of application programming interfaces (API) that allowed programming languages to interact with Exchange services. All these technologies in turn are based on a standard API called Messaging Application Programming Interface (MAPI), which is a standard produced by Microsoft.

CDOs expand on the capabilities of previous versions of the external interface to Exchange. CDOs can access calendar information through Outlook or Microsoft

Schedule+. If you are new to CDOs, the most important thing to understand about them is that they are standard COM components.

Collaboration Data Objects as COM Components

The Common Object Model (COM) is the standard component model for all Microsoft products and platforms. You don't have to understand anything but the basics of COM to use CDOs. A COM component, as the name implies, is an object that can be created and reused in a variety of common languages, such as Visual Basic or Visual C++. After you create a component, you can use it by setting its properties and calling its methods. A *property* for an object is an attribute for that object. The name of a folder is a property of the *Folder* object, for example. A *method* is a function that operates on an object. To add a recipient to a Recipients *collection*, for example, you use the *Add* method to add a new *Recipient* object to the collection.

Most COM objects are actually hierarchies of objects. You start using a CDO by creating a session object, which controls all the operations of a particular session. You can then create subsidiary objects as children of the main session object by using the methods of the session object.

COM objects use dot notation to represent the methods and properties of an object hierarchy. If you were to try to set the PROP1 property of the Child object of a Parent object, the syntax would look like this:

```
Parent.Child.Prop1 = value
```

The files that you need to use CDOs are included with Exchange Server 5.5 or later and with recent client software for connecting with Exchange, such as Outlook 98 and Outlook 2000. You learn how to integrate these files with a development environment later in this chapter.

The Structure of Collaboration Data Objects

CDOs, like all COM objects, are composed of a hierarchy of objects. The structure of the CDO hierarchy is shown in Figure 26-1.

Note There are actually two CDO libraries: the standard library, which is discussed in this chapter, and the CDO Rendering library, which is used on a server to help in displaying CDO objects and collections in HTML for transmission over the Web. For the rest of this chapter, the term *CDO library* refers to the actual CDO library itself, not to the CDO Rendering library, because the CDO Rendering library is beyond the scope of this chapter.

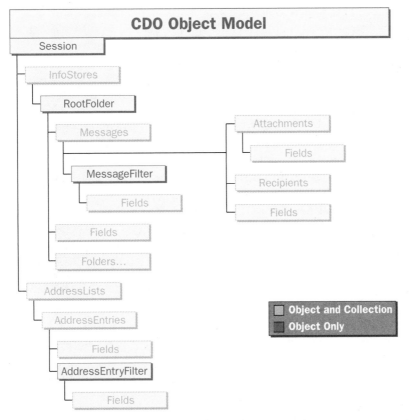

Figure 26-1. *The object hierarchy of CDOs.*

Each level in the CDO object hierarchy is either a single object or a collection of objects. A *collection* of objects, as shown in Figure 26-1, consists of one or more instances of a particular object. Each instance of the object has the structure indicated in the figure. This combination of a multilevel hierarchy with the added dimension of collections allows a very complex structure to be described in a fairly straightforward manner, which is one of the virtues of COM objects.

You don't need to digest all the information about the structure of the CDO object library immediately. When you are working with CDO objects in Visual Basic, the language will be able to give you a listing of the children at each level in the object hierarchy automatically, as part of its IntelliSense help feature.

Note The IntelliSense feature works in conjunction with dot notation. After you enter an identifier for an object and the dot that precedes one of the object's methods or properties, the Visual Basic development environment displays a list of properties and methods. As you enter the first few letters after the dot, the list scrolls to the appropriate property or method name. When the correct entry is displayed, press the Tab key to accept it.

However, you should understand the basic structure of the main levels of the CDO hierarchy as a foundation for your understanding. At the top of the hierarchy is the *Session* object. Everything in the CDO library is associated with a particular session. A *session* is the equivalent of a MAPI session, which maps to a single connection from a client to an Exchange Server. In essence, the *Session* object establishes the overall context in which everything takes place.

The session itself supports three main objects at the next level of the hierarchy: the *AddressLists* collection, a *Folder* collection (which is not displayed in Figure 26-1), and the *InfoStores* collection. The *AddressLists* collection contains all the objects needed to work with the address lists offered by an Exchange address book. The *AddressLists* collection contains an *AddressEntries* collection, which in turn contains an *AddressEntry* object, which holds an address that is contained in an address book, and an *AddressEntryFilter*, which can contain a filter that limits the addresses you see when you query the *AddressEntries* collection for its contents. Keep in mind that a CDO object is mapped to a complete Exchange object. You can limit the addressees that you see in an address book in Exchange clients, so the CDO library must supply the same functionality.

Notice that an *AddressList* object contains an *AddressEntries* collection, which contains a *Fields* collection, and that each *AddressEntries* contains an *AddressEntryFilter* object that has its own *Fields* collection. Although seeing the same *Fields* collection at so many places in the CDO hierarchy may be confusing, you can easily tell them apart with dot notation when you are actually programming with CDO objects.

Note In fact, every instance of the *Fields* collection has the same properties that help you navigate the *Field* objects that are a part of the collection. You can use the same set of methods and properties for the *Fields* collection to examine and set any *Field* objects associated with the collection. This commonality, in turn, makes it much easier to deal with a wide variety of objects that have a wide variety of properties.

The *Folder* object also exists at two levels in the CDO hierarchy, although only one of them is shown in the diagram. As a child object of the *Session* object, the *Folder* object can represent either the Inbox or the Outbox. These two folders are essential to the operation of Exchange, so they can be accessed directly from the *Session* object. A *Folder* object also exists as a member of the *InfoStore* object, which is a child of the *InfoStore* object. The *InfoStore* object points to a particular Information Store to which the Exchange Server has access. Each *InfoStore* supports a hierarchy of folders, each of which is represented by a *Folder* object.

Each *Folder* object in turn contains a *Messages* collection, which can contain any of the types of messages supported by Exchange: a standard mail message (*Message* object) or an appointment in an Exchange calendar (*AppointmentItem* or *MeetingItem*). Each *Message* object supports a wealth of child objects, such as a *Recipients* collection and an *Attachments* collection.

You now have a grounding in the structure of CDOs, so you can move ahead with creating a Visual Basic application that uses them. Because you understand the hierarchical structure of the CDO object library, and because you can easily get online help within the Visual Basic development environment, you do not have to memorize all the components of the CDO library. If you program with the library often enough, you will become very familiar with the objects that you use most frequently, as well as with the methods and properties associated with those objects.

Building the Application

You will use Visual Basic, one of the most popular Microsoft programming languages, to create your custom application. The chapter assumes that you have a fundamental knowledge of Visual Basic. The remainder of this chapter focuses on creating a Visual Basic application that uses CDOs to access the Exchange environment.

> **Note**   Microsoft Press has many titles on Visual Basic for programmers, such as *Microsoft Visual Basic 6.0 Learning Edition* (1998) and *Microsoft Visual Basic 6.0 Developer's Workshop* (1998). Beginners may want to check out *Microsoft Visual Basic 5.0 Step by Step* (1997).

The Goal of the Application

Before plunging into any coding, though, you should review the goals of the application that you will create. You have been implementing custom applications to address the needs of the co-authors Rick and Walter. All the applications that you created in earlier chapters existed in the Exchange system. When you used a discussion group or a routing application, your basic client was an Outlook client.

At times, however, you may have to leave the confines of the Outlook system because you want to implement some type of functionality that is outside the range of the system. In this particular case, Rick and Walter want to create a client application for their chapter submission process. In Chapter 24, you created a form in Outlook to gather the basic information for each chapter submission. You still had to do the work of attaching all the material for a chapter submission to a posting, however.

Rick and Walter keep all the materials for a chapter in a directory on the file systems of their own machines. For this reason, they could easily instruct an application to attach all the files in a particular directory to a chapter submission. This functionality not only makes the chapter submission process easier, it also makes it more accident-proof. A custom application never misspells the name of a file or overlooks one. The application that you build in this chapter accomplishes the chapter submission task more smoothly than the one you built in Outlook.

Setting Up the Application Development Environment

One great thing about COM objects is that they are easy to blend into the development environments of any of the languages that support COM. To use CDOs in a Visual Basic application, all you have to do is to add to the standard Visual Basic development environment a reference to the libraries that contain the CDO objects.

> **Note** To add a reference to the CDO libraries, you must be sure that you have the dynamic link libraries (DLLs) installed for the CDO libraries. Make sure that the MAPI32.DLL and CDO.DLL libraries are in your %WINDOWS%\SYSTEM32 Directory. If you installed Outlook 98 and Service Pack 1 of Exchange Server 5.5, the proper libraries should be installed on your client and server machines.

You will begin the entire development process by starting Visual Basic, adding the reference to the CDO library, and saving the project and initial form.

1. Open Visual Basic and select Standard EXE, the default, as the project type. Choose References from the Project menu, and the References dialog box appears, as shown in Figure 26-2.

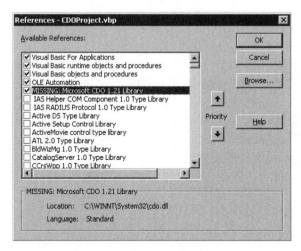

Figure 26-2. *The References dialog box in Visual Basic 6.0.*

2. Scroll down the list and select the Microsoft CDO 1.2x Library check box, and then click OK.

3. Choose Save Project As from the File menu to save the project and the form that you will use to create your Visual Basic application. For this example, use the names CDOFORM and CDOPROJECT for the form and project, respectively. After you add the reference to the CDO library, you are ready to design the user interface form for the application.

Note The CDO 1.21 library comes with Outlook 98, whereas the CDO 1.2 library comes with Outlook 97. Either of these libraries works for these examples, although you should make sure that you also have the 1.21 CDO library installed on the server with Exchange 5.5 Service Pack 1.

Designing the User Interface

The basic purpose of this application is to replicate and supplement the functionality of the Outlook form that you designed in Chapter 24. This form had a spin control to set the chapter number, a text box field to accept the chapter title, a drop-down menu to specify the status of a chapter, and a text area for entering a message. In this section, you create a user interface form that contains all these objects as well as an object that lets the user specify the directory that contains all the materials for the chapter. Using the steps that follow, you will accomplish this task.

Real World   Creating an Application with Visual Basic

If you are a Visual Basic programmer, you should not have a problem creating the application in this chapter. If you are not familiar with Visual Basic, it is still worthwhile to read through the material and get an understanding of how you can use CDOs to interact with Exchange, but you probably don't want to make this your first Visual Basic project.

The completed Visual Basic application is included on the accompanying CD in the Chapter 26 folder within the Examples folder under the name of CDOProject. You can open the CDOPROJECT.VBP project in Visual Basic to see the completed project and switch to the CDOForm (code) window to see the code for the application. If you don't have ready access to a Visual Basic environment, the code for the application is also included in a text file, CDOCODE.TXT.

1. Maximize the project area and the form within the project to get the largest amount of screen real estate for designing the form. Find the Properties sheet for the form, which is usually located on the right of the Visual Basic main window, as shown in Figure 26-3. Use the Properties sheet to set the Name property of the form to CDOForm and the Caption property to Chapter Submission Form, as shown in Figure 26-4.

2. Select the Label tool (the A icon) in the toolbox and add a label object to the top of the form by dragging and sizing the object. Set the Name property of the label to lblChapterNumber and the Caption property of the label to Chapter Number:. You should also resize the label to fit.

Note In Visual Basic, the name of a control is customarily preceded by a three-character abbreviation for the type of control, such as "lbl" for label controls.

3. Select the TextBox tool (the abl icon) in the toolbox, and add a TextBox control to the right of the lblChapterNumber label. Set the Name property of the field to txtChapterNumber and the Text property to 1. Set the Locked property to True to prevent the user from changing the value without using the control that you are about to add.

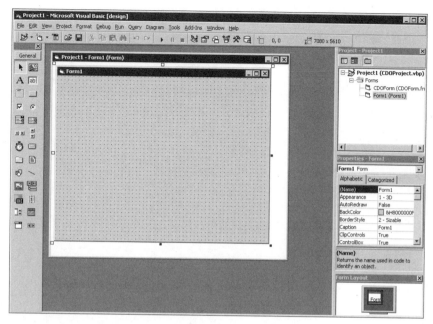

Figure 26-3. *Location of the property sheet in Visual Basic.*

Figure 26-4. *The property sheet for the CDOForm in Visual Basic.*

4. Choose Components from the Project menu to display the Components dialog box, shown in Figure 26-5.

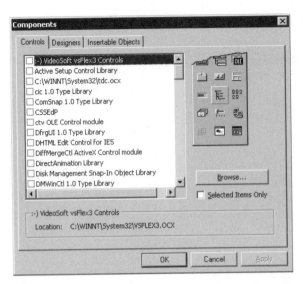

Figure 26-5. *The Components dialog box in Visual Basic.*

5. Scroll down the list of components and select the Microsoft Windows Common Controls-2 6.0 check box, as shown in Figure 26-6, to add an up-and-down button to the toolbox. (If you are using Visual Basic 5.0, you should choose the Common Controls-2 5.0.) Click OK to add the controls to the toolbox.

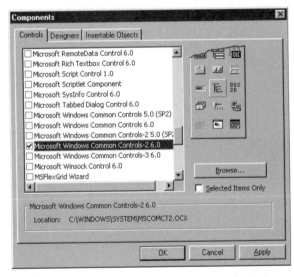

Figure 26-6. *Selecting the Microsoft Windows Common Controls-2 6.0.*

6. Select the UpDown control from the toolbox and draw it next to the txtChapterNumber field.

7. Set the Name property to udChapterNumber, the BuddyControl property to txtChapterNumber, and the SyncBuddy property to True. (This control serves the same purpose as the spin control in the Outlook form.)

8. Add a label and TextBox field for the chapter title below the controls for the chapter number. Set the Name properties of the label and the text control to lblChapterTitle and txtChapterTitle, respectively. Set the Caption property for the lblChapterTitle to Chapter Title:. Delete the value for the Text property for the text box. To have the user set the type of the submission, you will use a group of option buttons instead of the combo box that you used in the Outlook form.

9. Select the Frame control from the toolbox and create a group box below the chapter title controls. Give the frame the name frmType and the caption Submission Type.

10. Select the option button control in the toolbox and add three radio buttons to the frame. Give the option buttons the names rbFirstDraft, rbEditing, and rbCompleted. Give the option buttons the captions First Draft, Editing, and Completed. Set the value of the rbFirstDraft radio button to True.

11. Add a label and a large text field for the message below the option buttons you just added to the form. Set the caption of the label to Message: and name the label and text field lblMessage and txtMessage, respectively. Set the MultiLine property of the txtMessage field to True and the ScrollBars property to 2 – Vertical.

12. Delete the Text1 value from the Text property. If the Text property shows (Text), you need to use the drop-down button to show the Text1. Your form should now look almost like the form shown in Figure 26-7.

13. To add logic that automatically attaches all the files in a directory to the posting, you have to add a control to identify the target directory. Add a label to the form just below the Message controls and give it the name lblDirectory and the caption Directory:.

14. Select the DirListBox control (it looks like a little folder icon) in the toolbox and add a DirListBox to the right of the lblDirectory label by dragging and sizing the control and give it the name dlbDirectory. The DirListBox is an example of the power of Visual Basic. This control provides all the functionality needed to allow a user to select a directory, which is exactly what you need to do in this case.

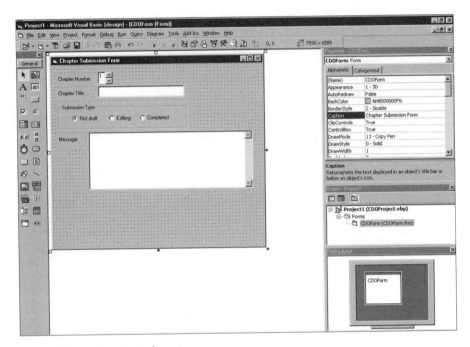

Figure 26-7. *The CDO form in progress.*

You have added all the controls that you need to accept input from the user, but you still have one thing left to do. You have drawn the form, but you still have to make it work:

15. Select the CommandButton control (the 3-D beveled button icon) in the toolbox and add a button to the right of the DirListBox control. Give the button the name cmdSend and the caption Send Chapter Submission. Save the changes to the form and the project by clicking on the Save tool in the toolbar.

Your user interface is complete. Your next step is adding some validation code to ensure that chapter submissions contain the proper information.

Validation Code for the User Interface

Most of the controls that you have added to your form have their own validation built in. The text box for the chapter number starts at 1 and can be changed only by the UpDown button, which ensures that the entry will be a number. A submission type will always be selected because the radio button group ensures

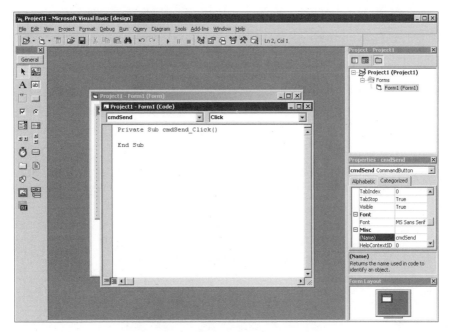

Figure 26-8. *The code window for the cmdSend button.*

that only one value in the group will be selected. The DirListBox begins with the current directory selected and always has a directory selected, so you do not need to force a value for that control. There is no requirement that a message be included with a chapter submission.

The only control that could possibly have an error is the txtChapterTitle. You must add code to ensure that the control contains a value:

1. Open the code window for the cmdSend button by double-clicking that button and add the following code to the cmdSend_Click() subroutine that appears when you open the code window, as shown in Figure 26-8.

```
If txtChapterTitle.Text = "" Then

  MsgBox "You must enter a value for the Chapter Title", _

    vbExclamation + vbOKOnly, "Chapter Title Required"

  txtChapterTitle.SetFocus

  Exit Sub

End If
```

2. Save the form by clicking Save on the toolbar, and then click the Start button on the toolbar to run the form.

3. Add some values to the fields in the form, but make sure to leave the Chapter Title field blank. Click Send. When the error message pops up, your form should look like Figure 26-9.

4. Click OK in the error message window, and the focus is sent to the Chapter Title control. Close the form by clicking the End button on the toolbar.

The code you add makes sure that the Text property of the txtChapterTitle control contains a value. If it does not, the code displays an error message box, sets the focus back to the control, and exits the subroutine. At this time, it may not make much sense to explicitly exit the subroutine. But the rest of the code in this subroutine, which you will add shortly, handles all the logic of creating and sending a message by using the capabilities of CDO, and you wouldn't want to allow that to happen if there is no chapter title.

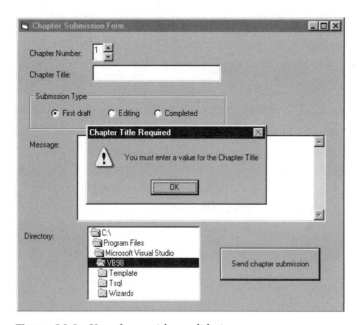

Figure 26-9. *Your form with a validation error.*

Everything appears to be in order. You are now ready to start working with the CDOs as you implement the functionality that will create and send the chapter submission.

Connecting to Exchange

As you remember from the discussion of the CDO object hierarchy earlier in this chapter, the first thing you must do when using CDO is create a session. All other CDO objects are children of a session, so you should also create a variable to hold the reference to the session.

It is good programming practice to include your variable declarations at the beginning of the subroutine or function of which they will be part. You will start your coding task by entering the variable declarations you will need:

1. Open the code window for the cmdSend command button by double-clicking on the object. Add the following variable declaration at the beginning of the cmdSend_Click() subroutine:

   ```
   Dim objSession As MAPI.Session
   ```

2. Add the code in boldface to the end of the existing code for the subroutine:

   ```
   Private Sub cmdSend_Click()

   Dim objSession As MAPI.Session

   If txtChapterTitle.Text = "" Then

      MsgBox "You must enter a value for the Chapter Title", _
         vbExclamation + vbOKOnly, "Chapter Title Required"

      txtChapterTitle.SetFocus

   Else

      Set objSession = CreateObject("MAPI.Session")

      objSession.Logon

      Set objSession = Nothing

   End If

   End Sub
   ```

Believe it or not, you have entered all the code that you need to connect to Exchange. You can create a session object and then call the *Logon* method for the object. You can call the *Logon* method in several ways—with a specific user profile, for example. But the easiest way is to call the method without any parameters, which causes the session object to display a logon dialog box. Note that the *Logon* method inherits the properties of the currently logged-in user.

It is always a good idea to set the value of an object to Nothing when you are done using it, to free any system resources that the object has been using. You also want to make sure that the last thing that a click of the Send button does is destroy the session object, because a user may click on that button again. You will add more lines of code immediately after the *Logon* method, so setting the object to Nothing is always the last line of code in the subroutine.

It's time to try out your first interaction between Visual Basic and Exchange:

1. Click the Start button on the toolbar and add some value to the Chapter Title field (because you have already seen the error handling working in the previous section). Click Send. You see a logon dialog box like the one shown in Figure 26-10.

2. Select a profile and click OK to log on. The login dialog box displays all the profiles that exist on your machine and gives you the ability to create a new profile or call up help. You can even click Options to select a profile as the default profile.

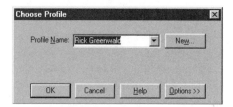

Figure 26-10. *The automatic login form.*

3. Exit the application by clicking the End button on the Visual Basic toolbar.

It is possible that you may receive an error if any of the Windows Messaging Subsystem components are not current.

You have just witnessed one of the great strengths of the COM model. A COM component can come with its own functionality. In the case of CDOs, the developers knew that users who access these applications have to log on, so they included the logon dialog box.

When the user is successfully logged on, you can start creating the message that will be sent to Exchange.

Creating and Addressing the Message

Now that you have established a connection to Exchange through a CDO session, you can create a message and transfer the information from the Visual Basic form that you just created to the message:

1. Your first step is to create a message that will be put in the user's Outbox for Exchange to pick up and send. Because you will refer to the properties and methods of this message repeatedly in your subsequent code, you want to catch the reference to the message object when you create it. Add the boldface line of code just after you create your session:

```
objSession.Logon

Set objMessage = objSession.Outbox.Messages.Add

Set objSession = Nothing
```

2. It is a good idea to make the subject of the message a combination of the chapter number, title, and status. Because the status is being determined by one of three radio buttons, you have to create some code to determine the state of those radio buttons. Add the following declaration at the top of the *cmdSend_Click* subroutine:

```
Dim sStatus As String
```

3. Add the code in boldface after you create the message to set the value of the *sStatus* string, right after your logon but before you create a message:

```
objSession.Logon

If rbFirstDraft.Value Then

    sStatus = "First Draft"

ElseIf rbEditing.Value Then

    sStatus = "Editing"

Else

    sStatus = "Completed"

End If

Set objMessage = objSession.Outbox.Messages.Add
```

4. To set the title and the message body for your new message, add the following declaration of a variable to the beginning of the *cmdSend_Click()* subroutine:

```
Dim sSubject As String
```

Note   Why not just directly assign the concatenated value for the subject to the message? First, using a variable makes it easier to debug the assignment, if necessary. Even more important, you want to assign the same subject string when you post the message later in the code, so assigning it to a variable makes it easy to reuse.

5. Add the following code after you give the *sStatus* string a value, just above the code where you set the *objMessage* variable:

```
sSubject = "Chapter " + txtChapterNumber.Text + _
    " - " + txtChapterTitle.Text + " - " + sStatus
```

Add the following boldface code, which sets the subject and message body of your message, after you create the message in your Outbox:

```
Set objMessage = objSession.Outbox.Messages.Add

objMessage.Subject = sSubject

objMessage.Text = txtMessage.Text
```

You have created the message that you want to send. Figure 26-11 shows all of the code so far that should be in your form. Take the time to compare your form to the form in the figure. The next step is to determine who will get this message and send it to that person.

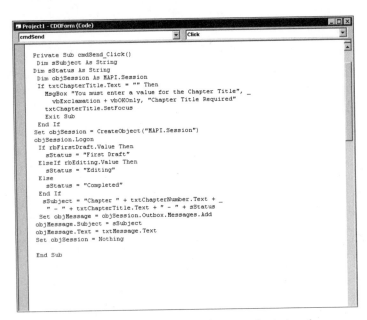

Figure 26-11. *Code listing for the chapter submission form.*

Note The complete code listing for the *cmdSend_Click()* subroutine is available in the CDOForm project on the CD-ROM that accompanies this book.

Sending the Message

Your first message created with CDO is almost ready to send to the Microsoft Exchange Server. All you have to do is to address the message to the appropriate recipients and send it.

As you remember from the customized Outlook form that you created in Chapter 24, some code automatically addressed the message to the co-author who was not the message sender. You can add the same type of code to your Visual Basic form. In the Outlook form, you had to use the following line of code to determine the message sender:

```
If Application.GetNameSpace("MAPI").CurrentUser = "Rick Greenwald"
```

When you are using CDOs, the identification of the sender is a bit less complex:

```
If objSession.CurrentUser = "Rick Greenwald"
```

As you would expect, the name of the current user is a property attached to the particular session object. The rest of the syntax for assigning recipients is also straightforward. Add the code in boldface to the existing code for the *cmdSend_Click()* subroutine:

```
objMessage.Text = txtMessage.Text

Set objRecipient = objMessage.Recipients.Add

If objSession.CurrentUser = "Rick Greenwald" Then

   objRecipient.Name = "Walter Glenn"

Else

   objRecipient.Name = "Rick Greenwald"

End If

objRecipient.Resolve

Set objSession = Nothing
```

This code adds a recipient object to the *Recipients* collection for the message object and then assigns a name for the recipient, based on the identity of the current user. When the recipient is added to the collection, you must explicitly resolve the recipient name to an Exchange address.

Note As with the examples in the previous chapters, this code assumes that you are creating this application for Rick and Walter. If you have not created these usernames for them on your system, please use your own names in this example.

You take a similar approach to determining whether the editor should be added to the recipient list for this message:

1. Add the following boldface code after resolving the first recipient's name:

```
objRecipient.Resolve

If rbCompleted Then

      Set objRecipient = objMessage.Recipients.Add

      objRecipient.Name = "Editor"

      objRecipient.Resolve

End If
```

This code checks to see whether the submission is a final submission. If it is (as indicated by the rbCompleted radio button), the Editor recipient is added to the list of addressees. You could have checked the value of the *sStatus* variable that you set earlier in this code, but it is probably better programming practice to refer to the definitive source of the submission type: the radio button group.

2. Add the following code after the code in bold that assigns recipients to your message and before the code that sets the session object to Nothing.

```
objMessage.Update

objMessage.Send

Set objSession = Nothing
```

With these two lines of code, you send the message to Exchange. When a message is sent, the object reference to it is automatically destroyed, so you do not have to set the object reference to Nothing. You can no longer use the object reference because the object that it points to has been destroyed.

3. Verify that your code is the same as shown below (or load from the included CD-ROM). If it is, save your project and form, and then click the Start button on the toolbar.

```
Private Sub cmdSend_Click()

 Dim sSubject As String

Dim sStatus As String

 Dim objSession As MAPI.Session

 If txtChapterTitle.Text = "" Then

   MsgBox "You must enter a value for the Chapter Title", _
```

```
            vbExclamation + vbOKOnly, "Chapter Title Required"
        txtChapterTitle.SetFocus
        Exit Sub
    End If
Set objSession = CreateObject("MAPI.Session")
objSession.Logon
    If rbFirstDraft.Value Then
        sStatus = "First Draft"
    ElseIf rbEditing.Value Then
        sStatus = "Editing"
    Else
        sStatus = "Completed"
    End If
     sSubject = "Chapter " + txtChapterNumber.Text + _
        " - " + txtChapterTitle.Text + " - " + sStatus
    Set objMessage = objSession.Outbox.Messages.Add
objMessage.Subject = sSubject
objMessage.Text = txtMessage.Text
Set objRecipient = objMessage.Recipients.Add
If objSession.CurrentUser = "Rick Greenwald" Then
    objRecipient.Name = "Walter Glenn"
Else
    objRecipient.Name = "Rick Greenwald"
End If
objRecipient.Resolve
If rbCompleted Then
        Set objRecipient = objMessage.Recipients.Add
        objRecipient.Name = "Editor"
        objRecipient.Resolve
End If
```

```
    objMessage.Update
    objMessage.Send
  Set objSession = Nothing
  End Sub
```

4. Set values for the chapter number and chapter title, enter a message in the Message field, and set the type of the submission. Click the Send Chapter Submission button.

5. If you receive an error, verify that your code matches the code shown in step 3.

6. If the application worked successfully, close the Visual Basic application and launch Outlook.

7. Log onto Exchange as the co-author who should have received the message. If things went well, you should see a message similar to the one shown in Figure 26-12.

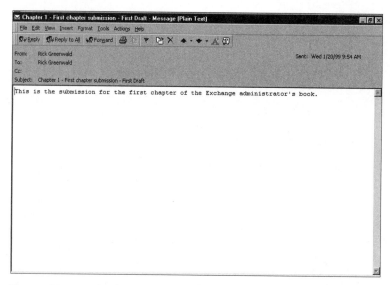

Figure 26-12. *The first message sent from your Visual Basic application.*

Success! You have accessed the power of Exchange from a Visual Basic application via the CDO COM interface. Your work is not quite done yet, however. You still have to send a copy of the message, with the attachments in the listed directory, to the public folder for the chapter. But because you will be posting that message instead of sending it, you must first add a little more code.

Posting the Message

In the custom form that you designed for Outlook in Chapter 24, you simply posted the message that you created to your co-author, the public folder, and possibly your editor. The same message, along with all the attachments, went to more than one location.

Because Exchange automatically stores attachments to multiple recipients on the same server in a single location, sending an attachment to multiple users is not much of a storage problem. A cleaner solution, however, is to keep the attached files in a single location and send the accompanying note to the other recipients.

In the preceding section, you sent the message to your co-author and editor. Posting a message to the public folder is also fairly easy because in the Visual Basic form, you have all the information you need to create and post the message. In fact, you can reuse some of the variables that you created for the mail message for the concatenated information.

Your first step is finding the folder that will receive the message posting. This step is a little more difficult than sending a message. To send a message, all you have to do is create a message in the Inbox, which is one of the folders that is directly associated with the session. Because there is no set structure for public folders, you have to find the public folder by searching through the available Information Stores.

> **Note**   Rather than have you go back to the top of the *cmdSend_Click()* button and add declarations for the variables used in this part of the code, this section, for the sake of simplicity, simply shows you the relevant code. You could directly use this code because you can declare variables on the fly, but a better practice is to explicitly declare your variables, as you do in the code sample at the end of this chapter. To absolutely ensure that variables are declared explicitly, you can use the Option Explicit statement. The Option Explicit statement must be placed before any other statements. It will then force you to explicitly declare all variables using the Dim, Private, Public, or ReDim statements. If you use an undeclared variable name, an error occurs at compilation, which forces you to go back and correct the variables that were mistyped.

You want to create the message that you will post before you send the accompanying messages to your co-author (for a reason that will be explained later in this chapter), so you should add the code for creating and posting the message just before the line of code that you wrote to add a new message to your Outbox, as outlined in the following steps.

1. Your first task is to locate the top of the Public Information Store. You have to first cycle through the Information Stores to find the IPM_SUBTREE Information Store, which is the root of all public folders, with the following code:

```
Set objInfoStores = objSession.InfoStores

For Each objInfoStore In objInfoStores

  Set objRootFolder = objInfoStore.RootFolder

  If objRootFolder.Name = "IPM_SUBTREE" Then

  End If

Next
```

2. After you find the public folder's root folder, find the top folder of the public folder hierarchy by searching for the folder known as All Public Folders in the hierarchy (which is the root folder for your organizations public folders) by adding the following boldface code. This code also includes the declaration of a constant, which allows you to use a more descriptive name, *IPM_PUBLIC_FOLDERS_ENTRYID*, rather than the less meaningful value *hex 66310102*:

```
Const IPM_PUBLIC_FOLDERS_ENTRYID = &H66310102

Set objInfoStores = objSession.InfoStores

For Each objInfoStore In objInfoStores

  Set objRootFolder = objInfoStore.RootFolder

  If objRootFolder.Name = "IPM_SUBTREE" Then

    strRootID =
      objInfoStore.Fields.Item(IPM_PUBLIC_FOLDERS_ENTRYID).Value

    Set objTopFolder = objSession.GetFolder(strRootID,
      objInfoStore.ID)

    Exit For

  End If

Next
```

3. Your last step in finding the proper folder is to drill down through the public folder hierarchy to get to the folder to which you wish to post. Add the following code after the code listed above to get to the appropriate chapter folder. The public folder named "Book" must exist in order for these programs to function correctly:

```
Set objFolder = objTopFolder.Folders("Book")

Set objFolder = objFolder.Folders("Chapter " +
    txtChapterNumber.Text)
```

Note If you are not familiar with Visual Basic, you might find this section of coding difficult. The only really complex part of the code is finding the All Public Folders root folder. If you needed this type of functionality frequently in Visual Basic, you could create a module with a function that could be called in a single line of code. That code would return this root folder or any other public folder for which you wanted to search.

---

4. Once you have located the appropriate destination folder, you must create a new message, because the previous message was destroyed once you issued a *Send* method on it. You can add code that is identical to the code you used to prepare the first message, except that this time the *sSubject* string has already been assigned. Add the following code after the previous *Send* method:

```
Set objMessage = objFolder.Messages.Add

objMessage.Subject = sSubject

objMessage.Text = txtMessage.Text
```

5. Your next step is to set some additional properties that are relevant for a posting. Add the following code after the code you just entered:

```
objMessage.ConversationTopic = sSubject

objMessage.TimeReceived = Time

objMessage.TimeSent = Time

objMessage.Sent = True

objMessage.Submitted = False

objMessage.Unread = True
```

6. The message is complete. All you need to do now is to send it, which you do with a simple method call. Add the following code after the creation of the posted message:

```
objMessage.Update
```

You have added all the code you need to post a message to a public folder. You should run your form now to see the result of the posting.

7. Run the Visual Basic application and send the message, with a title and message text, to a recipient and to a public folder that exists for a chapter. When you go to Outlook, the posted message should look like Figure 26-13.

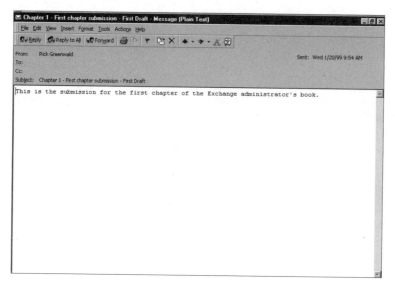

Figure 26-13. *A posting to a public folder from your Visual Basic application.*

The last step in creating your Visual Basic application is adding all the attachments to your posting.

Adding Attachments

Adding attachments to your posting is quite easy. You can easily get the directory that contains the files that you want to attach to your message. The code for attaching a message should look familiar. You use the *Add* method for the *Attachments* collection to create the attachment; then you set some properties and call a method for the new attachment:

1. You start by creating a complete path for the attachments and calling the Visual Basic *Dir* function to get the first file in the directory. Add the following code just before the *Update* method that officially posts the message.

   ```
   sPath = Dir1.List(Dir1.ListIndex) + "\"

   sFile = Dir(sPath + "\*.*")
   ```

2. The next step is to create an attachment for the posting. The following code creates the attachment; sets the type, source, and position of the attachment; and reads the value for the attachment from the complete file name you just retrieved:

   ```
   sCompleteFileName = sPath + sFile

   Set objAttachment = objMessage.Attachments.Add
   ```

```
objAttachment.Position = 0

objAttachment.Type = CdoFileData

objAttachment.Source = sPath + sFile

objAttachment.ReadFromFile (sCompleteFileName)
```

3. This code will work just fine if you had only a single file in the directory. In order to get all the files in the directory, you must call the *Dir* command repeatedly. Add the following boldface code to create a Do loop to iteratively add attachments:

```
Do

    sCompleteFileName = sPath + sFile

    Set objAttachment = objMessage.Attachments.Add

    objAttachment.Position = 0

    objAttachment.Type = CdoFileData

    objAttachment.Source = sPath + sFile

    objAttachment.ReadFromFile (sCompleteFileName)

    sFile = Dir

Loop
```

4. This code works well, but it doesn't know when to stop working. You want to exit the Do loop as soon as the *Dir* command comes up empty. Add the boldface code to leave the Do loop at the appropriate time:

```
Do

    If sFile = "" Then

        Exit Do

    End If

    sCompleteFileName = sPath + sFile

    Set objAttachment = objMessage.Attachments.Add

    objAttachment.Position = 0

    objAttachment.Type = CdoFileData

    objAttachment.Source = sPath + sFile

    objAttachment.ReadFromFile (sCompleteFileName)

    sFile = Dir

Loop
```

This code will also catch those cases when there are no files in the selected directory. If you enter the loop without a value for the *sFile* variable, you will immediately exit the loop based on the test for a value.

You have added all the functionality you will need in your Visual Basic program. It's time to try out this nearly complete version of the program. Save your application and then run it. Choose a directory that has a limited number of files, add a meaningful title and message body, and send the message. When you open the posting in Outlook, the message should look like Figure 26-14.

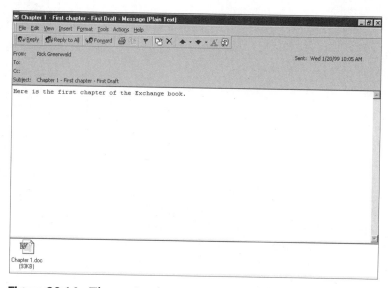

Figure 26-14. *The posting from your Visual Basic program, with attachments.*

Error Checking for the Message

You've accomplished your goal of creating a Visual Basic application that makes it easy to submit the materials for chapters. But your application, as it stands now, could still have a problem when it is used.

When you have run your program, you may have accidentally selected a chapter number that did not have an existing public folder. You may have indicated that a chapter submission was for Chapter 2, for example, but there was no public folder called Chapter 2 inside the public folder called Book. The current application would post the message to an invalid name but would not return an error. The result would be that your co-author, and maybe even your editor, would receive a message that a chapter had been submitted but would find nothing there. If your co-author read the message carefully, he would be able to check and see that the folder for the chapter did not exist. But why allow this type of error to occur? You can easily check to see whether the folder exists and let the user create a new folder from your program.

Your first task is to find out whether the public folder that you are looking for exists:

1. You start by creating a string from the Chapter Number Text field, because you will reference this value repeatedly. Add the following line of code immediately after you set the objFolder variable to the Book public folder:

```
sChapterName = "Chapter " + txtChapterNumber.Text
```

2. Next, you must cycle through all the folders underneath the Book folder and compare each one with the value of the *sChapterName* variable. You can cycle through the *Folders* collection under the Book folder by using the For ... Next syntax and comparing the value of the selected folder item's *Name* property with the variable. If the variable is found, you exit the For loop. You can accomplish this with just a few lines of code that you add after you have set the *sChapterName* variable:

```
For i = 1 To objFolder.Folders.Count

If objFolder.Folders.Item(i).Name = sChapterName Then

Exit For

End If

Next i
```

3. The next step is to check to see if the code exited the For loop having found a match for the folder name or not. The easiest way to do this is to check the value of the *i* variable that you were using to cycle through the *Folders* collection. If the *i* variable is greater than the count of the items in the *Folders* collection, you know that you exited the loop without finding a match. To prepare to take corrective action for this situation, add the following code after the completion of the For loop:

```
If i > objFolder.Folders.Count Then

End If
```

4. There may be more than one reason that the public folder the user is searching for does not exist. It could be that the folder has not yet been created, or it could be that the user simply forgot to specify the correct chapter number in the form. For this reason, you must use a Visual Basic

message box to prompt the user to confirm the creation of the new folder, which the following code will do:

```
If i > objFolder.Folders.Count Then
    If MsgBox("Would you like to create a new folder called " _
+ sChapterName + "?", _
        vbYesNo, "Make a new folder?") = vbYes Then
            objFolder.Folders.Add (sChapterName)
        Else
            Set objSession = Nothing
            Exit Sub
    End If
End If
```

If the user does not want to create the folder, you simply clean up the existing session and leave the subroutine. You don't have to worry about setting the appropriate properties for the new folder, because it will inherit most of the properties of its parent folder, the Book folder.

> **Note** Now you know why we put the posting before sending the corresponding message in the example program. If the user doesn't want to create a public folder, you can just exit the user out of the entire subroutine and not send the mail messages.

To test this code, save and run the completed form. Set a chapter number for a folder that does not exist. You will be prompted as to whether you want to create a new public folder. Send the chapter and click Yes, as shown in Figure 26-15. You should check for the existence of the folder in Outlook, and you should try to refuse to create a new folder.

Enhancements for the Program

You could add a great deal to this application. It would probably be helpful to add some information about the attachments to the body of the message, which you could easily do by counting the attachments or creating a list of files added and appending it to the value from the txtMessage field. You might want to add

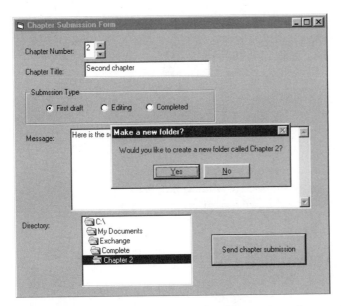

Figure 26-15. *Prompting the user for the creation of a new folder.*

a greater level of user feedback so that you could ask the user whether he or she really wants to send a message with a large number of attachments. Also, you could add a great deal of error-handling functionality.

So far, you have learned how to handle some of the standard errors that you can anticipate. In the real world, however, a wide variety of unexpected errors occur. Those errors could be caused by anything from a machine that is not properly configured to a server that is not running to a needed file that has been corrupted. Your application doesn't include any code that captures and addresses these types of errors.

To make this application production-ready, you have to add code for most of the calls to a CDO object to account for these unexpected situations. You also have to add some error-handling code at the end of the cmdSend_Click() button to deliver these errors to the user in an understandable fashion and allow the user to take corrective actions, if possible.

Creating any application involves three stages: adding the functionality that you want, preventing planned errors, and handling unplanned errors. The first stage is the fun part of development, the second stage is the necessary precursor to rolling out an application to production, and the last stage extends from the end of the development process until the end of time. This last stage can seem like pure drudgery, but to your users, an application that is protected from the vagaries of their environment is a great one.

Benefiting from the Application

You have now taken a whirlwind tour of CDOs, created a user interface in Visual Basic, and added code to enable the functionality that you needed. The application that you created and the process of creating it have delivered some important benefits:

- **Limits and cleanses the information gathered from the user**   When you create your own application, you can design the user interface to collect only the information that you want. Using the DirListBox, you give the user a handy graphical way to select a directory and a way to ensure that the directory the user selected is valid. The resulting application performs all the tasks that you need to submit a chapter and its associated materials.

- **Performs multiple functions**   With a single form, you were to mail messages to your co-author (and, when appropriate, to your editor) and to post a similar message to the appropriate folder. If you were using an Outlook form, this process would be more difficult. Because Visual Basic is a much more robust development product than the Outlook form development environment, you can shape the functionality of your applications more easily when you use Visual Basic. Your Visual Basic application is not integrated into a particular Exchange client, of course.

- **Run without any specific Exchange client**   The ability to run your application as a stand-alone is an advantage in some ways. If you had an environment with a mixture of Outlook 97, Outlook 98, Outlook 2000, and Exchange clients, you could still run your application on any Windows platform. In fact, you can run the application on an offline client, if the profile for the client is properly set up.

- **Requires relatively little code to implement**   You really didn't have to write much code to implement all the functionality of your application. You can credit this to the power of Collaboration Data Objects.

Summary

Although you may have occasionally been confused with all the coding in this chapter, you have really accomplished something. You have been able to open up the power of Exchange to the outside world by accessing CDOs through Visual Basic. However, this chapter just skimmed the surface of the power of CDOs. If you have needs in your environment that call for customized interfaces to the information in your Exchange environment, you will be able to use one of the most popular development languages in the world, Visual Basic, to create any type of application you want, easily blending in Exchange services when they are required.

The application that you wrote with Visual Basic and CDOs works well in a traditional client/server environment. Chapter 27 helps you understand and create another extension to the standard Exchange environment—one that works in the World Wide Web.

Chapter 27
Using the Active Server Platform

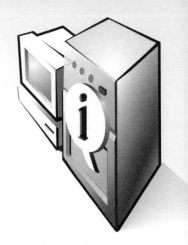

You've reached the last chapter in this book, and you've covered a lot of ground—from basic concepts through installation and administration of Exchange and its clients and through extending the reach and power of Exchange by creating your own custom applications. In this final chapter, you learn how to utilize the functionality of Exchange in conjunction with the hottest new computing platform around: the Internet.

Introducing the Active Server Platform

Before you can really appreciate the architecture and use of the Active Server platform, you should understand how using the Internet as the underlying networking platform is different from using the traditional client/server computing architecture.

In previous chapters in this part, you created applications based on Exchange using a variety of tools, both inside and outside the standard Exchange environment. All of these applications existed in the same basic world—the world of client/server computing. A diagram of the architecture of client/server computing is shown in Figure 27-1.

Figure 27-1. *Client/server computing.*

Client/server computing is distinguished by a few basic characteristics:

- Both sides in the client/server environment are complete computers— usually a personal computer on the client side and a high-powered server on the other side.

- Some form of network connects these two sides of the system, although these networks can span large geographic areas with the addition of wide area connections.

- The standard for user interface display is the Windows graphical environment.

- The client computer and the server computer remain connected via an application. This means that each side of the system is actively aware of the other throughout the interaction in the application. This constant and lasting connection, in turn, allows client/server applications to easily have repeated interactions as part of a single operation.

The Internet—more specifically, the World Wide Web (WWW or the Web)—introduced a different type of computing system, as shown in Figure 27-2. Web topology as a platform for application systems has a different set of characteristics:

- The client for the Web is a browser, which has limited computing capabilities.

- The network implemented with the Internet is extremely widespread—in fact, the universality of the Internet is one of its key attractions—but it is significantly slower and more prone to traffic bottlenecks than most local

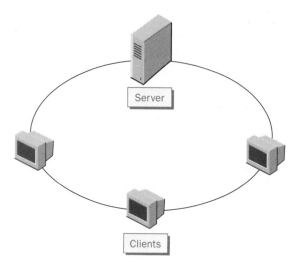

Figure 27-2. *World Wide Web computing on the Internet.*

area networks. This means that you will have to minimize the traffic between the Internet client and the Internet server in order to achieve an acceptable level of performance.

- The user interface display standard for Web computing is the HyperText Markup Language (HTML) standard.

- The Web uses a connectionless communication protocol, HyperText Transfer Protocol (HTTP). An HTTP topology differs from the connection-oriented topology of normal client/server computing. Each communication between the client and the server must be complete in itself.

All of these factors contribute to the creation of a new type of platform that can be used with the World Wide Web: the Active Server platform. As you saw in Chapter 14, Exchange version 5.5 has many features that relate to the Internet. These features have been designed to integrate Exchange and the Internet. When you want to use Exchange as a set of services that can be called by a World Wide Web client, you can use the Active Server platform, as shown in Figure 27-3.

Four basic components make up the Active Server platform. The first component is the browser, which is the client. This client is capable of interpreting HTML code and some basic logic implemented with a scripting language such as Visual Basic Scripting Edition (VBScript) or JavaScript (Jscript). The client is connected to the other components of the Active Server platform via the Internet, using the HTTP protocol.

On the server side, Microsoft's Internet Information Server (IIS), the second component of the Active Server platform, receives the communications from the client. IIS is capable of hosting the third component of the Active Server platform, Active Server Pages (ASPs), which implement the server-based logic.

Note Microsoft's Personal Web Server (PWS) can also run ASPs, but because you must have a Windows NT Server to run Exchange Server 5.5, and because the Windows NT Option Pack comes with IIS, we use IIS in all of the examples in this chapter. If you want to implement the examples in this chapter, you must make sure that the Active Server Pages component of IIS, which comes with the NT Server Option Pack, is installed. These features work with IIS versions 3.0, 4.0, and 5.0, although the screen shots in this book represent IIS 4.0 only.

Active Server Pages use a scripting language that is actively interpreted when the client calls the pages. The scripts in Active Server Pages can be directly interspersed

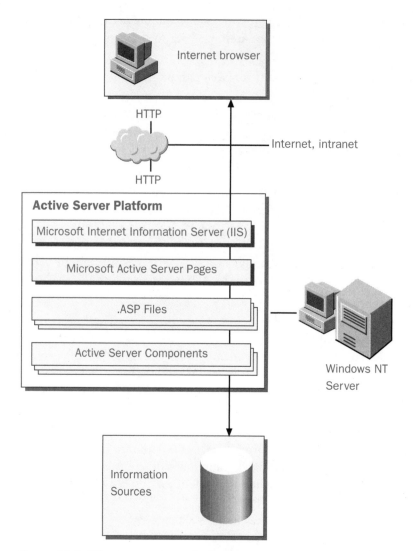

Figure 27-3. *The Active Server platform.*

with standard HTML code, which gives them the ability to combine static HTML code in a page with HTML code that is dynamically generated by the script.

ASPs can also call the fourth element of the Active Server platform: Active Server Components. Although this may be a new name for you, you worked with Active Server Components in Chapter 25. Active Server Components are simply Common Object Model (COM) components by another name. You can call virtually any standard COM component, such as Collaboration Data Objects (CDOs), from your ASPs. Although you can use CDOs as objects that are called from your ASP, Microsoft has also introduced an even simpler COM object specifically designed for use in the Active Server platform: Collaboration Data Objects for NT Server, or CDONTS. CDONTS, as you see later in this chapter, are specifically designed to make it easy for ASPs to use the Exchange mail services that are most likely to be implemented in an Active Server platform application system.

The main point of the Active Server platform is to optimize the development and performance of Internet-based applications. By implementing the logic of the application in ASPs on the server side, the Active Server platform removes the burden of processing from the browser-based client. By returning only HTML-based pages to the client, the Active Server platform makes it easy to use any browser on any computing platform. Furthermore, by making it easy to integrate existing COM components into applications, the Active Server platform makes it easy to leverage and extend existing components and the services they represent into applications.

In order to build applications on the Active Server platform, you use ASPs, which are described in the next section and used extensively throughout the rest of this chapter to implement the sample application.

Introducing Active Server Pages

ASPs are designed to allow you to create HTML pages with dynamic content. An HTML page, by definition, is nothing more than a static set of text and markup tags. There are many occasions on which you will want to deliver pages that are tailored to the needs of individual users. You want to be able to dynamically create some of the information in the page and combine it with predefined static pieces of HTML.

ASPs give you this ability by allowing you to intermix standard HTML code and scripts that can implement logic and generate HTML code. The ASP is processed by IIS, which reads the ASP from the top of the page to the bottom. When IIS comes to a part of the ASP that contains a script, it interprets the script and then moves on to the rest of the page.

Typically, the scripts that are part of an ASP contain logic that ends up generating HTML code. The code is inserted into the HTML page at the point at which the script should be executed. Once IIS has processed the script, it removes the script from the page that is sent back to the browser. The output from an ASP is a standard HTML page, which can contain any HTML that can be properly interpreted by the client browser, including client-side scripts that are interpreted in the browser.

The server-side implementation of ASPs means that the browser-based user can never see the script that is used to generate the HTML page. Any logic that you put in the ASP is executed on the server and goes no further, so even if a user examines the HTML code for the returned page, he or she will see no trace of the ASP scripts that were used to create the page.

Using Active Server Pages

As stated earlier, an ASP is composed of two basic types of code: standard HTML code and scripts. This chapter does not teach you the basics of HTML, because there are so many sources for that information and because our example application uses very simple HTML tags.

Note Microsoft's Internet Information Server comes with extensive online HTML documentation. To find it, simply enter *http://localhost/iishelp* in your browser's location window.

An ASP page can contain one or more scripts. Normally, these scripts are written in one of two languages, VBScript or JScript, although you can also get scripting engines for other languages, such as PerlScript, REXX, and Python, from third-party providers. The scripts within an ASP are contained within their own special tags: <% to mark the beginning of the script and %> to mark the end. Although it is not required that you include in your ASP page HTML comments that describe the actions of the scripts, it is good programming practice to document the basic purpose of any and all scripts within an ASP.

All ASPs are called by a Uniform Resource Locator, or URL, with which you are no doubt familiar from surfing the Web. A URL can contain information about the user who is requesting the page, and the request can also contain information that is sent from the browser. For instance, an HTML page can have text entry fields as part of a form. When a user clicks one of the buttons in the form, the data entered into the fields is sent to the destination URL.

ASPs are stored as files in one of the virtual directories defined for IIS. IIS knows that a particular file is an ASP because the file has an extension of .ASP. If a file does not have the correct extension, IIS will not process it as an ASP.

You can see the virtual directories that are defined for your IIS server when you start the Internet Service Manager by choosing the Start menu, then choosing Programs, then Windows NT 4.0 Option Pack, and then Microsoft Internet Information Server. As shown in Figure 27-4, the Internet Information Server is a "snap-in" for the Microsoft Management console. The server is listed below the Internet Information Server heading. The virtual directories are listed in the left pane beneath the Web site under the server name.

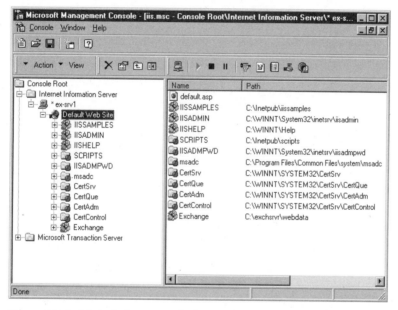

Figure 27-4. *Virtual directories listing within the Default Web Site of IIS.*

The easiest way to understand the syntax and implementation of an ASP is to create an ASP page that you can call from a browser. Because you will be creating a fairly simple application for the Active Server platform, and because our space in this chapter is limited, we use the simplest tool available to write our ASPs: Notepad.

If you are already familiar with HTML and VBScript, you know all that you need to know to be able to implement ASPs. If you are not familiar with either one of these technologies, you should be able to follow the code through the development cycle because the examples in the rest of this chapter use a subset of the code and functionality available in VBScript.

1. Open Notepad or some other ASCII editor and enter the following code for your first ASP:

```
<html>

<head><title>Your First Page</title></head>

<body>

<h2>Your First Page</h2>

Your first Active Server Page is nothing to get excited about!

</body>

</html>
```

Note   The complete code for this ASP has been included on the CD that accompanies this book, as are all the scripts and HTML pages mentioned in this chapter. For this specific ASP code, go to the Examples folder of the CD-ROM and look in the Chapter 27 folder for "SAMPLE1.ASP." Save the code as "SAMPLE1.ASP" with quotation marks so that Notebook does not automatically give the file an extension of .TXT. Move the file to one of the virtual directories defined for IIS on your Windows NT Server. The code you have entered looks just like a normal HTML page. In fact, it is—there is no requirement that any ASP have scripts included in it.

When you install IIS, it creates a number of standard virtual directories, including one called *scripts*. Because you will only be creating a few ASPs, you could place them in this standard directory for the time being, or you could create your own virtual directory by clicking Action, then New, then Virtual Directory in the Internet Service Manager. Make sure that Execute permission is granted for the directory you will use for your ASPs. You can check on the status of the Execute permission by opening the property sheets for the Virtual Directory. The Execute option is one of the Permission option buttons at the bottom of the sheet, as shown in Figure 27-5.

2. If you have been using a stand-alone machine, switch to a client machine that is connected to the NT Server with IIS. Enter the following line in the location text box at the top of the browser, where the *servername* keyword is replaced with the name of your server and the *directory* keyword is replaced with the name of the Virtual Directory into which you placed the ASP file:

```
http://servername/directory/SAMPLE1.asp
```

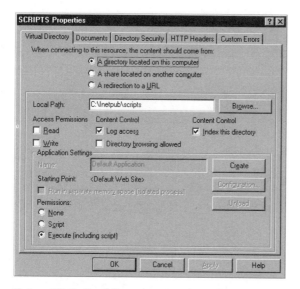

Figure 27-5. *Enabling execute access for ASPs in a directory.*

The page returned to your browser should look like Figure 27-6, a very simple Web page created using Active Server Pages. You can modify your ASP page to add some dynamic information to the page.

> **Note** The syntax provided in the preceding code allows you to directly access your server. If you have a DNS server in place in your network, you could use the DNS name of the server instead of the server name. You can also use the IP address if you prefer.

3. Open the SAMPLE1.ASP page in a text editor. Add the code shown in boldface below to the existing code:

```
<html>
<head><title>Your First Page</title></head>
<body>
<h2>Your First Page</h2>
Your first Active Server Page is nothing to get excited about!
<p>
Today's date is <%= Date %>, and it is a <%=
    WeekdayName(Weekday(Date)) %>.
</body>
</html>
```

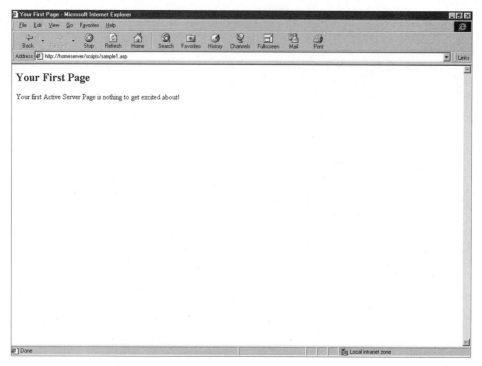

Figure 27-6. *Your first simple ASP page.*

You can see that there are two places where VBScript is used in the ASP. In the first piece of code, you used a simple VBScript function, *Date,* to cause the date to show up in the page. Notice that you used an equal sign after the first ASP code tag to indicate that the value will be calculated from VBScript.

The second bit of code takes the value returned by the *Date* function and subjects it to two other VBScript functions. The *WeekDay* function returns a number between 1 and 7 to identify the day of the week, and the *WeekdayName* function converts this number to a text string. You can have nested functions in VBScript as well as conditional and repeated logic, but you will not need to use conditional or repeated logic for the simple application you will create in this chapter.

4. Save the script under the name SAMPLE2.ASP, and then call the SAM-PLE2.ASP from your browser. The page that is returned looks like Figure 27-7.

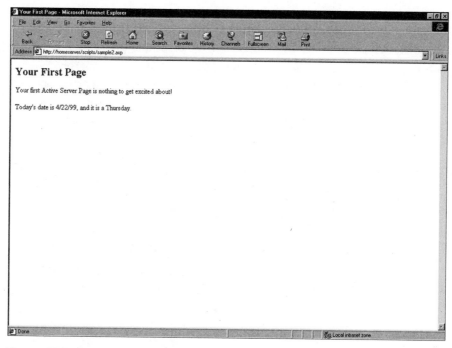

Figure 27-7. *Your second ASP page.*

Your second page is a little bit more exciting. You can see that the *Date* functions you added in your VBScript have done their job properly; the day of the week and the date are showing up correctly in the page. If you open the page to view the source in the browser, you see the following code. Of course, your date and day of the week will be different:

```
<html>

<head><title>Your First Page</title></head>

<body>

<h2>Your First Page</h2>

Your first Active Server Page is nothing to get excited about!

<p>

Today's date is 1/27/99 and it is a Wednesday.

</body>

</html>
```

There is no trace of the VBScript or the tags that were used to create the HTML—just the HTML that was delivered as a result of the code. The consumer of a page created with an ASP has no way of knowing what ASP code was used in the page except when the extension .ASP is seen. The consumer doesn't even know which of the HTML code was static and which was created by the ASP logic. The disappearance of the source code makes the use of ASP code intrinsically more secure than using client-side code for a page.

> **Note** You have used the simplest method to create your Active Server Pages. Microsoft has a robust development environment called Visual InterDev, which is designed for creating applications that are deployed over the Internet. With Visual InterDev, you can easily create applications that use both server-side ASPs and client-side scripts and dynamic HTML.

> **Note** For more information on Active Server Pages, you can look at *Programming Active Server Pages* (1997) from Microsoft Press. To learn more about Visual InterDev, we recommend *Inside Visual InterDev* (1997), also from Microsoft Press.

You have learned all you really need to know about the basics of ASPs. You understand how to create tags to identify ASP code and how that code is processed. There is quite a bit more to using ASPs, including the ability to create and use COM objects and the object model that is used by an ASP to get information from an incoming URL. You will learn about these facets of ASP technology as you build a sample application in the remainder of this chapter.

Building Your Application

Before beginning any programming project, it is always good practice to state what you hope to accomplish and try to anticipate potential problems.

The Goal of the Application

The basic goal of the application you are about to create is to implement the same type of interface with the discussion group you created in Chapter 25 over the Web. The application you create will allow the users of this book to send questions to Rick and Walter and have these questions automatically placed in a public folder that will act as a discussion group. This Web interface gives the discussion a worldwide reach while still controlling the way readers can interact with the public folder within the Exchange environment.

You could, of course, simply give your e-mail address to the world. But you want to be able to control the way that questions from the outside enter and interact with your Exchange system—the same way that the forms you designed in earlier chapters specified and limited the information that a user could send to you.

There are three main steps to creating your application. First, you must create a standard HTML form to accept the information from a user through a standard browser interface. The next step is to create an ASP that will take the information submitted with the form and use it to create a message that will be posted to the discussion folder. The final step is to create the HTML code that will be sent back to the users to confirm that their questions were properly submitted.

Creating an HTML Form

Because the purpose of this chapter and its sample application is to demonstrate how to use the Active Server platform with Exchange, you don't need to create anything fancy for the submission form. You can create a basic form by following these steps:

1. Open your favorite text or HTML editor. For the purposes of this application, we use that old standby, Notepad. Enter the following code:

   ```
   <html>

   <head><title>Questions?</title></head>

   <body>

   <h2>Questions for Rick and Walter</h2>

   <p>

   You can send a question to the happy co-authors by simply filling
       in the

   text boxes below and clicking on the push button.

   <FORM ACTION="sample4.asp" METHOD="POST">

   <b>Subject: </b>

   <p>

   <INPUT TYPE="text" NAME="QuestionSubject" SIZE="60"
   ```

```
     MAXLENGTH="200">

<p>

<b>Question:</b>

<p>

<textarea name="Question" Cols=60 rows=10></textarea>

<p>

<b>Your E-mail address:</b>

<p>

<INPUT TYPE="text" NAME="Emailaddress" SIZE="60" MAXLENGTH="200">

<p>

<INPUT TYPE="submit" NAME="QuestionSubmit" VALUE="Submit Your
   Questions">

</FORM>

</body>

</html>
```

The form isn't fancy—it simply has a text field to accept the subject for a question and an e-mail address as well as a text area for users to enter their detailed questions. The form has a single push button at the bottom of the page that users can click to submit information.

Notice that the Action for the form is the name of another ASP script, SAMPLE4.ASP, which you create in the next section of this chapter. The SAMPLE4.ASP script uses the data entered into the fields in this HTML form.

2. Save the file with a descriptive name and an extension of .ASP such as "SAMPLEFORM.ASP" in the directory you used for your other ASP scripts. Although this page does not contain any scripting tags, it makes sense to use a consistent naming scheme for all the components of a Web application.

3. Call the form in your browser. The completed form will look like Figure 27-8.

Real World   **Error Checking**

For the purposes of our sample application, this form works just fine. In the real world, you might want to add client-side code to ensure that the user provided a value for all of the data entry fields.

Figure 27-8. *The form used to submit data to an ASP.*

Now that you have created a user interface to submit a question, you can write the code that will accept this data and post it to a public folder.

Creating the Active Server Page Called by the Form

In this section, you create the ASP that will actually submit the posting to your Exchange environment. In order to make the process easier to understand, we divide the overall task into several separate steps, which are described in the following sections.

Creating a New Public Folder

1. Your first step is to create a new public folder that will accept the questions submitted from the HTML form you just created. You could allow your readers to submit questions directly to the technical discussion folder you created in Chapter 25, but it would be better to segregate

users' questions into their own folder, because Rick and Walter will be answering most of them. In addition, you must give the anonymous user access to the folder, because the people submitting questions to you will not be part of your Exchange environment. Using Outlook, create a new public folder at the top level of the All Public Folders hierarchy. Give it the name "Questions."

2. Start the Exchange Administrator on your server and select the newly created public folder in the Public Folder Resources container in the Public Information Store container. Double-click on the new Questions folder to bring up the properties sheet, and click Client Permissions.

3. In the Client Permissions window, select the user named Anonymous and give it the role called Contributor, as shown in Figure 27-9. This choice allows an anonymous user to post items to this folder.

Figure 27-9. *Giving permission to an anonymous user.*

Logging into Exchange

Now that you have created a home for the incoming questions, you can start to create the ASP that will take the information from the HTML form and use it to create and send a posting to the new folder:

Open Notepad again and enter the following code:

```
<html>
<head><title>Thanks!</title></head>
<body>
<%
set objSession = CreateObject("MAPI.Session")
objSession.Logon "", "", False, True, 0, True, _
    "/o=Book/ou=Home/cn=Configuration/cn=Homeserver" &  vbLf & vbLf
    & "anon"
%>
</body>
</html>
```

Does this code look familiar? If you have been reading this book in sequential order, it should. It is almost identical to the code you used in the last chapter to connect to Exchange. The reason this code is so similar is quite simple: You are using the same Collaboration Data Object you used on the client in Chapter 26, except that this time you are creating it on the server.

There is one significant difference between this code and the code in the previous chapter. The code for the *Logon* method in this ASP is different from the code in Chapter 26. The Visual Basic application you were running could interact with the user, so you could just call the basic *Logon* method, which would open a logon dialog box. Because this CDO is running on the server, and because the user submitting the question probably does not have a profile for your Exchange environment, you use the following line of code, which logs on to Exchange as an anonymous user:

```
objSession.Logon "", "", False, True, 0, True, _
    "/o=Book/ou=Home/cn=Configuration/cn=Homeserver" &  vbLf & vbLf &
    "anon"
```

Note   This code uses the /o=Organization, /ou=Site, and /cn=Objects naming structure. In this case, the Exchange Organization is Book, the Site is Home, and the "anon" user is located on Homeserver in the Configuration container of the site. These items should be replaced with the names of your organization, site, and server, respectively, in order for the code to function as expected.

Finding the Public Folder

Your next step is to locate the public folder that will accept the user postings. Add the code to the end of the code you wrote in the previous step but before the ending *</body>* and *</html>* tags.

```
<% Set objInfoStores = objSession.InfoStores

For Each objInfoStore In objInfoStores

   Set objRootFolder = objInfoStore.RootFolder

   If objRootFolder.Name = "IPM_SUBTREE" Then

      ' Get the top folder of the public information store

      strRootID = objInfoStore.Fields.Item(&H66310102).Value

      Set objTopFolder = objSession.GetFolder(strRootID,
      objInfoStore.ID)

      Exit For

   End If

Next

Set objFolder = objTopFolder.Folders("Questions") %>
```

This code is slightly different from the code you wrote in the previous chapter. Instead of defining a constant for the hex value of &H66310102, which is used to identify the top folder in the Public Information Store, you simply used that value when you found the ID for that top folder. Once you found the top folder, you simply set the *objFolder* variable to hold the reference to the Questions public folder. Now you are ready to create the actual message for posting.

Creating the Message

Before you jump into creating your message, you should learn a little bit about the objects available to you in your ASP.

You already used an object in the ASP you are writing when you called the *CreateObject()* method to create a CDO session object. ASPs also come with six built-in objects: the *Application, Server, Session, Response, ObjectContext,* and *Request* objects. These objects act as interfaces to the various types of information that are associated with an HTML-based interaction:

- *Application* object   The *Application* object is used to store global application settings as well as sharing information to all users of ASP applications.

- *Server* **object** The *Server* object provides access to properties and methods on the server. Methods used include COM components, timeout periods for scripts, URL or HTML encoding to strings, and mapping virtual directories to physical directories.

- *Session* **object** The *Session* object stores information pertaining to a particular user session. This information is maintained even when the user switches to different pages in an application. When the session ends, the information is discarded.

- *Response* **object** The *Response* object is used to send information back to the user. Two uses include redirecting the browser to a different URL and setting values in cookies.

- *ObjectContext* **object** The *ObjectContext* object is used to commit or abort transactions that have been initiated by an ASP script.

- *Request* **object** The *Request* object is used to gain access to information that is passed by an HTTP request. Examples of information that can be accessed using the *Request* object are cookies, client certificates, binary data such as uploads, and data passed from an HTML form, regardless of whether it uses the *POST* method or the *GET* method.

The only object you will have to use in this script is the *Request* object. The *Request* object contains a number of collections that reference information included in the HTML request. You will be using the *Form* collection, which holds the values entered into the form objects on the calling HTML page.

Begin by adding the following code after the previous code, but make sure that you add it before the ending:

```
<% Set objMessage = objFolder.Messages.Add
objMessage.Subject = Request.Form("QuestionSubject")
objMessage.Text = Request.Form("Question") + vbLf + vbLf + "Reply to:
   " _
+ Request.Form("Emailaddress")
objMessage.ConversationTopic = Request.Form("QuestionSubject")
objMessage.TimeReceived = Time
objMessage.TimeSent = Time
objMessage.Sent = True
objMessage.Submitted = False
objMessage.Unread = True %>
</body> </html>
```

Once again, this code looks quite familiar. You have created a message object and assigned values to the various properties of the message. The Subject property of the message object is the text entered into the QuestionSubject text field, and the ConversationTopic is the same value.

For the Text property of the message object, you concatenate the information entered in the Question text area with the e-mail address entered in the E-mail Address text field. The *vbLF* shown in the code is a VBScript constant that represents a line feed. To finish this part of the ASP, all you have to do is to post the message and destroy the message object. Add the following code after the previous code, but make sure that you add it before the ending *</body>* and *</html>* tags:

```
<% objMessage.Update

Set objSession = Nothing %>

</body>

</html>
```

This last piece of code is exactly the same as the code you used in the previous chapter with your Visual Basic application.

Now save the code you have written in the same directory as your previous HTML form. Give the file the name "SAMPLE4.ASP." Remember that this was the name of the ASP that you referenced in the SAMPLEFORM.ASP, so you must make sure it is correct. To ensure your code is correct, verify it against the code contained in Figure 27-10.

Note The complete code for this ASP is included on the CD that accompanies this book. It appears under the Examples folder in the Chapter 27 folder with the name SAMPLE4.ASP.

You're finished implementing the first stage of your first application based on the Active Server platform. Now let's check it out:

1. Open the HTML form you created earlier in this chapter. Fill in the text entry fields with some information that will let you easily identify the message that will be sent to the public folder.

2. Click Submit Your Questions.

3. Open Outlook and go to the Questions Directory. Your message should show up and look like Figure 27-11.

Success! With just this little bit of code, you have been able to implement a user interaction with an Exchange public folder based on the Active Server platform.

```
sample4 - Notepad
File  Edit  Search  Help
<html>
<head><title>Thanks!</title></head>
<body>
<%
set objSesion = CreateObject("MAPI.Session")
objSession.Logon "", "", False, True, 0, True, _
        "/o=Book/ou=Home/cn=Configuration/cn=Homeserver" & vbLf & vbLf & "anon"
%>
<% Set objInfoStores = objSession.InfoStores
For Each objInfoStore In objInfoStores
  Set objRootFolder = objInfoStore.RootFolder
  If objRootFolder.Name = "IPM_SUBTREE" Then
    ' Get the top folder of the public information store
    strRootID = objInfoStore.Fields.Item(&H66310102).Value
    Set objTopFolder = objSession.GetFolder(strRootID, objInfoStore.ID)
    Exit For
  End If
Next
Set objFolder = objTopFolder.Folders("Questions") %>
<% Set objMessage = objFolder.Messages.Add
objMessage.Subject = Request.Form("QuestionSubject")
objMessage.Text = Request.Form("Question") + vbLf + vbLf + "Reply to: " _
+ Request.Form("Emailaddress")
objMessage.ConversationTopic = Request.Form("QuestionSubject")
objMessage.TimeReceived = Time
objMessage.TimeSent = Time
objMessage.Sent = True
objMessage.Submitted = False
objMessage.Unread = True %>
<% objMessage.Update
Set objSession = Nothing %>
</body>
</html>
```

Figure 27-10. *Complete code listing for SAMPLE4.ASP.*

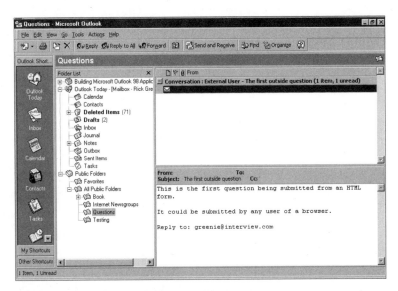

Figure 27-11. *The message your ASP posts.*

You may feel as though there is something missing. You were left with a blank page in your browser after you submitted the form. You can definitely do something about that.

Responding to the User Question

As you recall, your ASP can also send normal HTML back to the calling browser. It is always a good idea to provide feedback to users, especially to browser-based users who may experience significant delays due to overall traffic on the Internet and the speed of their connection.

Because you can include HTML as part of your ASP, it's easy to create an appropriate page to send back to the user:

1. Add the following code after the previous code and just before the ending *</body>* and *</html>* tags:

```
<h2>Got it!</h2><p>

Your question

<p><blockquote><i>

<% =Request.Form(“Question”) %>

</i></blockquote><p>

was received on

<% =WeekdayName(Weekday(Date)) %>

<% =Date %>

<p>

The response will be sent to

<p><blockquote><i>

<% Response.write Request.Form(“EmailAddress”) %>

</i></blockquote><p>

Thanks for submitting your question to Rick and Walter.
```

Most of this code is just standard HTML syntax. The only thing specific to ASPs in this piece of code are the four pieces of information that use VBScript functions and ASP objects to list the current day and date and recap the information sent in the message. Remember to save the new version of the ASP script.

2. Call up the HTML form again. Add some identifying information into the text fields and click the Submit button. This time, you get a page returned from the server in reply to your form, as shown in Figure 27-12.

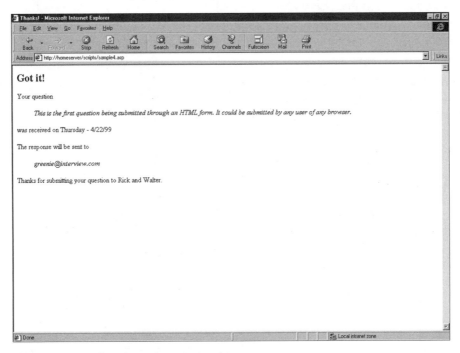

Figure 27-12. *The page your ASP sends in response.*

You have successfully implemented an application that operates in the world of the Active Server platform for Exchange.

Real World   Finishing the Application

As with the application in the previous chapter, the intention of this little exercise was to educate you about using the Active Server platform, not to build a complete and robust production-quality application. If you want to roll out this application to the real world, you have to add error handling to your ASP because the success page is returned to the user, even if the message is not posted successfully. If the ASP encounters an error creating an object, it may or may not return a VBScript error to the user. Receiving a confusing VBScript error is bad enough (one learns the hard way, through experience), but it is not as bad as getting an indication of a successful posting when the message did not in fact get to the public folder.

Collaboration Data Objects for NT Server

We used Collaboration Data Objects on the server as the way for an ASP to access the Exchange environment. We did this because we explained the basic structure and functionality of CDOs in the previous chapter, and all of that information also applies to CDOs running on the server.

But there is another object library available on the server for your use. This other object library, mentioned earlier, is called Collaboration Data Objects for NT Server, or CDONTS. CDONTS is installed by default when Exchange Server 5.5 is installed. If CDONTS.DLL is not present on your Exchange Server 5.5, another program may have uninstalled it.

The purpose of CDONTS is twofold. First, CDONTS has a higher-level interface than the standard CDO library because it is designed specifically for sending mail. In fact, using one of the objects in CDONTS, you can create and send a mail message with only four lines of code:

```
<% Dim myMail

Set myMail = CreateObject("CDONTS.NewMail")

MyMail.Send Request.Form("From"), Request.Form("To"), _
    Request.Form("Subject"), Request.Form("message")

Set myMail = Nothing %>
```

The other purpose of CDONTS is to leverage Internet standards for messaging. The support of Internet standards means that the CDONTS library lacks many of the Exchange-specific features, like working with calendars, which CDO has. In addition, CDONTS requires the use of Simple Mail Transfer Protocol (SMTP), an Internet mail protocol, in order to operate properly.

Exchange does support SMTP, but you will have to install the Internet Mail Service (IMS) option in order to use CDONTS. If you have installed this capability, you can find out more about CDONTS in the CDO help file. If your aim is to send mail from a Web browser, you may find that CDONTS will do the trick. The authors did not want to force you to install IMS to learn about the Active Server platform, so we chose to simply use the CDO library with which you became somewhat familiar in the last chapter.

Real World **Why Use the Active Server Platform?**
If the Internet is a part of your overall Exchange platform, you have no doubt installed IMS. Furthermore, if you want to use the Active Server platform, you are probably planning on making the Internet a part of your Exchange platform.

In the real world, the primary determinant of whether you want to use the Active Server platform is strictly whether or not you want interaction with your Exchange environment from a standard browser environment.

Benefiting from the Application

In this chapter, you took the power of Exchange a step further by creating a link between the worldwide reach of the Internet and your own Exchange organization. The application you created has delivered a number of important benefits:

- **Limits the information gathered from the user** As with the other applications you designed in earlier chapters, the HTML form acted as the user interface for collecting information. Because you created a structured form, the user could submit only three pieces of information, thus ensuring you do not receive extraneous or unnecessary data.

- **Integrates information from the outside world with your Exchange environment** The fact that Exchange can operate as a self-contained environment is, by and large, a good thing. By using ASP technology, you make it possible for anyone with a browser to add information to your Exchange environment.

- **Does not open your Exchange environment to the outside world** Even though this application made it possible for anyone to post a message to a bulletin board maintained inside your Exchange environment, you were able to control and limit access to Exchange through the intermediary of your ASP. Your entire Exchange organization could be located behind a firewall, fully secure, and still interact with the unsecured world of the World Wide Web.

This application will allow anyone with access to the World Wide Web to submit questions, which will be automatically integrated into your Exchange environment. There are many more possible applications for Active Server platform technology. You could take this approach; you know enough now to continue exploration on your own.

Summary

In this chapter, you learned how to use the technologies available in the Active Server platform to create customized Web forms that can interact with your

Exchange environment. The Active Server Pages that you created used the same Collaboration Data Objects that were used in the Visual Basic application you created in Chapter 26. You also implemented the appropriate practices to segregate the information coming in from outside sources into its own folder, to protect the security of your normal Exchange folders.

And now, we've reached the end...

We hope you have learned enough about administering Exchange to be able to do it—your way. We know that no book can provide all the answers to all the questions, but we have tried to answer the most obvious and important questions and to give you a firm grounding in Exchange so that you can investigate additional possibilities easily and efficiently.

Index

MICROSOFT LICENSE AGREEMENT

Book Companion CD

IMPORTANT—READ CAREFULLY: This Microsoft End-User License Agreement ("EULA") is a legal agreement between you (either an individual or an entity) and Microsoft Corporation for the Microsoft product identified above, which includes computer software and may include associated media, printed materials, and "online" or electronic documentation ("SOFTWARE PRODUCT"). Any component included within the SOFTWARE PRODUCT that is accompanied by a separate End-User License Agreement shall be governed by such agreement and not the terms set forth below. By installing, copying, or otherwise using the SOFTWARE PRODUCT, you agree to be bound by the terms of this EULA. If you do not agree to the terms of this EULA, you are not authorized to install, copy, or otherwise use the SOFTWARE PRODUCT; you may, however, return the SOFTWARE PRODUCT, along with all printed materials and other items that form a part of the Microsoft product that includes the SOFTWARE PRODUCT, to the place you obtained them for a full refund.

SOFTWARE PRODUCT LICENSE

The SOFTWARE PRODUCT is protected by United States copyright laws and international copyright treaties, as well as other intellectual property laws and treaties. The SOFTWARE PRODUCT is licensed, not sold.

1. **GRANT OF LICENSE.** This EULA grants you the following rights:

    a. **Software Product.** You may install and use one copy of the SOFTWARE PRODUCT on a single computer. The primary user of the computer on which the SOFTWARE PRODUCT is installed may make a second copy for his or her exclusive use on a portable computer.

    b. **Storage/Network Use.** You may also store or install a copy of the SOFTWARE PRODUCT on a storage device, such as a network server, used only to install or run the SOFTWARE PRODUCT on your other computers over an internal network; however, you must acquire and dedicate a license for each separate computer on which the SOFTWARE PRODUCT is installed or run from the storage device. A license for the SOFTWARE PRODUCT may not be shared or used concurrently on different computers.

    c. **License Pak.** If you have acquired this EULA in a Microsoft License Pak, you may make the number of additional copies of the computer software portion of the SOFTWARE PRODUCT authorized on the printed copy of this EULA, and you may use each copy in the manner specified above. You are also entitled to make a corresponding number of secondary copies for portable computer use as specified above.

    d. **Sample Code.** Solely with respect to portions, if any, of the SOFTWARE PRODUCT that are identified within the SOFTWARE PRODUCT as sample code (the "SAMPLE CODE"):

    i. **Use and Modification.** Microsoft grants you the right to use and modify the source code version of the SAMPLE CODE, *provided* you comply with subsection (d)(iii) below. You may not distribute the SAMPLE CODE, or any modified version of the SAMPLE CODE, in source code form.

    ii. **Redistributable Files.** Provided you comply with subsection (d)(iii) below, Microsoft grants you a nonexclusive, royalty-free right to reproduce and distribute the object code version of the SAMPLE CODE and of any modified SAMPLE CODE, other than SAMPLE CODE, or any modified version thereof, designated as not redistributable in the Readme file that forms a part of the SOFTWARE PRODUCT (the "Non-Redistributable Sample Code"). All SAMPLE CODE other than the Non-Redistributable Sample Code is collectively referred to as the "REDISTRIBUTABLES."

    iii. **Redistribution Requirements.** If you redistribute the REDISTRIBUTABLES, you agree to: (i) distribute the REDISTRIBUTABLES in object code form only in conjunction with and as a part of your software application product; (ii) not use Microsoft's name, logo, or trademarks to market your software application product; (iii) include a valid copyright notice on your software application product; (iv) indemnify, hold harmless, and defend Microsoft from and against any claims or lawsuits, including attorney's fees, that arise or result from the use or distribution of your software application product; and (v) not permit further distribution of the REDISTRIBUTABLES by your end user. Contact Microsoft for the applicable royalties due and other licensing terms for all other uses and/or distribution of the REDISTRIBUTABLES.

2. **DESCRIPTION OF OTHER RIGHTS AND LIMITATIONS.**

    - **Limitations on Reverse Engineering, Decompilation, and Disassembly.** You may not reverse engineer, decompile, or disassemble the SOFTWARE PRODUCT, except and only to the extent that such activity is expressly permitted by applicable law notwithstanding this limitation.

    - **Separation of Components.** The SOFTWARE PRODUCT is licensed as a single product. Its component parts may not be separated for use on more than one computer.

    - **Rental.** You may not rent, lease, or lend the SOFTWARE PRODUCT.

    - **Support Services.** Microsoft may, but is not obligated to, provide you with support services related to the SOFTWARE PRODUCT ("Support Services"). Use of Support Services is governed by the Microsoft policies and programs described in the user manual, in "online" documentation, and/or in other Microsoft-provided materials. Any supplemental software code provided to you as part of the Support Services shall be considered part of the SOFTWARE PRODUCT and subject to the terms and conditions of this EULA. With respect to technical information you provide to Microsoft as part of the Support Services, Microsoft may use such information for its business purposes, including for product support and development. Microsoft will not utilize such technical information in a form that personally identifies you.

- **Software Transfer.** You may permanently transfer all of your rights under this EULA, provided you retain no copies, you transfer all of the SOFTWARE PRODUCT (including all component parts, the media and printed materials, any upgrades, this EULA, and, if applicable, the Certificate of Authenticity), **and** the recipient agrees to the terms of this EULA.

- **Termination.** Without prejudice to any other rights, Microsoft may terminate this EULA if you fail to comply with the terms and conditions of this EULA. In such event, you must destroy all copies of the SOFTWARE PRODUCT and all of its component parts.

3. **COPYRIGHT.** All title and copyrights in and to the SOFTWARE PRODUCT (including but not limited to any images, photographs, animations, video, audio, music, text, SAMPLE CODE, REDISTRIBUTABLES, and "applets" incorporated into the SOFTWARE PRODUCT) and any copies of the SOFTWARE PRODUCT are owned by Microsoft or its suppliers. The SOFTWARE PRODUCT is protected by copyright laws and international treaty provisions. Therefore, you must treat the SOFTWARE PRODUCT like any other copyrighted material **except** that you may install the SOFTWARE PRODUCT on a single computer provided you keep the original solely for backup or archival purposes. You may not copy the printed materials accompanying the SOFTWARE PRODUCT.

4. **U.S. GOVERNMENT RESTRICTED RIGHTS.** The SOFTWARE PRODUCT and documentation are provided with RESTRICTED RIGHTS. Use, duplication, or disclosure by the Government is subject to restrictions as set forth in subparagraph (c)(1)(ii) of the Rights in Technical Data and Computer Software clause at DFARS 252.227-7013 or subparagraphs (c)(1) and (2) of the Commercial Computer Software—Restricted Rights at 48 CFR 52.227-19, as applicable. Manufacturer is Microsoft Corporation/One Microsoft Way/Redmond, WA 98052-6399.

5. **EXPORT RESTRICTIONS.** You agree that you will not export or re-export the SOFTWARE PRODUCT, any part thereof, or any process or service that is the direct product of the SOFTWARE PRODUCT (the foregoing collectively referred to as the "Restricted Components"), to any country, person, entity, or end user subject to U.S. export restrictions. You specifically agree not to export or re-export any of the Restricted Components (i) to any country to which the U.S. has embargoed or restricted the export of goods or services, which currently include, but are not necessarily limited to, Cuba, Iran, Iraq, Libya, North Korea, Sudan, and Syria, or to any national of any such country, wherever located, who intends to transmit or transport the Restricted Components back to such country; (ii) to any end user who you know or have reason to know will utilize the Restricted Components in the design, development, or production of nuclear, chemical, or biological weapons; or (iii) to any end user who has been prohibited from participating in U.S. export transactions by any federal agency of the U.S. government. You warrant and represent that neither the BXA nor any other U.S. federal agency has suspended, revoked, or denied your export privileges.

DISCLAIMER OF WARRANTY

NO WARRANTIES OR CONDITIONS. MICROSOFT EXPRESSLY DISCLAIMS ANY WARRANTY OR CONDITION FOR THE SOFTWARE PRODUCT. THE SOFTWARE PRODUCT AND ANY RELATED DOCUMENTATION ARE PROVIDED "AS IS" WITHOUT WARRANTY OR CONDITION OF ANY KIND, EITHER EXPRESS OR IMPLIED, INCLUDING, WITHOUT LIMITATION, THE IMPLIED WARRANTIES OF MERCHANTABILITY, FITNESS FOR A PARTICULAR PURPOSE, OR NONINFRINGEMENT. THE ENTIRE RISK ARISING OUT OF USE OR PERFORMANCE OF THE SOFTWARE PRODUCT REMAINS WITH YOU.

LIMITATION OF LIABILITY. TO THE MAXIMUM EXTENT PERMITTED BY APPLICABLE LAW, IN NO EVENT SHALL MICROSOFT OR ITS SUPPLIERS BE LIABLE FOR ANY SPECIAL, INCIDENTAL, INDIRECT, OR CONSEQUENTIAL DAMAGES WHATSOEVER (INCLUDING, WITHOUT LIMITATION, DAMAGES FOR LOSS OF BUSINESS PROFITS, BUSINESS INTERRUPTION, LOSS OF BUSINESS INFORMATION, OR ANY OTHER PECUNIARY LOSS) ARISING OUT OF THE USE OF OR INABILITY TO USE THE SOFTWARE PRODUCT OR THE PROVISION OF OR FAILURE TO PROVIDE SUPPORT SERVICES, EVEN IF MICROSOFT HAS BEEN ADVISED OF THE POSSIBILITY OF SUCH DAMAGES. IN ANY CASE, MICROSOFT'S ENTIRE LIABILITY UNDER ANY PROVISION OF THIS EULA SHALL BE LIMITED TO THE GREATER OF THE AMOUNT ACTUALLY PAID BY YOU FOR THE SOFTWARE PRODUCT OR US$5.00; PROVIDED, HOWEVER, IF YOU HAVE ENTERED INTO A MICROSOFT SUPPORT SERVICES AGREEMENT, MICROSOFT'S ENTIRE LIABILITY REGARDING SUPPORT SERVICES SHALL BE GOVERNED BY THE TERMS OF THAT AGREEMENT. BECAUSE SOME STATES AND JURISDICTIONS DO NOT ALLOW THE EXCLUSION OR LIMITATION OF LIABILITY, THE ABOVE LIMITATION MAY NOT APPLY TO YOU.

MISCELLANEOUS

This EULA is governed by the laws of the State of Washington USA, except and only to the extent that applicable law mandates governing law of a different jurisdiction.

Should you have any questions concerning this EULA, or if you desire to contact Microsoft for any reason, please contact the Microsoft subsidiary serving your country, or write: Microsoft Sales Information Center/One Microsoft Way/Redmond, WA 98052-6399.

Register Today!

Return this
Microsoft® Exchange Server 5.5 Administrator's Companion
registration card today

Microsoft Press
mspress.microsoft.com

OWNER REGISTRATION CARD   **0-7356-0646-3**

Microsoft® Exchange Server 5.5 Administrator's Companion

FIRST NAME   MIDDLE INITIAL   LAST NAME

INSTITUTION OR COMPANY NAME

ADDRESS

CITY   STATE   ZIP

(   )

E-MAIL ADDRESS   PHONE NUMBER

U.S. and Canada addresses only. Fill in information above and mail postage-free.
Please mail only the bottom half of this page.

**For information about Microsoft Press®
products, visit our Web site at
mspress.microsoft.com**

Microsoft·*Press*

BUSINESS REPLY MAIL
FIRST-CLASS MAIL   PERMIT NO. 108   REDMOND WA

POSTAGE WILL BE PAID BY ADDRESSEE

MICROSOFT PRESS
PO BOX 97017
REDMOND, WA 98073-9830

NO POSTAGE
NECESSARY
IF MAILED
IN THE
UNITED STATES